The
UNMANAGEABLE CONSUMER

SAGE was founded in 1965 by Sara Miller McCune to support the dissemination of usable knowledge by publishing innovative and high-quality research and teaching content. Today, we publish more than 850 journals, including those of more than 300 learned societies, more than 800 new books per year, and a growing range of library products including archives, data, case studies, reports, and video. SAGE remains majority-owned by our founder, and after Sara's lifetime will become owned by a charitable trust that secures our continued independence.

Los Angeles | London | New Delhi | Singapore | Washington DC

20th Anniversary Edition

The
UNMANAGEABLE CONSUMER

Yiannis Gabriel
& Tim Lang

SAGE

Los Angeles | London | New Delhi
Singapore | Washington DC

Los Angeles | London | New Delhi
Singapore | Washington DC

SAGE Publications Ltd
1 Oliver's Yard
55 City Road
London EC1Y 1SP

SAGE Publications Inc.
2455 Teller Road
Thousand Oaks, California 91320

SAGE Publications India Pvt Ltd
B 1/I 1 Mohan Cooperative Industrial Area
Mathura Road
New Delhi 110 044

SAGE Publications Asia-Pacific Pte Ltd
3 Church Street
#10-04 Samsung Hub
Singapore 049483

Editor: Matthew Waters
Editorial assistant: Molly Farrell
Production editor: Sarah Cooke
Copyeditor: Gemma Marren
Proofreader: Nicola Marshall
Marketing manager: Catherine Slinn
Cover designer: Francis Kenney
Typeset by: C&M Digitals (P) Ltd, Chennai, India
Printed and bound by CPI Group (UK) Ltd,
Croydon, CR0 4YY

© Yiannis Gabriel and Tim Lang 2015

First published 1995
Second edition published 2006
This third edition published 2015

Library of Congress Control Number: 2015932257

British Library Cataloguing in Publication data

A catalogue record for this book is available from
the British Library

ISBN 978-1-44629-851-0
ISBN 978-1-44629-852-7 (pbk)

CONTENTS

PREFACE TO THE THIRD EDITION

The Unmanageable Consumer was originally published in the mid-1990s, a period dominated by claims of the triumph of the consumerist West. In the midst of excitement about what was seen as an uncontestable hegemony of consumer capitalism, the book warned that 'any triumphalism about Western style consumption is misplaced. The future of global consumption must remain the object of questioning on economic, cultural, environmental and moral grounds'. Unlike some, we felt that the 1990s was a 'troubled time in the world'. Two decades later, few would dispute that times are indeed troubled or that Western-style consumerism is both facing and creating serious threats. These range from ecological crises such as climate change, resource shortages (from water to oil) and waste, to financial and geo-political uncertainties, including escalating religious and ideological divides.

Recent years have seen extraordinary military and political upheavals, and a major financial crisis in 2007–8 whose impact continues. Yet consumption continues to thrive as a social, economic and ideological force worldwide. The emergence of China, India and other developing countries as huge consumer markets and producer hotspots has extended the reach of contemporary consumerism. Political realignments worldwide have spawned new outposts of consumption and new black holes of deprivation, while debt and concerns over the costs and consequences of consumption have tempered some consumers' appetites. The seismic shift in consumption brought about by the internet has turned homes into retail outposts. It has also turned consumers into workers, often doing unpaid work for corporations. Consumers now have to work hard to service their needs, to develop new products or new uses for existing ones, to advise other consumers, and generally to self-service and replace other employees. At the same time, many objects that used to feature in consumption have dematerialized. Books, music, films and images are now consumed in electronic forms. Education and health services have become ever more commodified, with students and patients being recast as consumers. Anti-globalization movements, sometimes with overtly anti-consumption messages, have intermittently assumed centre-stage in politics, offering at least a glimpse of opposition to mainstream consumer capitalism. Alongside this opposition have emerged new forms of 'soft' opposition, framed around alternative exchange practices and a distaste for the global domination of markets, brands and corporations. These don't escape the grips of consumerism but generate counter-currents within it. Despite such eddies and currents, overall it has to be acknowledged that the last 20 years have seen a substantial expansion of consumerism worldwide.

Academics have watched this emerging picture with fascination. There has been an outpouring of writing on consumption and the accompanying fetishization of the consumer in new journals, books and debates. Cultural studies as an academic subject has thrived on consumption as a distinct and new terrain which, when cross-fertilized with marketing research, has spawned a large consumer culture theory (CCT) as a major field of academic inquiry. While CCT has been dissecting shopping malls as cathedrals of consumption, students of organization have focused on the limits of the ethos of customer service. As academic engagement with consumerism and consumption has intensified, other academic discourses have been colonized by the language of consumption. Identity construction has come to be viewed increasingly through the prism of lifestyles. Choice, modelled on the affluent consumer experience, has become the central tenet of many political and ethical discourses. At the same time, there is an increasing awareness among academics of the ecological limits to the consumerist orgy, which are already alarming observers of climate change, eco-systems, resource use, and the fragility of natural resources such as soil, water and air. Alongside the orgy, billions of people in low income countries subsist at a level of bare survival, and hundreds of millions of people in affluent societies quietly sink into new forms of poverty, dejection, debt and exclusion. Marketers, aware of this social phenomenon, have invented a new consumer category referred to as 'the bottom of the pyramid', which is to be pursued with messages and social packaging appropriate to straightened circumstances: thrift, ultra-cheap, aspirational to climb up.

When we originally wrote *The Unmanageable Consumer*, we put forward an unfashionable thesis. We argued that the notion of the consumer was an intellectually unstable entity, which summed up a central dilemma for late 20th-century capitalism – whether to treat people as controllable or free. We proposed, not least in the title of the book, that, in spite of the best attempts to seduce them, coax them or chide them, consumers consistently proved themselves unpredictable, contradictory and unmanageable – that they displayed many different faces and images. We also argued that far from disappearing from sight, work remained a fundamental part of people's everyday experience and that production and consumption were intrinsically interlinked through the socio-economic deal pioneered by American automobile magnate Henry Ford. What we termed the Fordist Deal offered alienating work in exchange for ever-escalating material standards and consumption. We observed that this deal, which had dominated the 20th century had, by the end of the 20th century, become fragile and could easily be disturbed by sudden events and cultural shifts. One such shift is the emergence of the working consumer, now often referred to as the 'prosumer', a word combining 'producer' and 'consumer' coined by futurologist Alvin Toffler to denote that the work process is being incorporated into the consumption process and vice versa. We also argued that citizenship is far from dead as a force in political arenas and that international relations could not be reduced to political deals aimed at improving consumer choice by removing trade barriers. We anticipated the continuation of a viable critique of rampant consumerism, building on the legacy of decades of struggles against the impact of industrialization and widening social divisions and inequalities.

Events in the last 20 years have strengthened our commitment to these arguments. An increasing number of academic voices now challenge the political and ideological primacy of 'the consumer'. The unmanaged and unmanageable dimensions of consumption signalled by our book have gained wider recognition, not least due to the urgency of environmental constraints, the growth of inequalities within and between societies and the impact of the 2007–8 financial crisis. That said, in certain ways our analysis of future trends could be accused of having been premature. In particular, in our concluding chapter, we were perhaps too eager to discern signs of a twilight of consumerism. As we have noted above, it has continued to grow and to flourish as a core feature of global capitalism for the 21st century.

Questions and doubts continue, however. Is consumer capitalism in the process of reinventing itself, in ways that transcend the crudity of mass production and mass waste? Could environmental and ethical costs be internalized into the prices of goods and services paid by consumers? Is the moral outrage against sweatshops sufficient to curb the worst excesses of consumer capitalism? Is consumerism now inextricably wrapped up in consumer debt? Is quality of life assuming a greater prominence over the sheer quantity of consumption? Or alternatively, is consumerism enlarging its grip and turning consumers into workers in pursuit of their dreams with the arrival of the prosumer? These are some of the questions which have prompted us to produce this new edition, while leaving the essential thesis, scope and arguments unchanged. We believe the unmanageable consumer continues to pose many threats for the survival of the planet, social justice and human happiness. We hope that the account we give here deepens engagement with the urgent policy debates on the containment of the negative aspects of consumerism, while enlarging and democratizing its positive aspects.

ABOUT THE AUTHORS

Yiannis Gabriel is Professor of Organizational Theory at the University of Bath and Visiting Professor at Lund University, Sweden. Yiannis has a degree in Mechanical Engineering from Imperial College London and a PhD in Sociology from the University of California, Berkeley.

Yiannis is well known for his work on organizational storytelling and narratives, leadership, management learning and the culture and politics of contemporary consumption. He has used stories as a way of studying numerous social and organizational phenomena including leader–follower relations, group dynamics and fantasies, nostalgia, insults and apologies. He has also carried out extensive research on the psychoanalysis of organizations. Yiannis is founder and co-ordinator of the Organizational Storytelling Seminar series, now in its fourteenth year (see www.organizational-storytelling.org.uk/), the author of nine books and numerous articles. He is elected to the board of EGOS and is currently Senior Editor of *Organization Studies*. His enduring fascination as a researcher lies in what he describes as the unmanageable qualities of life in and out of organizations.

Tim Lang has been Professor of Food Policy at City University's Centre for Food Policy since 2002. With a PhD in Social Psychology from Leeds University he became a hill farmer in Lancashire, North of England, in the 1970s. Over the last four decades he has engaged in public and academic research and debate about food policy: what sort of food system do we want? What do we mean by progress? He has written and co-written ten books and many reports and papers on the trends, problems and policy frameworks in the food system. A constant theme is how public health, environment, social justice and consumer rights do and don't connect. Besides his academic work, he has been an advisor to many bodies including the World Health Organization, the EU Environment Commissioner, the Mayor of London and many civil society organizations. He was the UK government's Sustainable Development Commissioner for food and land use in 2006–11. All this enquiry and engagement spawned and retains his keen interest in the issues analysed in *The Unmanageable Consumer*.

ACKNOWLEDGEMENTS

In writing this book, from its inception to this third edition, we have been helped by many people who have encouraged us to develop our thoughts; or discussed all or parts of our thesis; or fed us ideas, papers and facts; or suggested avenues of reading and research; or all of those! Our thanks to them all, and in particular to our academic colleagues in our own universities as well as our many friends around the world. We also thank everyone in the world consumer movements with whom we have talked and debated with over the years, also too numerous to mention! Our thanks, too, to our editors and all the people at SAGE.

INTRODUCTION

THE FACES OF THE CONSUMER

The consumer is now a god-like figure, before whom markets and politicians alike bow. Everywhere it seems, the consumer is triumphant. Consumers are said to dictate production; to fuel innovation; to be creating new service sectors in advanced economies; to be driving modern politics; to have it in their power to save the environment and protect the future of the planet. Consumers embody a simple modern logic – the right to choose. Choice, the consumer's friend, the inefficient producer's foe, can be applied to things as diverse as soap-powder, holidays, healthcare or politicians. And yet the consumer is also seen as a weak and malleable creature, easily manipulated, dependent, passive and foolish. Immersed in illusions, addicted to joyless pursuits of ever-increasing living standards, the consumer, far from being a god, is a pawn, in games played in invisible boardrooms.

The concept of the consumer sits at the centre of numerous current debates. Policy-makers, marketers, politicians, environmentalists, lobbyists and journalists rarely lose the consumer from their sights. The supermarket has become a metaphor for our age, choice its mantra. In the 20th century a new way of thinking and talking about people has emerged, which engulfs all of us. By the beginning of the 21st century, we had learnt to talk and think of each other and of ourselves less as workers, citizens, parents or teachers, and more as consumers. Our rights and our powers derive from our standing as consumers; our political choices are votes for those promising us the best deal as consumers; our enjoyment of life is almost synonymous with the quantities (and to a lesser extent qualities) of what we consume. Our success is measured in terms of how well we are doing as consumers. Consumption is not just a means of fulfilling needs but permeates our social relations, identities, perceptions and images.

The consumer has also assumed centre-stage in academic debates. If the 19th century tradition of social theory and political economy approached people primarily as workers and creators of wealth, consumption is the focus of much 21st-century theorizing. Psychologists have redirected their sights towards an understanding of what drives modern consumers. Cultural theorists have increasingly recognized the spirit of our age (whether described as late modernity, postmodernity or advanced capitalism) not in modes of production, government, class structure or art but in modes of consumption, lifestyles and identities. Following the collapse of Communism in the 1990s, consumerism was commonly described as the unchallenged ideology of our times. Its scope constantly stretched to incorporate new geographical areas, such as Far Eastern countries; new spheres of social relations, like health and education; and new social spaces, like homes and the countryside.

Discussions about consumption and consumerism are rarely value-neutral. Some commentators celebrate the rise of the consumer; having lost faith in religious or political recipes of salvation, the consumer is seen as the mature individual who seeks to enjoy life by making choices and exercising freedom. Others lament consumerism as the final stage of commodification, where all relations between people are finally reduced to usage and exploitation, in which the consumer is easily co-opted. The consumer is not merely an object of theorizing, but almost invariably a central character from a story; now a hero or a heroine, now a victim, now a villain, now a fool, but always central. In some stories, consumers feature as sovereign, deciding the fate of products and corporations at a whim, in others they feature as duped victims, manipulated by producers, advertisers and image-makers. In some, they feature as callous villains, indifferent to the plight of the planet or those less fortunate than themselves, in others as addicts, pursuing a chimera that only reinforces their despair.

This book was written because we believe that the word 'consumer' is now so extensively used that it is in danger of collapsing into a meaningless cliché. At one level, to state that someone is a consumer is almost as meaningless as acknowledging that she or he is a living being. We all consume the same way that we all breathe, since life without consumption is as impossible as life without respiration. Plants and other animals consume too. Why then has 'the consumer' in our culture become so loaded with meanings, assumptions and values? From where does this idea draw its power?

In this book, we argue that different traditions or discourses have invented different representations of the consumer, each with its own specificity and coherence, but wilfully oblivious to those of others. Neo-liberal economists, for example, have celebrated the consumer as a rational decision-maker and an arbiter of products while some consumer activists look at the consumer as a vulnerable and confused being, in need of help. Many cultural theorists look at the consumer as a communicator of meanings sustaining the social fabric, while most ecologists reproach consumers for their reckless and selfish behaviour. In this way, the concept of the consumer appears to have lost its specificity. It can enter different social and cultural agendas, including those of cultural theorists, Marxists, neo-liberals, journalists, publishers, marketers, advertisers and politicians across the spectrum with apparent equanimity, in seemingly perfect accord. The consumer can mean all things to all people.

The theoretical softness of the concept of the consumer (its readiness to act as an obedient and polite guest in almost any discourse) is accompanied by a moral hardness which it can readily assume. In reviewing what other thinkers have written and after considering the common usage of the term, we became and still are impatient with one-dimensional views of the consumer, whether they demonize or romanticize the consumer as if in consuming, people transcend every other level of social existence, as if consumption alone defines them. Perhaps surprisingly, love and fear of consumption cross conventional political, ideological and economic boundaries. Religious authorities can side with environmentalists in denouncing excessive consumption, while co-operative socialists and free market conservatives can join hands to celebrate consumer power.

We believe it is time that different traditions of defining the consumer started to acknowledge each other. Our first objective therefore is to identify, disentangle and juxtapose approaches to contemporary consumption that are rarely found within a single book or debate. Our discussion will address diverse features of consumption ranging from gifts and bargain-hunting to cashless systems of exchange, from fashion and fads in the developed world to the effects of Western consumerism on the developing world, from the class dimensions of consumption to children as consumers, from the semiotics of modern advertising to the scope and limitations of the law as an instrument of consumer protection, from the concept of choice to debates about free trade and protectionism.

The book's structure is an attempt to organize a truly prodigious, though sometimes chaotic, array of arguments according to the underlying image of the consumer which inspires and drives them. Thus, after Chapter 1, which investigates the emergence and spread of contemporary Western consumption, each subsequent chapter until the final one presents a distinct portrait of today's consumer, as it emerges from the writings of academics, journalists, advertisers, consumer advocates, policy-makers and others. We portray in succession the consumer as chooser, as communicator, as identity-seeker, as victim and so forth. It will quickly become evident that each of these portraits highlights a different feature of the consumer's physiognomy, while at the same time obscuring others. We discuss the tensions and contradictions inherent in each portrait and examine the tendencies of each to mutate into or confront different ones. We observe how critical discontinuities and anomalies in a particular tradition of consumer studies are overcome by simply switching from one consumer representation to another. We look, for example, at how the consumer as explorer turns identity-seeker or how the consumer as chooser turns into victim or the consumer as activist is seduced into being a consumer as worker. We argue that each one of these portraits has strengths as well as weaknesses and we try to evaluate each.

Our own purpose, however, is not merely to recreate these images, compelling though they be, nor to criticize each one of them from the vantage point of another. In spite of their considerable complexity, we shall argue that all of these portraits are too tame, predictable and one-sided, failing to come to terms with the fragmentation, volatility and confusion of contemporary consumption. By stirring various traditions together, we are seeking to reclaim some theoretical recalcitrance for the concepts of consumption and the consumer. We would thus like to re-inject some critical edge and prickliness into the notion of the consumer that it has lost by being all things to all people. We introduce the concept of the 'unmanageable consumer' to express this recalcitrance, a refusal on our part to allow the idea of the consumer to become domesticated and comfortable within parcelled discourses.

But there is another quality that we seek to capture through the concept of unmanageability, one that pertains not to the concept of the consumer as it features in academic, political and cultural discourses, but rather to the vital unpredictability that characterizes some of our actions and experiences as consumers, both singly and collectively. As consumers, we can be irrational, incoherent and inconsistent just as we can be rational, planned and organized. We can be individualist or may be driven by social norms and expectations. We can seek risk and excitement or may aim for comfort and security. We can be deeply moral about the way we spend our money or quite unfettered by moral considerations. Our feelings towards consumption can range from loathing shopping to loving it, from taking pride in what we wear to being quite unconcerned about it, from enjoying window-shopping to finding it utterly boring, from being highly self-conscious about the car we drive to being quite indifferent to it. Such fragmentations and contradictions should be recognized as core features of contemporary consumption itself, hence the pertinence of the idea of the unmanageable consumer.

To portray consumers as unmanageable does not seek to overlook the difficulties many people have in making ends meet, the lack of choice that we experience due to the oppressive burden of social expectations or the indignity of rank poverty. Nor does it skim over the immense resources and effort deployed to observe, monitor, survey, forecast and control our behaviour as consumers, in short, to manage us. Like today's worker, today's consumer is over-managed, prodded, seduced and controlled. Never before has one's every purchase been so closely observed, each credit card transaction so closely dissected, each movement monitored on close-circuit TV. In the pages of this book, we will encounter countless modes of consumer management coming from diverse quarters. Consumers, however, do not always act as predictably as would-be managers desire. The very fragmentations and contradictions that characterize our actions as consumers enable us from time to time, in devious, creative and unpredictable ways to dodge management devices and evade apparatuses of monitoring and control.

Ultimately, our actions and experiences as consumers cannot be detached from our actions and experiences as social, political and moral agents. The fragmentation and contradictions of contemporary consumption are part and parcel of the fragmentation and contradictions of contemporary living. Being a consumer dissolves neither class membership nor citizenship; it is not the case that at one moment we act as consumers and the next as workers or as citizens, as women or men or as members of ethnic groups. We are creative composites of several social categories at the same time, with histories, presents and futures.

But the most important reason for writing this book has been our desire to explore the qualities of fragmentation and unmanageability of contemporary consumption as part of a long-term historical process. Today's Western consumer is often treated as the terminus of a historical process, which will be duplicated in other parts of the world. Alternatively, Western consumption is viewed as culpable for the escalating plunder of vast sections of the developing world and the continuing deprivation of its inhabitants. We want to emphasize that today's Western consumerism is itself but a stage towards something different. The fact that no one can be sure about what lies ahead does not imply that we should treat today's Western consumer as the summation of a historical development. This is a mistake made by some political ideologues in their romanticization of consumer choice and inability to imagine a future different from the present. We wish therefore to reassert the importance of the debate about the global and historical implications of Western modes of consumption and the legacy that it is likely to leave for future generations.

The meaning of consumerism is framed by its wider political and social context. The demise of the Soviet Union and the end of the Cold War at the end of the 1980s signalled to many observers the triumph of Western consumer capitalism. Equally, the spectacular rise of the economies of the Asia Pacific region was seen as confirmation that the only meaningful choice left to nations (now that the choice of capitalism versus socialism was foreclosed) was that between consumer capitalism and poverty-ridden, corruption-rife under-development. Instead, we argue that any triumphalism about Western-style consumption continues to be misplaced. The future of global consumption must remain the object of questioning on economic, cultural, environmental and moral grounds. The rapid globalization of production and markets heralds a decline in some of the conditions that fuelled the rise of modern consumerism: steady jobs, full employment, high wages, rising standards of living and so on. Following the economic and banking crisis of 2007–8, the efforts of politicians, marketers, advertisers, publishers and trend-setters to entice people to resume the riotous pace of debt-based spending have not been consistently successful. Major economies like those of Japan and the Eurozone have faltered, while the USA itself stuttered and has lumbered itself with still more debt. In the wake of insecurity about jobs and pay, fed by countless cautionary tales of debt, homelessness and bankruptcy, many commentators talk about consumers suffering from spending reluctance and a return to thrift. Some politicians are quick to despair about consumers doing their bit for the economy. Many consumers have become nervous of unaffordable consumption. As earlier generations of workers had been accused of being work-shy by their bosses, so consumers today can be castigated for being spend-shy and failing in their duty to keep the economy going.

The core assumptions of consumerism have also come under scrutiny. The foolishness of pretending that the natural environment contains inexhaustible resources and has unlimited tolerance to abuse has become patently clear to an increasing number of analysts. The notion that everyone in the world could 'enjoy' Western standards of living without leading to an environmental and ecological catastrophe seems increasingly blinkered. Indeed, many giant corporations reliant on consumption now acknowledge that they need to reduce their resource use and environmental 'footprints'. Even the axiomatic equation of quality of life with wealth has started to be questioned, as some vanguard consumer groups advocate 'consume less'. A sizeable number of people are also heeding the call and voluntarily simplifying their lifestyles. While we cannot see the end of consumerism yet, its future and pattern can no longer be taken for granted. For the time being, consumerism, far from resting on its laurels, seems to be going through a period of well-earned malaise.

This book argues that the fragmentation and unmanageability of the consumer are features of this malaise. As long as the consumer could confidently look forward to a future of greater prosperity and affluence, the issue of defining the consumer seemed pedantic. Today, however, defining the consumer has become like a Rorschach Test, the psychologist's tool, where individuals are invited to say what they 'see' in the shape of an inkblot; the idea is that what they each 'see' betrays their state of mind. Similarly, to ask what the consumer is invites us to explore ourselves, our notions of society and our outlook on life. One's tendency is always to search for meaning, cohesion and transparency where there may be doubt, ambiguity and uncertainty. By accepting fragmentation and unmanageability, this book invites the reader to unravel some of the paradoxes that make up contemporary consumption and to assess their implications for the future. Are we going to witness the consumer's resurgence, metamorphosis or demise?

1

THE EMERGENCE OF CONTEMPORARY
CONSUMERISM

There is little sign that most of the populace wish for anything other than a continual increase in the availability of such products and the benefits felt to be received by their possession. (Miller, 1987: 185)

CORE ARGUMENTS

Consumerism emerged as a leading ideology in the 20th century and looks certain to play a major role in the 21st century. Identifying the good life with people's ability to meet their desires through the accumulation of goods, consumerism elevates individual choice to a supreme value. It proclaims free markets as the guarantors of technological innovation, economic growth and political freedom. This ideology originated in the West but has now gone global. Consumerism was underpinned by a 'Fordist Deal', the deal behind the rise of mass production and mass consumption under which enhanced standards of living compensated for alienated work. This deal has unravelled with a global division of labour and new technological forces such as the internet which have seen jobs become more precarious and mobile. The major challenges for consumerism in the future look likely to arise from economic and political forces that depress wages and increase job insecurity; from increasing awareness of the adverse environmental impact of consumption; and from the failure of consumption to deliver the happiness and well-being that it promises.

Since the 14th century, the word 'to consume' in English has had negative connotations, meaning 'to destroy, to use up, to waste, to exhaust'. By contrast, the word 'customer' was a more positive term, implying 'a regular and continuing relationship to a supplier'. The unfavourable connotations of the word 'consumer' continued to the late 19th century. Gradually, the meaning of 'to consume' shifted from the object that is dissipated to the human needs that are fulfilled in the process (Williams, 1976: 69). It is mainly since the 'Roaring Twenties' (1920s) in the USA that the meaning of consumption has broadened still further to resonate as pleasure, enjoyment and freedom (Lasch, 1991). Consumption moved from a means towards an end – living – to being an end in its own right. Living life to the full became increasingly synonymous with consumption.

By the 21st century, this has changed. The consumer is a totem pole around which a multitude of actions and ideologies now dance. Whether *en masse* or as an individual, the consumer is no longer a person who merely desires, buys and uses up a commodity. Instead, as we shall see in subsequent chapters, we encounter the consumer in turn as one who chooses, buys or refuses to buy; as one who displays or is unwilling to display; as one who offers or keeps; as one who feels guilt or has moral qualms; as one who explores or interprets, reads or decodes, reflects or daydreams; as one who pays, who gets into debt or shop-lifts; as one who needs or cherishes; as one who loves or is indifferent; as one who defaces or destroys.

Like the words consumption and consumer, the word consumerism has emerged as the umbrella term that captures the centrality of consumption in life. It has become part of the vocabulary of different intellectual traditions which carry different nuances but share the conviction that consumption provides the key to understanding of a wide range of issues in economics, psychology, cultural studies and politics. At its heart, consumerism is an ideology on a par with religion and politics – even overtaking them on some fronts. It looks at consumption as the source of meaning, identity and pleasure. Unlike politics and religion, consumerism is based on a relatively narrow conception of self-interest and personal choice. As a moral doctrine, therefore, it overcomes the Puritan ethic of self-denial; it celebrates and emphasizes the right of each person to search and find happiness in the use and display of commodities that they freely choose and acquire. Consumption has emerged virtually unchallenged as the essence of the good life and the vehicle for freedom, power and happiness. The claims of style, taste, fantasy and sexuality are at the forefront of this ideology, in which gender makes an intermittent appearance and class can vanish.

As an economic ideology, consumerism is seen as the force fuelling technological innovation and disseminating it globally. Following the collapse in the 1990s of the Communist bloc and its productionist rhetoric ('forever more tons of steel per head'), consumerism emerged uncontested as the ideological force behind the hegemony of free markets. It championed the pursuit of ever-higher standards of living from ever-less regulated markets, ushering in a new period of capitalist accumulation. It has become a key feature of international relations from trade and aid to foreign policy. The rise of the consumer and, relatedly, free markets are seen as the key to economic development everywhere.

Consumerism has long been the hallmark of neo-liberal politics but it has been increasingly embraced across the political spectrum in high-, medium- and low-income countries alike. The modern state has emerged as a guarantor of consumer rights and minimum standards while facilitating the 'free' operation of markets. In this process, large sections of the state itself – including the provision of health and education services – come under the sway of market forces; indeed, they are turned into quasi-markets. Almost all political parties have adapted accordingly, shifting their rhetoric from paternalism and protection to choice and freedom. Consumerism is the guarantor of access to marketplaces that supply glamorous, stylish goods and personalized services in contrast to the shabby, run-down state services left over from a previous political era. In this new world, the role of the state is to create and defend markets and to ensure fair market disciplines are applied.

A now discarded meaning of consumerism referred to a variety of social movements that sought to promote and protect the rights of consumers collectively. Consumer advocacy, dating back to the co-operative movement in the 19th century, developed as the patterns and the scope of consumption changed. This attitude to consumption emphasizes the vulnerability of individual consumers and the need for collective defence, education and representation. Neither state nor free markets, according to this view, can entirely be trusted to work for the consumer. While this tradition has endured and assumed new forms of consumer activism in our time, it has increasingly come to be associated with ethical consumerism, sustainable consumerism or even anti-consumerism. Thus consumerism – in spite of its global reach and ideological supremacy – is neither uncontested nor unproblematic. Even more contested and problematic are the images of the consumer that emerge from different academic traditions that are mesmerized by contemporary consumption. Thus some academics approach the consumer as a sovereign choice maker, others as a creature of habit rarely venturing beyond the familiar; some as conformist, easy fodder for marketers and advertisers, others as rebel, forever seeking to subvert or appropriate brands; some as rational and calculating, and others as capricious and impulsive.

Each of the chapters of this book introduces a different face of the consumer. We embrace the variety and nuances in the idea of 'the consumer' in order to develop a more complex account of consumerism, as a phenomenon that both describes social reality and also shapes perceptions of social reality. In all its meanings, consumerism is neither ethically nor politically neutral, and is therefore a terrain to be contested and argued over. Our object is not merely to clarify current and past debates on consumerism, consumers and consumption, but to explore the contradictions harboured by contemporary consumption patterns, the limits to consumerism and the forces that are likely to oppose it in the future.

The rest of this chapter sketches the emergence of Western consumerism and some of the contradictions that it faces today. We examine the circumstances that fostered it in the early phase of mass production and mass consumption in the 20th century. We trace its development through a period of mass media and advertising, examine its mutation in post-Fordist regimes and what some argued was a postmodern phase, and its resurgence in the era of the internet, and finally its possible dissolution into what some analysts already refer to as 'post-consumerism' (Lansley, 1994: 234–8; Gilbert, 2008; Cohen, 2013). The contradictions created within consumerism by environmental, population and political forces are cited by some commentators as the reasons for it moving in this direction.

The Fordist Deal and the rise of 20th-century consumerism

How did it all start? Contemporary consumerism in all its current diversity is unthinkable without the unwritten deal pioneered by Henry Ford for his employees: *ever-increasing standards of living in exchange for a quiescent labour force.* Ford offered his workforce the carrot of material enjoyment outside the work-place as compensation for the de-skilling, control and alienation that he imposed in the workplace. He also recognized the potential of his workers as customers, once they rose above mere subsistence. 'If you cut wages, you just cut the number of your customers' (Barnet and Cavanagh, 1994: 261). Since that deal was struck, consumerism has come to signify a general preoccupation with consumption standards and choice as well as a willingness to read meanings in material commodities and to equate happiness and success with material possessions (Lebergott, 1993).

The Fordist Deal linking consumption to the labour process highlights three dimensions of 20th-century consumer capitalism that are rarely addressed together. They will be at the forefront of our discussion throughout this chapter. The first is its *historical* character. Consumerism did not appear already shaped and formed in advanced industrial societies. It was prefigured in earlier societies (McKendrick et al., 1982; Williams, 1982; Mukerji, 1983; McCracken, 1988). Contemporary consumerism is the product of long-term historical changes. Fordism (as a phenomenon embracing both production and con-sumption) signalled the transformation of consumerism from an elite to a mass phenomenon in the 20th century in advanced capitalist societies (Williams, 1976). A very different picture emerges if, instead of approaching contempo-rary consumerism as the terminus of economic and cultural trends, it is seen as transitional, that is, having to reinvent itself or being overtaken by other social forces.

The second dimension of contemporary consumerism is its *global* nature. While consumerism touches the minutiae of everyday life, it is a global phenom-enon in many different ways. It underlines the interconnectedness of national economies, it affects rich and poor alike, it shapes international trade and (as the wars in the Middle East have demonstrated) politics and peace. The major play-ers in the consumerist game, the transnational corporations, are global players, the stakes are global stakes and the implications of the game itself are global

(Barnet and Cavanagh, 1994; Castells, 1996; Held, 1999; Brewer and Trentmann, 2006). By the end of the 20th century, just 200 corporations accounted for a fourth of global economic activity (Anderson and Cavanagh, 2000: 3).

This connects with the third dimension, sharply highlighted by the Fordist Deal, the vital links between contemporary consumerism and *production*. To be sure, a central feature of consumerism is the separation of the at times squalid circumstances of the production of commodities from their glamorized circulation and sale (Frenkel et al., 1999; Klein, 2000; Korczynski, 2001a; Korczynski, 2001b). Yet, patterns of consumption are crucially linked with developments in the nature of production. The consumer is ultimately the same person as the worker or manager now threatened by continuous mechanization of production and distribution or by the flight of capital to lower wage economies. Equally, international capital has a lot at stake in seducing the displaced peasant and exploited workers of low income countries and converting them into consumers aspiring after Western standards (e.g. Sklair, 1995; Prahalad, 2004; Seabrook, 2004).

The emergence of contemporary consumerism

As a mass phenomenon, consumerism may be a distinctly 20th century one, but particular patterns of consumption have held important social meanings throughout history, something explored by a number of scholars. In a pioneering study, McKendrick explored the consumption of the affluent in the early part of the industrial revolution, when the commercialization of fashion turned the British middle class into avid spenders (McKendrick et al., 1982). Rosalind Williams looked at the rampant consumerism of the Parisian bourgeoisie and the arrival of mass consumption through the institution of department stores in the late 19th century (Williams, 1982). Mukerji went further back and examined conspicuous consumption among Elizabethan nobility, fuelled by the discovery of 'fashion' and the arrival of nouveaux riches (Mukerji, 1983). What sets modern consumption apart from earlier patterns is not merely the growth of spending power across social classes and strata, but, more importantly, the experience of *choice* as a generalized social phenomenon. No earlier period afforded social masses the choice of what to spend surplus cash on after the means of subsistence had been met. This is well illustrated by the decline in the proportion of household expenditure on food. In Britain, at the start of the 20th century, working-class consumers were spending around a half to two-thirds of their income on food (Burnett, 1969). By the middle of that century, food on average claimed only a third of household expenditure. By the beginning of the 21st century it was nearer one tenth (Defra, 2014).

Most commentators on consumption agree that, following the Second World War, there was an explosion of consumption in the industrialized nations. Many industries, such as automobiles, chemicals, domestic appliances, electrical and electronic goods, took off, fuelling as well as feeding off a culture of consumerism. The basic bargain on which consumerism flourished was a more docile workforce in exchange for ever-increasing standards of living, referred to earlier as the Fordist Deal. Because Fordism makes the reproduction of labour power and mass consumption a decisive basis for the process of accumulation and valorization, it must aim for a tendentially unlimited expansion of consumption, it systematically institutionalizes 'wish production' and it constantly extends needs. These can only be satisfied in commodity form, which produces ever-new needs. The 'endlessness of needs' introduced with Fordist society, the limitless nature of consumer demands inherent in the Fordist model of consumption, contains an inbuilt tendency to a material '"demand inflation" ... [This] binds the structure of the Fordist individual with consumerism, which may certainly be politically stabilising, but also has an economically precarious effect' (Hirsch, 1991: 168).

Governments became vital parties to the Fordist Deal, leading some commentators like Hirsch (1991) and Jessop (2001) to speak of the 'Fordist State'. Governments became guarantors of full employment: 'Work and you will be able to consume; consume and you will be in work' (Bunting, 2004). Following the post-Second World War reconstruction, politics in the affluent world came to be dominated by governments' credibility, whatever the hue, to deliver on promises to improve living standards (Hobsbawm, 1994: 579ff). Political economy became a constant 'compare and contrast' exercise between the different types of contract with consumers (Hampden-Turner and Trompenaars, 1993). This was signalled in the UK by the defeat of the Labour government in 1950–51 whose seemingly endless policy of frugality since 1945 was swept aside by the Conservatives' promise of a better deal for the consumer (Hennessy, 1992) and in the USA by the post-war rediscovery of the American Dream or way of life that it represented (Mander, 1991). Throughout the period referred to by Hobsbawm (1994) as the Golden Age of the West (1947–72), this policy was highly successful, with ever-increasing opportunities for consumers to spend on goods such as records, clothes, homes, cars. By the 1960s, standards of living as measured by traditional indicators of consumption had improved spectacularly, with the USA, as so often, leading the way. In 1920, 16 per cent of US households had a phonograph; by 1960, 31 per cent had one (Lebergott, 1993: 137). In 1900, only 20 per cent of US households had a horse. In 1920, 26 per cent had a car and by 1989, nearly 90 per cent had one. In 1925, 10 per cent of US households had a radio; by 1990, 99 per cent had one and 98 per cent had a television. By 2010, the average number of television sets per US household had risen to nearly three.

The emergence of modern consumerism can hardly be reduced to spending patterns. Equally, it should not be studied outside the ideological context of the Cold War. Throughout this period, glamorized consumption in the West, as depicted in advertisements and celebrated in television series, was at least as potent an ideological weapon in the super-power confrontation as space exploits or gold medal hauls in the Olympic Games. The patent effectiveness of Western free enterprise in supplying a plethora of constantly mutating and highly desirable consumer products was held as final evidence of the superiority of capitalist market forces, entrepreneurship, free trade and political systems. Chronic shortages of consumer goods, perennial queues and the absurd inefficiencies of the Soviet system became as important a part of Western propaganda as civil rights abuses and political oppression. Since then, of course, the Chinese economic success has indicated that its brand of Communism was not intrinsically hostile to expanding consumer markets; certainly, it seized the opportunity to recast itself as the efficient low-cost labour force, reliable source of cheap luxuries to the rest while also fuelling its own consumerist boom.

But the eulogies of Western consumerism set against the alleged bleakness of the Communist system did not merely originate with the propagandists of the Cold War. Scorning a long sceptical and critical tradition from the 19th century to the present, which included Alexis de Tocqueville, Max Weber, Georg Simmel, Thorstein Veblen, R. H. Tawney and culminated in André Gorz and Herbert Marcuse, many Western economists found much to celebrate in consumerism. To them, the planned economies of the Soviet bloc provided a tangible model against which positive comparisons could be made. Milton Friedman and Friedrich Hayek, for instance, argued that consumers under Soviet-style command economies can only walk down the 'road to serfdom'. Command economies offer next to nothing, Friedman argued, compared to Western economies, which gain under 'co-operation through voluntary exchange', that is, voluntary associations through the free market's price mechanism (Friedman and Friedman, 1980: 3–14). Raymond Aron, no uncritical celebrant of Western consumerism, noted that under the old Soviet system:

> consumer choice has been almost completely eliminated. The distribution of national resources between investment and consumption is dictated by the planners, and even the distribution of resources between various sectors of industry, or between industry and agriculture, is not determined by the consumers. (Aron, 1967: 109)

In Soviet economies, it was a political choice not to give consumers choice. The state controlled the price of goods, taxing the difference between what it bought and sold products for. Thus planners had the power to decide 'whether or not to satisfy the desires of this or that category of consumers' (Aron, 1967: 110). Socialist economists joined in the critique of Soviet-style planned economies. In what reads as commonsense today, left-wing economic Professor Alec Nove, long before the demise of the USSR, pilloried the idiocy of giving the planner primacy over the end-user. Power over economic activity in the USSR, argued Nove, would ultimately have to be given to the consumer. 'To influence the pattern of production by their behaviour as buyers is surely the most genuinely democratic way to give power to consumers. There is no direct "political" alternative' (Nove, 1983: 225).

Throughout the Reagan–Thatcher years of the 1980s, a backlash against Keynesian economics in the West ushered in a phase of almost unchallenged supremacy for the free market. Consumerism shifted from an ideological weapon in the Cold War to an ideological weapon for the New Right. It became fashionable for apostles of the free market to view consumers as the storm-troopers of freedom. Their foes were no longer Soviet-style planners, but social-democratic politicians who supposedly wished to tax citizens, in order to provide whatever provisions – housing, health, education, railways, parks, roads – they believed were needed. The 1970s and 1980s saw the spectacular resurrection of Adam Smith, a selective reading of whose ideas provided the gospel of the New Right. Markets work, leave everything to the market, became the cry.

> It is not from the benevolence of the butcher, the brewer, or the baker that we expect our dinner, but from their regard to their own interest. We address ourselves, not to their humanity but to their self-love, and never talk to them of our own necessities but of their advantages. (Smith, [1776] 1970: 119)

Adam Smith's prototypical consumers did not have to contend with advertisers enticing them to have a second and a third dinner, let alone to 'graze' on snacks all day long; nor were they faced with different brands of meat, beer and bread, each proclaiming its own personality. But Smith's latter-day enthusiasts believed that neither the increasing concentration of economic activity nor the effects of mass media and advertising undermine the fundamental value of markets in ensuring efficient economic activity, value-creating innovation and satisfaction of human needs.

Consumerism and the mass media

The role of the mass media and advertising in fuelling and sustaining contemporary consumerism has been widely debated and contested. What is beyond doubt is that consumerism, in its many guises, found in the mass media the ideal vehicle both for its self-definition and for its dissemination. Modern consumerism really takes off with the growth of effective advertising and marketing campaigns, where the systematic attempt to mould consciousness can take place. Modern media of mass communication enabled advertisers to capture the attention and imagination of billions, to stop chance dictating how a product is seen and to shape thoughts and actions in particular ways. Raymond Williams suggested that the development of modern commercial advertising is highly significant in the creation of consumerism. Under late 19th-century capitalism, mass manufacture was related to the satisfaction of relatively fixed needs. Early forms of advertising were primarily meant to notify potential customers about available supply (Williams, 1976: 69). Modern advertising, on the other hand, is forged on the assumption that consumers have different means of satisfying needs; indeed, that consumers can derive pleasures and satisfactions that have little to do with needs. Modern advertising makes no secret of its aim to stimulate desire rather than to propose the means for satisfying needs (Campbell, 1989; Lury, 2004).

Much has been written about the genius and creativity of marketing as well as about the effectiveness of the techniques used. These techniques have become increasingly indirect and sophisticated, relying on product placements, texting, the creation of rumours and systematic manufacture of fashion in goods. Advertisers regularly counter criticisms that they manipulate the public and generate artificial needs for spurious products by pointing at the numerous failed campaigns and at advertisements that backfired. They also like to argue that today's 'sophisticated consumers' are not easily taken in by crass sales techniques, that advertisements today are a subtle art form, stimulating thinking and providing humour and entertainment. Some of these arguments will be examined in detail in the chapters that follow. While it is wrong to attribute to advertisers demonic powers of deception and persuasion, it is equally wrong to overlook the cumulative effect of advertising and marketing on culture. Irrespective of whether a campaign is successful, whether an advertisement is witty or mundane, whether it is addressed to a mass or a niche market, the cumulative effect of advertising is to associate commodities (and especially brands) with meanings, that is, to turn commodities into what Baudrillard called 'sign-values' (Baudrillard, [1970] 1988). Whether one is looking for happiness, identity, beauty, love, masculinity, youth, marital bliss or anything else, there is a commodity somewhere that promises to provide it. Through advertising, meanings are spuriously attached onto commodities, which are then presented as the bridges to fulfilment and happiness (McCracken, 1988; Cluley and Dunn, 2012).

The effects of advertisements on the 'unsophisticated' consumer are even more far-reaching. Mendelson and his co-researchers in the early 1990s voiced a common concern that children were especially vulnerable (Mendelson, 1992). Advertisers, they argued, used two approaches to sell products to children: normal advertisements and programme-length commercials that promote action figures and products related to the show.

Young children are unable to distinguish between programs and commercials and do not understand that commercials are designed to sell products. This observation suggests that any advertising directed at young children is inherently unfair. (Mendelson, 1992: 343)

The internet and ubiquity of product placement and sponsored websites and web content has accelerated this trend, with a blurring of the distinction between advertising, education and entertainment. Thus the culture of consumption is reproduced within each generation. This culture has been exported even to the lowest income economies. In her study of Ladakh culture in Nepal in the late 1980s, Helena Norberg-Hodge examined the impact that television had on a society previously locked into its extraordinary frugal subsistence way of life for centuries. Within a few short years from the introduction of television, children, aged six or less, started to see their own food as primitive and backward, refusing to eat what had been eaten for centuries and had been regarded with pride. In many other areas of consumption, Western goods came to be regarded as modern, civilized and desirable while their traditional counterparts were dismissed as backward and uncivilized. In a couple of decades, that culture was broken up irreversibly (Norberg-Hodge, 1991). While Norberg-Hodge acknowledged the role of other agents in such a cultural invasion, her research highlighted the power of the media and Western advertising and acts as a particularly striking reminder of the likely effects on local cultures of further globalization of the mass media through satellite and cable systems (Barnet and Cavanagh, 1994: 137–160).

The 1980s is now recognized as the moment of triumph for consumerism. The old moral restraints on consumption (such as remnants of frugality and thrift associated with the Protestant work ethic, guilt, or vestiges of snobbery vis-à-vis conspicuous consumption) were swept aside by an extraordinary, credit-led consumerist boom (Lee, 1993). Successful businessmen, and a few businesswomen, emerged as cultural super-heroes, temporarily joining film and sports stars. Greed lost some of its pejorative, puritanical connotations. The other side of the coin in the 1980s in the West was a crumbling social infrastructure, a squeeze on social services and a sizeable proportion of the population that was kept out of the consumer party (Mack and Lansley, 1985; Townsend, 1993). At the end of the 20th century, according to Zygmunt Bauman (1992) the 'new poor' were defined not by absolute standards of deprivation but by the lack of choice and their dependence on state provisions. In a strange way, the new poor not only did not spoil the party for the rest, but on the contrary tended to make it sweeter. According to Bauman, the poor were seen as failed consumers who stumbled in their exercise of choice and were then forced to accept the state's choices on their behalf:

> *The radical unfreedom of welfare recipients is but an extreme demonstration of a more general regulatory principle which underlies the vitality of the consumer-led social system. (Bauman, 1988: 69)*

The consumerist party ended abruptly with the end of the 1980s boom. It was ironic that just as the collapse of the Soviet empire came as final confirmation for some analysts of the superiority of the Western economic and social system (at least for Francis Fukuyama (1992) and those like him), the West was entering a period of recession, which generated some unease. The 1990s recession had several distinct features compared to earlier ones. For one, it affected strata of society – managerial, professional, home-owning, thoroughly middle class – which had rarely experienced the reality or even the threat of unemployment previously. Hardship, privation and feelings of profound economic insecurity became more widespread and more pervasive. The 1990s witnessed the appearance in Europe of US-style cheap mass retail outlets, substantially undercutting the prices of both high-street shops and out-of-town hypermarkets. Words like 'savings', 'value', 'free', 'unrepeatable offer' and so on, reappeared in advertisements. These trends made us ponder in the first edition of this book whether that phase marked a blip, a crisis or the twilight of consumerism. In retrospect, our diagnosis of generalized uncertainty owed more to our focus on North American, British and Japanese consumerism than on the rest of the globe.

Since the first edition of this book, the emergence of the internet has spearheaded a renewal of global capitalism and new and unexpected variants of consumerism. The worlds of consumption and retailing have been revolutionized by the arrival of on-line shopping, social media, Web 2.0 and interactive opportunities. Advertising has been able to target specific segments and market niches with far greater accuracy. Geographical distances have shrunk as information and the capacity to communicate in cheap ways have grown. Huge areas of consumption – music, messaging, books, films, newspapers and images – have been dematerialized. New enterprises and corporations have emerged seemingly overnight, such as Google and Facebook, which deal in these immaterial goods and services. And old companies have scrambled to reinvent themselves for the internet age or risk going out of business as happened to venerable names like Kodak, the photographic company, and others. In the process, the very distinctions between worker and consumer have become blurred, as companies sought to take competitive advantage of their capacity to 'crowdsource'. In the mid-2000s, the manufacturers of the highly successful European 'mini' car, the Fiat 500, used consumer feedback and suggestions in a systematic way to develop and configure the car. In a few months consumers supplied 170,000 design suggestions, 20,000 specific comments to develop the product, 1,000 ideas for accessories, and a mascot (Kleemann et al., 2008). Since this, the Fiat Mio was labelled the 'first crowdsourcing car'.

During the same period, however, new forces challenging or opposing global consumerism have emerged. Notable among these forces are the impact of the Islamic revival, the anti-consumer movement following the Seattle World Trade Organization talks (1999) and – perhaps most significantly – the collapse of consumer confidence in the Great Recession of 2007–13, following the financial meltdown of 2007–8. The Islamic revival has presented a moral and political challenge to consumerist value of self-interest and materialism not seen since the heyday of Soviet Communism (Gray, 2003). Sporadic challenges to consumerist values have also been seen in riots and occupations such as the Occupy movement on Wall Street from 2008 and at Seattle in 1999. Nothing, however, compares to the challenge posed by the more generalized inhibition and reluctance of consumers worried about debt, job insecurity, widening income inequality, volatile financial markets and general malaise (Cohen, 2013). Add to these ethical consumerism and other critical positions which have collectively dulled the appetite for wanton spending, resulting in large groups of people adopting lifestyles proclaiming voluntary simplicity, downshifting or anti-consumption (Wilk, 1997; Schor, 1998; Shaw and Newholm, 2002; Etzioni, 2009).

Several commentators have concluded that these amount to more than a temporary blip in the onward march of consumerism, auguring a new chapter of capitalism, which may be called austerity consumerism or the new age of thrift; some proponents of consumer capitalism recognize the systemic nature of this change (Piercy et al., 2010). Flatters and Wilmott, market analysts, have argued that, chastened by debt, consumers will 'seek simplicity in products and services; take companies' boardroom ethics into account in purchase decisions; pursue "discretionary" thrift (virtuous but not essential cost cutting); flit capriciously from brand to brand; make green consumption more a matter of reducing waste than purchasing premium products; and steer away from frivolous, extreme leisure experiences in favor of wholesome, authentic ones' (Flatters and Willmott, 2009: 106). In light of such analysis, it is no wonder that many see the return to debt-fuelled consumerism as increasingly unlikely and some are even arguing that the Great Recession is merely the forerunner of more extensive meltdown (Ivanova, 2011; Cohen, 2013).

There is thus no agreement on whether the current mixed picture for consumerism will continue or whether we are at the point of a more fundamental structural change in the nature of consumption. American neo-Cons, like their partners elsewhere in the world, are determined to keep their faith in the market to right itself and are unwilling to be dragged by faint-hearts back into Keynesian state investment to create demand. Keynesians for their part have supported measures such as quantitative easing as the way to stimulate or just maintain demand, and lead to a revival. Others anticipate a bleaker future.

Production and consumption

When writing the first edition of this book, we envisaged two major structural obstacles to the continuing hegemony of the Fordist Deal and Western consumerism at the end of the 20th century. These were, first, the new global division of labour, following the loosening of trade barriers at regional and global levels, and second, environmental limits, exhaustion and degradation associated with rampant consumption. In the 21st century, looking back, we can say that we over-emphasized the importance of the first factor and under-emphasized, if anything, the second. In spite of the continuing drain of jobs from the industrial to the developing countries, new areas of economic activity – especially opened up by the internet – have provided substantial compensation and opportunities for earning in the West. Many Western consumers may no longer enjoy 'jobs for life' enabling them to make long-term spending plans. However, in Anglo-Saxon countries, work opportunities in the new knowledge and information industries, the media, education, health, tourism, sport and entertainment, have enabled many of them to maintain if not expand their standard of living. With millions experiencing lower incomes either due to actual wage cuts or just the steady erosion of spending power due to inflation, the middle class has been squeezed towards the bottom of the pyramid. In countries such as Greece, Ireland, Spain, Cyprus, Portugal, unprecedented levels of private deprivation and breakdowns of community relations and civic institutions have been witnessed.

The precept 'the producer is also the consumer, the consumer is also producer' held somewhat different meanings to Henry Ford and Karl Marx. Yet they were both clear that work and consumption are closely interlinked activities. Unlike some sociologists who have viewed consumption as supplanting work as a source of meaning and identity in people's lives, work and consumption form a unity that becomes reconfigured in different historical periods. If the Fordist Deal offered stable, well-paid, deskilled, alienated jobs in exchange for uniform and methodical mass consumption, post-Fordism augurs a new deal whereby unpredictable employment in highly visible front-line jobs fuels a wide variety of lifestyle consumption patterns. Identities, instead of emerging out of steady jobs, steady class positions and predictable consumption aspirations, are being forged from a variety of transient lifestyle options that include work, sexuality, leisure pursuits, choice of brands and so forth.

In *The Corrosion of Character: The Personal Consequences of Work in the New Capitalism*, Richard Sennett argued that new flexible work arrangements promote a short-term, opportunistic outlook among employees, one that undermines trust and loyalty (Sennett, 1998). Insecurity and fear are endemic. Careers become spasmodic and fragmented, their different steps failing to generate cohesive or integrated life-stories. Exposed to intrusive monitoring of performance, employees feel constantly on trial, yet they are never sure of the goals at which they are aiming. There are no objective measures of what it means to do a good job, and those celebrated for their achievements one day easily find themselves on the receiving end of redundancy packages the next. Showing eagerness, being willing to play any game by any rules, looking attractive and involved, while at the same time maintaining a psychological distance and looking for better prospects elsewhere, these are the chameleon-like qualities of the new economy.

Above all, the opportunism of the new economy means being constantly on the lookout for new opportunities and never being satisfied with what one has. The missed opportunity represents the ultimate failure in this state of affairs. Constant job moves, preoccupation with image and the look of CVs/resumés, absence of commitments and sacrifices, these stand in opposition to traditional family values of duty, commitment, constancy and caring.

Choice is once again the key word and experience – choices of lifestyles, of brands, of partners and so forth. Opportunism rules along with an acceptance of highs and lows. Instead of a coherent linear life story, today's consumers, just like their alter-egos, today's producers, accept uncertainty and insecurity, creating multiple and overlapping storylines with themselves as central characters. Thus the volatility of consumer demand and the flexibility of organizations and consequent casualization of work feed off each other, creating a new configuration for the unity of production and consumption that, far from undermining consumerism, sustains it.

This argument highlights a further area into which consumerism has spread – the construction of *each individual employee as a brand* and the marketing of this brand to prospective employers. This idea was first captured in Erich Fromm's concept of the 'marketing orientation', the mindset of a person who sees himself or herself as a commodity and is only concerned with maximizing its value to an employer (Fromm, [1947] 1965). This worker, Fromm suggests, becomes subsumed by their employer and is consumed as a commodity. Although first outlined three quarters of a century ago, this analysis captures the overlap between consumption and work that in the 21st century has assumed a growing significance. No longer is a person a worker at the workplace and a consumer at home, as under the Fordist Deal. Instead, people are consuming and being consumed in the workplace, and working – often for free – while consuming at home and in their private lives. Here we see a sketch of a post-Fordist Deal which blurs the boundaries between work and leisure, resulting in widespread workaholism and finding its apotheosis in the idea of the 'prosumer', the working consumer and the consumer at work. This latter notion was first sketched by futurologist Alvin Toffler (1970), resuscitated by marketing guru Philip Kotler (1986) and is currently being fully painted in Technicolor by authors such as George Ritzer (Ritzer, 2014; Ritzer et al., 2012). This emerging face of the consumer which we had not considered in our original 1995 publication is the topic of an additional chapter in the present edition of the book, two decades later.

Environmental limits to consumerism

If casualization of work has not brought about the collapse of consumption that at one moment it appeared poised to do in the mid-1990s and again in the Great Recession (2007–13), the severity of the looming ecological crisis is likely to prove a more serious obstacle. It has now become almost universally uncontested that environmental factors threaten future unbridled consumption and that many people are alive to this threat. To consume is to use resources. There is no aspect of consumption that does not have an environmental implication not just for resource depletion but for the balance and sustainability of eco-systems. Making, moving and marketing goods all have a footprint, using space, energy and human labour and creating waste. When this book was first written, the evidence was already strong that there might be finite limits to population growth, to availability of oil, water and other resources, and to the earth's capacity to absorb pollution and waste. With time, this evidence has grown stronger (Millennium Ecosystem Assessment (Program), 2005; UNEP, 2011; World Bank, 2012; UNCTAD, 2013). And the emergence of evidence for 'new' pressures, notably climate change, has persuaded even short-termist politicians and commentators to see the connections between consumption and environmental degradation. The environmental impact of consumption is prompting the reformulation of what is meant by human and social progress (Jackson, 2009).

The challenge of creating modes of sustainable consumption that are at least environmentally benign, and at best environmentally beneficial, is now something that preoccupies many concerned citizens, academics, companies and policy-makers. Since the 1970s, an emerging environmental movement coupled with then noisy hippie reaction to materialism had decried the ecological impact of unfettered consumption (Roszak, 1970; Meadows et al., 1972; Fritsch, 1974). As one of the earliest and most trenchant critiques put it, 'the combination of human numbers and per capita consumption has a considerable impact on the environment, in terms of both the resources we take from it and the pollutants we impose on it' (Goldsmith et al., 1972).

Nearly half a century on, the questions regarding the capacity of the earth to maintain its population persist. The debate is no longer just about absolute levels of population or just about the exhaustion of particular types of raw materials, but about the scale of the continuing impact on the ecosystem from reckless consumption in the developed world and desperate attempts to escape poverty and hunger in the developing world. Even if the planet could sustain twice its present population, it is patently unequipped to sustain it at the present level of the wasteful and polluting lifestyles of the affluent nations, and international political institutions currently appear to be ill-equipped to meet the needs of the poor globally. Early pessimists argued starkly that 'if we attempt to preserve the consumer economy indefinitely, ecological forces will dismantle it savagely' (Durning, 1992b: 107). Early optimists, on the other hand, placed their faith on technical fixes (cleaner cars, recycling, energy conservation, etc.), on the resourcefulness of markets in finding rational solutions (von Weizsäcker et al., 1996) and, less conspicuously, the determination of governments to see that the poor, the disenfranchised and the starving, at home and abroad, are kept at bay.

Since the birth of a modern environmental movement (Pearce, 1991), the environmental critique of consumerism has moved from being a minor irritant to being a major challenge to corporations and states. The Western model of consumerism was originally based on environmentally unsustainable premises; this is something on which there is widespread agreement. Analysts vary over which environmental factor they judge to be most critical. Some point to energy, others to food, others to water or land, others to the over-riding impact of climate change. Still others point to the interactive and cumulative effects of human-induced changes to the environment as a whole. One authoritative analysis by Rockström and colleagues proposed the concept of planetary boundaries and identified at least nine such key boundaries within which humanity can operate safely. They argued that data suggest humanity has already transgressed three of the nine, with three others becoming critical, creating serious risks for the future (Rockström et al., 2009a; Rockström et al., 2009b). Such analyses lend themselves to the view that irreversible 'tipping points' can be reached, beyond which corrective action is difficult if not impossible (O'Riordan and Lenton, 2013). Jared Diamond has illustrated the impact of such collapse at regional levels, identifying numerous examples of thriving civilizations that imploded due to systematic abuse or misuse of eco-systems (Diamond, 2005).

Capitalism has responded to the growing evidence of the adverse environmental impact of consumption in a variety of ways. Many companies have embraced an environmental agenda – some more, some less – and are adapting their products, procedures and marketing to reduce the damage caused by their activities. This has been partly a response to the strength of the environmental case, and partly an attempt to protect or enhance the value of their brands by association with sustainability. Consumers, for their part, have responded in a wide range of ways to increased awareness of the environmental consequences of their choices. Many – possibly even 25 per cent according to some estimates of Australia and Britain (Hamilton, 2003; Hamilton and Mail, 2003) – have 'downshifted', limiting both their income and their expenditure, using their buying power to reward environmentally responsible companies, and to punish those they view as reckless. Some have gone further, organizing boycotts or trying to restrict their purchases to offerings that carry a badge such as Fairtrade. A smaller number, sometimes referred to as 'voluntary simplifiers', have radically reconfigured their consumption altogether to minimize its environmental impact. Yet consumers on the whole remain confused and inconsistent in where and how they apply particular ethics. Governments, like corporations and consumers, have varied in how they have sought to address environmental consequences of contemporary consumption. Many have taken some measures – for instance banning particular chemicals with harmful effects – or restrained environmentally damaging practices – for instance setting quotas for fish capture or on logging. Most governments are nervous about pushing such 'choice-editing' to a level which harms the competitiveness of national companies, and seek, if at all, international agreements. Here the European Union has been important, slowly setting new frameworks for economic activity and cross-national agreements, in pursuit of what is called the 'circular economy' (Ellen Macarthur Foundation and McKinsey, 2013; European Commission, 2014). However, at the global level, attempts to create such new frameworks have often met the difficulty of national interests of different countries and company lobbies. Often, the rhetoric simply puts responsibility onto the consumer, or on government regulation, or on responsible corporate practices, instead of recognizing the interconnections between these actors. Consumers by themselves cannot save the planet.

The elusive pursuit of happiness

In the previous two sections we have argued that consumerism faces major economic, political and environmental challenges. These are brought into sharper relief by the overwhelming evidence of its enduring failure to raise the overall levels of happiness and well-being for the bulk of the population in every society that has attained a certain level of affluence. Economists, psychologists, cultural theorists and even marketing experts have produced convincing evidence that, above a certain minimum, increasing affluence does not produce more well-being for individuals, groups and societies. On the contrary, there is much evidence that indicators of social and psychological distress – including alcoholism, drug use, depression and anxiety, eating disorders – increase with increasing affluence, especially if accompanied by growing inequalities (Kasser, 2002; Layard, 2005; James, 2007; Alvesson, 2013). If anything, the crucial designator for societal happiness and well-being is relative equality within a society. The more equal societies and economies become, the better they seem to perform across a wide range of indicators such as crime, physical and mental health, violence, educational performance and family cohesion (Wilkinson and Pickett, 2009).

Not only has consumerism failed to deliver its promise of increased happiness but, as many cultural analysts have pointed out, it acts as a machine for creating unhappiness, envy and unrealizable desire. The panoply of mass media with its constant glamorization of celebrity lifestyles – movies, TV, journals, websites, gossip columns, etc. – creates an endless fascination with the unobtainable or the ephemeral. Instead of people comparing themselves to their close reference groups, friends, neighbours or family, they endlessly seek to match themselves against the lifestyles of celebrities. Instead of keeping up with the Jones's, people seek to emulate stars whether of sports, film, music or television. The fashion world epitomizes this. No sooner is a celebrity or royalty seen in a particular garment, than a range of replicas are identified or produced by turn-round stores; and then the celebrity stops wearing it and the cycle of desire moves on. Like other ideologies (e.g. religions), what sustains consumerism is its ability simultaneously to create desire and frustrate desire. However, when compounded by the economic challenges outlined above – insecure jobs, stagnant wages, debt, etc. – and the environmental challenges – resource depletion, pollution, climate change, etc. – we can begin to see a moment when the charms of consumerism may prove unable to contain the discontents it causes. This takes the discussion of consumerism back into the mainstream of debates about politics and the ability and willingness of different societies to chart diverse futures for themselves.

Looking ahead

In the first edition of this book, we noted that Western consumerism was then facing uncertainty. It was threatened by technological, economic, environmental and demographic forces. In the intervening 20 years, much has changed. As we have seen in this chapter, consumerism has colonized new territories. The Fordist Deal has unravelled as corporations have been able to outsource production and distribution. Employment in many industrial countries has become increasingly precarious and insecure. At the same time, the rise of the internet has unleashed new opportunities both for wealth creation and consumption, and has dematerialized entire sections of the economy. The encroachment of the 'market' into ever wider sections of social and economic life – education, healthcare, social services, public space – has continued. Environmental awareness has increased and many people have sought to reappraise their consumption through the prism of sustainability. The Great Recession has confronted many hitherto prosperous consumers with debt and even bankruptcy. Whether by choice or force of circumstance, a sizeable number of consumers have opted for voluntary simplicity, downshifting, or even complete withdrawal from particular areas of consumption. The fragility of consumerism today is even more marked than the mid-1990s when this book was first conceived and written.

Despite these developments, we remain convinced that the consumer continues to be unmanageable – our core thesis. As we shall see in the chapters that follow, the consumer presents many faces which easily morph, blend or fragment. This is as true today as it was 20 years ago. The rest of this book explores each face in turn and can, therefore, be seen as a variation on a theme, probing deeper into what is meant by the consumer and consumerism. In the last chapter we shall return to address the questions raised at the beginning of the book.

2

THE CONSUMER AS CHOOSER

The ancient Greeks were right. The ideal of the chosen life does not square with how we live. We are not authors of our lives; we are not even part-authors of the events that mark us most deeply. Nearly everything that is most important in our lives is unchosen. The time and place we are born, our parents, the first language (Thaler, 1980) we speak – these are chance, not choice. It is the casual drift of things that shapes our most fateful relationships. The life of each of us is a chapter of accidents. (Gray, 2002: 109)

CORE ARGUMENTS

Choice is the concept that has virtually come to define contemporary consumption, assuming different psychological, cultural and economic dimensions. Choice lies behind the contemporary notion of freedom that underlies the political philosophy of neo-liberalism that has dominated political life since the 1970s. The menu becomes emblematic of a society in which individuals are constantly invited to exercise choice. However, there are now serious questions about whether choice constitutes a supreme and uncontested value for individuals, societies and environment. While constituting the basis of today's freedom and driving economic development and progress, choice is shown to have a darker side as well as different negative consequences for individuals and economies.

Choice lies at the heart of consumerism, both as its emblem and as its core value. The principal advantages of choice can be summed up in a few brief notions:

- Choice means freedom. All choice is good; the more choice we have the better.
- Choice is good for the economy; consumer choices in free markets are the driving force for efficiency, innovation, growth and diversity.
- A social and political system based on choices is a political system based on citizen freedom. Democracy is the system where citizens freely choose their political rulers. Choice is a supreme political value, lending legitimacy to power relations.
- Consumer capitalism means more choice for everyone. It brings an ever widening part of social and personal life – including identity, reproduction and fertility, gender and sexuality, career and work, even when and how to end one's own life – under the ambit of choice.

In this chapter, we explore where the idea of choice draws its extreme power and ask why it seduces consumers, politicians and intellectuals alike. We question whether all choice is the supreme value that it claims to be, by examining three distinct intellectual traditions that address it: psychological, cultural and economic. We do not deny the reality of choice for many people, nor do we diminish its importance. We do, however, argue that choice has limitations and even that there is a dark side to choice. In particular, we argue that:

1. Choice without information is not real choice. Almost everyone agrees with this. The contention starts over what sort of information is appropriate, how much, in what format and given by whom.
2. Choices are conditioned by what is available, what is easily accessible and what appears in front of our eyes. It is easy to overlook possibilities that do not explicitly confront us as choices.
3. Choice between similar options is only choice in a marginal sense, like choosing between Tweedledum and Tweedledee. It can be psychologically significant for the chooser, but may obscure other choices that do not happen to be 'on the menu'. We opt to use the word 'selection' for this type of choice.
4. Choice limited only to those with resources undermines the benefits of choice for all. It can disenfranchise the poor from large areas of social life and can lead to a relentless competition among the others that rarely results in greater happiness or well-being.
5. The overabundance of choices leads to diminishing returns. It prompts fears of failing and worries about choosing the right option. Anxiety can be caused by major decisions (for example, marriage, career, house) but also by trivial ones (for example, choosing a wine at a restaurant).
6. Choice can be used as a smoke screen for shedding responsibility or for deception. If one is seen as actively choosing a particular option, one is expected not to complain when it goes wrong; for example, if a cosmetic operation leads to complications or if a used car breaks down.
7. Choice may be seen as the reason for different actions which are in fact the result of habit, instinct or impulsive emotion.
8. Every choice has consequences, some of which are not intended. These may lead to further choices or forced actions, as in a chess game. Choices often appear singly, but in reality one choice leads to another and, collectively, they can generate entrapment where damaging courses of action continue to be pursued because the costs of extrication appear to be too high.
9. Choice is not always a guarantee for freedom. Certain choices expose us to discreet and other forms of control and the exercise of choice exposes us to forms of surveillance that may undermine our privacy and our freedom.

The allure and power of choice

It is hard to stand back from the idea of choice. Choice is inextricably linked with morality, questions of right and wrong, good and evil. Without choice there would be no stories and no drama; there would be no heroes making 'hard choices' and seeing them through to triumph, nor victims suffering the consequences of their own 'bad choices' or the choices of others. Without choice, there would be no nations going to war, no revolutions, no adventure, no journey, no change. Uttering the word 'no' or the word 'yes' is every child's and every adult's way of making a choice known to others. Even animals exercise choice when they jump a fence to seek greener pastures on the other side or when they refuse to budge taking no account of carrots or sticks. There are, of course, those who deny the reality of choice. Determinists would argue that many or even all the choices we experience as having are illusions – their outcomes are already determined at the physical, biological or psychological level. Yet, even those who deride choice as a mere illusion would be up in arms if their choices of newspapers or books, let alone political representation or fertility treatment, were restricted.

Choice is something we get used to, something we take for granted until suddenly we find ourselves denied it. This is why choice is a sensitive issue. As individuals, we all like to believe that we have choices, even if we choose not to exercise them. We will sometimes choose to fight battles defending our right to make choices that we do not plan to exercise. We will vociferously defend our right to vote, even if we choose not to turn up at the poll booths at election time. But many of us would react strongly to being *forced* to vote (for example, as a precondition to being issued with a passport) – our choice *not* to vote is as important as our choice of *who* to vote *for*.

Choice is desirable. Many of us will prefer an airline that offers us a choice of three meals over one that offers us but a single one, *even if* none of the options of the former is as good as the single option of the latter. Arguably, one of the last things that we will surrender when everything else is lost is our right to make choices. The right to choose when and how to die seems to sum up the value we have come to accord to choice. In the ancient Greek myth, Pandora's Box was Zeus' gift to Pandora, a valuable receptacle containing all the blessings of the gods; when opened, everything escaped, last of all hope. Like Pandora, today we may be at risk of losing all the blessings for the sake of retaining choice.

The rise of the menu society

The logic of 'the more choices the better' is now permeating every aspect of life. A food shopper a century ago would have found the idea of a hypermarket with 40,000 different items on sale inconceivable. Even more inconceivable would have been the idea of internet bookshops like Amazon, which, at the time of writing, listed 44,466,265 different books for sale in the UK. The department store of the past has been supplanted by the innumerable internet outlets offering countless fashion items, household goods, designer objects and entertainment opportunities. Hundreds if not thousands of TV channels have become available via satellite, cable and internet, challenging the few terrestrial channels that dominated television even 20 years ago. The logic of choice has spread to education and health provisions. University courses now come in an unparalleled range, with varieties ostensibly to cater for every taste. Within each course there are ever increasing numbers of 'electives' for students to choose. Patients are offered different options of treatment by a choice of hospitals. New fertility treatments have extended the range of choices over child-bearing. New medical procedures have created ever wider ranges of choices over a person's gender, appearance and body shape. The internet has opened up previously unimaginable ranges of choice – product choices, love choices, game choices, network and club choices, sex choices and identity choices, virtual and 'real'.

This proliferation of choice is often seen as a cause for celebration by consumers themselves, but also by market enthusiasts and politicians of all political colours, by cultural and social theorists, by media pundits and consumer advocates who are never short of products and ranges to compare. *The menu*, in the view of sociologists Korczynski and Ott, becomes a dominant metaphor of our times, not only in the sphere of consumption, but also in those of production and even citizenship. It also dominates nearly every form of electronic activity. The restaurant menu, they argue, is meant to enchant and appeal to the customer who is naturally cast in the role of a sovereign figure choosing between alternatives. 'This ritualised emphasis on autonomous choice can make the act of choosing as delicious as the actual food consumed. The customer here consumes the enchanting myth of sovereignty' (Korczynski and Ott, 2006: 912).

This fetishization of choice is not without costs and headaches for the consumer. The enormity of choices create formidable difficulties. Consumers find this enormity almost impossible to navigate and must rely on a number of resources in order to guide them, including their own skills, various sources of information and advice, as well as the prompts or 'nudges' offered by producers themselves. The internet has opened up unprecedented opportunities for information sharing. It also creates difficulties of its own, like information overload or the questionable validity and reliability of sources. Traditional ways of eliciting information about the quality of different commodities relied on stories and experiences of friends or relatives. These now find their online parallels, as people turn to internet communities and trusted websites.

The rise of the menu society is complemented by the growth of packages and offers. The selling and marketing skills of modern firms are refashioned into supplying their customer with what marketing scholars Firat and Dholakia (1998) term 'structures of available alternatives'. These organize choices into patterns, guided by 'packages', 'best buys', 'special deals', etc. Just as a waiter may highlight specific items on a menu to a customer, the menu itself may offer various packages or combinations of courses, dishes and drinks that ostensibly simplify the customer's choice, but also generate a measure of control over these choices. In a similar way, company websites are now learning to prompt or guide consumers into particular pathways of choice, particular combinations of products and so forth. In this way, choices can be structured or 'nudged' through various default configurations and manufacturers' or suppliers' recommendations (Goldstein et al., 2008). A nudge theory has thus recently emerged, suggesting that mass behaviour, including consumer choices, can be shaped to specific ends:

> *A nudge ... is any aspect of the choice architecture that alters people's behavior in a predictable way without forbidding any options or significantly changing their economic incentives. To count as a mere nudge, the intervention must be easy and cheap to avoid. Nudges are not mandates. Putting fruit at eye level counts as a nudge. Banning junk food does not. (Thaler and Sunstein, 2008: 6)*

Nudging emerges as a vital strategy through which choice becomes a mechanism for managing the consumer, while perpetuating the illusion of consumer sovereignty. 'The choice is yours' proclaims the menu, ostensibly placing the consumer in the position of power, an invitation of such seduction that few can decline.

The menu society does not only offer the seduction of choice as a veil for subtle or not so subtle controls. It also individualizes consumption. You may be at a table with others but you are each meant to make your own choice. You can all suit your own taste and risk your own disappointment. Yet, as anyone who has shared a restaurant table with others knows, individual choices are also shaped by the preferences expressed by others around the table and by wider social conventions and personal commitments. To a vegetarian or a vegan, a wide range of options on many a restaurant menu can be entirely meaningless. The menu society also creates hierarchies of privilege and exclusion. For somebody who finds themselves in a restaurant far more expensive than they can afford, the opulence of the menu and the variety of offerings on the wine list, far from enchanting, can turn into a veritable nightmare.

For all its downside, the menu opens up an unprecedented type of freedom, one which spreads way beyond consumer choices as the model for decision-making in everyday life. Choosing politicians, choosing occupations, choosing a university, choosing an apartment, choosing a partner, indeed choosing an identity, all are opened up by this freedom. The market has become the underpinning of this freedom to choose. It is a freedom for the sake of which people will make many sacrifices and which its proponents declaim as an inviolable principle for the good life (Friedman, 1962; Friedman and Friedman, 1980). This idea of freedom is quite distinct from other interpretations of freedom. These include philosophical and theological discourses of free will, political conceptions of freedom of speech, self-determination and association, and the intellectual value of freedom of inquiry and thought. All of these have tended to be marginalized in public discourses under the dominance of the neo-liberal consumerist concept: the freedom to choose among options on a menu.

In the last few years, we have also become aware of another danger that the menu society engenders. Our choices are constantly monitored by public and private agencies, generating data that commands a high price. A woman who orders an online pregnancy testing is liable to be bombarded with advertisements for a variety of related pregnancy and maternity products; indeed, she may also risk the offer of a job, should a prospective employer become aware of her condition. A man who seeks help for a chronic medical condition from a friendly agency on the internet may soon find that insurance companies raise their health premiums or refuse him coverage altogether. As our movements and actions are ever more closely followed, it is now becoming apparent that the exercise of free choice may seriously jeopardise our privacy and indeed curtail our freedom.

Choice in different academic disciplines

Academics have approached choice in a number of different ways, generating different insights and theories. The rise of consumerism has made consumer choice a major area of inquiry, submitting it to relentless scrutiny. Companies stand to make massive gains if they can accurately forecast consumer choices; they stand to make even bigger gains if they can influence these choices. The image of the consumer as chooser is thus constantly invented and reinvented, as insights from different academic disciplines are seized by marketing and consumer behaviour experts. In this way, we can encounter

- the rational thrifty consumer who thinks carefully before every purchase and tries to maximize value for money
- the impulsive spendthrift consumer who cannot resist a well-packaged temptation
- the crowd-following consumer who will follow the dictates of fashion, whatever they happen to be
- the individualistic consumer who will strive for uniqueness and difference
- the timid consumer who needs constant reassurance and reinforcement
- the adventurous consumer who longs for risk and excitement
- ... and many others.

The rest of this chapter will examine consumer choice as it is approached from three different perspectives. The first perspective has theorized the cognitive and social psychological processes by which consumers make decisions or judgements. The second has focused on the social and cultural context within which consumer choices are made. The third has debated the centrality of choice for political economy and for the operation of markets. We shall examine each one in turn.

The psychology of choice

Throughout the 20th century, many psychologists approached choice through laboratory studies of decision-making. An ever increasing part of these studies addressed consumption: why is one product chosen over another? What shapes the direction of choice? How can choice be influenced by extraneous factors? Which factors are more significant to different groups? More recently, market researchers have gone into ever finer gradations of the factors that influence consumer choices. In addition to laboratory testing, new product ideas are now also widely tested on focus groups. Whereas laboratory studies explore discrete 'objective' factors, focus groups invite participants to voice their own interpretations and views. An immense amount of material has emerged from both research traditions, often summarized in consumer behaviour or marketing textbooks. In a sense, the consumer has become the guinea pig on which new market ideas are tried and where new product ideas are sought. The trajectory of psychology, like other human sciences, from a discipline interested in Big Ideas to a discipline concerned about 'marginal differences' in behaviour is illuminating.

Writing in the 1890s, William James argued that 'the mind selects' (James, 1891: 285), and 'no two men are known to choose alike' (James, 1891: 289), but many of his successors seemed determined to identify trends and similarities. Psychology started the 20th century with grand promises – the unlocking of human motivation, no less – but a large part of it ended the century as a servant to mass consumer enterprise. Whereas Sigmund Freud, for example, pioneered studies of the *unconscious* in Vienna, his nephew Edward Bernays sought to apply such insights to create the discipline of public relations in New York as the systematic attempt to shape the *consciousness* of consumers (Tye, 1998). The rise and fragmentation of psychology's interest in consumer choice has an important tale to tell. In the 20th century, which saw the rise of the rhetoric of choice, applied psychologists spent much of their time studying the factors that determine choices and the ways such factors can be controlled. Motivation theory, whether applied to the individual as producer or consumer, became the key to constraining, guiding and controlling choice. Psychologists became merchandisers of meaning (Sievers, 1986). For much of late 20th-century psychology, the study of behaviour had become a study of control, along the path laid by F. W. 'Speedy' Taylor, the father of Scientific Management. For Taylor, the purpose of what became known as industrial or occupational psychology was to remove the unpredictability of the human factor in production. The uses of modern psychology emerged as remarkably prosaic. When applied to consumers, this psychology was to help producers understand how consumers discriminate between products. Such was the point of studies like that of R. L. Brown in the 1950s on whether the wrapper on a loaf of bread can influence consumer perception of freshness; consumers judged wrapped bread, whether one day or two day old, as equally 'fresh' as freshly baked bread (Brown, 1958). The core objective of management was to control and manage both consumers and producers using insights from psychology, little realizing that both of these actors would find ways of escaping the clutches of managerial control.

A different intellectual tradition of psychology came to dominate the middle part of the 20th century – behaviourist psychology. This chose to ignore the reasons people give for their actions and focused exclusively on their behaviours. From their perspective, behaviour is substantially the result of learnt conditioning, prompted by incentives and punishments (Skinner, 1972). Decisions are therefore conditioned by earlier experience, habits and context. Choice is merely learned behaviour, an act of discrimination between stimuli (Hull, 1974). From this perspective, choice was almost an illusion, the consumer lapsing from choice-maker to a target for behaviour modification.

Another major tradition in psychology, depth psychology, found the promise of marketing applications even more alluring than did the behaviourists. Since the 1950s, a part of depth psychology was applied to promote specific products by connecting them to unconscious desires or by presenting them as substitute gratification for repressed or unexpressed wishes. If you are unconsciously longing for power and prestige, there is a product somewhere that will make you feel powerful and important. If you are unconsciously craving love and affection, there is a consumer experience that will make you feel loved and appreciated. Thus, advertising engaged in its titanic campaign to charge and supercharge everyday products and experiences with powerful meanings. The sexualization of everyday objects (fast cars, cigarettes, lipsticks and so on) was one of the outcomes of this campaign (Dichter, 1964). Thus, within psychology, there was a strange truce on the subject of choice between the two dominant schools, psychoanalysis and behaviourism, with both stressing the management of and, on occasion, the constraints on choice.

Even as these two schools of thought were availing themselves to the management and control of choice, a third school, humanistic psychology, could naively argue that, other things being equal, humans always choose love rather than hate, affection and creativity rather than fear and obedience (Maslow, [1954] 1970: 275ff). Freed from constraints by oppressive social conventions and expectations, people, according to this view, mostly make the right choices seeking growth and happiness for themselves and those around them – a far cry from the brash world of marketing psychology. Ironically, humanistic psychology has spawned its own 'self-help industry' of books, support programmes, coaching and psychotherapy, whose core promise was to liberate people from their anxieties and fears and put them back in control of their own lives. This has come under considerable criticism for creating a 'self-sustaining market' that accentuates the very anxieties which it purports to alleviate (Davis, 2008; Salecl, 2010).

The rise and rise of brands

Brands epitomize the kind of choices confronting today's c
noted by numerous commentators (see, for example, Kle
2005; Arvidsson, 2006), also epitomizes the enduring success
chology in charging everyday consumer products and exp
conscious and unconscious meanings. The power of brands is well c
Sir Michael Perry, ex-chairman of Unilever, one of the world's bigge
owners, in a presidential address to the UK Advertising Association:

> In the modern world, brands are a key part of how individuals define themselves and
> their relationships with one another. The old, rigid barriers are disappearing – class and rank;
> blue collar and white collar; council tenant and home owner; employee and housewife.
> More and more we are simply consumers – with tastes, lifestyles and aspirations that
> are very different. It's a marketing given by now that the consumer defines the brand.
> But the brand also defines the consumer. We are what we wear, what we eat, what we
> drive. Each of us in this room is a walking compendium of brands. You chose each of
> those brands among many options – because they felt 'more like you'. The collection
> of brands we choose to assemble around us have become amongst the most direct
> expressions of our individuality – or more precisely, our deep psychological need to iden-
> tify ourselves with others. (Perry, 1994: 4, emphasis added)

Brands are instantly recognizable. They stand out from a crowd by having a
unique personality, a personality associated with any number of qualities – tradition,
success, drive, beauty, economy – and supported by a variety of images, stories,
characters, slogans and logos associated with them. In this way, brands reflect the
rampant individualism of consumerist cultures, where there is a brand or a family
of brands to suit every taste and every lifestyle. Their diversity embodies the
dynamism of consumer capitalism, their ubiquity stands for its democratic ethos –
the president of the United States can be seen holding the same can of fizzy drink
or sporting the same brand of running shoes as anyone else.

Brands are infiltrating every aspect of life. People brand themselves in their
search for employment; and organizations now brand themselves to their
employees as much as to their customers. Employees for their part, especially
those visible to the customers, become features of a corporate brand, their looks
and personality capable of enhancing it or contaminating it (see Chapter 11,
'The Consumer as Worker'). A large part of a corporation's valuation today
resides in the value of the brands it owns or in its own name and logo as a brand.
The value of brands like Google or Facebook are currently millions of times
greater than the value of any material assets they own. Companies that have
never produced any profit can be worth billions of dollars purely on the value
of their brands. Aware of the importance of brand value, companies seek to control (not always successfully) the meanings, images and emotions evoked by

.. They construct stories for their brands and rehearse these stories through ertisements, product placements and various marketing campaigns in the iss media and, increasingly, the social media. Managing a brand becomes ery bit as important as managing employees and customers.

How then do brands affect consumer choice? Brands are both objects of choice and filters of choice. They present the consumer with numerous dilemmas as they compete for affection and attention, but, once a consumer has declared loyalty to a particular brand, the realm of choice becomes more limited. A brand can then appear to offer an anchor of security and stability in an unstable world. Yet, brands constantly stir up new temptations and new insecurities. Faced with a profusion of brands, the relentless emergence of new ones, the decline and disappearance of some old familiar ones and the sudden resurgence and revival of others, consumers can become confused, fascinated or repelled (see Chapter 3, 'The Consumer as Communicator'). They may fall in love with some brands, experimentally play with others, distance themselves from yet others or try to ignore them. Some consumers construct their entire identity by embracing a handful or even a single brand, while others develop a deep abhorrence and mistrust of brands altogether opting instead for unbranded goods and services. Yet, it has become impossible to ignore brands as they fill and saturate our homes, our screens, our cities and even our minds.

The phenomenal success of Naomi Klein's book *No Logo: Taking Aim at the Brand Bullies* (2000) expressed deep discomfort with the ever increasing domi- nance of brands and branding. No longer is it unfashionable to argue, as we did in the first edition of this book, that brands are oppressive and gloss over their more complex and toxic consequences. Klein's book became a focal text for an anti-consumerist ethos that sought to challenge the hegemony of brands and the insipid violence they engender. It also captured a mood that was first expressed in a politically significant way in the protests against the General Agreement on Tariffs and Trade (GATT) trade talks held in Seattle in December 1999 (Solnit et al., 2009). Klein's book was thus instrumental in capturing an anti-corporate sentiment and helped voice a dissatisfaction with the power of brands. This was not what the brand psychologists had either anticipated or wanted in the decades of brand build-up and ascribing monetary value to brands.

The 'No Logo' ethos, despite the book's success, has not made much of a dent in the continuing rise of brands (Gilmore, 1999; Gilmore, 2003). Nor has the economic downturn of the last few years, which has possibly favoured some brands and encouraged others to move on with the times. 'Own label' products have grown on the back of the retailers' increasing power at the expense of manufacturers (Seth and Randall, 2001). Changes in retailing have encouraged some consumers to purchase retailers' 'own label' products, thus elevating these labels as new brands associated with thrift and savvy consumerism (Flatters and

Willmott, 2009; Piercy et al., 2010). For all this, the fierce campaign to capture consumer spending and link it with particular brands continues. Belief in consumer choice and the power of brands to meet the consumer's needs for meaning and identity remain articles of faith not only for market researchers and their psychological gurus, but also for corporations and most consumers.

Brands rise and fall, they come and go. They are resisted by sections of the populations on ideological, price or other grounds, but they continue to be major influences on consumer choice. In an uncertain world, brands symbolize stability and continuity. In a highly standardized world, brands symbolize individuality and uniqueness. And in a highly unequal world, brands symbolize egalitarianism and democracy. In their ability to reconcile deep-seated contradictions in contemporary consumerism, brands, like the myths of traditional societies, can be seen as archetypal emblems arousing and sometimes meeting deep-seated emotions. This is the ultimate source of their power.

Advertising: a systematic creation of false choices?

As we stated at the opening of this chapter, information is a precondition for meaningful choice. One can make choices but if one lacks information about alternatives, their pros and cons, their uses, side-effects and dysfunctions, the results of these choices can range from inadequate to catastrophic. Moreover, information can create false choices or guided choices concealing rather than elucidating the full range of options. The relationship between information and choice is captured in the Chinese story recounted by Gregory Bateson (1972: 208). A guru shows a stick to his pupil and says 'if you say this is a stick, I will beat you with it; if you say this is not a stick, I will beat you with it'. The lesson the guru was trying to impress on the pupil is not to fall for false choices. A sensible pupil should say anything she or he wished other than the two 'choices' proffered by the master. Is the advertisers' project anything other than the drawing up of false choices?

Is the message from psychology that consumer choices are nudged and manipulated? Most academic researchers would say yes. Practitioners, however, like advertising and marketing experts, are more equivocal. On the one hand, they argue that their professional skills can work (or they would be out of a job). On the other hand, when accused of manipulation, they emphasize that their powers are limited. Consumers today are meant to be sophisticated. They can see through attempts to manipulate them; they resist and even mock clumsy attempts at persuasion. These battle lines are old and heat up periodically, notably over advertising that targets children, enticing them, for example, to eat sugary, unhealthy foods (Hawkes, 2007).

An unalloyed notion of choice becomes untenable. For consumers to be 'sovereign', they would have to have a wide range of options, an unlimited amount of information, good education and a sound understanding of their own needs and wants. They would have to be immune to temptation. In the words of E. J. Mishan, an economist, nothing is further away from reality.

> [U]nless the wants of consumers exist independently of the products created by industrial concerns it is not correct to speak of the market as acting to adapt the given resources of the economy to meet the material requirements of society. In fact, not only do producers determine the range of market goods from which consumers must take their choice, they also seek continuously to persuade consumer to choose what is being produced today and to 'unchoose' that which was being produced yesterday. Therefore to continue to regard the market ... as primarily a 'want-satisfying' mechanism is to close one's eyes to the more important fact, that it has become a want-creating mechanism. (Mishan, 1967: 147ff)

Even if consumers were not susceptible to the temptations and false choices presented to them by advertisers, obtaining accurate information about different products is deeply problematic. The old-fashioned ways of eliciting such information relied on advice from experts as well as the experiences of friends and relatives. In the 1970s, the economist J. K. Galbraith argued that, with the demise of the extended family, consumers lost a source of consumer experience and know-how in the home (Galbraith, 1974: 59–60). Today, however, consumers have no shortage of online sources of information and advice, both from experts and from other consumers like themselves. Gone is the local travel agent with vested interests in recommending particular holiday packages, but trusted for having provided several happy holidays in the past; in comes the trip feedback advisory website. Gone are the personal recommendations of a university or a course; in come new ranking systems which shake up old reputations, student satisfaction surveys, impact indicators and media evaluations.

As more information becomes available, the options open to the consumer become more numerous and more complex calling for still more information. Thus information itself does not simplify, let alone resolve the conundrum of choice. A vicious circle emerges of ever increasing options and information overload, one that intensifies anxieties – there will always be a better deal somewhere, a better product, one that would make our current choices look foolish. In this way a chronic insecurity and anxiety comes to characterize many consumer choices; people spend more and more of their time searching and have less and less confidence that they have landed on the best option for them. They agonize long over trivialities and are caught unprepared for the consequences of their choices. Alternatively, they act impulsively and are caught short when the bill arrives. In summary then, a consumer society, glorifying choice, bombards its consumers with information rationalized as an aid to choice; this simultaneously underlines how under-informed they are and creates an information overload that often inhibits rather than aids their decision-making. It is not surprising then that many psychologists have started to talk about 'the paradox of choice' (Schwartz, 2004) or even the 'tyranny of choice' (Salecl, 2010).

Choice in cultural studies

The second tradition that has systematically explored consumer choice is cultural studies. Instead of examining how consumers make different choices and what obstacles and resources they find along the way, cultural studies explore choice as part of a zeitgeist, the spirit of our times, indeed as a defining feature of con-temporary culture, politics and society. Where cultural studies fundamentally differ from psychology is in acknowledging that choices, even when they seem to be made by individuals, are socially situated. People do not merely make choices. They also constantly judge the choices made by others and they worry about how their choices will be judged by others. Whether they acknowledge it or not, choices are made 'through the eyes of others' (Salecl, 2010). Even when an action is not the result of a conscious choice, it is likely that others will see it as precisely this – a conscious decision.

The seductiveness of choice is a point on which numerous cultural theorists of consumption converge. Many of these writers were strongly influenced by postmodernist thinking, fashionable throughout the 1980s and 1990s, that emphasized the plurality of meanings, the importance of language and the social construction of reality (e.g. Baudrillard, 1983; Baudrillard, 1988; Harvey, 1990; Featherstone, 1991; Bauman, 1992; Bertens, 1995; Firat and Venkatesh, 1995; Elliott, 1997). The postmodern world is highly relativistic without abso-lute standards or unshakable truths. Bauman and Baudrillard, two key figures in this area, argued that much modern consumption unfolds in the realm of seduction, where goods are not chosen for their uses but as objects of fantasy. Choice itself is an illusion, but like all illusions it serves as a mechanism of control. Seduction is one major mode of control that applies to those people with the means to scrutinize, to fall in love and to purchase goods, that is, those who can easily persuade themselves that they are choosing. By contrast, the 'new poor', disenfranchised from choice, by being dependent on the state for their livelihood, a livelihood devoid of choice, are controlled through repres-sion (Bauman, 1998). Whether living in our midst or in developing countries, the poor, living without choices, become a spectacle at once fascinating and terrifying, but a spectacle that reminds us what fate awaits us were we to ever surrender our ability to choose.

Bauman's theory linking consumer choice with freedom is sophisticated but also profoundly ambiguous. Choice and especially consumer choice, he argued, is the foundation of a new concept of *freedom*: 'In our society, individual freedom is constituted as, first and foremost, freedom of the consumer ...' (Bauman, 1988: 7ff). This freedom, however, is not distributed evenly: '[t]hose who rule, are free; those who are free, rule' (Bauman, 1988: 23). Modern capitalism, says Bauman, opened up the possibility of choice to ever-increasing numbers of people, offering 'a wider than ever space ... the rapidly expanding, seemingly limitless, world of consumption' (Bauman, 1988: 57). By the same token, however, the very system that offers 'a lot of choice and makes him a truly "free" individual, also generates on a massive scale the experience of oppression' (Bauman, 1988: 50ff). Bauman argues that precisely because of the importance of choice, those excluded from making choices automatically become disenfranchised and oppressed.

The key to this type of freedom is not a political struggle for the acquisition of communal rights (like those that emerged from the French and American Revolutions, the anti-colonial struggles in 20th-century India or the anti-apartheid movement in South Africa), but the marketplace. 'The consumer market as a whole may be seen as an institutionalized exit from politics', argued Bauman (1988: 82). Yet, this freedom is no less sweet than what drove the French Revolution:

> What makes the freedom offered by the market more alluring still is that it comes without the blemish which tainted most of its other forms: the same market which offers freedom offers also certainty. It offers the individual the right to a 'thoroughly individual' choice; yet it also supplies social approval for such choice, thereby exorcizing that ghost of insecurity ... People are thus pulled to the market by a double bind: they depend on it for their individual freedom; and they depend on it for enjoying their freedom without paying the price of insecurity. (Bauman, 1988: 61)

This double bind of choice lies at the heart of Bauman's ambivalence. Here is the price of consumer freedom:

> Thick walls are an indispensable part of consumer society; so is their inobtrusiveness for insiders. ... Consumers rarely catch a glimpse of the other side. The squalor of inner cities they pass in the comely and plush interior of their cars. If they ever visit the 'Third World', it is for its safaris and massage parlours, not for its sweatshops. (Bauman, 1988: 92)

Bauman's approach to choice resonates with approval and disapproval. Choice, even when exercised, has its downside. Like other cultural theorists, Bauman acknowledges the contradictions of choice. Choice is imagined, yet real; choice liberates some, but exacerbates the oppression of others.

Like Bauman, Giddens placed choice squarely at the centre of his discussion of contemporary culture. The interest in his argument lies in his attempt to link choice to individuals' struggle for identity and selfhood. Unlike people in traditional societies whose identity was fixed by social position, tradition and habit, the contemporary individual pursues an unending project of self-creation by continuously making choices. His or her identity is never fixed but always in the making through a large number of every day choices.

> *On the level of the self, a fundamental component of day-to-day activity is simply that of choice. Obviously, no culture eliminates choice altogether in day-to-day affairs, and all traditions are effectively choices among an indefinite range of possible behaviour patterns. Yet, by definition, tradition or established habit orders life within relatively set channels. Modernity confronts the individual with a complex diversity of choices and ... at the same time offers little help as to which options should be selected. (Giddens, 1991: 80)*

For Giddens 'we all not only follow lifestyles, but in an important sense are forced to do so – we have no choice but to choose'. Lifestyles are routinized practices around which consumers define themselves:

> *Each of the small decisions a person makes every day – what to wear, what to eat, how to conduct himself at work, whom to meet with later in the evening – contributes to such routines. All such choices (as well as larger and more consequential ones) are decisions not only about how to act but who to be. (Giddens, 1991: 81)*

Giddens, like Bauman, acknowledges that choice is not open to everyone. 'To speak of a multiplicity of choices is not to suppose that all choices are open to everyone' (Giddens, 1991: 82). Yet, the rise of choice is an indicator of the demise of traditional society. The world is now characterized by an accentuation of difference and the opportunity for people to create their own niches, rather than be controlled by tradition or by mass markets. Consumption is an opportunity to create and display one's identity (see Chapter 5, 'The Consumer as Identity-seeker'). Many postmodern theorists stress the creative opportunities of contemporary consumption, how individuals can forge a unique sense of selfhood out of resources available to them.

Other cultural theorists take a more equivocal view: people seek both uniqueness and similarity; culture both opens up choices but also restricts them. Bourdieu (1984) uses the term 'habitus' to indicate a modest but significant elbow room for choice afforded to each individual by his or her social class or stratum. Tastes in food, films, music, art, photographs and so on, are social demarcators, generally accounted for by a person's 'cultural capital', that is, his or her educational level, occupation, physical appearance and so forth. A quest for similarity and a quest for difference seem to exist side by side. One of the authors visited the car park of a prestigious financial institution and was surprised by the array of cars parked next to each other – they all happened to be black BMWs. Coincidence? Were all financial high-fliers behaving like a herd of animals? Did they all make the same choice by accident? Then he noticed that not all black BMWs were identical. To his untutored eyes, dissimilarities like insignia SE and Gran Coupé and tiny differences in trim and finish seemed unimportant. Yet, to their owners such differences may have been deeply significant, possibly even reflecting differences in status and earnings. Was the car park a site of likeness or one of difference? Bourdieu may well have seen it as a both, a space, a habitus, where both can be practiced.

These tensions – choice as a quest for difference versus choice as a quest for similarity, culture as opening up choices versus culture as closing down choices – are endemic in cultural approaches of consumption. Interest in them can be traced back to Veblen's and Simmel's pioneering accounts of fashion at the start of the 20th century (see Chapter 3, 'The Consumer as Communicator'). What was new in postmodern theorizing in the 1990s was its single-minded emphasis on difference. Thus Rutherford argued that the rules of consumer choice were changing: 'It's no longer about keeping up with the Jones's, it's about being different from them' (Rutherford, 1990: 11). Baudrillard argued that difference was the *only* object of consumer choice, in other words, people bought solely for the purpose to be different from others. The futility of this project is self-evident, yet this obsessive pursuit of difference defined the postmodern consumer (Baudrillard, [1970] 1988: 45). The postmodernists' fascination with difference sometimes seemed to turn choice into mere whim and caprice. Choosing between goods became a cerebral in-joke, an impudent gesture, a defiant rejection of anything as boring as calculation and the embracement of 'why not?' as the ultimate rationale for choice. 'Anything goes' became the postmodern slogan, *par excellence*.

Since the 2001 attacks by Al Qaeda on New York and Washington DC, the more extreme forms of postmodernism which denied the existence of any objective reality or facts went into tail-spin. By 2013, leading marketing experts Cova, Maclaran and Bradshaw proclaimed the end of postmodernism in consumer studies (Cova et al., 2013). The number of books and articles that used 'postmodern' in their title declined from 1,610 in 2000 to 928 in 2013, according to Google Scholar, a very significant decline given how slowly trends filter through publishing outlets. Maybe even more significant is the fact that postmodern claims that seemed exciting or plausible during the movement's high noon now sound dated, affected and even juvenile. The legacy of postmodernism, however, with its deconstruction of tacit power relations and meanings, its close scrutiny of the way language is used to create hierarchies of privilege and exclusion, and its general mistrust of anything that proclaims itself as commonsense or natural, has endured. The lasting insight of postmodernism on thinking about choice is that the ubiquity of choice and brands should be mistrusted; choice is not a fact, but a way of looking at our experiences and the situations we face. These experiences and the power structures from which they emerge must be critically and relentlessly assessed.

Choice in economic theory

In contrast to cultural theorists, economists start with the assumption of rational choice and explore its implications. The basic tenet of modern economics is that people on the whole act rationally in pursuit of their self-interests, whether as consumers, workers or producers. Economists prefer to speak of preferences, not needs or desires, and people's preferences are formed independently of the options available to them – they are 'exogenous' to the economy. Resources are scarce and human wants are infinite, so choices must be made between competing alternatives. On the basis of the best available information, people choose the optimal course of action to maximize their welfare, after a careful consideration of all options, under their existing 'budget constraints'. In this way, economic theory has generally approached the behaviour of consumers as one of 'constrained optimization'.

This approach to consumer choice is quite consistent. Many economists describe it as 'elegant' and it has dominated mainstream economics for decades. It is summed up in Samuelson's confident assertion that modern economics is the study of 'how ... we choose to use scarce productive resources with alternative uses, to meet prescribed ends ...' (Samuelson, 1970: 13). This approach has been criticized for assuming an ideal world (where individuals have perfect information, where they know exactly what their needs are, where they act consistently and rationally and so forth) that does not correspond to reality. 'The theory merely assumes the individual to be acting rationally, in that his choices are consistent with each other and stable over the short time that is relevant' (Douglas and Isherwood, 1978: 19). What consumers actually choose is often systematically different from what economic theory predicts that they would choose.

Since the pioneering work of Herbert Simon, many economists have acknowledged that in most practical situations human beings cannot act as perfectly rational men and women. Simon's concept of 'bounded rationality' sought to highlight that even 'rational' actors will come to a decision when they find an alternative deemed *good enough* instead of endlessly seeking the perfect option (Simon, 1947). But, as prospect theory (Kahneman and Tversky, 1979) has demonstrated, people are not 'even rational'. When presented with situations involving risk, people's judgements are fundamentally and systematically biased – in other words, they evaluate risk and make decisions in systematically different (and inconsistent) ways from what economists would expect them to do. In particular, we all have an exaggerated tendency to avoid risk where gains are concerned and seek risk where potential losses are concerned. We generally prefer certain outcomes over uncertain ones, even when uncertain ones offer the promise of far greater rewards (Thaler, 1980; Kahneman and Tversky, 2000; Kahneman, 2011). Others have shown that, when purchasing goods that give pleasure, consumer choices are governed by very different factors from the choices they make when they purchase things that are merely 'useful' (Dhar and Wertenbroch, 2000). All in all, the idea of rational beings making rational choices to best meet their needs has come under considerable criticism, even though it continues to function as a fundamental assumption in a great part of mainstream economic modelling and forecasting.

Some economists have expressed still more fundamental reservations, by questioning the centrality of *all choice* as a determinant of economic behaviour. Deaton and Muellbauer, for instance, wrote that 'the part played by preferences in determining behaviour tends to be overestimated' (Deaton and Muellbauer, 1980: 3). Other factors influencing economic behaviour are more important than choices between alternatives: budgets, availability, information, uncertainty. Consumers have no way of knowing which companies offer the 'best' prices for a particular good (Deaton and Muellbauer, 1980: 410); they often have to make decisions in an information vacuum which is only partially filled by the data and advice that consumer organizations supply through their testing procedures and publications (now mostly done online). Nor is this data and advice consistent. Deaton and Muellbauer are right; many consumer 'choices' can be little more than stabs in the twilight whose full ramifications do not become evident until later. Every action taken by a consumer can have unintended ramifications, pleasant as well as unpleasant. Uncertainty 'is pervasive in almost all decision-making', they say (Deaton and Muellbauer, 1980: 380), a view which surely resonates with at least some experiences of every consumer.

Some institutional economists, such as Galbraith, have moved still further in questioning how economics address the issue of choice. In particular, they have challenged the assumption that preference formation is unrelated to the actual goods and services produced by an economy, especially in a society dominated by mass advertising. Choice is not an act carried out countless times every day by each and every consumer, as mainstream economics would have us believe. Instead, anticipating later consumer theorists, Galbraith views it is an *ideology*, a belief about how decisions are made, a belief increasingly at odds with actuality, especially as markets become increasingly oligopolistic. This fetishization of choice is highly convenient to those in power (Galbraith, 1974). It serves dominant economic interests, in upholding the belief that free marketplaces allow sovereign consumers to determine the success and failures of products, services and those who sell them through their everyday decisions. It sustains a rampant faith in free markets as the guarantee of freedom, progress and democracy. It supports each individual's belief that his or her dollar, euro or rupee will command the same market power as those of anybody else. It also offers a degree of immunity to any choice, however immoral or distasteful, so long as there is a legitimate market in which to pursue it. It becomes the duty of any consumer to pursue the choices that purport to offer best value for his or her dollar, euro or rupee – irrespective of ethical, environmental or political considerations.

Not surprisingly then, the fetishization of choice as a supreme economic value has attracted stinging critiques by environmental economists like Jackson (2009) and Ekins (1999). Critiques of choice as the foundation of economic activity and the resulting questioning of free markets as the guarantors of economic progress and prosperity have now become fairly common, even among economists themselves. They tend to draw economic theory towards other theoretical disciplines, notably social and cultural studies, psychology and politics. They also seek to reintroduce an ethical dimension to economic theory, something that that has been stubbornly resisted by most economists, i.e. the view of economic behaviour as linked to the idea of the pursuit of a good and happy life in a thriving community (Etzioni, 1988; Sen, 1988; Panigyrakis and Zarkada, 2014). In truth, however, these critiques have scarcely dented the dominance of economics, Thomas Carlyle's 'dismal science', in government and policy-making, a dominance that, if anything, has been reinforced during the prolonged recession that followed the 2008 economic crash.

Choice, the state and the New Right

Inspired by the theories of Adam Smith and David Ricardo, neo-classical economists have long argued that politicians' duty is to remove barriers to perfect competition in order to allow growth and the market to work its wizardry over scarce resources and infinite wants. For these economists, choice is no longer just a means, whether towards economic development or individual happiness. It has become an end in its own right. Choice means freedom, and it has to be defended at all costs. Nowhere is this clearer than in the writings of the political economists of the New Right who were so influential in shifting political culture from the corporatism of post-Second World War Keynesian economics to the anti-statism of the Reagan–Thatcher years. Economists such as Hayek and Friedman attacked the Keynesian view as the engine of economic growth, placing their faith instead on the market and individual's right to choose. The purpose of the new political economy, they argued, could only be justified if it increased choice:

> *An essential part of economic freedom is freedom to choose how to use our income: how much to spend on ourselves and on what items; how much to save and in what form; how much to give away and to whom. (Friedman and Friedman, 1980: 65)*

The main barrier to choice according to these thinkers is the state, which however well intentioned almost inevitably both reduces freedom and fails to deliver what is promised. Far better, therefore, to remove the burden of the state and to structure society to maximize choice and consumer power. Daily experience, said the Friedmans, suggests that consumers can make both sensible and elegantly simple choices.

> *When you vote daily in the supermarket, you get precisely what you voted for, and so does everyone else. The ballot box produces conformity without unanimity; the market-place, unanimity without conformity. (Friedman and Friedman, 1980: 65ff)*

By intervening in the marketplace through taxation, legislation, subsidies and other means, the state stops consumers from expressing their values and from using resources accordingly. Critics of state-dominated economies do not necessarily deny the need for social welfare; but they do argue with others over how it should be produced, controlled and delivered (Gray, 1993; Gray, 1994). One of the more intriguing and pervasive ideas from the New Right has been the application of consumer choice to the state sector itself. Since the national or local government provide many services – schools, health, welfare benefits, transport, etc. – monopolies tend to build up. This leads to a diminution of consumer choice and the growth of a bureaucracy supposedly out-of-touch with the needs of its constituents, and few motivations to cut costs. The New Right's solution to this conundrum was to push for wide-ranging privatization of public utilities and to introduce markets and quasi-market mechanisms into the supply of state-led and state-funded provision. This was designed to enable consumers to choose among alternative providers, forcing competition and ostensibly driving costs down and quality up.

The political and ideological obsession since the 1980s with applying choice to all spheres of government has continued to gather momentum. Provision of choice is a key rationale – a sales pitch, almost – for the privatization of public utilities, for applying market logic to sectors whether or not they were inappropriate (Hutton, 1995). Public sector bodies, it was argued, are unresponsive to consumer preferences, have no incentive to raise quality, to lower costs or to innovate. This was epitomized by the idiocies of the planned economies, which not only failed to get goods to their consumers, but gave their consumers no control over what or how goods are produced. Free markets, on the other hand, offered the optimum mechanism for allocating resources, for driving innovation, cutting costs and meeting social needs.

The increasing marketization of public services led to the New Public Management movement (Ferlie et al., 1996), which sought to introduce management techniques from the private sector into public administration such as benchmarking against 'best practice', total quality management, outsourcing, performance league tables and individual pay scales. In the UK, the previously homogeneous welfare system was separated into 'purchasers' and 'providers' of services. Purchasers have the state-funded budgets with which to buy services from competing providers – increasingly from the private or charity sectors. The key purpose of this purchaser–provider split is to engender a contractual relation within welfare services.

The purchasers' task is to find the best value-for-money on offer from providers and to ensure the delivery of 'packages of care' to the customer.

This application of the notion of choice to public administration ranks as one of the great political experiments by the state machine. This could only happen through a strong central state. It is also a wholly ideological phenomenon. As a result, perhaps, the love affair with choice in welfare began to raise questions about whether choice is transferable from goods to services, and from the private to the public sector (Pollock and Leys, 2004; Fotaki et al., 2008; Fotaki, 2011). Overall, privatization and the introduction of market disciplines into the public sector continue to arouse powerful controversies and lie at the heart of whether choices made by individuals or decisions made by public bodies offer a better route to social and economic welfare. There is now a substantial body of opinion among experts suggesting that there are many circumstances when people prefer a reliable and universal state provision for everyone (health, primary education, public transport) paid out of taxation over having to make choices in a confusing and unreliable marketplace (Fotaki, 2006; Clarke et al., 2007; Carmel and Papadolpoulos, 2009).

The economic crisis of 2008 and Great Recession that followed it have prompted a renaissance of interest in Keynesian economics and an acknowledgment of the crucial role of the state in forging the way out of economic slump. They offered reminders that markets by themselves can sometimes lead to dramatic collapses and enormous social and economic sufferings for hundreds of millions of people. Far from being spaces for rational decision-making, markets can be gripped by fantasies and overwhelming contagious emotional forces of greed, panic and herd-like imitation (Lewis, 2014). So our review of the political economy of choice returns to where it began; that choice, where it is felt to exist, occurs within limits, that much of the rhetoric about choice is misplaced, that there is a downside to consumer choice, that choice is a political affair. In practice, there is a tendency for producers to coalesce, for markets to be oligopolistic and dominated by large producers, and for information to be dominated by interests of the seller. We have seen that from the second half of the 20th century, wholly new opportunities for highly suspect, though systematic, moulding of consumer choices were opened up. We have also seen that, for all the faith ascribed to rational choices by neo-liberals, these choices can have calamitous ramifications when markets operate in an unfettered and thoughtless way.

Which? Or whether?

From our review of the field of consumer choice, we cannot escape a sense that one type of choice has monopolized the attention of writers, whether psychologists, economists or cultural critics. We prefer to use the word 'selection' for this sort of choice. It corresponds to the notion of the menu society, which we introduced earlier. Choices, however, come in many forms and some reach far deeper, involving dilemmas and morality, issues of right and wrong, good and bad, rather than tastes and whims or a desire for difference. Such deeper choices range across important matters in life such as choosing which career to pursue, whom or whether to marry, whether to have children, whether to become a whistleblower, whether to donate a kidney, or whether to drop out of consumerism and donate half one's salary to the needy.

So much that is referred to as consumer choice in mature markets and developed economies boils down to relative trivialities compared to matters of life and death, political and civil rights or the future of the planet. To us as individuals, it does, of course, matter whether we download Mozart or McCartney from the internet, or buy this linen suit rather than that cotton one, or eat this food rather than that. The glorification of consumer choice in the post-Second World War period, fuelled by aversion to state-driven production and consumption, created a blind spot in Western cultural values. It focused the idea of choice resolutely on *which* product or service we select and deliberately forgot about *whether* and *how* to consume. It narrowed the domain of choices to items appearing on menus and induced a systematic blindness to choices that question the menu mentality itself. By casting consumers as choosers, it silenced those billions of fellow humans who were excluded from such privilege for lack of money to be able to exert choice – it even turned them into items on the menu of charities competing for funds by using the latest marketing techniques. It also silenced alternative ways of seeking a good and happy life among those who *can* exert choice.

The image of the consumer as chooser features directly or indirectly in every discussion of contemporary consumption. While the nature and extent of the choice is widely debated, choice itself is assumed. What we find interesting, and what we pursue in subsequent chapters, is how easily the face of the consumer as chooser mutates into other faces, such as explorer, identity-seeker, hedonist or citizen. Even when consumers are seen as victims, questions are often raised as to whether they have chosen this status, and whether anyone has the right to deny them. To that extent, choice remains *a* central if not *the* central theme of contemporary consumerism.

3

THE CONSUMER AS COMMUNICATOR

Goods assembled together in ownership make physical, visible statements about the hierarchy of values to which their chooser subscribes. Goods can be cherished or judged inappropriate, discarded, and replaced. Unless we appreciate how they are used to constitute an intelligible universe, we will never know how to resolve the contradictions of our economic life. (Douglas and Isherwood, 1978: 5)

CORE ARGUMENTS

The objects we consume can be seen as a live communication system, through which cultural meanings are conveyed and contested. In this way, fashion creates distinctions of social status, supplanting older distinctions based on family lineage or wealth. Goods, such as clothes and cars, as well as services, such as holiday destinations and meals in restaurants, tell stories about those who consume them; goods also communicate emotion and social prestige when exchanged as gifts. The meanings and messages emitted by particular objects and services, individually or in combination with others, are widely but imprecisely affected by advertising that seeks to create stories and narratives within which to cast them. How fixed are the meanings and messages communicated by different objects? There is a continuing argument in the social sciences over this question. Many scholars emphasize the stable and predictable attributes of material culture, while cultural theorists, especially postmodern ones, emphasize the transient, volatile and interactive nature of meanings that characterize today's consumer culture.

Few images have dominated discussions of consumption to the same extent as that of the consumer as communicator of meanings. This may be seen as the by-product of the current dominance of language in every cultural debate. It is not merely fashionable to talk of food, clothes, cars, buildings, organizations, politics or even our bodies *as* 'texts', carrying messages. The idea, according to many cultural theorists, is that all culture *is* text, using different codes and subjects to different rules of syntax and grammar. Language no longer serves as a metaphor for understanding culture (let alone as a mere tool); it has become the *core* paradigm furnishing core concepts and ideas that then migrate into numerous other cultural debates, redefining the terms of these debates. This chapter explores the strengths and shortcomings of looking at consumption and the world of objects as a system through which we communicate to others as well as to ourselves.

Images of consumers as communicators, using material objects to express social differences as well as personal meanings and feelings, considerably pre-date the present privileged position of language within the human sciences. Simmel's ([1904] 1971) theory of fashion as well as Veblen's ([1899] 1925) critique of conspicuous consumption both approach material goods not as useful objects aimed at satisfying different human needs, but as signs defining social status, establishing differences and similarities. More recently, anthropologists and sociologists have examined how social differences and status become encoded in systems of dress and clothing, food, transport and other areas of consumption (Sahlins, 1972; McCracken, 1988). An emerging tradition in historiography is currently re-evaluating consumption in the 15th and 16th centuries, revealing not only ostentatious displays of wealth, but also a keen awareness of fashions and a rampant consumerism (McKendrick et al., 1982; Mukerji, 1983). Even the supposedly ascetic Protestants in the 17th and 18th centuries are gradually being discovered to have cultivated tastes for 'great country houses on their newly acquired estates and filling them with lovely artefacts (portraits, chairs, murals, and chinaware) that testified to their high social position' (Mukerji, 1983: 3). All of these trends have had the effect of dislodging material objects from their automatic linkage with physical and social needs and placing them within a communicative package as carriers of meaning.

Since the 1980s, a vast body of literature has focused on the idea of *material culture*; in other words, the meanings carried by material artefacts, visual representations, images and so on. Since Barthes' ([1966] 1977; 1973) pioneering work on narratives, we have come to appreciate the ability of such artefacts to tell stories that become embedded in the life-stories and identities of the people who use them, display them or appropriate them. Consumer culture, in other words, the sum total of meanings carried by objects, images and signs, is now seen by many as a defining feature of late modernity and the societies many of us inhabit (e.g. Miller, 1987; Appadurai, 1990; Featherstone, 1991; Lury, 1996; Slater and Tonkiss, 2001). More recently, an entire school of consumer studies has emerged known as consumer culture theory (CCT) which has placed consumption squarely at the centre of all cultural practices, and has used consumption as the lens through which to study almost any phenomenon, including work (Firat and Venkatesh, 1995; Arnould and Thompson, 2005; Holt, 2012; Cova et al., 2013). In order for objects and images to assume their dominant position as cultural signifiers, their association with human needs had to be dislodged – an item of clothing could not be seen as telling a story about its wearer as long as its primary function was seen as keeping him or her warm, nor could an automobile establish the rank of its owner, as long as it was seen as merely a machine carrying people from A to B.

The idea of needs goes out of fashion

Material objects are and have always been central to human communication. We communicate through words, but we also communicate through body language and manners, through gifts, through clothes, through food and through the innumerable items that we use, display and discard every day. Large sections of Homer's *Iliad* and *Odyssey* are devoted to detailed descriptions of material objects, armour, swords, shields as well as domestic objects, each object telling a story (Homer, 1974). At a less poetic level, even a sword may serve its aim without actually being used, by communicating deterrence. This appears so self-evident that it is surprising that entire areas of the human sciences have ever been able to study the material world that surrounds us without looking into communication. Yet, large areas of psychology, sociology and economics have in different ways done precisely that. Whether a coat is seen as an item to keep one warm, as the product of a deskilled mechanical process or as an item on an inventory – in all of these instances, its communicative qualities are either ignored or denied. Consider, for example, the opening of Marx's *Capital*:

> The wealth of those societies in which the capitalist mode of production prevails, presents itself as 'an immense accumulation of commodities,' its unit being a single commodity. Our investigation must therefore begin with the analysis of a commodity. A commodity is, in the first place, an object outside us, a thing that by its properties satisfies human wants of some sort or another. The nature of such wants, whether for instance, they spring from the stomach or from fancy, makes no difference. Neither are we here concerned to know how the object satisfies these wants, whether directly as means of subsistence, or indirectly as means of production. (Marx, [1867] 1967: 35)

Marx and many of those who followed him approached material objects, in the first place, in terms of their usefulness, hence the term 'use-value', and subsequently as things that can be exchanged or traded, hence the term 'exchange-value'. Marx held no naive naturalistic views of the ways objects fulfil human needs, being fully aware both of the social nature of these wants and of the polymorphous usefulness of objects. Nevertheless, he did not inquire into the factors that make objects useful or the manner in which they may satisfy human wants. A weapon, a machine, a coat, a clock, a table and a jewel, are all useful objects having use-values; they cannot be compared with each other until they are treated as exchange-values. Political economy takes no interest in what makes them useful or what uses they may have. 'To discover the various uses of things is the work of history' (Marx, [1867] 1967: 35).

Subsequent authors have distinguished between luxuries and necessities, but the essential link between the usefulness of the object and need of the consumer remained (see Lebergott, 1993). Conservatives prefer the term 'utility' to the Marxist 'use-value'. As we saw in Chapter 2, the two have argued endlessly whether the state or the individual is a better judge of these needs, and whether a socialist or a capitalist production system is better able to satisfy them. Nevertheless, they agreed on seeing objects as the means of satisfying material, psychological and social needs, that is, as things whose primary *raison d'être* lies in their uses.

Baudrillard has vigorously contested this view, arguing that use-value was always a flawed concept which foreclosed any theoretical study of consumption (Baudrillard, [1968] 1988; Baudrillard, [1970] 1988). By short-circuiting the uses of objects with putative human needs, use-value reduces consumption to a series of tautologies: 'I buy this because I need it; I need it because it is useful to me', 'I buy this because I like it; I like it because it is nice', and so on. The shortcomings of the idea of use-value are laid bare by consumption patterns in the industrial West. The word 'useful' is surely being stretched to excess when applied to computer games, olive paté, kitchen gadgets, cigarettes, Spotify subscription, as well as numerous other objects we consume daily. To describe an expensive pair of running shoes as 'useful for running' or a perfume as 'useful for enhancing one's self-image' collapses either to tautology or to absurdity – a theoretical impasse. To argue retrospectively that such objects fulfil human needs merely highlights the impasse. (For more equivocal arguments than Baudrillard's on the demise of use-value, see Kellner, 1989; Lury, 1996.)

An earlier generation of social critics had also expressed reservations about the idea of goods as use-values. Adorno, one of them, argued that under capitalist accumulation the exchange-value of commodities dominates or even obliterates their use-values. Objects are produced if they can be sold at a profit, rather than because of any social or individual uses they may have. Most commodities, argued Adorno, become detached from their use-value; use-values persist as distant memories lost in the noisy symbolic clout of consumer society, whereas commodities acquire new symbolic meanings and associations (Rose, 1978).

The demise of the concept of use-value, precipitated by Western consumers' apparent willingness or even eagerness to purchase commodities with only the most tenuous use-value or no apparent use-value at all, has opened several possibilities. One is to argue along with Packard ([1957] 1981), Marcuse (1964) and Lasch (1980; 1984) that consumers are *victims* (see Chapter 7, 'The Consumer as Victim'), duped into buying more or less useless objects by techniques of mass manipulation and marketing. A less pessimistic option is to argue that the attraction of objects in advanced capitalism lies not in their function but in their aesthetic qualities, the consumer being essentially an *artist* whose purchases constitute the brush-strokes of an on-going creative process; for example, one's home becomes one's creative expression (see Chapter 6, 'The Consumer as Hedonist'). Yet another option is to approach the consumer as an *explorer* of objects, as one who goes out shopping 'just to look' or who purchases without any clear notion of what lies ahead but in the hope of discovering something exciting and unexpected; for example, buying a book because you like the cover or title (see Chapter 4, 'The Consumer as Explorer').

The meanings of goods

None of these less pessimistic images, however, has quite the currency enjoyed by the image of the consumer as *communicator*. At the core of this image lies the idea that material objects embody a system of meanings, through which we express ourselves and communicate with each other. We want and buy things not because of what things can do for us, but because of what things mean to us and what they say about us. According to this view, goods tell stories and communicate meanings in different ways but every bit as effectively as words. In the first place, material objects stand as evidence that certain events took place, removing ambiguity and fixing meanings. A wedding ring, for example, is the material object that establishes marital status, turning two separate people into husband and wife; its 'use' lies primarily in the story it tells about those wearing it. According to this view, whether a car is a useful device to carry you from A to B is largely irrelevant. There are many ways of going from A to B, and in any event the reasons why one wishes to go from A to B may be related to the availability of a car. A car, therefore, is not a carrier of persons so much as a carrier of meanings about itself, its owner, its manufacturer and the broader culture. It is a part of a symbolic nexus made up of material goods (McCracken, 1988; Firat and Venkatesh, 1995; Firat and Dholakia, 1998; Shah et al., 2012).

The study of consumption as communication proceeds from the cultural values of goods and the meanings that they embody. Economic (exchange) values ultimately derive from cultural values, not from biological or social 'needs':

> One cannot sell objects that do not have meaning to other people. A wad of paper or ball of fluff does not have economic value, unless adopted by an artist for an artwork or otherwise used as a raw material ... But objects do not have to have absolute cultural meanings in order to sell. A Mexican blanket may be bought in Mexico to be used on a bed for warmth while it may sell in the United States as a wall hanging. People need only find ways to make objects meaningful to make them economically valuable (without necessarily depending on the meanings of their creators). (Mukerji, 1983: 13)

The recognition that goods are parts of a communication system opens great possibilities of explaining the seemingly insatiable character of modern consumption without recourse to concepts of greed and envy, of exploring how different goods may combine to generate composite stories, and of explaining why people may make do without necessities in order to afford 'luxuries'. Finally, it opens the possibility of assessing the impact of image-makers and 'merchandisers of meaning' (Sievers, 1986: 347) without resorting to the idea of manipulation or deception, discussed in Chapter 2.

Communication and consumption: some early views

Two of the earliest theorists to focus on the communicative qualities of commodities were Thorstein Veblen and Georg Simmel, both of whom were fascinated by the emerging metropolitan lifestyles at the start of the 20th century, especially the ostentatious displays of wealth pursued by the nouveaux riches. In *The Theory of the Leisure Class*, first published in 1899, Veblen explored how, at least for the newly rich, everyday objects lose their functional qualities and become objects of display, establishing the social standing of their owners and users. For the members of the leisure class, the functions of objects are not defined by their uses; their function is to signify that their user does not work with his or her hands, or indeed does not work at all. Goods become status markers, indicating a certain level of income and a lifestyle of leisure. Veblen's conception, as McCracken has argued (1988: 36), did not involve any elaborate theory of communication or any genuine symbolic depth. Goods are 'prima facie evidence' of income, rather than symbols. Fashionable clothes are *insignia* of leisure. Any sensible observer can deduce the wealth of a person by the cost of an item of clothing they wear, without any intricate interpretation or clever decoding.

Veblen shrewdly managed to detach consumption, especially ostentatious and 'excessive' consumption, from notions of greed or acquisitiveness and to account for its driven qualities by linking it to social status. At the heart of his conception lies emulative spending, a heightened propensity to consume in order to keep up with the Jones's. Unlike the image of the consumer as chooser (see Chapter 2), the decision to buy an expensive car or a holiday in an exclusive destination is more likely to be imitating someone of high status than a choice of alternative options. People are dominated by fashion, because falling behind the fashion implies one's social decline. McKendrick et al. (1982) have pointed out that what Veblen observed and described is what pioneering entrepreneurs like Josiah Wedgwood had realized and exploited for well over a century – selling pottery pays, not because of its use-value but because of its snob value (Wernick, 1991). Conspicuous consumption may be aggravated by capitalism, but can be seen as a feature of all cultures; it is based on Veblen's central assumption, that social competition for status induces imitation.

Imitation is a central feature in the other early theory of fashion, developed by Georg Simmel. Like Veblen, Simmel approached consumption essentially as a process whereby social status and rank are established and communicated. Display is no side-effect of consuming, according to these two views, but its very essence. In an article called 'Fashion' (Simmel, [1904] 1971), Simmel argued that social groups forever seek to emulate the clothing patterns of their social superiors. However, Simmel argued that status competition inspires not only imitation but also differentiation. The higher social strata seek to distance themselves from their close subordinates by endlessly adopting new fashions and new trends. These act as the new status markers, while yesterday's status markers fall into disrepute to them, even as they are adopted by social groups below them. In this way, imitation and differentiation drive fashion. He wrote:

> The peculiarly piquant and suggestive attraction of fashion lies in the contrast between its extensive, all-embracing distribution and its rapid and complete disintegration; and with the latter of these characteristics the apparent claim to permanent acceptance again stands in contrast. (Simmel, [1904] 1971: 322)

Leading social groups set new trends in an attempt to distinguish themselves from the masses; the new trends are then adopted by those next in the pecking order until eventually they 'trickle down' to lower social groups. By this time, the trend-setters have moved onto new pastures. Even more than Veblen, Simmel was able to show that acquisitiveness, the seemingly irrational change of fashions, the psychological obsolescence of outmoded, though perfectly functional commodities and the obsessive interest in style, fashion and trends are all fuelled by an underlying competition for social status and prestige.

Veblen's and Simmel's ideas have had considerable influence on subsequent theories of consumer behaviour. Their plausibility, when applied to many of the goods we consume in everyday life, is remarkable. Consider, for example, the plight of parents whose children nonchalantly discard yesterday's expensive toys only to embrace a new fad, smartly displayed by their friends in the school yard. In the early 1990s, parents of all incomes and classes fought pitched battles in toy shops to obtain the precious sets of 'teenage mutant ninja turtles'; a mass marketing exercise had induced turtle mania to children throughout the Western world. The coveted turtle logos featured on every conceivable item of children's clothes, furniture, kitchenware and so on. It may seem ridiculous, but any child who failed to sport at least some turtle merchandise could be described as culturally deprived. What was even more remarkable was the speed with which turtles became passé. Within a few months, what had been treasured objects turned into objects of derision. Children who turned up at school still wearing clothes with turtle logos or carrying turtle-emblazoned bags or pencil-cases found themselves teased and ridiculed. It was now the turn of the turtles to become symbols of cultural deprivation. There is nothing new about this phenomenon; whole commercial empires have been built on it, most conspicuously that of Disney (Goulart, 1970).

Holiday destinations can also be seen reflecting status competition among different social groups. New tourist resorts are 'discovered' by the trend-setters, who scorn to visit the mass destinations. Yet, these new resorts gradually trickle down to become mass destinations themselves. Snobbery, hardly concealed contempt and disparagement are reserved for those who cannot afford the new fashionable resorts, even worse for those who have not realized that the resorts they visit are no longer fashionable. Like children's toys, holiday destinations are not innocent or risk-free; they are part of a process whereby meanings of social worth are established and elaborate hierarchies of social standing are sustained.

Simmel, like Veblen, did not develop a theory of how particular meanings come to be attached to particular objects, how meanings migrate across different categories of objects or the changes they undergo as they are interpreted and decoded. Nor did he explore the circumstances under which subordinate groups may choose to reject the fashions set up by their social superiors and set up fashions of their own (something central to the work of Bourdieu and Douglas). He did, however, argue very cleverly that rejection of fashion and affected indifference to it very quickly becomes 'imitation, but under an inverse sign' (Simmel, [1904] 1971: 307), that is, a fashion in its own right. His views on the fickle, arbitrary quality of fashion anticipated current thinking on 'the arbitrariness of signs' and 'free-floating signifiers', as we shall see. But the paramount value of his work on fashion lies in its convincing portrayal as at once irrational, capricious, tyrannical, but also a central force in our lives as consumers:

> *Judging from the ugly and repugnant things that are sometimes in vogue, it would seem as though fashion were desirous of exhibiting its power by getting us to adopt the most atrocious things for its sake alone. The absolute indifference of fashion to the material standards of life is well illustrated by the way in which it recommends something appropriate in one instance, something abstruse in another, and something materially and aesthetically quite indifferent in a third. (Simmel, [1904] 1971: 297–298)*

More recent views

The pioneering qualities and originality of Simmel's and Veblen's work is widely acknowledged. Their theories suffer from a number of theoretical shortcomings (McCracken, 1988), yet the fact remains that by looking at the goods that we consume, not as material necessities or useful objects, but as markers of social standing, Veblen and Simmel placed consumption at the heart of social theorizing, long before this became a theoretical fashion in its own right. Their views prefigure many current ideas regarding consumption as a system of communication.

An oft-quoted statement of this position has been provided by the anthropologist Mary Douglas and the economist Baron Isherwood in *The World of Goods: Towards an Anthropology of Consumption* (1978). Unlike Veblen and Simmel, however, Douglas and Isherwood argued that there had been too much sniping at excessive consumption. For too long, the study of consumption had suffered from 'a tendency to suppose that people buy goods for two or three restricted purposes: material welfare, psychic welfare, and display' (Douglas and Isherwood, 1978: 3). Much of the sniping would be silenced if consumption was seen as a *live information system*, through which cultural meanings are conveyed and contested. The essence of objects lies in the social symbolism that they carry.

> *Instead of supposing that goods are primarily needed for subsistence plus competitive display, let us assume that they are needed for making visible and stable the categories of culture. It is standard ethnographic practice to assume that all material possessions carry social meanings and to concentrate a main part of cultural analysis upon their use as communicators. (Douglas and Isherwood, 1978: 59)*

Douglas and Isherwood are more concerned than the earlier theorists about the fine nuances of meanings that may be communicated through material objects, as well as about the creative choices which consumption requires.

> *The housewife with her shopping basket arrives home: some things in it she reserves for her household, some for the father, some for the children; others are destined for the special delectation of guests. Whom she invites into her house, what parts of the house she makes available to outsiders, how often, what she offers them for music, food, drink, and conversation, these choices express and generate culture in its general sense. (Douglas and Isherwood, 1978: 57)*

Instead of passive imitation or compulsive differentiation, they argue that 'the most general objective of the consumer can only be to construct an intelligible universe with the goods he chooses' (Douglas and Isherwood, 1978: 65). Goods not only communicate social categories and hierarchies (for example, superior/subordinate, avant-guard/conservative, new-rich/old-rich) but a highly varied, specific and symbolically charged range of meanings. In this sense, they are far richer than signs or insignia and more like stories through which we communicate with each other and express our emotions. As Miller has noted (1987: 99), children are able to articulate a wide variety feelings and desires through objects at a much earlier age than through purely linguistic symbolism, and although language may supplement the usefulness of material objects in communication, it never quite nullifies it.

Consider, for example, the range of meanings communicated through food, an area of consumption to which Douglas devoted considerable attention over many years. In her classic article 'Deciphering a meal' (1975), she examined in detail what exactly constitutes a meal. She argued that the definition of a meal varies across cultures and has little relation to the nutritional qualities of what is being consumed. Instead, it depends on the types of utensils used, the kinds of ingredients used, the type of cooking and so on. These not only differentiate meals from other occasions when food and drink is taken (for example, 'drinks', 'snacks', 'quick bites') but also define what kind of meal is being consumed as well as what the relations are among those who participate. To most middle-class Britons, a sequence of soup and fruit simply does not constitute a meal, just as eating without utensils was not regarded as a meal until the arrival of US-style fast food. A dish with two staple items on a plate, for example, potatoes *and* rice, sounds a discordant note, just as a misspelt word on a printed page or a mispronounced word in a sentence.

Food on a plate, then, constitutes a system of communication, with its own rules and its own ambiguities. It is a coded message.

> If food is treated as a code, the message it encodes will be found in the pattern of social relations being expressed ... Food categories encode social events. (Douglas, 1975: 249)

Particular types of meal are signalled through the use of special dishes or trimmings. The use of special items, such as turkey with all the trimmings at Christmas, a roast on Sunday, or a first course followed by an entrée for a dinner party, communicate specific messages. For Douglas, unlike Veblen, ostentation does not necessarily imply social competition, but rather a fixing of meanings. Social and moral judgement is withheld. The use of special cutlery or luxury china during a meal may be less a means of impressing an important guest than a way of stating that a meal is a special one in comparison to other ones.

While Douglas has been persistently critical of Veblen (Douglas and Isherwood, 1978: 4 and *passim*), Veblen's argument about competitive imitation can be seen as a special case of Douglas's more general view that goods establish social categories. For it can hardly be denied that one of the range of social categories which *may* be communicated through a meal is social superiority, especially if a highly ostentatious meal is served to a visitor who can hardly reciprocate at the same level. Nevertheless, Douglas's argument considerably enlarges the communicative potential of material goods, well beyond the establishment of social hierarchies to the general maintenance of meanings. Without material goods, argues Douglas, meanings become unstable, ambiguous, they tend to drift or even disappear. Meanings require rituals to sustain them, and rituals depend on material objects:

> More effective rituals use material things, and the more costly the ritual trappings, the stronger we can assume the intention to fix the meanings to be. Goods, in this perspective,

are ritual adjuncts; consumption is a ritual process whose primary function is to make sense of the inchoate flux of events. (Douglas and Isherwood, 1978: 65)

Douglas and Isherwood carry the argument well beyond those of Veblen and Simmel, by highlighting the interconnections of material objects as a feature of their communicative potential, instead of treating each object as a separate icon. Objects do not make individual statements, but rather they communicate together with other objects, just like individual items on a menu or on a plate acquire their significance in the light of the other items. Silver cutlery next to crystal wine glasses and expensive porcelain tells a very different story from silver cutlery in the midst of rustic tableware.

The Diderot effect and product constellations

The combined effect of material objects is graphically captured in what McCracken (1988) terms the 'Diderot unity', prompted by an intriguing observation made by the great French thinker Denis Diderot (1713–84). In a little essay entitled 'Regrets on parting with my old dressing gown', Diderot describes how upon receiving a gift of a magnificent scarlet robe, he discarded his 'ragged, humble, comfortable old wrapper'. He then started getting dissatisfied in turn with every other item in his study for failing to live up to the splendour of the new item. He therefore set about replacing chairs, engravings, bookshelves and everything else. With every new acquisition, however, he found new things to be dissatisfied with, so that eventually he looked back nostalgically at his study the way it used to be, crowded, humble, chaotic but happy. 'Now the harmony is destroyed. Now there is no more consistency, no more unity, and no more beauty', he reflected (quoted in McCracken, 1988: 119).

McCracken, prompted by Diderot's reflections, observes that objects do not communicate in isolation but in concert with other objects (the 'Diderot unity'). Once a particular component is replaced, the harmony is undermined, precipitating further changes. According to this view, individual purchases are not motivated by envy or social competition or display, but by an urge for consistency and completeness. The quest for completeness, consistency and unity, is, of course, a driving force in every collector; but it is also a more general cultural phenomenon. The owner of a new Rolex watch may soon begin to be discontent with his or her modest motor-car and starts dreaming of 'upgrading' it. This phenomenon is well known to advertisers who perennially try to entice us with offers of products that complement or 'bring out the best in' what we already have. Product constellations can be seen as objects that somehow reinforce each other's message and reduce the scope for ambiguity or conflict. Even more commonly, we are enticed with 'complete sets', packages or collections which have already been designed to communicate in unison.

Moving from the public statements of goods in Mary Douglas's arguments to the solitary concerns of Diderot, it may be thought that we have lost sight of the consumer as communicator. After all, Diderot's study, like his dressing gown, was private, not meant for public display. Are there some forms of solitary, personal consumption that simply repudiate the idea of consumption as communication? Douglas and McCracken do not think so. Douglas argues that even the solitary consumers submit to the rules and categories of their culture, when, invisible to others, they eat their meals with knives and forks and shirk away from beginning with pudding and ending with soup, or eating mustard with lamb and mint with beef (Douglas and Isherwood, 1978: 67). Somewhat similarly, McCracken describes goods both as 'bulletin boards for internal messages and billboards for external ones' (McCracken, 1988: 136). Through the goods that we consume, we may be communicating with ourselves, reinforcing social categories and classifications. Like old family photographs that are not for public display, we may use those private goods to remind ourselves of who we are, what we have achieved, what we have lost and what we may wish for the future.

It is questionable, however, whether many consumer goods fall into this category of purely personal story-telling, entirely devoid of a social dimension. Consider, for example, some increasingly popular types of consumption in the West, such as body piercing jewellery or tattoos in intimate places. The very fact that such practices are now seen as fashionable indicates that, for all their privacy and intimacy, they comply with the trends described by Simmel and elaborated by Douglas and McCracken. Like whispered secrets, private and hidden jewellery and tattoos can be seen as a unique type of communication, confirming the special standing of both those who don them as well as those allowed to see them.

Gifts

Even Diderot, in his solitary study, was hardly removed from a process of communication. In the first place, he was interpreting his friend's opulent gift as a message confirming the eminence he had attained, rather than purely as a token of esteem or as a mere luxury in which he might indulge without further ado. Moreover, through the hapless sequence of subsequent replacements, he might have been seeking to communicate to himself an image of himself as someone who, adorned by his magnificent scarlet robe, deserves something more sumptuous for his den than his simple study of old. His friend's gift turned inadvertently into a Trojan horse.

If virtually all goods carry meanings, gifts are self-conscious of their meaning-carrying capacities. By their essence, gifts are laden with symbolism, punctuating important ritual occasions, such as weddings, anniversaries, birthdays, name-days, bar mitzvahs, christenings, house moves, Christmas, Mother's and Father's days, Valentine's days. Gifts must not be regarded as a small class of objects and exchanges at the margins of consumption. From the 'treats' indulged by parents on deserving children, to flower bouquets dispatched by Interflora, to the purchasing of rounds of drinks or the holding of parties, to corporate hospitality, to the generalized consumer delirium as Christmas approaches, gifts are an important feature of Western culture and a cardinal feature of many others. The gift shop has confidently taken its place in shopping malls, high streets, airport lounges and museums. Whole areas of the economy from jewellery and perfumes to book and music tokens, are now fuelled by gift-giving. It is not accidental that the study of gifts has attracted considerable research interest and offers important insights into the consumer as communicator (Belk, 1982).

Since the pioneering work of Marcel Mauss ([1925] 1974), it is widely accepted that gifts, unlike donations, are not just free goods, but parts of reciprocal exchange relations. Gifts reflect the nature and importance of the occasion; they communicate meanings and emotions (such as respect, gratitude, love, and even pity and scorn), as well as defining the social and emotional distance between giver and receiver. The meanings of gifts are often ambiguous and far from easy to interpret and the choice of gifts can become a cause of major headaches. Yet the very ambiguity in the meanings of gifts makes them highly effective. Like myths, gifts can carry meanings that are at once ambiguous and powerful. And like myths, gifts can reconcile the irreconcilable (Barthes, 1973), bridging vast differences of culture and interest, though of course they can equally lead to gigantic misunderstandings and conflict. For this reason, most of us treat gifts with special respect, as if we recognize that they are a risk. A gift is something that both the giver and the receiver will be judged by. It is also something through which both giver and receiver will judge the other's opinion of them, as well as the importance that the other accords to the occasion. It is not surprising, then, that the amount of time we spend in choosing a present is considerably greater than that which we spend in buying similar items for personal consumption (Pandya and Venkatesh, 1992).

Gifts communicate in many ways and are judged by many of their qualities. Consider one of the simpler ones: price. The price of a gift is an important part of its meaning, yet it can be highly ambiguous. An inexpensive gift from a rich relative may be interpreted as a rebuff, as a discourtesy, as a sign of a loss of money or status on the part of the giver or as a sign of increasing social and emotional distance that the giver tries to establish. Yet an inexpensive gift may equally be accepted with relief for not imposing too severe demands for its recip-rocation. A costly gift from a rich relative may be gratefully received with an acknowledgement of the relative's superior economic and perhaps social standing. It may, however, be interpreted as an attempt to humiliate, since it may not be reciprocated in kind. Gifts are a highly delicate area of consumption.

Price is not the only feature by which gifts are judged. Appropriateness, originality, presentation and personal time are highly valued qualities in gifts, as is the personal touch. Children may delight their parents with presents that they make themselves, until somehow they get the idea that things that they make themselves and that are not paid for are not 'real presents'. A less well-off relative may be able amply to reciprocate an opulent present with a less expensive but very well-chosen one, a beautifully wrapped one, an exotic one or one which required a lot of his or her time. Skill, judgement and, above all, time can all enrich the meanings of a gift, compensating for its low cost. As Bourdieu (1979) has argued, time can be the most precious of gifts, and the time it takes to locate, to choose, to wrap and to present becomes part of the story that the gift tells. The wrapping, the ribbons and cards that accompany a gift are no mere ornaments, but of the very essence.

Nor do gifts cease to communicate once the ritual of presentation has taken place. Some remain as reminders of the occasion or of the giver, keeping or even increasing their symbolic power as the years go by. These are treasured objects, whose damage, theft or loss is experienced as a personal injury by their owner. The anthropologist Levy-Bruhl (1966) noted that in some cultures, everyday objects such as ornaments, clothes and tools, become literally incorporated in the self. In a similar way, Belk (1988) has argued that certain objects (especially things like cars or houses) become vital elements of our identity as if they were physical extensions of our bodies. He has stretched this idea for the digital world, noting that a large part of the self today is constructed through digital interactions online (Belk, 2013). These arguments provide a bridge between the consumer as communicator and the consumer as identity-seeker (see Chapter 5, 'The Consumer as Identity-seeker'). Most gifts, however, have more mundane careers, being used and forgotten, or being sold as second-hand goods at knock-down prices, being given as 'half-gifts' to new receivers or simply being thrown away.

In an intriguing work on consumerism in Japan, Clammer describes how shopping habits are conditioned by the gift economy, 'a perpetual and enormous circulation of commodities – a gigantic kula-ring-like cycle of obligations and reciprocities' (Clammer, 1992: 207). Gifts, exchanged by the Japanese on a considerably larger scale than most Western Europeans or Americans, come mostly to an inglorious end:

> *A certain day each month is 'heavy rubbish day' when unwanted large objects can be put on the sidewalk for collection by the municipal rubbish collectors or by private contractors. The most astonishing variety and volume of things are discarded – furniture, TVs, bicycles, golf-clubs, all kinds of electrical appliances and just about everything that a modern household needs ... often in almost mint condition. (Clammer, 1992: 208–209)*

While from an economic point of view, endless rounds of gift-giving may represent waste and may be dented by recession, in Japan, they strengthen networks of social relations and define social hierarchies in an effective way (Clammer, 2011). In these respects, gifts highlight Douglas's and McCracken's arguments concerning the consumer in the capacity of gift-buyer and gift-receiver as someone who essentially creates, communicates and interprets meanings.

Gifts to oneself?

Is it possible to give gifts to oneself? Mick and DeMoss (1990) and Levy (1982) have argued that self-gifts differ in character from other personal consumption; they are quite common in Western cultures. Self-gifts can mark special occasions, like private anniversaries or special visits. Souvenirs are often purchased in this way, as markers of specific events. Even more commonly, they appear as rewards for achievement or consolations for failure, reasserting pride and self-respect. Pandya and Venkatesh give this graphic example:

> In the film 'Crimes of the Heart', Diane Keaton, a lonely middle-aged single woman, thinks her family has forgotten her birthday. She gets a cookie for herself, lights a candle on it and sings 'Happy Birthday' to herself. She gives herself a birthday party the others forgot to give her. Her gift to herself accentuates her loneliness but also affirms her selfhood. There are many such examples of self-gift in real life like vacations as a reward after a year of hard work. But when families discuss their vacations with their friends these often become signs of their status, competition and success. (Pandya and Venkatesh, 1992: 152–153)

Such self-gifts can be seen as part of a continuing dialogue one has with oneself. One can almost imagine old Diderot, ruminating in his study on what should replace the threadbare tapestry hanging from the wall, finally deciding to treat himself to a fine new one. The need we have to present special purchases as treats or rewards highlights the symbolic importance of the objects we purchase. In this way, we use objects to construct meaningful stories about our efforts, our successes and failures and this is one of the factors that doubtless drives modern consumerism. A new pair of gloves may be thought of as an unnecessary luxury that we resist. If, however, we can present it as the just dessert for a successful effort or as the rightful consolation for an unsuccessful one, it becomes irresistible.

A recent development in the discourse on self-gifts is the notion that ethical consumption is a form of self-gift, a reward for acting responsibly. Ethical consumption is way of communicating to oneself and others the caring attitudes one holds. Ethical consumption can also be a reward for resisting the temptation to consume in the mainstream.

One could very well ask: why do success or failure need be marked in this way, through the use of a newly acquired object? Is it impossible to construct meaningful stories about ourselves and others without the assistance of the objects? For example, is it necessary to mark an important anniversary with a costly gift rather than a kiss and a hug? Why are singing, dancing, poetry and speechmaking not adequate enough rituals for a wedding, without having in addition an arsenal of gifts? Is it impossible to construct a story of a meaningful holiday without the material reminders of photographs, souvenirs and other costly tourist paraphernalia?

Objects and sign-values

Mary Douglas has argued that material objects are indispensable for fixing the meanings and the categories of events. Long after the singing and the dancing at the wedding have finished, the wedding ring will still be the material evidence of the event. Primitive cultures as well as modern cultures rely on material objects to fix meaning. Baudrillard, whose early studies into consumer culture have much in common with Douglas's, takes a different view. Like Douglas, Baudrillard viewed material objects as forming a system of classification, though his assessment of their value is more ambivalent:

> *Objects are categories of objects which quite tyrannically induce categories of persons. They undertake the policing of social meanings, and the significations they engender are controlled. (Baudrillard, 1988: 16–17)*

Having convincingly challenged the concept of objects as use-values, Baudrillard approached each object as the carrier of a sign-value. This is where his argument departs from Douglas's view of physical objects as material depositories of social meaning. For Baudrillard, the sign-values of objects are mobile and precarious, more so since the beginning of the industrial era, and infinitely more so at the present time. Like neurotic symptoms, where each symptom can easily be replaced by another (for example, a neurotic cough may be replaced by colitis), the sign-value of objects can quickly migrate from one commodity to another:

> *A washing machine serves as equipment and plays as an element of comfort, or of prestige etc. It is the field of play that is specifically the field of consumption. Here all sorts of objects can be substituted for the washing machine as a signifying element. In the logic of signs, as in the logic of symbols, objects are no longer tied to a function or to a defined need. This is precisely because objects respond to something different, either to a social logic, or to a logic of desire, where they serve as a fluid and unconscious field of signification. (Baudrillard, [1970] 1988: 44)*

Baudrillard is arguing here that for the individual consumer, the desire for a washing machine may inexplicably be transferred onto a desire for a dress, a record or a car, just as the signifying effect of the washing machine may be achieved through a dishwasher, a carpet or a ring. Unlike Douglas, who stresses the stabilizing influence of objects, Baudrillard views sign-values as fleeting and migratory. For Douglas, a wedding ring is solid, timeless, reassuring; for Baudrillard, a wedding ring is a transmitter of spasmodic, indistinct and ambiguous messages. This is what makes sign-values both fiercely contested as well as ideally malleable material in the hands of advertisers and marketers. This is also why, in the last resort, they are unable to provide the basis for real identity or selfhood. Ultimately, goods lose all signification, standing for nothing whatsoever beyond themselves. From being depositories of social meaning they become black holes into which meaning disappears (Baudrillard, 1983).

Brands, advertising and the destruction of meaning

> *If I can describe a cake, a cigarette, a fishing rod, or a bottle of whisky in such a way that its basic soul, its basic meaning to modern man, becomes clear, I shall, at the same time, have achieved direct communication. I shall have established a bridge between my advertisement and the reader and come as close as possible to motivating the reader or listener to acquire this experience via the product which I have promised him. (Dichter, 1960, quoted in Lee, 1993: 150)*

Selling things by making them tell stories was well known to Dr Ernest Dichter, Director of the Institute of Motivational Research. He saw advertising as the art of making commodities communicate to us, by making goods speak with human voices (see Chapter 2, 'The Consumer as Chooser'). Brands were humanized and brand names became condensations of stories. Like the 'crown', which stands metonymically for all things royal, majestic and imposing, brand names become embodiments of special qualities, values and images. Meaning travels from the whole to the part and from the part to the whole. A small bar of soap carrying the logo of Harrods, the famous London department store, becomes the embodiment of the Harrods values, tradition, soundness and quality, the best of Old British values. By purchasing the small bar of soap, one purchases all that Harrods stands for and makes these attributes of Harrods one's own. Exploiting these metonymic qualities of goods has long been the task of advertisers and market analysts; it has been explored by academics, such as Williamson (1986), Lee (2000) and McCracken (1988):

> *Advertising works as a potential method of meaning transfer by bringing the consumer good and a representation of the culturally constituted world within the frame of a particular advertisement. The creative director of an agency seeks to conjoin these two*

elements in such a way that the viewer/reader glimpses an essential similarity between them. When this symbolic equivalence is successfully established, the viewer/reader attributes certain properties he or she knows to exist in the culturally constituted world to the consumer good. The known properties of the world thus come to be resident in the unknown properties of the consumer good. The transfer of meaning from the world to good is accomplished. (McCracken, 1988: 77)

McCracken argues strongly that material objects act as a means of encoding and communicating meanings, but do *not* constitute a language. One of the main differences between language and objects is that objects are constrained in the range of meanings they can assume. In language, onomatopoeic words apart, a particular sound may signify virtually anything, there being no necessary connection between signifier and signified, between word and meaning. Objects, on the other hand, 'bear a "motivated" and "non-arbitrary" relationship to the things they signify' (McCracken, 1988: 132). In this view, a Rolex watch cannot signify a poor man, since a poor man could not afford to buy one. Equally, an inexpensive 'unglamorous' pair of shoes may signify parsimony or poverty or inverted snobbery or various other qualities, but it *may not* by its very nature signify certain things such as wealth, power or discriminating taste in shoes.

Not so, argues Baudrillard, who, since his early book *The System of Objects* ([1968] 1988) has seen brands as capable of telling virtually *any* story, however unconnected to any putative need or use. Even a Rolex may be but a cheap fake, bought at a hundredth of the price, though looking similar. And even a 'real' Rolex may appear as nothing but the kind of model that is much imitated and faked. Once Rolex watches, real and fake, are worn on the wrist of any taxi-driver, the meaning carried by them becomes malleable. This argument develops Simmel's idea on the whimsical nature of fashion, whereby anything can become fashionable, provided that it stands out from the rest. Baudrillard takes this argument to its logical conclusion, that signification means simply difference and nothing else. The only meaning that signs retain is their difference from other signs; and this is the end of meaning:

> *Diverse brands follow one another, are juxtaposed and substituted for one another without an articulation or transition. It is an erratic lexicon where one brand devours the other, each living for its own endless repetition. This is undoubtedly the most impoverished of languages: full of signification and empty of meaning. It is a language of signals. And 'loyalty' to a brand name is nothing more than the conditioned reflex of a controlled affect. (Baudrillard, [1968] 1988: 17)*

The more brands like McDonald's, Marlboro, Harrods and Nike become temporary depositories of 'meaning', the more emaciated and burnt out the meaning becomes. The more obsessively we interpret, analyse and classify others in terms of the messages emitted by their shoes, their clothes and their preferred drinks, the less we know about them. Ultimately, medium becomes message, signifiers float freely and meaning implodes. Nike, the ancient Greek goddess of victory, no longer stands for victory, for the meaning of victory is swallowed up by the shoe. Clio is no longer an ancient Greek muse; nor do her classical qualities survive in the product; she has become momentarily a French motor-car, a pretty girl, a youthful longing, a clever advertisement, before she is drowned by the noise of other brands, lost and forgotten.

In Baudrillard's view, within the media-dominated world of Western societies, boundaries between reality and representation, substance and image, have imploded, just like the difference between the real and the fake Rolex. A photograph no longer captures the essence of a real event, nor does it claim to do so. A photograph becomes pure image, the product of a photo-opportunity, a staged event that may link, for example, a perfume brand to a tropical island or a politician to a cause – all touched up and beautified with the aid of Photoshop. The viewer of the picture is aware that the picture is the product of a temporary and imaginary marriage of convenience between two free-floating signifiers, which will soon go their separate ways. Ultimately, the perfume, the tropical island, the politician and the cause lose any meaning, outside the photograph. Like photographs, other consumer goods cease to express meanings and they too become self-referential. The gift is no longer the material proof of Christmas, nor is the wedding ring the material proof of the wedding. Both become opportunistic carriers of ever-decreasing fragments of meaning. Christmas becomes *the* gift; its meaning apart from gifts, photo-opportunities, TV images, drink and food opportunities shrivels to almost nothing. What makes you a mother is not having had a baby but the fact that you shop at a specialist shop called Mothercare. The wedding ring and paraphernalia procured from a shop called Pronuptia become *the* marriage. Disneyland is the photographs and merchandise one brings back. Ultimately Christmas, marriages, Disneyland and the other institutions of consumer society become photo-opportunities, object-opportunities, spending-opportunities and little else.

Advertising

The names adopted by rock bands, seemingly laden with meaning, yet ultimately completely meaningless, highlight Baudrillard's notion of the arbitrariness of the sign. They are entirely self-referential, making no attempt at signification or classification, their only point being to make a temporary impact on our consciousness, without getting lost in the general clamour of which they are but an infinitesimal part. The same can be said of the new wave of advertisements since the 1980s. These advertisements, pioneered by a number of new advertising agencies that challenged the functional and pragmatic approaches of the older more traditional agencies, eschewed both hard-sell and soft-sell approaches in favour of images and compositions from which 'selling' is effectively banned (see Lee, 1993; Lury 1996; 2004). Instead of appealing to our reason or to our emotions, such advertising, along with other 'postmodern' artefacts, celebrated visual images, 'decontextualising "great" works of art and established aesthetic conventions, raiding the iconographies of religious beliefs and political struggles, or incorporating the forms of other cultures into its own discursive frame and for its own ends' (Lee, 1993: 149).

Many of these advertisements are intertextual, openly borrowing text or ideas from other advertisements and adding an often humorous twist. Alternatively, they are reflexive, being essentially advertisements about advertising. 'Aren't conventional ads a bore', they seem to say. 'Do they not treat consumers like dullards, presuming to manipulate their choices through silly images and naive stories? Now *we* know that *you* would not fall for such crude tricks, would you? In fact, we know that you cannot be manipulated at all. You are cool, sophisticated. So, let's forget about us selling you a product. Forget about the product altogether. Let's have some fun together.' Such is the message of this generation of advertisements. Fun assumes the form of a joke, a pun, a parody of a competitor's advertisement or product, a puzzle, a guilty pleasure or the breaking of a taboo. Such fun undoubtedly creates a degree of solidarity between the advertiser and the reader/viewer based on a shared sense of non-conformism, cleverness, originality, rebelliousness. A conspiracy is sometimes orchestrated between clever advertiser and smart consumer at the expense of supposedly dull advertisers, dumb consumers, or even the very manufacturer who is paying for the commercial. Whether consumers are flattered by such treatment and whether they appropriate the positive qualities residing in the hyper-text are as questionable as whether such advertisements help sell products at all.

According to Davidson (1992), these advertisements tell no story about a product; their stories are at best about themselves and those who conceived them, at worst they would seem to have no story at all. They are pure signs without meaning, signs that almost coincidentally collide with 'products' (that are themselves but signs) only to destroy them, part of the 'hyper-real' world of the mass media, which in Baudrillard's later arguments completely defines the 'real' world. In the hyper-real world, everything mutates into everything else, all is image, appearance and simulation. The TV soap opera is more real than the viewers' own personal reality, the brand is more real than the product. In this hyper-real world, the consumer is no longer a communicator, nor are commodities sign-values. The consumer becomes a Pavlovian dog salivating mechanically at the sight of simple images, his or her emotions are conditioned responses to the sight of brands. Communication dissolves into seduction.

Baudrillard's insights unlock some of the mysteries and mystifications of modern advertising, mass media and communications, pointing at a very real crisis of meanings and signification. They highlight the fragility of systems of signification that are built around seemingly solid objects. They also act as a constant reminder that when we believe that we are most aware that we know what is going on, that we have objective, up-to-the-minute information from CNN, the BBC and other media organizations, we are in fact being transported in a world of special effects, simulations and virtual reality (see, for example, Baudrillard's discussions of the First Gulf War as a consumer spectacle, Baudrillard and Gane, 1993). At the same time, one cannot escape the impression that Baudrillard's views on the omnipotence of modern media, their ability to shift signs and signifiers, to define reality and to destroy meaning, these are the products of one who is fixated on the mass media, living through the media and ultimately becoming himself part of the hyper-real world which alone interests him. 'I live in the virtual. Send me into the real, and I don't know what to do' (Baudrillard and Gane, 1993: 188), was Baudrillard's response to an offer to go to the Gulf and see for himself what was going on during that war.

Even if a good deal of modern consumption unfolds in the realm of virtual reality, simulations and make-believe, Baudrillard underestimates the consumers' ability to *alter* rather than just receive and carry messages. It may be quite true that everyday reality is cluttered by the noise of commodities, signs and images, yet most of us have learned to ignore much of this noise, screen it out and live with it, just as we can enjoy listening to music over the noise that surrounds it. We also learn to experiment with objects, to try them in different ways, and discover meanings in the *uses* we find for them. As de Certeau (1984) has argued, through makeshift arrangements and creative combinations of objects, we learn both to discard the spurious significations of the media and to redefine objects, replenishing them with meanings and significations. (See Chapter 8, 'The Consumer as Rebel'.) Advertising agencies today are only too aware how deft consumers have become at subverting some sign-values, ridiculing others or appropriating others for the 'wrong' purposes.

In the age of the internet and social media, consumers are exposed to more subtle and finely targeted messages from advertisers. At the same time, they have learned to become advertisers in their own right, advertising their scorn and derision of offers, ads, people. They discover and define new brands as being cool. And they trash venerable brands. In some ways, this suits the advertising industry well, in that consumers are now outsourced, unpaid, crowdsourcing workers. The price is that the industry risks losing control of the brand (Holt, 2002; Arvidsson, 2006).

In conclusion

Theorizing on advertising practice has tended to focus on glamorous, fashionable and highly charged commodities like perfume, upmarket clothing and cars. It disregards the mundane and functional areas of consumption, yet this area, as we saw in Chapter 2, is precisely what became more important in the Great Recession, as people turned to thrift and value-for-money offerings. Consumer culture theorists may not be interested in the likes of discounter supermarkets, but the practitioners are, and some of the prize-winning advertisements were in fact those celebrating those values. A washing machine *is* after all a device for washing clothes, and one can hardly imagine doing without one if one can afford it, sign-value or no sign-value. Many of the ordinary, unbranded, quiet, unobtrusive objects that surround us never seem to quit the mundane realms of the real for the fantasy world of simulations. And even when they become fantasy objects, they are just as likely to take on the robust cultural symbolic qualities highlighted by Douglas (1975) (a Valentine card stands for romantic love and roast turkey for Christmas) than the volatile, nervous and transient qualities of the hyper-real.

Consumption as communication opens numerous windows into our relations to the physical objects that surround us and the ways we use these objects to express meanings, feelings and social distinctions. This approach can account for the seemingly endless and absurd variety of products that we seek and use, without resorting to tautologies regarding the use-values of such objects or reducing everything to greed. Once we recognize that goods tell stories, that these stories resonate with symbolism and express meanings that cannot be expressed effectively through language, consumption becomes strangely re-humanized. Even irrational, absurd consumption, can be seen as a muddled, ambiguous, contested but ultimately sensical activity, rather than a zombie-like delirium. This is part of being human.

In spite of its remarkable ability to explain numerous aspects of consumption, the image of consumer as communicator presents only a partial picture of consumption. Gifts, status symbols, fashion and branded goods, designer products and goods that are self-consciously displayed, these are objects for which it seems tailor-made. For goods which are consumed without fuss, in privacy, it is less illuminating. The idea of self-gifts, which turns personal consumption into part of self-dialogue, seems more like an excuse or rationalization for behaviour rather than an explanation of it. The fact that an object can equally be a self-reward for success or a consolation for failure would support this scepticism. Unless we accept unconditionally Baudrillard's challenge and provocation, a hyper-real world of simulations and mirages, of fleeting signifiers and black holes of meaning, it is not clear from the idea of consumer as communicator why objects that require payment have such unique significance in our lives, what drives our desire for them and why we need excuses for purchasing them. Unlike myths, with which we argued commodities have much in common as carriers of symbolism, the resonance of most objects that were once desired and subsequently purchased fades away quickly. The image of consumer as communicator simply fails to account either for the kick we get when we acquire a new and much longed-for commodity or for the frequent disappointment we feel for yesterday's purchases. The portrait of the consumer we next move to, that which portrays the consumer as explorer, holds the promise of insights into these excitements and disappointments.

4

THE CONSUMER AS EXPLORER

When you start on your way to Ithaca, then pray that the road is long, full of adventure, full of knowledge. ... Stop at Phoenician markets, and purchase fine merchandise, mother-of-pearl and corals, amber and ebony, and delicious perfumes of all kinds. ... And if you find her poor, Ithaca has not deceived you. With the wisdom you have gained, with so much experience, you have surely understood what Ithacas mean. (Kavafis, 'Ithaca')

CORE ARGUMENTS

Marketplaces offer consumers many opportunities to explore new product lines, fashions and experiences. Under the rule of consumerism, cathedrals of consumption, such as shopping malls and theme parks, attract people escaping boredom and seeking excitement. These are spaces that consumers are invited to explore for new products and new experiences, with which to create meaning in their lives. Different quests go on in these sites – quests for bargains, quests for difference and even quests for spiritual fulfilment. The internet has become an additional vast arena for consumer explorations, turning the home into a temple of consumption in its own right.

Who could fail to experience the eternal fascination of exotic markets, their strange displays, their unfamiliar smells and sights, their mystifying rituals of coaxing, bargaining and bluffing? There are no signs anywhere around you, no empty Marlboro packets, no Coca-Cola logos on refrigerated displays. American Express is not known here. These markets are ageless, chance alone has taken you there. You are surrounded by unfamiliar things; or familiar things in unfamiliar guises, at unfamiliar prices. These are not generally friendly places. Excitement is mixed with danger. Are things what they appear to be? Is the amber real or might it be a clever plastic imitation? Would you be taken for a ride if you paid the asking price for a local wood-carving? And what would it look like back in your house, miles away from its siblings and forced to mix with your other valuable possessions? A good topic of conversation or an eyesore?

Now picture yourself in a shopping mall, not perhaps the one you visit regularly whose features you know well, but one slightly less familiar. It may have been purpose-built or it may be housed in an old canning factory or a converted and 'preserved' warehouse. This too is a place to explore, a place to discover, but it is certainly more user-friendly. This is a space that has been *designed* for exploration. An invisible hand has planned everything for your delectation. The reassuring quality of its familiar brands, the accommodating array of boutiques next to the intriguing shop selling Peruvian parrots and Colombian hammocks, the bars, the restaurants, the soft background music, the discreet lighting, the comfortable climatization, the instantly meaningful signs – this is a synthetic oasis, and none the less stimulating for being designed with people like you in mind. It is a clean, genial, graffiti-free space, where a cultural oxymoron can be acted out, relaxed exploration. There are no worries here, no pushy salespeople, no invisible pickpockets, goods have fixed price-tags and are covered by legislation aimed at protecting consumers. If you run short of cash, plastic money is welcome. To be sure, this is a fantasy world; it brings exotica to the consumer instead of taking the consumer to the exotic. Yet it is a space of exploration.

Exploring and shopping have become one. Bargain hunting, discovering new lines, new fashions, new 'product ideas' and new forms of fun; these are all part of the excitement of shopping. Exploration can begin before you leave your home; it can take place in a relaxed, poised manner, merely flicking the pages of glossy magazines, brimming with new ideas for entertaining guests, decorating your home or stimulating your partner (Barthes, 1973: 86). You can explore the lives of the rich and famous, study the interior of their houses and scrutinize every particle of their face. You can savour dream-like cuisine and be transported to magical places, hardly needing to leave your armchair or strain your purse. Internet shopping brings the excitement of high-street exploration onto your own screen, opening up unprecedented possibilities. The 'Internet Explorer' is, of course, Microsoft's aptly named web-browser, which promises to carry you into new worlds, converting a simple mouse click into the key that unlocks them.

Alternatively, you may join the armies of energetic explorers, travel to distant places and fill your bags with souvenirs and your camera with digital images. Or you may explore the latest changes in your own high street's array of shops, window displays, signs and street life. Whether we envisage the consumer browsing a magazine or touring, it is hard to imagine consumption without exploration or exploration without consumption.

This chapter looks at contemporary consumers as explorers of goods, marketplaces and signs. We examine the curiosity that is manifest in the act of shopping in all its diversity and the quest for novelty that drives some of our consuming behaviour. Some of the approaches we introduce may seem far-fetched and removed from the world of mundane day-to-day shopping. They lend themselves to easy ridicule as hopelessly indulgent and aspirational, oblivious to the world of poverty and privation, as portrayed by analysts like Townsend and Gordon (2002) and Seabrook (1985). Nevertheless, the image of the consumer as explorer is implicit in much of the work on consumption done by cultural theorists since the 1980s. It also inspired an entire generation of retailers and their designers, who sought to transform shopping areas, from hypermarkets to boutiques, into terrains of exploration. By making explicit what has hitherto been implicit, that is, the view of the consumer driven by insatiable curiosity, we seek to highlight both the strengths and, later, the serious deficiencies of these approaches.

Bargain hunting

Exploration takes many forms. Bargain hunting is perhaps the most evident. Even unfamiliar foreign markets may contain goods that can easily be obtained 'back home', though perhaps at different prices. Prices exercise undoubtedly a strange fascination on consumers. How is it possible that exactly the same item of clothing, the same bar of chocolate, the same shampoo, can cost different amounts in different shops? How is it possible that exactly the same train journey can incur dozens of different fares? How can the price of an electronic toy be halved in less than a year? Or a pack of 12 batteries retail for less than a pack of four identical ones on display in the same shop? Not for nothing did Marx argue in his concept of commodity fetishism that commodities assume mystical qualities. This was long before marketers adopted price as one of the four Ps (the others being product, place and promotion) of their *métier* and decided to make these things still more confusing for consumers.

In spite of the growth of non-utilitarian, esoteric advertising, words like 'free', 'extra', 'more', 'value', 'savings' and, above all, 'bargain' dominate numerous commercials. What is a bargain? Clearly a bargain is in the first place quality at low price; good value for money. But this cannot make bargains the subject of a hunt, or fuel the kind of fever that is generated by the sales of large department stores, let alone explain the joy and delight generated by the discovery of a bargain, which parallels that of discovering a secret or sharing a good joke. Dry beans may represent excellent value for money, especially if value is defined in nutritional terms, though they could hardly be described as a bargain. Conversely, discovering a designer scarf at half its normal price may seem like a great bargain, even if the last thing you want is another scarf. A free bottle of wine with every dozen you buy can look irresistible. Bargain hunting has little to do with sound management of household budgets and more to do with discovering a secret, which few may share, a secret of getting something for nothing, in a world where everything has to be paid for. For years immemorial, the secret of commerce has been spotting bargains, buying cheap and selling dear. Whole areas of trade, from antiques to houses, and from second-hand cars to coin or stamp collections, are driven by the craving for bargains. The discovery of a bargain performs great services to our self-esteem. It is not uncommon for individuals to fashion their identities around their uncanny ability to spot bargains and take advantage of them. Their exploits are often recounted to others (who may feel bored to tears or, alternatively, envious at having missed an opportunity) and embroidered for greater effect, while the spoils of their adventures are displayed with considerable pride.

While much energy and money is spent by advertisers to inform consumers of the bargains on offer, it seems to us that, like secrets, bargains cannot be known to everybody. Nor can a shop, a retailer or an airline be perceived to make a living by always offering bargains, although particular brands or sites may become well known as bargain-hunting terrains. A discounted Italian designer suit may be a bargain, a cheap suit is not. Looking for a bargain then, is not the same as looking for value for money. It is more like looking for opportunities to discover anomalies in the market and take advantage of them. The bargain spotter is akin to a trickster figure who exposes fissures in the system and triumphs against its dictates through cunning and opportunism. Bargain hunters are not always solitary creatures. Informal networks of information exist through which individuals can share their discoveries with friends and neighbours. This sharing of secrets and exploits with like-minded people is grist to the mill of social media such as Twitter or Facebook. Finding a bargain marks the triumph of opportunism, like scoring an undeserved goal, which is all the sweeter for being undeserved.

A duty to explore?

It is paradoxical that bargain hunting, which is central to value-for-money consumerism and to consumer advocacy (see Chapter 9, 'The Consumer as Activist'), has attracted limited attention in studies of consumption (Furnham and Okamura, 1999; Tatzel, 2002; Cox et al., 2005). Economists, in particular, have been reproached for ignoring *curiosity* as one of the consumer's motives. Scitovsky, one of the few economists who has introduced the concept of exploration in the discussion of modern consumption, has criticized other economists for failing to recognize

> *that most important motive force of behavior, including consumer behavior – man's yearning for novelty, his desire to know the unknown. The yearning for new things and*

ideas is the source of all progress, all civilization; to ignore it as a source of satisfaction is surely wrong. (Scitovsky, 1976: 11)

By contrast, however, curiosity was a notion of considerable interest in cultural theory circles, coupled with the idea of difference. When applied to the study of consumption, these generated immense excitement: the consumers' quests for new pleasures, new meanings and even new identities, through tiny differences in what they purchased, through their sorties to the market, were endlessly probed. Today's Western consumer is constantly exhorted to savour new tastes, to discover new pleasures and to explore new worlds. As Baudrillard, a major figure in this trend, noted:

> *the modern consumer, the modern citizen, cannot evade the constraint of happiness and pleasure, which in the new ethics is equivalent to the traditional constraint of labor and production ... He must constantly be ready to actualize all of his potential, all of his capacity for consumption. If he forgets, he will be gently reminded that he has no right not to be happy. He is therefore not passive: he is engaged, and must be engaged, in continuous activity. Otherwise he runs the risk of being satisfied with what he has and of becoming asocial. A universal curiosity (a concept to be exploited) has as a consequence been reawakened in the areas of cuisine, culture, science, religion, sexuality etc. (Baudrillard, [1970] 1988: 48)*

Being true to oneself as a consumer means being eager to browse and to explore. A vast number of consumer products, ranging from books, magazines and films, to holiday packages, have materialized arousing consumer curiosities, exciting them, nurturing them and satisfying them. Newspapers are filled with curiosity features, exotic places, exotic cuisines, exotic people and so on. 'I don't like travelling' is an instant conversation stopper at parties, just as 'I don't have a TV' can be an instant conversation starter! Facebook and YouTube have become curiosity spotting arenas where people spend huge amounts of time exploring curios in all aspects of life. The local grocery store has been metamorphosed into the hypermarket, which may stock up to 40,000 different items. This jungle of consumption offers a bewildering array of goods – whose prices, packages, sizes, formats and names, to say nothing of contents, are constantly changing – and makes brands a feature of permanence acting like signposts in the jungle. Thus, shopping for groceries turns from a habit or a rational choice into an exploration (see Chapter 2, 'The Consumer as Chooser').

Consumer explorations are not searches into deep unknowns, inner or outer. Instead they are explorations of minute variations, of infinitesimal idiosyncrasies of style, products, brands, signs and meanings. This type of exploration is the discourse of *difference*, the discovery of difference, the establishing of difference and the appropriation of difference. Even modest bargain hunting is a quest for a certain type of difference (that is, to be the person who spots the bargain) and the reading of meaning into this difference.

The quest for difference

Images of consumers as explorers, restless and impatient, driven by insatiable curiosity, constantly looking for difference, underscore the ideas of numerous prominent cultural theorists, including Bourdieu, Bauman, Featherstone, McCracken and the early Baudrillard. Reekie argues:

> *shopping appears to have undergone re-skilling, from a management task defined by the shopper's ability to select 'bargains' (or quality at low cost), to a creative task defined by the shopper's ability to locate unusual, unstandardized or personalized goods. (Reekie, 1992: 190)*

Difference drives the modern consumer, argues Baudrillard, effectively obliterating the concept of *needs* that can be satisfied through material objects, since 'a need is not a need for a particular object as much as it is a "need" for difference (the *desire for social meaning*)' (Baudrillard, [1970] 1988: 45).

Consumer explorations routinely assume this form of a quest for difference. It is not surprising, then, that even our local mall, our local supermarket and our local high street can be places of exploration, where the consumer pursues difference, just like the primitive hunter pursues his prey (Ginzburg, 1980). And just like the primitive hunter, the consumer/explorer is avidly and restlessly looking for tiny clues and disturbances, for signs that a new fashion may be about to explode on the scene, that a new pleasure has been discovered or that a new signifier has been born.

The quest for difference has all the compulsive qualities of the 'Spot the Difference' game, something that manufacturers and advertisers have long appreciated. The consumer is presented with countless puzzles to unlock, countless riddles to decode, countless knots to untie. Examples of semiotic puzzles include:

- misspelt words or brand names
- puns, word games, double entendres or innuendoes, especially in advertisements and corporate logos
- unpronounceable words, especially in brand names
- ambiguous newspaper headlines
- advertisements that do not display the name of a brand or conceal the product in a collage of images.

The current trend among some car manufacturers, following BMW, of *not* marking their products with prestigious model signs is another play on difference. To the 'untrained' eye, two cars may seem identical, yet, to the connoisseur, tiny details of trim reveal enormous differences in price, specification, 'cool' and prestige. Such devices highlight the importance of the minuscule, heighten the consumer's state of alertness, provoke curiosity and reward perseverance.

Freud's concept of the 'narcissism of minor differences' captures well the symbolic and emotional importance of tiny details, especially when they distinguish social groups and individuals that are geographically and socially close to each other (Freud, [1921] 1985; Freud, [1930] 1985). In such situations, group members are held together not by the force of shared ideals and powerful leadership, but rather through the signs that differentiate them from their immediate neighbours. It is to those little badges, emblems and colours that the group's and the individual's self-esteem become, as Freud would put it, condensed. Postmodern theorists would say that they act as metonymies for the group (Culler, [1981] 2001). Under the regime of the narcissism of minor differences, signs become essential differences and, therefore, essences. This is how small differences become big differences. Being able to read such differences is vital, since these differences become sources of in-group solidarity and out-group hostility. In this way, supporters of a football team reserve the highest hostility for supporters of the team based in a neighbouring part of the same town (Gabriel, 1999). Local accents, slang, anecdotes, badges, stories, websites, myths and folklore can also provide similarly charged symbolic differences, as can consumer products. In this way, clothes, watches, shoes, cars, bikes and other visible products offer the symbolic means of self-identification through which individuals align themselves emotionally with those sharing their lifestyles, forming what Maffesoli aptly described as 'neo-tribes' (Maffesoli, 1995). These neo-tribes are transient and volatile, mutating and cross-fertilizing, but they are a reliable source of narcissistic satisfaction for their 'members'(Cova et al., 2007). They have prospered with the rise of social media and the internet generally (Kozinets, 1999; Cova and White, 2010).

Being able to identify and decode what to others may be imperceptible differences between products, solving those semiotic puzzles that either defeat or escape others, gives people a sense of uniqueness. In this way, they can become sources of narcissistic pleasure, similar to the pleasures of people who solve the *New York Times* crossword puzzle before breakfast or complete a Sudoku on the bus or hack their way into any secure computer for the thrill of unlocking what is seemingly impregnable. This may explain the compulsive puzzle-solving responses generated by unmarked products, cryptic advertisements, unorthodox hairstyles and other mildly unusual signs of difference. The ability to decipher such signs, as well as a selection of the signs themselves, are incorporated in the consumers' idealized images of themselves – what Freud calls 'egos-ideals' (Freud, [1921] 1985) – which fuel their further explorations. Being street-wise means being able to recognize instantly signs like those above.

If Freudian theory may indicate that narcissism is the fuel of the individual's quest for difference and compulsive puzzle-solving, Simmel's trickle-down hypothesis (see Chapter 3, 'The Consumer as Communicator') offers an interesting sociological parallel, linking these phenomena with the impersonal qualities of modern urban life and the decline of traditional fixed status markers. For Simmel (as indeed for Veblen), consumption turns into an arena for status explorations, where subordinate groups constantly seek to imitate the consumption patterns of superordinate groups, which, in turn, strive to differentiate themselves by adopting new fashions and generating new status markers. Imitation and differentiation act as a motor for social change. Discovering *difference*, becoming different and discovering ways of becoming different are all, in Simmel's view, responses to the pervasive *indifference* of urban cultures.

> This leads ultimately to the strangest eccentricities, to specifically metropolitan extravagances of self-distantiation, of caprice, of fastidiousness, the meaning of which is no longer to be found in the content of such activity itself but rather in its being a form of 'being different' – of making oneself noticeable. (Simmel, [1903] 1971: 331)

In this remarkable passage, which anticipates the concept of 'cool' as well as theories of free-floating signifiers, Simmel captures two important themes; first, that consumers set interpretative puzzles for each other so that manufacturers and advertisers may be seen merely as riding rather than causing this tendency; and, second, that difference is not a fact, but a way of looking. When consumers are looking for difference, they are in effect looking for different ways of looking. Whether or not two pairs of trousers are alike or different has less to do with the qualities of the trousers themselves than with the meanings attached to them by different groups. A pair of jeans may stand out from an ocean of grey suits; a pair of bleached jeans may stand out from a sea of jeans; a pair of torn and bleached jeans may stand out from the rest ... only to the practised eye. In this way, 'decoding the minutiae of distinctions in dress, house, furnishing, leisure lifestyles and equipment' (Featherstone, 1983, quoted in Tomlinson, 1990: 21) turns into a compulsion for all of us. It is because we strive for difference that we become compulsive 'readers of signs', experimenting with different interpretations.

The shopping space becomes a jungle of signs and symbols where products and people alike seek to present themselves as what the marketers would call, 'unique selling propositions'. Shoppers are at once explorers and explored. New shopping design incorporates the shoppers as part of the adventure, as they try different clothes, stare at themselves in mirrors, or simply display their enigmatic hairstyles, clothes or 'looks' (Nixon, 1992).

> Shopping is ... adventure, safari, carnival, and contains unexpected 'risks' in what you may find and who you may meet. It is a kind of self-discovery. And by its very nature it possesses theatricality: one dresses up to go out and one shops to acquire the new persona, to modify the old one or to perfect the setting in which one is seen and known. (Clammer, 1992: 203–204)

Consumption sites such as theme parks, cruise ships, casinos, tourist resorts, hotels, restaurants and, above all, shopping malls, are referred to as 'cathedrals of consumption' by George Ritzer to indicate their quasi-religious, enchanted qualities. Ritzer (1999) views them as the core institutions of late modernity, which have redefined the nature of society. The great sociologists of modernity, including Weber and Durkheim, emphasized its rationalizing qualities that dissolve traditional elements, such as superstition, myth and folklore. Ritzer argues that where modernity led to a Weberian 'disenchantment of the world', a stripping away of myth, folklore and fantasy, late modernity reintroduces these into social life through 'hyper-consumption', mass festivals of consumption taking place in its spiritual homes, the modern cathedrals. Ritzer's central thesis is that contemporary management sets its eyes firmly not on the toiling worker, but on the fantasizing consumer. What management does is to furnish, in a highly rationalized manner, an endless stream of consumable fantasies inviting consumers to pick and choose, thus creating the possibility of re-enchanting a disenchanted world through mass festivals in the new cathedrals of consumption.

Ritzer offers prodigious illustrations of the ways in which consumption is constantly promoted, enhanced and controlled in these new settings, not so much through direct advertising, as through indirect means such as spatial arrangements, uses of language, festivals, simulations and extravaganzas, as well as the cross fertilization ('implosion') of products and images. Above all, consumption gradually colonizes every public and private domain of social life, which become saturated with fantasizing, spending and discarding opportunities. Thus, schools, universities and hospitals are converted from sober, utilitarian institutions into main terrains of consumption, treating their constituents as customers, offering them a profusion of merchandise and indulging their fantasies and caprices. Hyper-consumption is a state of affairs where every social experience – romance, learning, celebration, mourning – is mediated by market mechanisms.

Before Ritzer adopted it as the centre point of his argument, the first edition of this book described the term 'cathedral of consumption' as a hackneyed metaphor. Some have ridiculed the idea that shopping (and web-shopping) can be spiritual experiences akin to visiting a real cathedral. Given the arrant materialism of contemporary consumption, to describe it as a spiritual experience may indeed be stretching the meaning of words. All the same, we should not forget that places of worship have long been places of trade and that promises of spiritual salvation have often come at a material cost. Remember Christ wielding the whip as he drove the money changers from the temple and overturned their tables (John 2:14 and 15).

One particular cathedral of consumption with pronounced religious and spiritual qualities is the re-invented football stadium. Stadiums like Bernabeu, Camp Nou, San Siro, Old Trafford and Stamford Bridge have become sites where footballers are accorded demi-god status among delirious fans, where watching the intricacies of the game on the field assumes secondary importance to the spiritual union with other fans, especially in the presence of evil, embodied by the supporters of the opposing team (Eyre, 1997; Edge, 1999; Sklair, 2010). Touching the players as they emerge from the tunnel or even appearing in a television shot with a player taking a corner kick becomes tantamount to coming close to God. At the same time, these spaces are very much spaces of consumption where a bewildering array of merchandise is available at exorbitant prices. Some of this, including a wide variety of clothes, shoes and trinkets, may be linked to the football team but others, such as food and drink, games, toys and so forth promote synergistic brands that are absorbed by association in the fans' spiritual experience.

Ritzer may be overstating the enchanted qualities of contemporary consumption, although if we view cathedrals as spaces of inner exploration as well as outer, as places, in other words, where novel experiences are to be had and new selves fashioned, the parallel between cathedrals of old and the consumption temples of today may not be far-fetched. Where the religious ascetics and visionaries may seek enlightenment in fasting, self-denial and faith, today's consumers may be seen as seeking to explore their own limits, physical, psychological and spiritual, through extreme experiences, induced by travel, drugs and spectacle. As Kyrtatas (2004) has suggested, spirituality today may be discovering new homes in tourist destinations, theme parks and all those earthly paradises that have replaced the great one in heaven.

Theme parks, malls and redesigned department stores are not the only spaces of consumer exploration and discovery. Browsing 'exciting new titles' of publishers, music retailers and film distributors online, one notices that many of these 'titles' present little semiotic puzzles to be deciphered, such as puns, metaphors, paradoxes, oxymora, caricatures or, most commonly, spoofs on famous titles. The books' covers – whether seen on paper or as images online – are equally exciting and inviting. Collages, distorted photographs, parodies of famous images, decontextualized cuttings all help to create the feeling that not only is the catalogue a space to be explored, but each book is itself a little mystery, having an utterly unique and personal story to tell. It is easy to regard these qualities as contemporary consumption phenomena. They have in fact been the hallmark of consumerism since its early phase, whether in Parisian department stores (Williams, 1982), the Army and Navy stores throughout the British Empire or the famous Sears catalogue to US homesteaders since the turn of the last century. Whether looking at goods directly or through their images in catalogues, contemporary consumers are constantly invited to become explorers of differences.

Goods and their stories: terrains for exploration

Just like goods in the catalogue, so too do other consumer objects cry out loudly that they have their own personal stories to tell (see Chapter 3, 'The Consumer as Communicator'). The consumer as expert semiotician can disentangle the voices of the different objects, and quickly reads the clues about their stories in their appearance, their name, their packaging, their relationships and, unnoticed to postmodern thinkers, their prices. If, as Baudrillard argues, commodities are sign-values rather than use-values, price is an important aspect of the story which they tell. For example:

'I am pricey, I know it and I invite you to find out for yourself if I am worth it.'
'I offer no-nonsense value for money; I may look plain, but if you choose me you will receive loyal and reliable service.'
'I am really inexpensive, but what do you lose by trying me?'
'I look pricey, but I am not really.'
'I am mean and nasty but I am the cheapest.'

Of course, price is by no means the only feature of goods which tells a story. The story told by a shampoo or a motor-cycle is fashioned by numerous other features as well: brand name, packaging, advertisers' images for the product, the images of people displaying or using the product, the images of those who eschew it, the images of other products with which it is associated or against which it competes. Still more, the stories that goods tell are fashioned by reports and recommendations constantly updated online, and instantly available by other consumers.

All these things and many others shape the stories told by a particular commodity. Consumers listen to these stories and make their own decisions about the products. Some goods are quickly discarded as boring, uncool, poor imitations of the 'real thing', sheep in wolves' clothes, phoney, unfashionable. Others are appreciated as clever challenges, for example, a witty advertisement, an amusing package, a clever spoof on an existing product or an imaginative new *product idea*. Being phoney does not necessarily diminish a product in the eyes of today's consumer, if it can be interpreted as an imaginative, cheeky or defiant simulation rather than as an inferior copy, seeking to conceal its inferiority or the fact that it *is* a copy. Such products may generate a desire to acquire them, not because their stories are untold to the prospective purchaser, but because they can provide semiotic tests to others. Will *they* be able to 'read' them, or will *they* be fooled by them? We go exploring for such objects, which will serve as puzzles that we enjoy setting for others.

There is another category of objects that appears more reluctant to reveal their stories to potential buyers. Such objects are either difficult to decode so long as they are not owned, or stimulate curiosity about, for example, the truthfulness of their claims. The resistance offered by these objects increases their aura and stimulates desire. They seem to cry out for further exploration, an exploration that cannot proceed unless the consumer can get them, either by paying for them, borrowing them or by 'liberating' them from their ownerless state (see discussion of shoplifting in Chapter 8 'The Consumer as Rebel'). A new arrival on a supermarket shelf or a new 'wonder' anti-ageing skin cream or health-enhancing food and drink acts in this manner.

Such objects cannot be fully consumed, that is, tell their full story, unless the consumer can make them his or her own and appropriate them. Objects that require no payment seem hardly worth exploring; their value in the eyes of the consumer is reduced, the quality of the exploration is diminished in his or her own eyes. How unalluring are the various free newspapers that are dispensed through our letter-boxes; how unexciting the various experiences on offer 'for free'; how insipid the water that comes out of our taps when compared to the sparkling glamour that pours out of a delicately tinted bottle that we have paid for! Notice that 'something for free' is not at all the same as 'something for nothing' which, as we saw, is the trademark of the true bargain. If the bargain represents a little symbolic triumph at the expense of the system, free handouts carry many of the dreary marks of philanthropy, the dispensation of second-hand or second-rate goods with a symbolic or moral catch. Payment, then, is far from incidental to consumer explorations. Paying for a product signals the start of a new phase of exploration, the exploration of the owned object or purchased experience. Think of the excitement of bringing a new acquisition back from the shop or of receiving an order in the morning's mail or attending the music festivals (rather than taking a free walk in the park). What will the new armchair look like in your sitting room? How will the new speakers perform with your entertainment system? What will the new blouse look like with your green skirt?

The careers of objects

Once a commodity – whether object or service – has been paid for, rented or received as a gift, it begins a new life as an object of consumer exploration; this life can assume several different twists. Many authors have commented on the tendency of objects to disappoint once they have been paid for and numerous explanations of this phenomenon have been offered (Galbraith, 1967; Baudrillard, [1968] 1988; McCracken, 1988; Campbell, 1989). In these instances, the consumer finds that the object has no story to tell, no secret to reveal. Like Kavafis's poem 'Ithaca', cited at the start of this chapter, it has no special magic of its own. Its promise is the journey, not the final destination. Such objects lose their charm instantly and sink into an anonymous existence, forgotten at the bottom of a drawer or quickly discarded in a dustbin. Occasionally, they may be rediscovered, as gifts to someone who unaccountably values them, as items of kitsch value, as antiques or even as souvenirs of one's consumer follies. Many end up in charity shops and jumble sales, where they can be discovered as bargains and start new careers.

Consumers may or may not feel cheated at such inglorious turns of events (see Chapter 7, 'The Consumer as Victim'). What is interesting is the extent to which they are prepared to weather disappointments; after all, exploration is full of dead-ends, and if they paid good money for what turned out to be quite ordinary or a dud, so be it; perhaps the price was worth paying for the satisfaction of knowing that the product was quite ordinary. Sometimes disappointment is swift. There are instances, however, where the consumer stubbornly refuses to relinquish faith in a product, against considerable evidence to the contrary as illustrated by the following experience of one of the authors.

> *I remember purchasing what had seemed like a marvellous Italian motor-car, much to the amusement of my friends and relatives who teased me endlessly about the car's poor reputation for reliability and its general 'tackiness'. No matter. Since my childhood this make of car, famous for its sweetly purring engine, had held an overwhelming fascination for me. It did not take long for me to realize that every allegation against the car was true, as hardly a week went by without the car needing garage attention. The story told by the car was very different from the one I was longing to hear. Yet, the car's aura refused to wane. Each time I took it to be repaired, I thought it would be the last visit, the one that would finally get the car back into full health. This was no love–hate relationship; it was straightforward love. I was prepared to forgive the car its every misbehaviour, as one forgives a pampered child. It took me fully 18 months before I was willing to recognize that the car was simply a fiasco. I employed every conceivable rationalization to defend the car, until I finally gave up and sold it. Yet, I felt no anger or disappointment for having bought it; I paid good money for what turned out to be a bad car. But I felt that I had owed it to myself to buy this car, and the money was spent to very good effect. It was like staking some money on a bet and losing. As a consumer-explorer, I was philosophical about losing money on bad bets.*

In addition to objects that sooner or later disappoint, there are objects that stubbornly refuse to yield their full stories. How often is it that we discover that having purchased something, we may not obtain full advantage of it unless certain accessories are purchased, which in turn emerge as nothing but preambles for further purchases. We may suspect that such objects are mere entrapments, that they try to lure us into impasses, yet, as in the case of the Italian car above, the temptation to throw good money after bad is powerful. Explorers find it very difficult to turn full circle and return to base.

There is yet another class of products, those with which we develop a relationship of sorts. Some of them are quickly absorbed in our self-perceptions; they pose no further puzzles but offer the prospect of quiet contentment. A new track suit in which we feel comfortable, a trusted brand of virtually anything, a no-nonsense watch – such items do not challenge us, although in their quiet way they may be important parts of our identity. Then, there are objects which cannot be incorporated so easily: a 'loud' jacket, a flash car, an eye-catching hat, a suggestive T-shirt. They maybe need to be used at first in private before we feel confident to present them as part of our public persona. These things may make us self-conscious, they cannot be readily accommodated in our identity, which needs to stretch or adjust itself in order to absorb them. It is then that exploration of the world of objects initiates an exploration of identity. The quest for outer difference becomes a quest for inner meaning. This will be the main focus of the next chapter, which examines the consumer as identity-seeker.

Boredom

The power of the image of the consumer as explorer is thrown into sharp relief by the experience of boredom. This may not be adequately recognized in consumer studies as a fuel of contemporary consumerism (for an interesting exception, see Shankar et al., 2006); yet, boredom is a threat against which many sorties into the marketplace promise relief. It is also a frequent experience that results from familiar shopping and familiar routines. Men report boredom when they go shopping with female partners for clothes, as do children when resisting parents' announcement of a shopping trip. Everyone knows that boredom is a regular experience of consumption, yet academics have not paid much attention to it. By contrast, retail planners and architects who designs shops, shopping malls and the internal layout of stores, and also website builders who design shopping websites, are keenly aware of the need for measured and unthreatening variety. They know that consumers have to be kept interested. The constant offer of new experiences, not least to keep the potential purchaser in the store or on the site, is a response to the fear of boredom above all. Retail analysts talk of store brands being 'tired', 'in need of a facelift', 'due for a makeover'. For them, boredom is the black hole into which profitability disappears.

Novelists and poets have long acknowledged the emotional depth and importance of boredom. In *Notes from the Underground*, based on his experience in a penal colony, Dostoevsky (1821–1881) described how, when faced with boredom, people will resort to any form of destructive or self-destructive behaviour. 'All humanity's problems stem from man's inability to sit quietly in a room alone', wrote Pascal (1623–1662). The search for stimulation and excitement leads people to every kind of adventure and folly, but it is also the spur to creative work and exploration. The concept of the 'flaneur' was first outlined by Baudelaire – and amplified by Walter Benjamin (Benjamin and Tiedemann, 1999) – as the city dandy who seeks to escape boredom by wandering the thronged streets, melding into crowds; watching other people's vitality became a substitute for the lack of his own. Benjamin, Simmel ([1903] 1971) and other cultural analysts of early urban living saw the city as providing an escape from the boredom of what Marx called 'the idiocy of rural life', but creating opportunities of boredom of its own.

Department stores and the increasing commercial activity of city streets offered numerous opportunities for escaping domestic boredom. At the same time, the impersonality of modern cities and their standardization and routinization exacerbated the opportunities for boredom.

The limits of exploration

Few images capture the driven qualities of modern consumption, its excitements and disappointments as attempts to escape boredom, as that of the consumer explorer. Few figures can so easily be ridiculed and disparaged as the explorer who never left his or her back yard, the explorer who dreamed it all up, who played safe. The worlds explored by modern consumers are certainly not natural worlds; the discoveries they make along the way are carefully orchestrated by producers, designers and retailers to greet them at the appropriate time in the appropriate place. Many surprises are premeditated, many wonders staged. Here lies one of the paradoxes of modern consumption – the experience of exploration can be genuine, even if the object is simulated and the subject knows that it is simulated, a theme that fascinated Baudrillard (Baudrillard, 1983; 1988). Why go looking for real alligators, unpredictable as they are, when you can catch a grand view of them in the theme park, where they are guaranteed to make an appearance? And why indeed go to the theme park, when you can put your face right inside the mouth of one through the lens of a camera or virtual reality?

Consumer 'explorations' easily end up in quotation marks, as simulated pseudo-explorations in virtual pseudo-realities generated by the magicians of postmodern spectacle societies. In such societies dominated by spectacle (Debord, 1977), many explorations are taken from the comfort of the armchair or bed. Yet, even if the insides of one's computer, theme parks, shopping malls, museums, galleries, tourist attractions and other sites are pre-arranged and manufactured, does this disqualify them from being sites of exploration? Does the fact that others, sometimes thousands or even hundreds of millions, have been there before, invalidate their experience of exploration, excitement and discovery? Hardly. It is perfectly possible to explore hand-made artefacts, whether they be the pyramids of Egypt, a Gothic cathedral or a Doris Lessing novel. If it is possible to explore a novel, a symphony or a building, why not a website, a suit or a shopping mall? Nor does the circumstance that many have been there before diminish the experience of one who, for the first time, 'discovers' Mahler or Kafka. With innocent eyes and ears, he or she may even discover a line of interpretation, a symbolic twist, a coded reference that has not been noticed before. A young student discovered an extended quotation from Pergolesi in Mozart's Requiem, which had escaped the notice of experts, who had spent lifetimes studying the piece. Young people are quick to spot the cultural reference in a celebrity's dress. Besides, leftovers by previous explorers can be fascinating in their own right; one may, for example, remember one's first forays into an area of literature through second-hand paperbacks, which have been read and underlined in different colours by several previous owners, each leaving their own comments on the margins. This can enhance one's experience of exploring.

In sum, neither the artificial quality of the terrains of exploration, nor the presence of numerous fellow-explorers detract from the aptness of a metaphor of exploration, not least as an escape from boredom. It captures admirably the restless, exciting, insatiable qualities of modern consumption, its endless fascination with tiny differences, and its obsession with puzzle-solving, interpretations, clues and signs. The face of the consumer as explorer highlights curiosity as a driving force of Western consumerism, the desire to know the unknown and the yearning for innovation and change, the pursuit of the new. In this sense, it accounts for the consumers' unique vulnerability to lucky draws, mystery presents, promises of exotic trips and other marketing gimmicks, which rely on our capacity to be excited and our longing for the unknown as a leverage for sales. Curiosity, once aroused, makes us highly vulnerable to the merchandisers' tease 'Discover x', where x can range from Turkey to a new brand of lavatory cleaner, a new food product or a new sanitary towel.

What the perspective of the consumer-explorer fails to do is to illuminate what makes things or spaces worth exploring in the first place and at what point they lose their charm and are discarded in favour of new ones, how attempts to escape boredom become boring in their own right. Equally, it obscures the wide range of instances when consumers appear to strive after the familiar and the safe. Brand loyalty would seem incongruous from a perspective that stresses neophilia, innovation and adventure. Surely one of the defining paradoxes of modern consumption is the consumer's need to mix the familiar with the unfamiliar, the simultaneous travel to exotic places with patronage of McDonald's and Holiday Inns (whose earlier logo promised 'No surprises'), the simultaneous capitulation to the comfort of habit and the pursuit of adventure. This is an instance of fragmentation in contemporary consumption that frequently goes unnoticed.

In general, the explorer metaphor presents a somewhat individualistic concept of consumption, underplaying its social character except for the interpretative puzzles that consumers set for each other, known as fashion. Even then, the metaphor is more successful at illuminating why individuals seek to decode and solve these puzzles than why they are inclined to set them for others. In these different ways, this metaphor draws attention to consumption in the first place as a range of relationships between people and things and only to a much lesser extent as relationships among people, consumers and producers or among consumers themselves (as highlighted in Chapter 3, 'The Consumer as Communicator'). The metaphor also fails to take notice of all those people who have become disenchanted with all aspects of consumerism, find every ad or marketing ploy profoundly boring, and have opted for different lifestyles.

All in all, it is a metaphor that creates rather too heroic an image of consumers. It is also too cheerful and, perhaps, frivolous an image. What if the driven qualities of modern consumption, instead of being a quest for novelty and adventure amount to little more than an attempt to escape reality, to find solace in fantasy and self-delusion? In any event, the sorrows, deprivations and frustrations of modern consumption are far from the sights of images of the consumer as explorer. The drudgery of routine shopping, the furtive sorties to shops between family and work commitments, the sacrifices necessitated by demanding children and social expectations, above all, the anxiety about making ends meet or whether to take on more debt, these things have no place in the realms of consumers as explorers.

No other image of the consumer studied in this book is quite as firmly aspirational and youthful as that of the consumer-explorer. One suspects that large numbers of people on the breadline would regard the idea of consumers as explorers as a cruel joke. One suspects that consumer-explorers, in their youthful enthusiasm and exuberance, their constant desire to experiment and try, their naive fascination with puzzles, signs and symbols and their obsession with difference, were a wish-fulfilling fantasy of glossy marketers and excitable semioticians. It is a fantasy on which, from time-to-time, some consumers became fellow-travellers.

5

THE CONSUMER AS IDENTITY-SEEKER

That which is for me through the medium of money – *that for which I can pay (that is, which money can buy) – that am* I, *the possessor of money. The extent of the power of money is the extent of my power. Money's properties are my properties and essential powers – the properties and powers of its possessor. Thus, what I am and am capable of is by no means determined by my individuality. I am ugly, but I can buy for myself the most beautiful of women. Therefore I am not ugly, for the effect of ugliness – its deterrent power – is nullified by money. I, in my character as an individual, am lame, but money furnishes me with twenty-four feet. Therefore I am not lame. I am bad, dishonest, unscrupulous, stupid; but money is honoured, and therefore so is its possessor.* (Marx, [1844] 1972: 81)

CORE ARGUMENTS

Identity has assumed centre-stage in discussions of contemporary politics, culture and consumption. Most commentators agree that psychological identity represents a difficult and precarious project for most people today, as established social categories of class, gender, occupation and so forth become eroded. Choice of occupation, of partner, of sexual preference, of goods to consume and so forth has opened up new possibilities of identity construction but also created new burdens. The material culture both supports and undermines efforts to create and maintain identities. On the one hand, many branded and unbranded goods become briefly parts of an extended self, at least temporarily boosting identity, self-image and self-esteem. In this sense, consumer culture is tailor-made for the narcissistic strivings of contemporary society. Several authors, however, have commented on the addictive quality of consumption – while temporarily assuaging narcissism and bolstering identities, consumer culture creates long-term dissatisfaction, dependency and meaninglessness.

Debates on Western consumption rarely stay clear of the theme of identity for long. Identity is Rome to which all discussions of modern Western consumption lead, whether undertaken by Marxist critics or advertising executives, deconstructionists or liberal reformers, advocates of multiculturalism or radical feminists.

The consensus of otherwise irreconcilable perspectives appears to be that, in late capitalism, consumption is the area where personal and group identities are fought over, contested, precariously put together and licked into shape. As previous chapters have indicated, the Western consumer readily transfigures into an identity-seeker. Whether choosing goods, exploring them, buying them, displaying them, disfiguring them or giving them away, consumers are, above all, frequently presented as thirsting for identity and using commodities to quench this thirst. This chapter examines this popular image of the consumer as identity-seeker, highlighting some crucial ambiguities in the concept of identity.

Identity, like stress, is a concept whose currency and expedience belies its relatively recent pedigree in psychology. It is a concept that we all feel that we grasp intuitively, and is accorded great explanatory weight in discussions of consumption. For these reasons, it is important to investigate how this idea achieved its privileged place in contemporary cultural discussions and then ask what it adds. We start by examining some of the ambiguities acquired by the concept of identity, as it migrated from objects onto people and as the quest of identity came to be regarded as the cause of most major social and individual problems. How did identity turn from a fact into a problem and what is its relevance to consumption? We will also indicate some of the ways in which the obsession with identity, brands and consumption among cultural theorists has hogged the limelight and obscured some other promising lines of study into the relationship between the individual, their sense of self and what they consume.

Fixed identities: from people to goods

Initially, the word 'identity', drawing on its Latin derivation, stood for the sameness, continuity and distinctiveness of things. It applied equally to humans, animals and material objects. Establishing the identity of a person, a flower or a mineral amounted to giving it a name and specifying its uniqueness and distinctiveness in terms of similarities with, and differences from, its relatives. Even in this early conception, identity is not merely a property of the object being identified; it is equally an expression of the interest of those who identify it. The identity of minerals or plants generally coincides with the name of their species – the particular specimen at hand generally requires no further identification to establish it as something singular and unique. This, however, is not the case with a famous diamond that has been given a name, such as the Koh-i-Noor; its identification, notably if stolen and recovered, is not complete unless confirmed to be the very specimen that is missing. Simply establishing the identity of a recovered gem as a diamond is not enough. It is immediately apparent that forensic investigations crucially depend on the identity of objects as absolutely unique items. And it is also apparent why identity cards have become an important issue in these days of vigilantly patrolled frontiers and stolen identities.

The identity of animals in many cases is adequately fixed by the species name alone, or species plus gender. Gardeners are quite happy to know the species of caterpillar that is ruining their crops without concerning themselves about the particular individuals that are most to blame. Knowing the species is enough to dictate the measures that may be taken against it. Likewise, bird spotters are generally content to establish the species and gender of a rare specimen that they catch sight of. Ornithologists, on the other hand, may be interested in knowing the habits and history of a particular specimen or pair; to do so, they may then seek to identify them through the use of coloured rings or other unique marks. Such marks would establish not just species identity, but individual identity and where they have been. In a similar way, family pets, race-horses or animal celebrities carry identities beyond their species and gender, names that establish them as unique individuals. As we shall see presently, the question of whether identity refers to species or specimen is not unconnected with the strivings of Western consumers.

People, too, are generally identified by names; but different people may have the same name, hence it is often necessary to specify the identities of the father and mother, the date of birth or some other feature to establish the identity of an individual. Identity, in this sense, is fixed. No matter what transformations are undergone by the individual, his or her identity cannot change. Nor is identity a matter of choice, will or desire; identity is the outcome of family lineage. Confusion over identity amounts to confusion over parenthood, confusion about facts not about meanings. This theme lies at the heart of drama, both in its tragic and comic senses. Establishing the identity of an individual, whether a person is accused of a crime, or is claiming to be somebody or to own something, is not always easy (especially before DNA identification), but essentially it is a technical, forensic question. Odysseus, returning home after 20 years, had to prove his identity and establish that he was the person he claimed he was. This he proceeded to do with the aid of signs – a scar on the knee as well as knowledge of several intimate secrets that no one else could know.

Why is this important? As Ginzburg (1980) reminds us, the problem of identity was in the first place a *political* one, not an existential one, as consumer theorists have narrowed it down to. Claims to power and property depended crucially on establishing the identities of individuals making the claims. Equally importantly, the maintenance of criminal records and the administration of legal justice and discipline hinge on establishing the identity of people as unique individuals. This can be an immensely difficult problem if individuals are unwilling to co-operate. In a memorable scene from Kubrik's film *Spartacus*, the Romans ask the captured rebels which one of them is Spartacus; to protect their leader, each and every one of the rebels claims to be Spartacus, to great dramatic effect. This was echoed by the Occupy movement's adoption of the Guy Fawkes/ Vendetta mask as a symbol of opposition to the wreckage caused by the 2007–8 banking crisis and to stop individual recognition by the authorities.

The branding of offenders was meant to establish their identity permanently, marking their criminal record, so to speak, on their bodies. Branding was not an option available to colonial administrators, though of course it was rediscovered by the Nazis in the 20th century. A different type of branding has now assumed great importance as a way of marking a product on consumer consciousness. The problem of identity was especially pressing for the administrators of the British Empire, having to administer what they saw as justice to 'natives' who seemed deceitful, disputatious and, to their Western eyes, all looked the same. Fingerprinting, introduced by Sir William Herschel in Bengal in the 1870s, seemed to provide a technical solution to the political problem of identity, a far more discreet but also more efficient solution than branding had been to slave-owners. Each person carried permanently on their fingertips indelible evidence of their identity; no subjective claim or denial could thenceforth discredit the objective evidence of ink on paper. The fingerprint was proof of the person's identity. Thus a person's identity is, in the first place, part of a system of political practices that seek to classify, distinguish and differentiate each individual from others. Gene typing has taken this many stages further.

The political dimension of practices such as identity cards, fingerprinting, random identity checks or unobtrusive surveillance of shopping malls and online activity has led to endless controversy surrounding their introduction. We shall refer to this conceptualization of identity as 'forensic identity' to underline its political nature, and to distinguish it in this chapter from the 'psychological' and 'group' identities. This discussion leads to two conclusions. First, we note that branding has shifted from being a mark to discriminate between people to being a device for according identity and individuality to products. Second, we note that forensic identity, unlike psychological identity, was a problem not for the individuals concerned, but for those who sought to control them. Even today, large corporations seek to manage their customers by maintaining detailed records of their shopping activities, preferences and profile.

Identity as a psychological and sociological concept

The migration of identity into psychology and sociology has maintained some of the qualities of forensic identity, reversed others, as well as introducing several new features of crucial relevance to consumption. It is interesting that psychoanalysis, which virtually invented the idea of psychological *identification*, did not seriously turn to identity until Erikson coined the expression 'identity crisis' (Erikson, 1959).

He used this term to describe the condition of soldiers severely traumatized by the battlefield during the Second World War. These soldiers appeared to have lost their sense of sameness and continuity with their former selves. This suggested to Erikson the idea that psychological identity is not something given or fixed, but something that one achieves with the aid of others. Subsequently, Erikson developed his theory that identity crisis is a normal stage of ego development in late adolescence and early adulthood that may lead to different outcomes. Some individuals uncritically adopt identities derived from their parents, others endlessly experiment with different identities – a process Erikson refers to as 'moratorium' – at times failing to emerge with any coherent identity – a process he refers to as 'diffused identity'. The happiest conclusion of this process is the achievement of an identity in which the individual is both conscious of his or her uniqueness and which provides him or her with an anchoring into the here and now (Erikson, 1968). In these ways, self-esteem and self-image, as Erikson has acknowledged, are conceptually very close to ego identity.

Erikson's ideas of identity crisis and identity confusion and diffusion gained substantial popularity in the 1950s, when the search for identity came to preoccupy psychologists, especially American ones, very considerably. This led to a very different concept of identity from the fixed, stable and immutable forensic identity. The new concept was to serve psychologists intent on delivering the consumer as a manageable package to merchandisers very well. This identity is subjective; it is an individual's answer to questions such as 'Who am I?' and 'In what ways am I different from others?' This is a changing, precarious and problematic entity, the product of an individual's perpetual adaptation to his or her environment. Uniqueness is not given, but is achieved; continuity can be undermined or ruptured. Psychological identity is the product of psychological work; it must be nurtured and defended, worked for and fought over. The importance of material objects to these processes was to prove seminal.

The sociological itineraries of identity took off from where psychological discussions left. Psychologists themselves had prepared the ground in their 'mass psychology', where it was argued that in crowds people lose their individual identities and become one with the mass, part of a collective mind, entirely derivative from it (Freud, [1921] 1985; Le Bon, [1985] 1960). The implicit assumption that identity is a free-flowing entity that pours from the collective to the individual characterizes much of the traditional sociological literature on the subject; by contrast, the pursuit of forensic identity has been to distinguish the individual from the masses. Thus, members of ethnic groups, sexual preference groups, political movements, occupational and professional groups are often seen as drawing their sense of social identity from their group, sharing its ideals and aspirations (Tajfel, 1974; 1979). A group's identity, like personal identity, is problematic; it must be fought over and forged out of shared experiences and traditions; it must discard attributions imposed upon the group by others;

it must discover and celebrate its own continuity with its past; it must choose who its friends and enemies are, where its boundaries lie, what its symbols are and so on (Omi and Winant, 1987; Hall, 1996; Hall and Du Gay, 1996). However, as groups shape their identities, their members' individual identity problems recede; individual identity derives from identification with the group.

Modernity and identity

Most cultural commentators agree that psychological and social identity is a uniquely modern problem. In a pre-modern society, psychological and group identities coincide with forensic identities, since they

> *are easily recognizable, objectively and subjectively. Everybody knows who everybody else is and who he is himself. A knight is a knight and a peasant is a peasant. There is, therefore, no problem of identity. The question, 'Who am I?' is unlikely to arise in consciousness, since the socially predefined answer is massively real subjectively and consistently confirmed in all significant social interaction. (Berger and Luckmann, 1967: 184)*

Urban living, anonymous organizations, impersonal work, mass production, social and physical movement, the proliferation of choice; in short, modernity itself conspires against fixed identities. In late modernity, the media of mass communication assume extraordinary significance in shaping our perceptions of the world we inhabit, saturating our physical and mental spaces with images, yet producing a massive vacuum to the individual's question 'Who am I?' With the exception of when we catch glimpses of ourselves on TV monitors in shopping malls or selfies posted online or occasionally in reality or other TV shows, our personal identities are hardly recognized or validated in a world saturated by information and noise.

Faced with a modern world that falls far short of providing the massive confirmation noted by Berger and Luckmann above, identity becomes a major and continuous preoccupation of each individual. Unlike Erikson, who saw identity crisis as a temporary phase, eventually resolved and left behind, current cultural theory approaches identity as an interminable project, involving not only crucial life-choices and decisions but, equally, their translation into a narrative, a life-story. One of the clearest statements on identity has been offered by Giddens:

> *In the post-traditional order of modernity, against the backdrop of new forms of mediated experience, self-identity becomes a reflexively organised endeavour. The reflexive project of the self, which consists in the sustaining of coherent, yet continuously revised, biographical narratives, takes place in the context of multiple choice as filtered through abstract systems. In modern social life, the notion of lifestyle takes on a particular*

significance. The more tradition loses its hold, and the more daily life is reconstituted in terms of the dialectical play of the local and the global, the more individuals are forced to negotiate lifestyle choices among a diversity of options. (Giddens, 1991: 5)

Identity, in this formulation, does not lie in any fixed attributes of personality or self, still less in certain fixed forms of behaviour. Nor can past achievements and glories form the basis of identity. As Schwartz reminds us, a '"has been" [is] somebody who once was somebody, but is no longer anybody' (Schwartz, 1990: 32). Instead, as Giddens states, identity lies now 'in the capacity *to keep a particular narrative going'* (Giddens, 1991: 54). Identity, then, can be seen as a story that a person writes and rewrites about him or herself, never reaching the end until they die, and always rewriting the earlier parts, so that the activity of writing becomes itself part of the story. In this sense, it is both reflexive and incomplete. Identity and identity-seeking are, at least in Western culture, essentially the same thing. In creating a story in which the author is a protagonist, the author creates himself or herself anew – author and protagonist co-create each other in an unending reflexive process.

Many authors believe that in our times, a variety of circumstances conspire to make the 'storying' of our lives particularly difficult. Thus for Boje:

Some experiences *lack that linear sequence and are difficult to tell as a 'coherent' story. Telling stories that lack coherence is contrary to modernity. Yet, in the postmodern condition, stories are harder to tell because experience itself is so fragmented and full of chaos that fixing meaning or imagining coherence is fictive. (Boje, 2001: 7)*

The theme that storying has become especially hard in our times is highly developed in Richard Sennett's work. He argues that new capitalism, with its emphasis on flexibility, opportunism and the powerful illusions of choice and freedom, fragments the continuity of today's life narratives, denying them the continuity and coherence enjoyed by the narratives of yesteryear (Sennett, 1998: 31). As Slater has noted, 'underlying such perspective is an ineradicable nostalgia or lamentation: consumer culture can never replace the world we have lost, or provide us with selves we can trust, or offer a culture in which we can be truly home' (Slater, 1997: 99).

Consumption, choice and identity

What then do individuals write in the precious life-stories that constitute their identities? How do they construct their selfhoods? What are the identity structures that distinguish late modernity from earlier periods? Various answers have been provided to these questions, although increasing emphasis is placed on consumption at the expense of personal and family histories, membership of occupational and professional groups, work and personal achievement, charac-ter and temperament, as the terrain in which identities are sought. Bauman (1988; 1992; 2001) has been one of the strongest champions of the view that the 'work ethic' has, at least in Western societies, been dislodged by a 'consumer ethic'. He argued:

> *If in a life normatively motivated by the work ethic, material gains were deemed secondary and instrumental in relation to work itself (their importance consisting primarily of confirming the adequacy of the work effort), it is the other way round in a life guided by the 'consumer ethic'. Here, work is (at best) instrumental; it is in the material emoluments that one seeks, and finds, fulfilment, autonomy and freedom. (Bauman, 1988: 75)*

Consumption, not only expands to fill the identity vacuum left by the decline of the work ethic, but it assumes the same structural significance that work enjoyed at the high noon of modernity.

> *The same central role which was played by work, by job, occupation, profession, in modern society, is now performed in contemporary society, by consumer choice. ... The former was the lynch-pin which connected life-experience – the self-identity problem, life-work, life-business – on the one level; social integration on the second level; and systemic reproduction on the third level. ... Consumerism stands for production, distribution, desiring, obtaining and using, of symbolic goods. (Bauman, 1992: 223)*

How do consumer choices fashion identity? At its simplest, the argument would suggest that individuals can buy identities off the peg, just as corporations can buy themselves new images, new brands and new identities by adopting new symbols, signs and other similar paraphernalia. Numerous commentators on consumption appear to regard this as self-evident, requiring little explanation or elaboration.

> *Shopping is not merely the acquisition of things: it is the buying of identity. (Clammer, 1992: 195)*

> *The identity of the consumer is tied with the identity not only of the brand, but of the company that produces it. (Davidson, 1992: 178)*

At their most mechanistic, such arguments suggest that images and qualities of products are simply transferred onto the consumer, either singly or in combi-nations. Identity is essentially a self-image resulting from the endless displacements and condensations of product images. 'Ours is a world in which it is our products that tell our stories for us', argues Davidson (1992: 15). The consumers' main preoccupation then is being able to afford those goods that they require to sustain their identities. This approach, however, disregards the reflexive qualities underlined earlier and only transposes the question 'Who am I?' On what basis do individual consumers make their choices? Why are some objects liked and others disliked? Why do some objects easily blend with individual identity and others do not? Why are some images convincing while others are rejected as phoney? And if the qualities of objects are mechanically transferred onto their owners, such as branding for slaves, why does the project of identity remain incomplete? What drives the consumers' desires for new products and new identities?

These questions can be foreclosed if we were to accept Baudrillard's argument that the *only* product image that today's consumers want is one that is perfectly unique, different from all others. Only this will make each consumer unique, forever standing out from the crowd. This is impossible, of course, though not merely because today's products are mass-produced and lack the required uniqueness. In a hyper-real world of self-devouring signifiers (see discussion of Clio and Nike in Chapter 3, 'The Consumer as Communicator'), where each new arrival on the scene consigns its predecessors to the undifferentiated state of also-rans, standing out from the crowd is a problematic project. Free-floating signifiers wreak havoc with our individual identities, which are ransacked by wave after wave of semiotic invaders. In this case, as Miller put it, 'our identity has become synonymous with patterns of consumption which are determined elsewhere. Taken to its logical conclusion (and the advantage of Baudrillard is that he does just this), this view entails a denial of all signification' (Miller, 1987: 165). The project of identity, once it has been hijacked by hyper-real consumerism, is doomed. Uniqueness, continuity and value will forever elude it.

Many of the writers exploring the connection between consumption and iden-tity have not shared Baudrillard's rather bleak view. Nor, however, do they take the view that identities can be constructed unproblematically by purchasing a particular set of images. Between the life-story that constitutes identity and the images of the consumer world, most of these authors seek to interpose human agency, a kind of creative *bricolage* whereby identities are fashioned through an active engagement with product images. This relationship between identity and the world of material objects is the main focus of the rest of this chapter.

Objects and extended selves

The view that material objects are a vital feature of every aspect of our identities is neither novel nor particularly original. Owning a *unique* object such as a work of art might have been solid proof of forensic identity as good as any branding or distinguishing mark. The qualities of material objects and their past history con-fers prestige and status onto their holders. Furthermore, there are some categories of objects, such as family heirlooms or valued gifts, which are so dear to us that they end up being parts of our extended self (Winnicott, 1962; Winnicott, 1964; Csikszentmihalyi and Rochberg-Halton, 1981; Belk, 1988; Dittmar, 1991; Lee, 1993). Winnicott (1964) noted that in early childhood certain objects, like teddy bears or pieces of soft rag, acquire a great significance for children. These objects, which he calls 'transitional objects', are half-way between the infant's inner and outer realities, providing *bridges* between the internal and external worlds. Transitional objects are instrumental in the child's development and may be replaced later by other objects which have the same bridging function. From a very young age, we learn to look at such objects as extensions of ourselves. In the words of George, a seven-year-old boy to his dad (one of the authors):

> My owl collection is very valuable to me; it is part of me. It's like my hair. If you lose your hair you are sad, if I lost my owls I'd be sad.

In this way, some material objects can become central characters of our personal histories, without which our histories would be unthinkable. The quest for a particular object, whether it be the Holy Grail or another owl in George's collection, may be an important part of a person's life-story, and the finding of the object may confer fame and generate pride. In this way, the search for particular objects, the adventures encountered along the way, the glory and fame achieved by their discovery, these can all become part of an individual's identity.

As we saw in Chapter 3 ('The Consumer as Communicator'), Levy-Bruhl (1966) noted that in pre-literate cultures, ornaments, clothes and tools are seen as parts of the self. Over a century ago, William James ([1892] 1961: 44) noted that a man's 'me' is made up of everything that he can call his, including his body and his mind, his clothes, his house, his wife, his children, his parents, his land, his yacht and his bank account. In all these instances, material objects become ensconced in our identity because of the closeness of our relationships with them, our physical and emotional *attachment* to them.

In contrast, however, to these instances, Western consumption is unique in that identity becomes vitally and self-consciously enmeshed in stories that are read by consumers in relatively mundane, mass-produced objects that they buy, use and discard. These unexceptional objects are not so much carriers of meaning, as carriers of vivid and powerful *images*, enabling us to choose them consciously from among many similar ones, promising to act as the raw material out of which our individual identities may be fashioned. Unlike children who form attachments to their cuddly toys, Western consumers do not establish profound relationships with the majority of the goods they consume. Instead, they use them in opportunistic but highly visible ways, being very conscious of the inferences that others will draw from them and by the ways their image will be affected by them.

Children spontaneously like certain things and dislike others; they do not construct identities around them (Baumeister, 1986). Yet by the time they reach school age, likes and dislikes lose their innocence. Liking unfashionable toys, making friends with unpopular children, wearing old-fashioned shoes, these things become tied to image and identity. By early adolescence, virtually every choice becomes tainted by image-consciousness. Smoking, drinking, eating, clothes, accents, hairstyles, friendships, music, sport and virtually every like and dislike become highly self-conscious matters. On Facebook and other websites, by ticking the 'like/dislike' box, one subscribes to a bundle of meaning.

For young people today, consumption appears as a key to entering adulthood. Abercrombie argues that 'young people will experiment with different identities, by ignoring the way in which class, gender and race construct the boundaries of identity' (Abercrombie, 1994: 51). Commodities, under consumer capitalism, rich in image, become young people's main accomplices in these attempts to reach adulthood. As Willis argues, adulthood 'is now achieved, it seems, by spending money in a certain way rather than "settling down" to a life of wedded bliss' (Willis, 1990: 137). Consumption becomes the core element in the rite of passage to adulthood. It is not enough for young people to be seen spending their own money on cigarettes, clothes and electric goods. What is more important is constructing out of these ingredients an individual style, a convincing image. Identity, then, does not mean the creation and projection of any image, but of one that commands respect and self-respect.

Shopping malls become the arenas for such explorations where young people try out different images and experiment with precarious selfhoods. Today's teenage identity-seekers are not a marginal social group; nor do they go through a temporary phase that will be overcome with triumphant entry into adulthood, as Erikson or anthropologists debating rites of passages might have envisaged. Instead, teenagers epitomize the contemporary search for identity. As Featherstone has argued, 'youth styles and lifestyles are migrating up the age scale and ... as the 1960s generation ages, they are taking some of the youth-orientated dispositions with them, and ... adults are being granted greater licence for childlike behaviour and vice versa' (Featherstone, 1991: 100–101). This is especially noticeable when adults go on holiday or even on business trips, when, relieved of the hardened personas they assume at work and at home, they experiment with different styles, images and identities. They wear strange clothes, develop unusual mannerisms, let their hair down and feel free to explore pleasures that they would otherwise deny themselves. The transformation of airport and hotel lobbies into Meccas of consumption can be seen as testimony of the travelling consumers' thirst for experimentation with identity as well as of the loosening of their inhibitions towards spending (see Chapter 4, 'The Consumer as Explorer').

Experimenting with identities and images of self can at times be seen to stretch into explorations of inner worlds, spiritual Ithacas and Idahos of the mind. Vast areas of the economy, including some of the so-called leisure industries, the hobby industry, the body industry, the personal growth industry, appear to be fuelled by the individuals' thirst for self-exploration (Lasch, 1984). Many of these explorations become quests for reaching one's own limits, whether in sport, art or learning. Occasionally buying or being given a new object, such as a trumpet, a tennis racket or a set of watercolours, may signal the opening of a new phase of selfhood. Yet, in truth, such inner explorations seldom go beyond ephemeral daydreams or volatile fantasies. Compared to the explorations of the colourful world of objects and their images out there which many consumers pursue with skill and virtuosity, inner explorations can seem murky, dull and not terribly productive. On the other hand, to many, they epitomize the quest for identity.

Postmodern identities, images and self-esteem

Images of the consumer as identity-seeker are compelling and feature centrally in postmodern theory. They account for the obsession with brands, the willingness to read stories into impersonal products, the fascination with difference, the preoccupation with signs, and above all the fetishism of images. They also account for the fragmented and precarious nature of selfhood, which has been a favourite theme of those writers who postulate a radical discontinuity between modernity and late modernity, the phase of human history we are currently meant to be inhabiting. One leading feature of this discontinuity concerns the demise of the idea of a sovereign self, the managerial self that reflects, compares, decides, creates and takes responsibility. Following Freud, Mauss and Foucault, many postmodernists argue that this image of the sovereign self is an illusion reflecting the grand narratives of modernity – such as work, gender, happiness, healthy life, moral choice and achievement – but fatally undermined by postmodernity. According to Firat, consumers of modernity fashioned their identities by purchasing products, whose stories and images echoed those grand narratives. By contrast:

> the consumers of postmodernity seem to be transcending these narratives, no longer seeking centered, unified characters, but increasingly seeking to 'feel good' in separate, different moments by acquiring self images that make them marketable, likeable and/ or desirable in each moment ... Thus occurs the fragmentation of the self. In postmodern culture, the self is not consistent, authentic, or centered. (Firat, 1992: 204)

Firat and other 'postmodern' cultural theorists of the 1990s and early 2000s saw fragmentation and discontinuity as dominant narratives, sweeping all in front of them and shattering the self into numerous self-images coming in and out of focus. If modern consumers could be seen as victims of self-delusions, their needs manipulated by image-makers, postmodern consumers were said to suffer from no such self-delusions. They did not search for authentic, integrated, wholesome selves. They did not demand that product images should be authentic, integrated or wholesome. They were sophisticated enough to recognize that these images are only fleeting mirages, spawned in the imaginations of clever image-makers who want to sell them things. But they did not mind. They were content with diverse personas, all products of artifice, all inauthentic, often at odds with each other. Schizophrenia became a leitmotiv for the postmodern consumer (Jameson, 1983).

Group identities, too, were seen as fragmented. Groups themselves lost their boundaries, becoming transient, ephemeral and largely fictitious. Individuals identified with each other through shared lifestyles or shared fantasies, their self-images temporarily shaped by memberships of imaginary clubs and societies, 'imagined communities' (Anderson, 1983), 'invented traditions' (Hobsbawn and Ranger, 1983) or 'neo-tribes' (Bauman, 1992; Maffesoli, 1995). Some of these groups are the ephemeral result of converging identity projects, sharing imagined heritages, qualities or interests. Others exist purely in individual imaginations.

Some postmodern thinkers drew rather optimistic conclusions from images of consumers as identity-seekers. Bauman, one of the most insightful theorists of the intersection of consumption, identity and postmodernity, saw in consumer freedom the possibility of a healthy competition, which does not disintegrate into warfare and destruction:

> In the game of consumer freedom all customers may be winners at the same time. Identities are not scarce goods. If anything their supply tends to be excessive, as the overabundance of any image is bound to detract from its value as a symbol of individual uniqueness. Devaluation of an image is never a disaster, however, as discarded images are immediately followed by new ones, as yet not too common, so that self-construction may start again, hopeful as ever to attain its purpose: the creation of unique selfhood. (Bauman, 1988: 63)

Can the idea of identity survive the many fragmentations and discontinuities celebrated by postmodern writers? Is the idea of the consumer as identity-seeker meaningful, when identity has turned into nothing more than a succession of mirages? And can Bauman talk plausibly of this succession of mirages as 'self-hood'? The above extract illustrates well some of the paradoxical implications of postmodern thinking that at once obliterates unity, sameness, continuity, fixity and independence, the features that defined identity as a concept, while at the same time giving it pride of place in cultural discussions. If, as Bauman correctly pointed out, the overabundance of signifiers undermines their value, is it possible to view identities as non-scarce goods? While there may well be an over-abundance of *images*, we think that there is a scarcity of *value-laden images*, images that command respect. While identity, in the fragmented, anarchic postmodern sense, may not be in short supply, the same could hardly be said of esteem and self-esteem. To individuals craving recognition and self-esteem, Bauman's pronouncement that 'identities are not scarce goods' sounds like the sanctimonious preaching of conservative politicians to those living on state benefits. If uniqueness is so highly prized as a prerequisite for esteem and self-esteem, the notion that any image can be the basis of identity begins to sound like a cruel joke.

Postmodern thinking scorned to distinguish between identity and self-image, self-image and self-love; it also cheekily conflated image and self-image. If identity is treated as narrative pure and simple, not only is the issue of authenticity obviated (any story can be valid *as a story*), but also the traditional concerns of sociologists and psychologists regarding the differences between self-identity and presentation of self to others melts away. If self-image and image are only mirages, to ask whether they coincide becomes irrelevant. Yet, contrary to postmodernist theorizing in the recent past, today's consumers *are* highly preoccupied both with the authenticity of their own identity and with the recognition of this authenticity by others. They spend much time scrutinizing each other for inauthentic personas, contrived styles, yesterday's fashion and false identities. They can punish – occasionally with venom – those they perceive as inauthentic or uncool, as is illustrated by the phenomenon of 'trolling'. To argue that in the consumerist carnival every mask adds to the generalized delirium fails to recognize the high levels of policing and self-policing that governs styles, fashions, images and identities. The follies of those who assume images above their station, those who seek to deceive others with cheap imitations or those who deceive themselves with studied and affected lifestyles attract the same ridicule and censure today as they did in the age of the Molière's *Le Bourgeois gentilhomme*, the classic statement of a man who makes a fool of himself by seeking to give the appearance of one above his station. The struggle for identity is much less benign than Bauman envisaged, and may indeed be ridden with malice, envy and contempt, clearly delineated by Veblen and Bourdieu (see Chapter 6, 'The Consumer as Hedonist').

To summarize: if Western consumers are to be seen as identity-seekers as numerous postmodern theorists invited us to do, the craving for authenticity, unity and consistency must be seen as intrinsic features of their searches. Any image will simply not do. While today's consumers may be willing to adopt multiple personas in different circumstances, as Giddens argued, lifestyles are 'more or less *integrated*' sets of practices, through which self-identities are constituted (Giddens, 1991: 81). Cohesion cannot simply be wished away from identity, simply because it has become problematic. (Bourdieu's concept of 'habitus' is pointing in a similar direction.) Identity that does not command the respect of others and does not lead to self-love is quite pointless; even if image is in ample supply, the same can be said of neither respect nor self-love. Without these qualifications, the theme of fragmented identities and the figure of the consumer as identity-seeker threaten to collapse into meaningless, though fashionable, clichés. Identity, self, image, self-image and subjectivity threaten to become free-floating signifiers, easily substituting each other, merging and dividing up, losing their moorings and distinctiveness.

Identity, the ego-ideal and narcissism

Can money buy us identity? If identity was seen as pure image or as the respect of anonymous others, then, as Marx surmises in this chapter's opening extract, money would rule supreme. In spite of reservations expressed by theorists like Bourdieu, since the decline of the aristocratic ideal, matters such as taste, style, refinement, adventure and image are things that may be bought, if one is not born with them. In today's world, it is not unknown for rock stars or footballers to become country gentlemen. Identity should then not be a serious problem for the rich. Yet one searches in vain for confirmation of this view (see McCracken, 1988). Instead, we propose that to the extent that identity constitutes a 'problem' or a 'project', it must encompass not only image (which may be purchased) and narrative (which may be constructed) but, contrary to some postmodernist thinking, meaning and value as well. This is far more problematic, for rich and poor alike. It involves the fashioning of an image in which one may admire oneself and through which one may gain the respect of significant others. Identity is no mere life-story but a life-story that commands attention, respect and emotion. Extending Giddens' idea of identity as narrative, we would see identity not merely as the story of who we are, but also a fantasy of what we wish to be like. Identity is not only an embellished account of our adventures, accomplishments and tribulations, but also that vital web of truths, half-truths and wish-fulfilling fictions that sustain us (Gabriel, 2000). This accounts for identity being at once fragmented and discontinuous, as well as united and continuous; it also brings the project of identity surprisingly close to the psychoanalytic concept of the ego-ideal, an amalgam of idealized images, phantasies and wishes against which we measure our experiences.

The ego-ideal can be built around different themes, frequently drawing on cultural or organizational achievements, nostalgic recreations of a golden past or utopian visions of glorious futures (Schwartz, 1990; Gabriel, 1993). The ego-ideal represents an attempt to recreate, in later life, the condition of primary narcissism, the period of our infancy when we imagined ourselves the centre of a loving and admiring world. Our primary narcissism is doomed to receive numerous blows, starting with the realization that the world is generally not a loving place and that, contrary possibly to the impression created by mother, we are not its centre (Freud, [1914] 1984; Schwartz, 1990: 17ff). We may still cling to the fantasy that we are unique and special, but this too will receive a cruel blow during our first encounters with schools and other impersonal organizations, which consign us to the status of a number on a register or a face among unknowns. Thereafter, we discover that admiration is hard to come by and love even harder. For this reason, the fact that young children have little problem of identity is hardly surprising. With every injury to their narcissism, however, the need to erect an ego-ideal becomes more pressing. The ego-ideal, then, emerges as a wishful fantasy of ourselves, as we wish to be, in order to become once more the centre of an admiring and loving world.

> *What man projects before him as his ideal is the substitute for the lost narcissism of his childhood in which he was his own ideal ... To this ideal ego is now directed the self-love which the real ego enjoyed in childhood. The narcissism seems to be now displaced on to this new ideal ego, which, like the infantile ego, deems itself the possessor of all perfections. (Freud, [1914] 1984: 94)*

At times, our ego-ideal merges with our ego; these are moments of triumph and joy when admiration and love is lavished on us, either for our individual achievements or for the achievements of groups, organizations or cultures with which we identify. Traditional societies supported individual ideal-egos with cultural ideals, powerful role models and overbearing symbols. Members of religious or political sects, today, may derive total narcissistic fulfilment through their membership of these organizations, which promise them not only omnipotence and salvation but also immortality in one form or another.

Western culture not only exacerbates the need for an ego-ideal by inflicting numerous injuries to our narcissism, but it also places formidable obstacles to its formation. Gone are the days of sweeping cultural ideals and moral certainties. Gone are the powerful role-models, untouched by scandal and corruption. Gone are the stirring symbols. Gone, too, are the great cultural accomplishments, artistic, scientific or military, in which we may take unalloyed pride. In a world where heroes are forever cut down to size and perfection remains elusive, the gleaming surfaces of material goods, their pristine packaging and virginal existence inevitably attract our attention, even before the image-makers get down to work. As Lasch (1980; 1984) has powerfully argued, the world of objects appears to hold the promise of delivery to our ailing narcissism. Consumerism promises to fill the void in our lives.

Lasch has provided vivid pictures of the narcissistic personality that he sees as dominating American culture. Today's Narcissus spends endless amounts of time looking at himself in mirrors, but is not lost in self-admiration. He is not happy with what he sees. He worries about growing old and ugly. He sets about busily constructing an ego-ideal around idealized qualities of commodities, aided and abetted by the propaganda of the makers of dreams. He pours money into anti-ageing cosmetics, plastic surgery and every conceivable beauty aid.

He yearns for admiration and recognition from others, striving for intimacy, yet he is unable to establish long-term relationships; after all his only interest lies in himself and his ego-ideal, forever elusive, yet forever appearing within reach. Although blemished, the narcissist always finds something to admire in himself; his life-story may not have been crowned with glory yet, but the happy end is within sight – if only he tries a little harder, gets a lucky break, or, above all, finds a bit more money.

The usefulness of material objects now becomes quite apparent – these objects hold the promise of bridging the distance between the actual and the ideal. The view of commodities as *bridges* has been developed by McCracken (1988), who regards them as instances of displaced meaning. 'If only I could buy that car I would be what I would ideally like to be'; the car becomes a fantasy bridging the actual and the ideal. The less accessible the car, the greater the promise it holds. As focal point of a fantasy, the longed-for car becomes a magnet for displaced meaning; the flawlessness of the paintwork, the power under the bonnet, the overwhelming sense of perfection that it radiates, are thinly disguised narcissistic delusions transferred onto the idealized object. Once acquired, the object may at least temporarily act as a powerful narcissistic booster. Grown-up men have been known to cry in the arms of their mothers, on seeing a tiny scratch on that gleaming bodywork. In such cases, the car is incorporated in the ego-ideal, its every affliction experienced as a personal calamity. In as much as it provides a reason for self-love and the respect of others, such an object can be said to support the consumer's identity quite effectively. Yet, as McCracken argues, once acquired, often at considerable sacrifice, the spell of the commodity is exposed to falsification.

> *The possession of objects that serve as bridges to displaced meaning is perilous. Once possessed these objects can begin to collapse the distance between an individual and his or her ideals. When a 'bridge' is purchased, the owner has begun to run the risk of putting the displaced meaning to empirical test. (McCracken, 1988: 112)*

Once the fantasy built around the product has accepted the test of reality, its value to the ego-ideal decreases; almost invariably, it is bound to be found lacking, not because the product is not good, but because such extraordinary expectations have been built on it. A new fantasy will already start to develop around some new product. It is this process on which consumer capitalism thrives.

Since the first edition of this book, postmodernism has faded as a dominant Western intellectual current; indeed some have argued that it has died (Cova et al., 2013). The number of references to postmodernism in academic publications has certainly dramatically declined. Two other developments have occurred in the last 20 years: the search for identity in the digital world of social media and the increasing number of people who search for their identity in spaces as far removed from contemporary consumerism as possible.

Belk, one of the early pioneers of the theory of extended self, has pointed out that social media and other internet avenues have affected the construction of the extended self. He singles out five major changes that have put a distance between the consumer's personae on and off line (Belk, 2013). Dematerialization is when one does not need to own the good but can experience it in a non-physical form. Re-embodiment is where avatars are used online to create multiple persona. Sharing is where a particular possession, such as digital music, is shared with other users. Co-construction of self is where attachment to virtual possessions in video games becomes part of oneself. And, finally, distributed memory is where the internet offers opportunities to archive 'narratives of self' that would previously have been held in one's head or material possessions (such as physical photos). In all of these ways, the digital world offers fresh opportunities to extend the self not only in physical space through the accrual of material possessions but also in virtual form, which can be every bit as meaningful.

The other development has been the widely acknowledged growth in affluent societies of people who have distanced themselves from consumerism and have sought meaning and identity elsewhere. These are people who inevitably consume in an everyday way just like everyone else, but they refuse to *define* themselves through their patterns of consumption. Some of these people would go as far as calling themselves anti-consumers (Rumbo, 2002; Zavestoski, 2002), not because they don't consume but because they actively oppose the ideology associated with it. They hold strong anti-consumerist sentiments verging on disgust. Wilk has highlighted how, in pursuit of their identity, such people explicitly engage in acts of non-consumption or avoidance, experiencing distaste towards all offerings of branded consumer culture (Wilk, 1997). Apathy is not a negative stance, he argued, but represents an active choice. Oppositional movements to contemporary consumerism are addressed in Chapters 8 ('The Consumer as Rebel') and 9 ('The Consumer as Activist'). We should note, however, the significant range of ideological positions that seek to detach identity-seeking from consumerism; these include voluntary simplifiers, boycotts, buycotts, downshifting and joining activist groups such as Adbusters or Occupy (Lasn, 1999). Anti-consumerists have been criticized as elitist, undemocratic, conservative and ultimately even consumerist by another name (Littler, 2005; Arnould, 2007). This suggests that it has become almost impossible to escape from being a consumer identity-seeker, if not in one's own eyes, in the eyes of everyone else.

Consumerism: addiction or choice?

In this chapter, we have argued that behind the consumer's ostensible quest for identity lurk more fundamental cravings for respect and self-love, born out of the injuries that modern life inflicts on us. These generate anxieties that cannot be allayed by image alone or narratives spun around commodities; they demand far more radical measures. These anxieties are the result of injuries sustained by our narcissism, whose healing requires nothing less than the formation of an idealized phantasy of the self, an ego-ideal, commanding admiration, respect and self-love. In a culture shorn of role models and ideals, consumerism throws up ephemeral images to identify with (pop-stars, sports people, TV celebrities) and a promise for boosting our ego-ideals, by proffering commodities around which fantasies of perfection, beauty and power may be built. These fantasies are wish-fulfilments that transform mundane everyday objects into highly charged symbols.

How successful is consumerism as the means of restoring our ailing narcissism? Cultural critics like Christopher Lasch are in no doubt that consumerism merely reinforces the discontents for which it promises consolations. Individuals become constantly more insecure and image-conscious, looking at themselves in mirrors.

> *A culture organized around mass consumption encourages narcissism – which [we] can define, for the moment, as a disposition to see the world as a mirror, more particularly as a projection of one's own fears and desires – not because it makes people grasping and self-assertive but because it makes them weak and dependent. (Lasch, 1980: 33)*

In the last resort, the self-illusions of uniqueness, power and beauty cannot be sustained in such a culture. As Horkheimer and Adorno put it in their memorable lament of lost individuality:

> *What is individual is no more than the generalities' power to stamp so firmly that it is accepted as such. The defiant reserve or elegant appearance of the individual on show is mass produced like Yale locks, whose only difference can be measured in fractions of millimeters. The peculiarity of the self is a monopoly commodity determined by society. (Horkheimer and Adorno, [1947] 1997: 154)*

In his past published work, Lasch argues that Western consumerism, sustained by mass production and celebrated in the mass media, amounts to a mechanism of addiction.

> *'Shop till you drop.' Like exercise, it often seems to present itself as a form of therapy, designed to restore a sense of wholeness and well-being after long hours of unrewarding work. 'I feel like hell and I go out for a run, and before I know it, everything's OK.' Shopping serves the same purpose: 'It hardly matters what I buy, I just get a kick out of buying. It's like that first whiff of cocaine. It's euphoric and I just get higher and higher as I buy.' (Lasch, 1991: 521)*

At this point, the consumer as identity-seeker turns into a victim, a willing victim, an unknowing victim perhaps, but a victim all the same. While the addictive qualities of consumption epitomized in the 'shopaholic' are widely recognized

(Baudrillard, [1968] 1988; [1970] 1988; Campbell, 1989; Lebergott, 1993), Lasch's pessimism is not shared by everyone. An earlier herald of the liberating potential of consumer freedom, Philip Rieff, had argued:

> Confronted with the irrelevance of ascetic standards of conduct, the social reformer has retreated from nebulous doctrines attempting to state the desired quality of life to more substantial doctrines of quantity. The reformer asks only for more of everything – more goods, more housing, more leisure; in short, more life. This translation of quantity into quality states the algebra of our cultural revolution. Who will be stupid enough to lead a counterrevolution? (Rieff, 1966: 243)

Rieff's views are echoed by numerous less eloquent conservative theorists, who view consumerism, not only as offering delivery from the drudgery of self-reliance, but also as the begetter of genuine variety, choice, freedom and true individuality. Such enthusiasts dismiss the arguments of critics like Lasch as sanctimonious nonsense, flying in the face of evidence. Lebergott (1993: 26–27) pours scorn on intellectuals who dismiss the choice presented by supermarkets while revering libraries full of unread tomes. The consumer's freedom to choose from 200 different beers, 600 different motor-cars or 160 different magazines is no less meaningful than the intellectuals' freedom to read or write what they please. Freedom of choice, in the view of conservative commentators, far from being empty or meaningless is the very foundation of our cultural identity, which has rejected apocalyptic messages and faith as the roads to the good life. The consumer Garden of Eden, according to this view, with its limitless choice, endows us with narcissistic pride, even if its most alluring packages remain beyond our reach. A brief look at the images of poverty, warfare, hunger and suffering on our TV, or at the plight of those surviving on state benefits, deprived of the freedom of choice, suffices to convince us of the spiritual superiority of the culture of the mall, the supermarket and the gleaming surfaces. (See Chapter 2, 'The Consumer as Chooser'.)

In conclusion

Our pursuit of the consumer as identity-seeker has brought us to a junction. In one direction, we can pursue the consumer exercising freedom, making choices, accepting satisfactions and set-backs, reaching compromises and, to a greater or lesser extent, succeeding in building an ego-ideal that commands the respect of others and inspires self-love; all this, through the act of consumption. In the other direction, we can pursue the consumer as an addict, unable to live without self-delusions, mediated by material goods, which ultimately aggravate his or her condition, and represent nothing but a daily fix. Difficult questions now confront us. Is identity a project or a consolation? Are material objects bridges to an ideal or bridges to nowhere? Do attempts to deal with the problem of identity outside the sphere of consumption ultimately lapse back into consumerism by another name?

The ambiguities of modern consumption are such that the face of the Western consumer is liable to change. Like the images we examined earlier, it is hardly surprising that the consumer as identity-seeker has the tendency to metamorphose into something else. Like them, it tends to present too monochromatic a picture of the consumer. Some of us may and do, from time to time, seek identity by browsing in front of shop windows, purchasing goods, internalizing their images and browsing the internet. These may prove disappointing or may provide considerable support to our ego-ideals and identities. At other times, however, our identities may be built around resistance to consumption and consumerism and the subversion of the symbolism carried by objects. Defying the slogans of advertisers and sneering at the propaganda of commodities may be a sound enough base for constructing an ego-ideal as the worship of the shopping mall. Alternatively, we can pursue our projects of identity by focusing our life-narratives elsewhere. At a time when workaholics compete with shopaholics, it seems premature to write off the work ethic. For many, work remains an arena (though of course not the only one) where identity is fashioned, as indeed is the family (single- or double-parent, extended or not, step- or blood) and other social networks that defy the neo-tribe sobriquet. Or would anyone sensible discount the power of religion to continue to act as a source of meaning and belonging for billions of people, as the resurgence of Islam and evangelical Christianity amply demonstrate? And who would discount social class as a source of identity when practicing marketers busily classify, monitor and target everyone in those terms? The organizations that we serve also nurture our ego-ideals, either by lending us some of their corporate aura (Schwartz, 1990) or by serving as objects of ridicule (Gabriel, 1999).

If the conflation of identity and consumerism is premature, might the conflation of self with identity be liable to exhaustion? Before closing this chapter, we may reflect briefly on the privileged position of 'identity' in contemporary discussions of selfhood. Is it not possible that identity has become itself a fashion, used to cover a multitude of sins? It certainly has some of the marks of a fashion: universal appeal, seeming inevitability, floating signifiers, a mass industry of media pundits, opinion-leaders and image-makers sustaining it and a stream of celebrities embodying it. One thing is certain, the prominence of identity since the 1980s has isolated cultural studies of consumption from addressing numerous types of consumer behaviour and action that have been of central importance to people ranging from financial analysts to consumer activists, to many consumers themselves. What if, for a number of us, unaffected by this suggestive apparatus, identity simply does not exist as a problem or as a project or as anything else? This is how Lévi-Strauss has described his own experience of self:

> I never had, and still do not have, the perception of feeling my personal identity. I appear to myself as the place where something is going on, but there is no 'I', no 'me'. Each of us is a kind of crossroads where things happen. The crossroads is purely passive; something happens there. A different kind of thing, equally valid, happens elsewhere. There is no choice, it is just a matter of chance. (Lévi-Strauss, 1978: 3–4)

Read as a literal and honest description, rather than as a mischievous structuralist aphorism or an Olympian utterance by a sage who stands removed from mundane matters, this statement suggests that identity may not be such a universal preoccupation, after all. It is certainly possible to think of ourselves in ways that do not depend on the output of the identity industry. Could it be that identity, like other fashions, will eventually exhaust itself, its appeal shrinking to a niche market kept alive by nostalgia? Some of us may look forward to the day when identity sheds its psycho-sociological identity and returns to its forensic-political roots. But what a challenge that would pose to brands!

6

THE CONSUMER AS HEDONIST

I will offer one thousand golden pieces to any man who can show me a new pleasure.
(Xerxes)

CORE ARGUMENTS

Most consumers claim to find pleasure in the goods and services they consume, and economists have defended the view that higher living standards represent greater happiness. The pursuit of happiness and pleasure is ensconced in the American Constitution but may require more than just money. Different types of pleasure are identified, including pleasure that results from fulfilment of needs and pleasure that comes with heightened emotional experiences and fantasy. Aesthetic pleasure, deriving from the consumption of stylish, 'cool' products often comes at a cost to those who fail to match the pronouncements of style gurus, and 'tastes' can become an instrument of social ostracism and exclusion. In a narcissistic culture, pleasure deriving from fantasy all too easily becomes associated with domination and violence, assuming sadistic qualities that occasionally get acted out.

Pleasure lies at the heart of consumerism. It finds in consumerism a unique champion that promises to liberate it both from its bondage to sin, duty and morality as well as from its ties to faith, spirituality and redemption. Consumerism proclaims pleasure not merely as the right of every individual but also as every individual's obligation to him- or herself.

> *The modern consumer, the modern citizen, cannot evade the constraint of happiness and pleasure, which in the new ethics is equivalent to the traditional constraint of labor and production. ... He must constantly be ready to actualize all of his potential, all of his capacity for consumption. If he forgets, he will be gently reminded that he has no right not to be happy. (Baudrillard, [1970] 1988: 48–49)*

Consumerism seeks to reclaim pleasure, not least physical, sensuous pleasure, from sanctimonious moralizing and the grim heritage of the Protestant ethic, which said, 'Work! Work! Work!' (Tawney, [1922] 1969; Weber, 1930). It celebrates the diversity of pleasures to be obtained from commodities, proposing such pleasures as realistic, attainable goals of everyday life. Enjoying life means consuming for pleasure, not consuming for survival or for need. If we fail to enjoy life, it may be that we are failing to look after ourselves, weighed down by self-inflicted hangups and inhibitions. The pursuit of pleasure, untarnished by guilt or shame, becomes the bedrock of a new moral philosophy, a new image of the good life. But how well does this image match the realities of contemporary consumption? How realistic is the project of attaining pleasure through material and virtual possessions? And to what extent do we, as consumers, answer the call of consumerism to enjoy ourselves? These are some of the issues that this chapter addresses.

The world of commodities and the pursuit of pleasure

Western consumption, Bauman, Bourdieu, Baudrillard and countless others have argued, is a realm of *seduction* – alluring and glamorous. Few can escape its temptations, certainly not the poor, whether they live in high-, medium- or low-income countries. Since the collapse of Eastern-style Communism, consumerism has emerged as a global hegemonic idea, underpinning capitalist accumulation, free trade and the riotous commodification of everything (see 'Introduction: The Faces of the Consumer'). Consumer capitalism raises commodity fetishism to heights undreamed of by Marx who coined the term (Marx, [1867] 1967). As goods leave the world of production to enter the sphere of display, circulation and consumption, they become objects of fantasy and instruments of pleasure. As Abercrombie has argued:

> Not only are the denizens of modern society consumers, they are also consumerist. Their lives are organized around fantasies and daydreams about consuming; they are hedonists, primarily interested in pleasure, and sensual pleasure at that; they are individualists, largely pursuing their own ends and uncaring about others. (Abercrombie, 1994: 44)

In *The Cultural Contradictions of Capitalism*, Daniel Bell (1976) identified the central contradiction of late capitalism as one between the discipline, rationality and asceticism required in production and the spend-happy hedonism and waste of consumption. For Bauman (1988; 1992; 2001), writing later, the contradiction has turned into symbiosis. Seduction becomes a mechanism of control; the consumer's pursuit of pleasure enables him or her to endure the rigours of life under the capitalist reality principle, that is, alienating work, the threat of unemployment or worse. Pleasure, for so long the enemy of the capitalist project, against which no resource of puritanical morality was spared, is now mobilized to support the project. Pleasure and reality principles are at last reconciled.

In the present consumer phase, the capitalist system deploys the pleasure principle *for its own perpetuation.* Producers *moved by the pleasure principle would spell disaster to a profit-guided economy. Equally, if not more disastrous, would be* consumers *who are not moved by the same principle. ... For the consumer, reality is not the enemy of pleasure. The tragic moment has been removed from the insatiable drive to enjoyment. Reality, as the consumer experiences it, is a pursuit of pleasure. Freedom is about the choice between greater and lesser satisfactions, and rationality is about choosing the first over the second. (Bauman, 1992: 50)*

In *Pursuing Happiness: American Consumers in the Twentieth Century*, Stanley Lebergott argues that 'in open societies, human consumption choices share one characteristic – they are made in pursuit of happiness' (Lebergott, 1993: 8). He then goes on to provide extensive economic documentation of the massive increases in US consumption since the end of the 19th century, for example, an hour's work in 1990 earned on average six times more than it did in 1900. Lebergott dismisses the notions both that consumers are manipulated into purchasing items that do not afford them pleasure and that the variety and glamour of these items represent economic inefficiency and waste. Instead, he views the immense variety of commodities on display in shops as evidence that American consumers have never had it so good in terms of the quantity, quality and variety of things they consume and that American workers 'exchanged their labor hours for goods and services at a better rate than workers did in almost any other nation' (Lebergott, 1993: 68). Aware of their privileges in comparison with the rest of the world, US consumers are both proud of their consumerist culture and capable of taking advantage of it, he says. They make expert choices, refusing to be lured by unrealistic claims, contemptuously killing countless products that do not make it in the marketplace.

Lebergott, writing in the Reaganite 1980s, is especially scathing in his criticism of Tibor Scitovsky, an economist who in the 1970s had challenged (a) the economic assumption of consumer sovereignty, that is, that consumers choose whatever best satisfy their needs, and (b) the view that American consumers are either capable or willing to spend their money and even more importantly *their time* on things that give pleasure. Scitovsky (1976), for example, had argued that Americans are far less concerned with the taste of the food they eat than its nutritional qualities and its convenience. To Scitovsky's idea that American consumers sacrifice pleasure for comfort, Lebergott countered:

The United States does indeed lack an official corps of tasters and chewers, to decide which dinners are 'good, representative.' But what of the vast, untidy party of amateurs who exhort and instruct in newspaper food columns? And what of the best-sellers in US bookstores for decades – cookbooks? This record hardly demonstrates any 'lack of interest in the pleasures of food'. (Lebergott, 1993: 9)

Unlike Scitovsky, Lebergott scorns to distinguish between necessities and luxuries. One of the most interesting features of his argument is that 'necessities' make as big a contribution to the consumers' pursuit of pleasure as luxuries, since they free consumers from the drudgery of housework and extend their free time. Thus convenience foods, such as tinned peas, which for Scitovsky epitomize the Americans' indifference to the pleasures of the palate, are for Lebergott vehicles of pleasure – through them consumers free themselves from the drudgery of shopping for, cleaning, cutting up and preparing fresh vegetables. The greatest increases in consumer expenditure since 1900, he notes, went to those items 'that promised to extend lifetime hours of worthwhile experience', for example, labour-saving devices, cars, convenience food, heating, lighting and more recently medicine (Lebergott, 1993: 36). He estimates that each American house-wife spent 32 fewer hours weekly on meals and cleaning up between 1910 and 1975 (Lebergott, 1993: 59). One question that arises is how consumers spend their 'free' time? In 'quality time' with their loved ones, in hobbies and other pleasure-imparting activities, as Lebergott implies, or in increased travel times to and from work, shopping centres and so on, or watching TV, as work by Gershuny (1992), Postman (1986) and others suggests?

While Lebergott builds an impressive argument on the back of the grim picture of the labour-intensive domestic chores that filled most people's (especially women's) lives in the early part of the 20th century, he fails to establish *pleasure* as the object of contemporary consumerism. True, the burden of doing the laun-dry or the washing up by hand, of fetching fuel and cleaning fireplaces, of baking bread and making and mending clothes, have been lightened. But can people today be said to be either happier or more pleasure-driven than their grandpar-ents? Discomfort avoidance, curiosity and status thirst (the first two endorsed by Scitovsky) could replace 'happiness' in Lebergott's arguments without any loss of coherence. Buying a dishwasher may have little to do with the pleasurable activ-ities that one may pursue while the machine gently washes away the grime, using up fossil fuel energy and polluting the world at the same time. Instead, one could see the purchase of a dishwasher as a discomfort-avoidance device, a status sym-bol or numerous other things. As we examined in the Introduction, neither washing machines nor the overall rise in consumer spending seems to have increased the aggregate level of well-being since the middle of the 20th century. Lebergott's arguments, therefore, would appear to fly in the face of the evidence that, even if consumers are seeking happiness, they are not achieving it.

Hedonism old and new

Like many economists, Lebergott uses a quasi-democratic argument against arbiters of taste who distinguish between high-brow and low-brow pleasures, to defend the axiom that ordinary consumers, rather than aesthetes, academics, state plan-ners, environmentalists, consumer activists and bureaucrats, or even producers, know best what pleases them. Lebergott's hedonism is axiomatic and, as a result, it adds little theoretical value, although it acts as a firm ideological support to enthusiasts of the free market. The axiom that what saves time is useful and what is useful is pleasurable is directly attacked by Campbell (1989), who developed one of the most advanced positions of contemporary consumption as a unique and highly elaborate form of pleasure-seeking. Campbell's account of consumerism stands out from other commentaries in numerous respects. First, Campbell refuses to separate the sphere of consumption from that of production, each characterized by its own 'ethic'. Unlike Bell and even Bauman, he argues that the same psycho-cultural forces that drive a pleasure-orientated consumption also account for the broad range of work attitudes, normally subsumed under the Protestant work ethic label. Second, Campbell, almost alone among contemporary cultural theorists, seriously explores the meaning of pleasure, both establishing its differences from utilitarian concepts such as need and satisfaction and identifying different modes of constructing and deriving pleasure. Third, Campbell provides a convincing and highly detailed picture of the original qualities of contemporary hedonism, which places it apart from traditional hedonism, yet maintains the centrality of pleasure. In this way, he provides an intriguing, though controversial, way of absorbing dissatisfaction, frustration and loss into an essentially hedonistic outlook on life.

The first of several astute distinctions made by Campbell is between pleasure and utility, conflated by utilitarianism and confused by economists. Like Baudrillard ([1970] 1988), Campbell criticizes the concept of utility by reviewing Galbraith's (1967) arguments. But while Baudrillard goes on to distinguish between use-values and sign-values of commodities, Campbell explores utility and pleasure as distinct motivational principles, the former deriving from need, the latter aiming at pleasure. Need represents the disturbance of a state of psychological equilibrium; it is based on absence, on lack, on necessity. By contrast, pleasure, argues Campbell, is 'not so much a state of being as a quality of experience' (Campbell, 1989: 60). Desire is triggered by the presence in one's environment of 'a recognized source of pleasure' (Campbell, 1989: 60). Campbell's account of the pleasure principle could hardly be more different from that of Freud (1920; [1923] 1984), who following Schopenhauer saw pleasure as essentially a negative phenomenon, a struggle to release oneself from unpleasure, pleasure being the lowering of tension that follows the gratification of an instinctual impulse. By contrast, the pursuit of pleasure, for Campbell, does not seek to restore an earlier state of disturbed equilibrium, but is a quest for a certain kind of stimulus that will bring about a pleasurable experience. Stimulation is therefore itself part of the pleasurable experience.

Both needs and desires drive consumption, although in modern societies desire assumes an ever-increasing role. Unlike Baudrillard, Campbell does not deny the continuing existence of needs or the merging of needs and desires.

Hunger is paradigmatic of need, sexuality of desire. The two often operate in tandem; a meal may both yield pleasure and satisfy hunger. More importantly, however, guaranteed satisfaction saps the potential for pleasure. In the presence of guaranteed satisfaction by regular meals or routine sex, the pleasure-yielding potential of eating or sexual activities is moderated. Comfort undermines pleasure. In spite of the fact that they may merge or oppose each other, needs and desires represent very different motivational principles. Needs are far more tied to specific means of satisfaction than desires. Hunger can only be met with food. Desire, by contrast, can be stimulated by a wide variety of objects and can migrate from one experience to another. More importantly, while needs are tied to objects, desires can wander into a world of fantasy and imagination; 'whilst only reality can provide satisfaction, both illusions and delusions can supply pleasure' (Campbell, 1989: 61). Campbell now draws a second crucial distinction, between traditional and modern or imaginative hedonism. Traditional hedonism is a hedonism of a multitude of pleasures, a hedonism of sensations attached to the senses, taste, smell, touch, sight and hearing. Modern hedonism, on the other hand, seeks pleasure not in sensation but in emotion accompanying all kinds of experiences, including what may be called sad or painful ones. Traditional hedonism is epitomized in the lives of luxury and opulence of potentates, princes and the super-rich. Their tables were spread with an abundance of exotic foods, their villas decorated with artistic masterpieces. Musicians, comedians and entertainers were on call to offer finer and higher pleasures; harems, jugglers and fools to gratify lower ones. But, as Xerxes' heart-rending pronouncement at the opening to this chapter makes plain, 'guaranteed satisfaction' jades the senses. Pleasure becomes the ultimate scarce commodity for the traditional hedonist. Boredom and dissatisfaction set in. Traditional hedonism also offers an explanation for some of the excesses of today's super-rich, and for why so many seem to be unhappy, unfulfilled or bored.

When comfort kills pleasure, pleasure may be sought in new stimuli, less predictable, less comfortable, more dangerous. Comfort must yield to adventure. Few potentates had the courage or the latitude of doing so, without risking their power, wealth and status. Some turned to hunting or to mixing incognito with lesser mortals as a means towards greater excitement; invading Greece seemed to provide Xerxes with the ultimate thrill in 480 BCE. Such pursuits are certainly not consistent with comfort, yet it is only through exposing oneself to hardships and dangers that the project of hedonism can stay on course; hence, far from being the opposite of hedonism, adventure, hardship and privation become, for Campbell, its logical culmination. These 'adventurous' pursuits provide the bridge between traditional and modern or imaginative hedonism. What sets modern hedonism apart from traditional hedonism is the emphasis on emotion and the submission of emotion to a special type of self-control that enables any emotion, including fear, pity, grief or nostalgia, to yield pleasure. This self-control disengages emotion from action and reinterprets it as a source of pleasure. Anger, for instance, can be greatly pleasurable if it can be stopped from turning into physical violence. Spectators of professional wrestling, for example, can be driven to paroxysms of rage by the orgy of evil unfolding in front of their eyes. As Barthes (1973) explains, this is highly enjoyable for the spectators, so long as they do not join in the mêlée, and even more so if the worst villains among the wrestlers meet with the most terrifying punishment. That terror itself can be highly thrilling is no more eloquently illustrated than by the successes of ever more frightening roller-coaster rides.

It can now be seen how important puritanism, with its emphasis on emotional control, was in promoting modern hedonism. By blocking feeling as a motive for action and replacing it with rational calculation, puritanism did not kill feeling; instead, it made it available to support a new mechanism of pleasure, one deriving not from the senses but from experience.

> Unlike traditional hedonism, however, [pleasure] is not gained solely, or even primarily, through the manipulation of objects and events in the world, but through a degree of control over their meaning. In addition, the modern hedonist possesses the very special power to conjure up stimuli in the absence of any externally generated sensations. This control is achieved through the power of imagination, and provides infinitely greater possibilities for the maximization of pleasurable experiences than was available under traditional, realistic hedonism to even the most powerful of potentates. This derives not merely from the fact that there are virtually no restrictions upon the faculty of imagination, but also from the fact that it is completely within the hedonist's own control. It is this highly rationalized form of self-illusory hedonism which characterizes modern pleasure-seeking. (Campbell, 1989: 76)

Consumerism and the new hedonism

If the key to modern hedonism is the quest for pleasure via emotional experience rather than sensory stimulation, then modern consumption can be seen as an elaborate apparatus enabling individuals to *imagine* the dramas that afford them pleasure, to *dream* the scenarios that fulfil their desires. What commodities do is to act as props for the imagination, as stimulants for a reverie in which longing and fulfilment coincide.

> In modern, self-illusory hedonism, the individual is ... an artist of the imagination, someone who takes images from memory or the existing environment, and rearranges them or otherwise improves them in his mind in such a way that they become distinctly pleasing. No longer are they 'taken as given' from past experience, but crafted into unique products, pleasure being the guiding principle. In this sense, the contemporary hedonist is a dream artist, the special skills possessed by modern man making this possible. (Campbell, 1989: 79)

Consider the fashion of South American hammocks. The importation of hammocks from Peru, Bolivia and Paraguay is a curious reversal of the 19th century, when hammocks mass-produced from Manchester wiped out South American production (Gott, 1993). Hammocks remain popular, allowing consumers to imagine themselves luxuriating in the sunshine, relaxing, at peace with themselves and with the world. The hammock becomes the stimulus for a longing reverie, at once unrealistic and unrealizable, frustrating and yet strangely fulfilling. If many of the hammocks sold are rarely used and if, when they are used, they fail to yield much relaxing time (since people who day-dream about hammocks are the very people unable to relax), these things hardly matter. To these people, the pleasure afforded by the hammock is at the level of fantasy, rather than as an object. The enjoyment of products as parts of fantasies and the fantasies about products are crucial features of modern consumerism and may explain why window shopping and browsing unaffordable items on the internet or in glossy magazines can be enjoyable.

Modern consumption, according to Campbell, is built around day-dreaming, 'envisaged as an activity that mixes the pleasures of fantasy with those of reality' (Campbell, 1989: 85). Desire becomes itself subject to control, nurtured, encouraged, stimulated so long as it affords pleasure. Deferred gratification is no sacrifice of pleasure but a state of increased excitation, at once frustrating and enjoyable, endured in the interest of heightened pleasures ahead. Disillusionment in hedonism of this type is not the result of dulling of the senses, as it is with traditional hedonism, but the result of the fact that imagined pleasures are always greater than actual ones, that as the poet John Keats said, 'heard melodies are sweet, those unheard are sweeter' (quoted in Campbell, 1989: 87). Dissatisfaction with reality, a generalized *tristesse*, becomes the back-cloth against which the consumer as a dream artist can embroider his or her fantasies. 'Thus the contemporary hedonist not only tends to welcome deferred gratification, but may also prematurely abandon a source of pleasure, as, by doing so, he maximizes the opportunities for indulging the emotions of grief, sorrow, nostalgia, and, of course, self-pity' (Campbell, 1989: 88). Campbell's account of hedonism reveals consumer culture to be a space where a wide range of emotions can be experienced, through a combination of real and imagined stimuli. A bungee jump, a visit to one of the numerous terror attractions (Madame Tussaud's, the London Dungeons and so on) or watching a horror movie are all experiences in terror; a visit to the Holocaust museum in Washington, DC becomes an experience in grief; the purchase of a gift for a loved one becomes an experience in romantic love and so on. Experiences fade with repetition, hence self-illusory hedonism is always seeking novelty, uniqueness and adventure, while at all times seeking to maintain control over the intensity of stimulation, balancing endurable longing with a kaleidoscopic survey of emotions and delectable morsels of pleasure.

The cycle of desire – acquisition, use, disillusionment, renewed desire – is a general feature of modern hedonism, and applies to romantic interpersonal relationships as much as the consumption of cultural products such as clothes and records (Campbell, 1989: 90). This type of hedonism finds its ideal in *romanticism*, which:

> had the effect of casting the individual of true virtue in the role of an opponent to 'society', whose conventions he must deny if only to secure proof of his genius and passion. At the same time, he becomes not merely a virtuoso in feeling but also in pleasure, some-thing he must prove by creating cultural products which yield pleasure to others. Pleasure indeed becomes the crucial means of recognizing that ideal truth and beauty which imagination reveals – it is the 'grand elementary principle' in life – and thus becomes the means by which enlightenment and moral renewal can be achieved through art. (Campbell, 1989: 203)

Modern hedonism and the aesthetics of everyday life

Under the romantic ethic, the modern consumer fuses hedonism with an aes-thetic attitude to life, seeking to emulate the artist in his or her pursuit of pleasures through the medium of imagination, repudiation of 'easy' pleasures or comforts in the interest of controlled stimulation and quest for a highly indi-vidual style. Here, Campbell joins an important tradition of consumer studies, which underlines the so-called aestheticization of everyday life, according to which everyday consumer objects are infected with aesthetic considerations, becoming signs of style and taste, and losing their functional qualities (see, for example, Miller, 1987; Ewen, 1990; Willis, 1990; Featherstone, 1991; Lury, 1996; Slater, 1997; Pountain and Robins, 2000). He also joins a tradition of marketing and consumer studies that, starting with Hirschman and Holbrook's (1982) influential paper, has sought to emphasize the pleasure-yielding qualities of a large section of contemporary consumption, a tradition that eventually gave rise to the consumer culture theory (CCT) (e.g. Firat and Venkatesh, 1995; Arnould and Thompson, 2005; Holt, 2012; Cova et al., 2013). This tradition challenged the 'traditional' utilitarian/economic perspective, emphasizing the sensuous, fantasy and emotional qualities of a large part of contemporary consumption, and sought to uncover the conscious and unconscious meanings carried by the fruits of consumerism. Like Campbell, Hirschman and Holbrook (1982) empha-sized that even painful experiences, like watching tragic films inspired by the Nazi holocaust or by slavery, can afford pleasure. Like Campbell, they also high-lighted the aesthetic qualities of contemporary consumption, noting that an ever increasing range of products, such as music, movies, books and sport, are capable of arousing intense emotions and an aesthetic appreciation. Western consumers can spend enormous amounts of time decorating their homes, choosing their clothes, food and other goods, planning their holidays, forever mixing ingredients, as if they were trying not merely to create works of art but to discover a uniquely individual style. To do so, commodities must appear to forget their use-values, and must appear exclusively as objects of pure taste. This, according to Bourdieu:

> asserts the absolute primacy of form over function, *of the mode of representation over the object represented, [and] categorically demands a purely aesthetic disposition which earlier art demanded only conditionally. The demiurgic ambition of the artist, capable of applying to any object the pure intention of an artistic effort which is an end in itself, calls for unlimited repetitiveness on the part of the aesthete capable of applying the specifically aesthetic intention to any object, whether or not it has been produced with aesthetic intention. (Bourdieu, 1984: 30)*

The corollary of the aestheticization of everyday life is the de-aestheticization of art. Surrealist painting initiated the project of stripping objects of art of their transcendental qualities and mystique, either by parodying well-known masterpieces (Dali adding a moustache to the Mona Lisa) or by presenting everyday objects as artwork (Duchamp presenting a urinal signed 'R. Mutt 1917' as sculpture). Many museums today routinely display 'ordinary' objects of everyday life, inviting the visitor to turn them into artistic works through the use of imagination.

The great advantage of Campbell's account over most others highlighting the artistic qualities of modern consumption is that it keeps both pleasure and dissatisfaction in the picture, built as it is on a sophisticated theory of desire and stimulation. Tastes and aesthetic preferences are not arbitrary social constructions, but are derivative of romantic sensibilities pursuing pleasure. Trivial objects of everyday life become charged with aestheticism, not because of Veblenesque status concerns, nor because individuals are influenced by taste-makers or 'new cultural intermediaries' working in media, design, fashion, advertising and information (Bourdieu, 1984), but because they become objects of emotion activating pleasurable reveries. Furthermore, Campbell offers strong arguments for why dissatisfaction, inextricably linked with the pursuit of pleasure, drives innovation. His hedonist-consumers are inexorably drawn to exploration and experimentation (see Chapter 4, 'The Consumer as Explorer'). Above all, Campbell offers one of the few convincing explanations of why consumers may be avidly pursuing horror, fright, anger, sadness and even pain as part of the pursuit of pleasure, why they may seek out ugly objects and failed artistic creations in the name of beauty.

The relative weaknesses in Campbell's account of modern consumption are paradoxically linked to his success in elucidating pleasure. His account of the pleasure principle is, as we saw, rich in insights, more dynamic and in some ways more convincing than the psychoanalytic account of the same concept, which is connected to homoeostasis and the reduction of tension. Yet, where Freud saw the world conspiring against individual pleasure, Campbell sees no such limitations. For Freud, the pleasure principle must be continuously modified, compromised and deflected according to the demands of reality:

> What decides the purpose of life is simply the programme of the pleasure principle. This principle dominates the operation of the mental apparatus from the start. There can be no doubt about its efficacy, and yet its programme is at loggerheads with the whole world, with the macrocosm as much as the microcosm. There is no possibility at all of its being carried through; all the regulations of the universe run counter to it. (Freud, [1930] 1985: 76)

Unlike the psychoanalytic account of libido forever torn between pleasure and social bonding, forever frustrated by necessity, Campbell's pleasure principle rules supreme:

> Modern hedonism presents all individuals with the possibility of being their own despot, exercising total control over the stimuli they experience, and hence the pleasure they receive. (Campbell, 1989: 76)

The main limitations on pleasure entertained by Campbell appear to be those originating in the nature of pleasure, the dulling effects of comfort and the diminishing intensity of pleasure itself. This view does not explain what happens when one individual's pleasure inhibits the pleasure of somebody else. Nor what happens when one individual's pleasure runs counter to the broader institutions of morality, religion or law. Finally, it seems that Campbell's individual can pursue his or her Quixotic adventures, oblivious to the necessities and hardships of life or any other external demands.

While much of Campbell's discussion occurs at the level of macro-social and cultural trends across several centuries, the picture he paints of the modern consumer is highly individualistic. The pleasure principle, as he conceives it, operates across classes, races, genders, ages and all other social and cultural distinctions. Unlike Douglas and Isherwood (1978), who view the solitary consumer as a fiction, consumers emerge from Campbell's discussions as solitary creatures, individually pursuing pleasure, absorbed in their reveries, more or less oblivious of each other. Campbell's severe criticism of Veblen, his contemptuous dismissal of Packard's ([1957] 1981) thesis of consumer manipulation, his steadfast refusal to relate fantasy with escapism or substitute gratification and his indifference to the social, political and communicative dimensions of consumption all underline his uncompromising commitment to pleasure as the totalizing principle at the heart of modern consumption. His account, however, serves as a warning of some of the absurdity that one ends up with, when seeing contemporary consumption through a single prism. It would be bizarre to envisage a lone parent or a poor person shopping for his or her weekly groceries as lost in a reverie of pleasure.

Social hedonism

To Campbell's uncompromisingly solipsistic hedonism, it is interesting to juxta-pose Bourdieu's social hedonism. Bourdieu's book *Distinction: A Social Critique of the Judgement of Taste* (1984) caused a substantial public debate when first pub-lished in France, partly because it was seen as debunking the concept of taste (notably 'high-brow taste') by re-integrating aesthetic consumption with ordi-nary everyday consumption. Bourdieu combines an emphasis on hedonism with an insistence that consumption is a set of practices establishing social differences, viewing consumers both as pleasure-seeking (like Campbell) and as hungry for distinction (like Douglas and Isherwood). Tastes, according to Bourdieu, emerge at once as avenues towards pleasure and as a class phenomenon, as a form of cultural capital and as an instrument of oppression.

Bourdieu's arguments draw on two extensive surveys on consumer tastes and lifestyles carried out in France in the 1960s. Judged on their own merit, these surveys are both outdated and methodologically mechanistic, suffering from all the familiar shortcomings of attempting to capture a person's lifestyle, tastes and meanings through standardized inflexible questions. Nevertheless, these surveys enable Bourdieu to argue that there are important differences in how different social classes, or even class factions, derive pleasure. The food and the drinks they consume, the films and TV programmes they watch, the cars they drive and the ways they furnish and decorate their homes are not merely governed by dif-ferent tastes but reveal fundamentally different modes of deriving pleasure, different aesthetics, different pleasure principles.

The key to these differences is what he calls the 'Kantian aesthetic', which is central to middle-class lifestyles, yet entirely absent from working-class lifestyles. For Kant (1952), the aesthetic experience occupies a position between morality and sensuousness and centres on the faculty of judgement. Judgement mediates between theoretical reason and practical reason, through the feeling of pleasure; its realm is art. Aesthetic experience rejects immediate *sensuous* pleasures in favour of *abstract* appreciation of the artistic, which comes through the faculty of imagination. Beauty, according to this view, is neither floating freely in an external world, nor the direct corollary of sensuous pleasure, but is creatively constituted through the work of imagination. Thus beauty can be discovered in an object's form as well as in the mode of its representation, if the object can be approached in a detached, disinterested manner that completely disregards its use or material composition. Even objects that could be classed as 'ugly', can therefore become beautiful.

A photograph of rotting vegetables, a painting of an ugly man or a grotesque interlude in the midst of a symphony can all afford great aesthetic delight if the object can be released from its bondage to both pleasure and usage and turned into a 'free' being, signifying nothing but itself, through the free play of imagination.

Bourdieu rejects the Kantian theory as a theory of aesthetic judgement (respectfully parodying, in the title of his book, Kant's *Critique of Judgement*, 1952) but accepts it as a description of bourgeois aesthetics. He regards the detached, aloof disposition of the Kantian aesthetic not as a mental faculty, but as an orientation concomitant to the affluence of today's bourgeoisie and an instrument of social distinctions. The crux of his argument is that while the middle class embrace the Kantian aesthetic, cultivating tastes for the abstract, the working-class aesthetic is that of popular culture, dictated by necessity and tied to both function and sensuous pleasure. This fundamental difference cuts across every aspect of taste. The working class invariably seeks direct gratification while the middle class seeks 'style'.

Bourdieu provides numerous illustrations of this dichotomy, ranging from food and drink to photography, from music to home decoration. A couple of his examples will suffice. Working people like food, plentiful in protein, nutritious, what Orwell in *The Road to Wigan Pier* described as 'a little bit "tasty"' (Orwell, 1962: 86). Pleasure is synonymous to an 'honest' and unfussy but abundant assortment of 'strong' food, which ultimately reflects the value of virility, rooted in physical work. By contrast middle-class tastes weigh heavily towards elaborately prepared food, sauces and so on, the uses of exotic ingredients (like rare mushrooms), or towards the extreme simplicity of nouvelle cuisine. These emphasize the 'higher and finer' qualities inherent in preparation and presentation and, in the extreme, seem to deny that food is anything quite as vulgar as nourishment.

Similar illustrations are offered by Bourdieu from music (working class prefer music with strong melodic and rhythmic content, middle class prefer avant-garde), photography (working class prefer pictures of garish sunsets or innocent children at first communion, middle class prefer pictures of dissected cabbages or car crashes) and others. In Bourdieu's account the aestheticization of everyday life is a middle-class affliction, rather than a totalizing principle of late capitalism as for some postmodern thinkers. If middle-class consumers approach their clothing, eating and home furnishing with an anti-functional, detached outlook, this is not the same for working-class lifestyles. 'Nothing is more alien to working-class women than the typically bourgeois idea of making each object in the home the occasion for an aesthetic choice' (Bourdieu, 1984: 47). For Bourdieu, even where the same commodity is consumed by different social classes, its meaning will vary. Where some movie-goers watch a 'Western starring Burt Lancaster', others have watched 'the latest Sam Peckinpah'; these are vastly different ways of seeing the same film, at once reflecting different tastes, generating different pleasures and producing social distinctions (Bourdieu, 1984: 28).

Consumers' tastes, for Bourdieu, have darker, less innocent qualities than they do for Campbell or indeed most economists. Aesthetic judgements act as a form of 'thought terrorism' (a favourite term of Bourdieu's) cutting across social classes and fractions.

> *Terrorism [lies] in the peremptory verdicts which, in the name of taste, condemn to ridicule, indignity, shame, silence (here one could give examples, taken from everyone's familiar universe), men and women who simply fall short, in the eyes of their judges, of the right way of being and doing; it [lies] in the symbolic violence through which the dominant groups endeavour to impose their own life-style, and which abounds in the glossy weekly magazines: 'Conforama is the Guy Lux of furniture', says* Le Nouvel Observateur, *which will never tell you that the* Nouvel Obs *is the Club Méditeraneé of culture. There is terrorism in all such remarks, flashes of self-interested lucidity sparked off by class hatred and contempt. (Bourdieu, 1984: 511)*

Insults rarely hurt more than when aimed at the adversary's 'taken for granted preferences'; few types of social humiliation can match the dismissal of someone's tastes. 'You like X? Oh dear, it's so passé/common!' where X can be anything from digital watches, dried tomatoes to yesterday's music idol or theories of Althusser or Baudrillard. Conversely, argues Bourdieu, a transgression of the aesthetic decrees of 'high culture' will outrage the bourgeois more effectively than the breach of a moral code. An improperly dressed person, for example, will incur more hostility than a sexual deviant. In this way, aesthetics becomes a major terrain of contest between social classes and fractions, a contest where much pleasure is derived from terrorizing the adversaries, either by passing judgements on their tastes or by violating aesthetic codes. If Campbell's hedonist-consumer is naturally driven towards the image of the consumer-explorer, Bourdieu's consumer tends to modulate from an aesthete into a snob, a sadist or a rebel. Pleasure becomes linked, not to discovery and innovation, but to class violence and aggression.

Bourdieu's account of the different classes' aesthetics has been criticized from both the left and the right; the left have accused him of diminishing the working-class lifestyle to a caricature, while the right have feigned horror at his questioning of their aesthetic taboos (see Jenkins (1992) for an overview). Yet he does not seek to evaluate these aesthetics, since he rejects any transcendental aesthetic qualities. Ultimately, all tastes are socially constructed, as are their 'high' or 'low' qualities, that is, distinctions between tastes. To be sure, the middle classes may sneer at the vulgarity and 'cheapness' of common culture, just as the working classes may, less blatantly, belittle the airs and affectations of the high-brows. But for Bourdieu, the two represent fundamentally different aesthetics. From the two, various social fractions and intermediate or marginal groups seek to mould their own aesthetics, for example, artlessly aspiring at high-brow or affectedly 'opting' for rustic simplicity. However, the mechanisms for deriving pleasure are essentially different. Working-class lifestyle is one of a 'realistic (but not resigned) hedonism' (Bourdieu, 1984: 49), while the middle-class lifestyle becomes ever more closely aligned to the Kantian aesthetic, concerned with style, form and distinction.

Bourdieu's account of consumerism is one that combines a discussion of pleasure with a class analysis of tastes and patterns of consumption. In its emphasis on class differences in consumption, it is only matched by Douglas and Isherwood's analysis (see Chapter 3, 'The Consumer as Communicator'). Many commentators, however, have found Bourdieu's class analysis not only inaccurate but also patronizing. Jenkins (1992) and Douglas and Isherwood (1978) have argued that style and cultivated/inane tastes are every bit as important for working-class people as they are for the middle classes. Numerous British commentators have established the importance of style, fashion and fantasy in consumption patterns of young working-class people, whose preferred tastes in music may be as perplexing to middle-aged, middle-class people as any avant-garde may be to a working-class audience (Fiske, 1989; Willis, 1990; Featherstone, 1991; Pountain and Robins, 2000). In sum, one suspects that the class dimension in Bourdieu's argument is at least outdated or more alarmingly a projection of his own middle-class presumptions; certainly, it is contentious.

Comparing Bourdieu's and Campbell's hedonistic accounts of modern consumption, one may be tempted to discern an equivalence between the two mechanisms of pleasure they each describe. Bourdieu's Kantian ethic and Campbell's modern hedonism hinge on the imagination and on deferred pleasure. Bourdieu's realistic hedonism and Campbell's traditional hedonism are both associated with instant sensuous pleasure. The former present the consumer as artist or aesthete, the latter as hedonist. This similarity, however, could be somewhat misleading. For Bourdieu, taste, culture and pleasure are not only class experiences but historically constructed ones. An individual *learns to enjoy* a wide range of objects and activities, from coffee to frogs' legs, from Chinese opera to heavy metal music, from jogging to foxhunting on rainy days. Many of these may appear curious to those 'uneducated' in these pleasures, yet membership of a social group and induction into its social tastes substantially determines an individual's '*habitus*', which Bourdieu sees as the range of tastes from which he or she will derive a personal repertoire. This contrasts with Campbell's far more individualistic account, where individuals must discover pleasure for themselves, their aesthetic responses being a matter of individual psycho-history rather than class or group membership.

Ethical hedonism

Drawing on a renewed interest in Aristotle and in particular his concept of 'eudaemonia', some theorists of contemporary consumption have argued that the pursuit of pleasure need not be slavishly attached to individual goals or disregard social values and virtues. One of the most advanced accounts of this position has been provided by feminist philosopher Kate Soper (2007; 2008; 2012) who has consistently advocated an 'alternative hedonism' as a possible corrective for the mindless pursuit of consumerist pleasure. Many consumers in affluent societies, argues Soper, have not only become aware of the damaging ecological effects of Western consumerism, but are becoming increasingly disaffected with its negative effects on their lives – stress, ill-health, frustration, pollution and congestion. Soper argues that puritanical appeals to self-denial and socially responsible consumption are unlikely to be successful unless complemented by what she calls a 'new hedonist imaginary'. This does not reject pleasure, but seeks to discover alternative sources of pleasure. Instead of spending, shopping and waste,

> *an anti-consumerist ethic and politics should therefore appeal not only to altruistic compassion and environmental concern but also to the more self-regarding gratifications of consuming differently: to a new erotics of consumption or hedonist 'imaginary'. (Soper, 2008: 571)*

Instead of rejecting pleasure, this alternative hedonism proclaims a new version of the pleasure principle, one that discovers well-being in a harmonious co-existence with others, with the natural environment and with our own well-being. The Italian Slow Food movement provides Soper with one of the examples of alternative hedonism – the relaxed preparation, presentation and enjoyment of food replaces the excitement of searching for ever more exotic and environmentally damaging foodstuffs. Instead of automatically using a car whenever we desire to travel, alternative hedonism seeks pleasure in riding a bicycle, in walking or in not travelling at all.

Eschewing fashion and brand-buying, bodily self-styling and other resource-hungry ways of satisfying needs for self-esteem and self-expression, alternative hedonism proposes a new attitude towards time, one that does not look at time as the ultimate scarce good. Contemporary consumerism forever denies us time, consigning us to ever more breathless work, not only for our employer, our families and friends but also for the very purposes of consumption (see Chapter 11, 'The Consumer as Worker'). A key demand of alternative, ethical hedonism according to Soper would be a demand

> *for reduction of the working week, a slower pace of living and more locally sourced provision. This could save us from the 'clone town' syndrome, restore children to a healthier and more carefree existence, and provide everyone with opportunities for forms of sensual experience denied by frenetic travel and work routines. It could also help to boost communities, reduce crime, and foster new forms of intergenerational cooperation and exchange. ... Utopian as these ideas may seem, they now have some anchorage in the feelings of those who are troubled by the undesirable by-products of their own formerly less questioned sources of gratification. Emerging 'alternative hedonist' frameworks of thinking about the good life might alter conceptions of self-interest among affluent consumers, thus sparking a relay of political pressures for a fairer global distribution of resources and allowing better understanding of the worst consequences of northwest 'overdevelopment' and how to avoid them. (Soper, 2012: 101)*

Soper is aware that her vision of an ethical hedonism might appear both unrealistic and elitist. Her focus on the blurred lines between alternative consumerism and anti-consumption underplays the implications this might have for employment in a world where millions of people rely on producing glamourized junk products and services for their livelihoods. This is the question that has preoccupied many environmental economists, for whom the key question is how to engender well-being and prosperity without growth (Hirsch, 1976; Daly, 1996; Jackson, 2009; Daly and Farley, 2011). This is an issue that draws the consumer as hedonist towards a different image of the consumer, that of the consumer as citizen, to which we shall return in Chapter 11.

Hedonism and sadism

For all their limitations, images of consumers as hedonists that emerge from work by Campbell, Bourdieu and consumer culture theorists have a compelling quality. As we stare at the clothes in a shop window, or as we visit a theme park or browse the motor-boats in our leisure magazine, or we salivate over the dishes pictured in our Sunday newspapers or at our neighbour's smart new car, we experience a feeling that can only be described as desire, a desire that is at once sweet and frustrating, a desire capable at times of convulsing our physical being as though it were purely sexual. Such objects seduce us as though they were sexual objects, sparking off strings of fantasies, which continue to prosper the longer the object remains inaccessible. As Freud ([1921] 1985) realized in his theory of the relationship between sexual gratification and romantic love, the denial of consummation enhances the idealization of the inaccessible object, just as in courtly love the longing was all the sweeter, the more aloof and unresponsive was the object of the lover's languor.

The accounts that we have explored in this chapter put pleasure at the centre of modern consumption and more generally as the central ethic of Western cultures. Happiness is increasingly defined not in terms of achievement or success, but in broadly hedonistic or aesthetic terms reflected in the 'quality of life' both at and outside the workplace. Happiness is seen neither as a reward for effort or virtue, nor as the result of fortune. Instead, as Rieff (1959) has brutally put it, human happiness is a question of the *management of pleasure* and, therefore, a *duty* to oneself. So long as one is not excluded from the seductive world of commodities by being dependent on the state for survival, being unhappy is inexcusable. It can only be due to one's ineptness at managing pleasure.

Neither Campbell nor Bourdieu would seek to vindicate such a position as an ethical hedonism, the true road to the good life, if such a thing exists. They both believe that consumers are deluding themselves in their espousal of the pleasure principle (in any guise), and their determination to pretend that the grey world of necessity has melted away. The very shrinking of individual women and men to the status of consumers, the willingness to define oneself and others through their standing as consumers, is indicative of this self-delusion. Yet, neither Campbell nor Bourdieu are remotely willing to entertain the notion that modern hedonism, though its roots lie in delusion, is a form of compensation for the greyness of life under the reality principle or an escapist form of substitute gratification. Consumerist fantasies may be detached from reality but the pleasure they afford is real. This is a position that has been criticized with considerable eloquence by Christopher Lasch. Lasch argued over many years that the pleasures of consumerism are innocent neither in their origins nor in their implications.

> Commodity production and consumerism alter perceptions not just of the self but of the world outside the self. They create a world of mirrors, insubstantial images, illusions increasingly indistinguishable from reality. The mirror effect makes the subject an object; at the same time, it makes the world of objects an extension or projection of the self. It is misleading to characterize the culture of consumption as a culture dominated by things. The consumer lives surrounded not so much by things as by fantasies. He lives in a world that has no objective or independent existence and seems to exist only to gratify or thwart his desires. (Lasch, 1984: 30)

At the heart of Lasch's critique lies the connection between hedonism and narcissism, a link widely discussed in psychoanalytic literature (for example, Lasch, 1984; Gabriel, 1999). The modern narcissist is the individual who, unable to love and unwilling to be loved, constantly seeks to derive pleasure from his or her own image. This she or he tries to do by embellishing her or his ego through the consumption of material and human objects, which become objects of fantasy and desire. Contemporary hedonism erects a massive edifice of *substitute gratifications* which, instead of obliterating, compounds the narcissism and lovelessness of modern life. As objects of desire, commodities and people are indistinguishable – they are objects to be used, abused and manipulated for one's personal enhancement.

> Contemporary hedonism ... originates not in the pursuit of pleasure but in the war of all against all, in which even the most intimate encounters become a form of mutual exploitation ... This hedonism is a fraud; the pursuit of pleasure disguises a struggle for power. (Lasch, 1980: 66)

Lasch tries to show the extent to which pleasure in our culture has become co-extensive with aggression; sex and violence become irredeemably intertwined in language, in fantasy and in reality. As ever increasing levels of violence and sex in films and TV demonstrate, this bonding becomes normalized. If individuals derive pleasure, aesthetic or otherwise, from violence or products associated with violence, this is not as Campbell might have argued because violence just happened to provide a springboard for pleasurable fantasies, in the same way that tenderness, love or romance might have done. Violence becomes one with pleasure, when pleasure becomes life's only business, detached from morality or order. If Bourdieu, following Veblen, clearly envisages the sadistic delights of both snobbery and aesthetic transgression, Lasch goes a step further. In the Marquis de Sade's explosive 18th-century utopia, where sexual pleasure leads to every humiliation of the other imaginable, even as far as mutilation, hacking, tearing, cutting and killing, Lasch finds both the prototype and terminus of modern hedonism, seeing no distinction between objects and people as instruments of pleasure. De Sade's message, coming at the outset of the French republican era, was that uncompromised hedonism, far from leading to an emotional polytheism, can only lead to one thing, unbridled aggression. Once moral restraints have been removed, the pursuit of pleasure quickly turns into violence.

> In a society that has reduced reason to mere calculation, reason can impose no limits on the pursuit of pleasure – on the immediate gratification of every desire no matter how perverse, insane, criminal, or merely immoral. For the standards that would condemn cruelty derive from religion, compassion, or the kind of reason that rejects purely instrumental applications; and none of these outmoded forms of thought or feeling has any logical place in a society based on commodity production. (Lasch, 1980: 69)

De Sade's vision has come closer to normalized reality 200 years later. Aggression has assumed a more central position in every aspect of Western life, including the predatory nature of personal relationships, the pitiless abuse of nature in pursuit of ever-higher standards of living, the use of commodities as weapons in a Veblenesque combat for status and the savagery of modern spectacles, including war itself. The fantasies of consumer culture, pleasurable though they may be, have little of the day-dreaming, bitter-sweet qualities envisaged by Campbell. The material or human object's resistance to being possessed, far from heightening the delights of yearning, spawn murderous fantasies of rape, pillage and destruction. These occasionally get a chance to be acted out as the dreadful photographs of sexual abuse of prisoners at the Abu Ghraib prison camp in Iraq have shown or the daily posting of decapitations or other hideous clips on YouTube. Sexuality becomes the basis of torture and humiliation, performed ceremonially in front of the photographic lens. If a narcissist cannot have something, whether it be the goods in a shop window, the neighbour's car or the object of his or her sexual interest, far from gently dreaming of acquiring it by seduction or payment, he or she dreams of smashing it, breaking it or destroying it. Any residual pleasure in the object rests in its annihilation. Vandalism and destruction are the flip side of consumer hedonism, something that often goes unnoticed among those who preach both the worship of commodities and respect for human values.

In conclusion

This bleak picture of pleasure from aggression and violence contrasts sharply with the more upbeat depictions of Western consumers as pleasure-seekers. But, like them, Lasch sees individuals today as much more likely to associate happiness with pleasure than with achievement, success or virtue. They are likely to envisage pleasure as residing in those objects that attract desire, and in doing so they may treat commodities or people in a similar manner, as stimulants for fantasies. Life assumes the character of an erotic simmer, a never-ending process of seduction, maintaining a constant level of desire that migrates from object to object as they each assume the spotlight in our fantasies.

Different accounts of consumer hedonism take different views on the nature of pleasure and the extent to which it differs across social classes and other groups. Nevertheless, there is wide agreement that consumer pleasure lies not so much in physical sensation as in total emotional experience, pleasure lies in the meaning of this experience. While this experience may be fantastic or delusory, the pleasure is not delusory at all. Thus the pleasure derived from a 'designer' ashtray lies in its imaginary qualities, which lift it above the mundane realities of its function, its substance, its price or its future uses. The object is idealized in much the same way as any object of infatuation is. It seduces us in exactly the same way that a person might.

Bourdieu and Campbell go some way towards providing an explanation for the thesis that everyday reality in Western cultures becomes aestheticized, with objects and activities assuming the qualities of art and losing their functional and material bearings. Style becomes more important than utility, which acquires a vulgar, common hue. The consumer as hedonist must be able to derive pleasure from every item with which he or she comes into contact and everything must be orientated to that end.

Starting with Lasch, our view is that consumer hedonism is neither entirely playful nor innocent. Instead it can be the outcome of a culture in which the market becomes the dominant institution regulating relations among individuals, and tastes reign supreme with little restraint from loyalty, morality, duty or love. Pleasure derived from material and symbolic manipulation of people and objects entails a substantial amount of aggression and the pursuit of this type of pleasure may be ultimately futile. The consumer becomes an addict capable of inflicting any amount of pain on others in order to obtain what he or she believes will satisfy his or her desires. Consumer hedonism can lead to a complete dead end, reinforcing the very discontents that drive it. Few have expressed this idea with the force and clarity of an old militant, interviewed by Seabrook:

> *People aren't satisfied, only they don't seem to know why they're not. The only chance*
> *of satisfaction we can imagine is getting more of what we've already got now. But it's*

what we've got now that makes everybody dissatisfied. So what will more of it do, make us more satisfied, or more dissatisfied? (Seabrook, 1978: 132)

Whether today's consumers are locked in a vicious circle of dependency, frustration and hate, or whether they enjoy in a limited but vital way the satisfactions available to them, in practice or fantasy, this remains a vital question at the heart of the debate on today's consumerism.

Hedonism is an idea that accounts for certain qualities of contemporary consumption; the thrill we get when we acquire an object we like, our insistence on what we like and what we do not like, and our ability to derive pleasure, thrills and fun out of seemingly disagreeable experiences. It also can elucidate different ways in which different social classes, including the very poorest, derive pleasure out of material objects. The underside of this is that hedonism is neither the only principle driving today's consumers, nor the liberating force celebrated by its apologists.

7

THE CONSUMER AS VICTIM

[C]onsumers are being manipulated, defrauded, and injured not just by marginal businesses or fly-by-night hucksters but by the US blue-chip business firms ... (Ralph Nader, 1968)

CORE ARGUMENTS

Victimhood is the flipside of consumer sovereignty. Even the staunchest proponents of consumer choice recognize the potential for consumers to be exploited in a free market. Consumers, free to make their own choices, are still liable to be defrauded, manipulated and short-changed. Victimhood, whether conscious or unconscious, has played a central role in Western debates about modern consumption. There are splits, however, between those who believe that victimhood is exceptional or endemic. There are also splits between those who argue that the law is needed to protect consumers and those who see the market by itself as capable of providing its own correction. The former group looks at state power as the guarantor of the level playing-field and the ultimate source of consumer protection. The latter group believes that markets and the free sharing of information empower consumers, enabling them to avoid unscrupulous providers and substandard goods. Information is a key to both groups. The chapter examines whether the market mechanism alone is sufficient for the provision of necessary information, or whether this too should be underpinned by regulation. Consumers face increased risks in a world of globalized markets, complex supply chains and multi-sourced products. Consumer co-operation has long been a mechanism for consumer defence, complementing the power of the state. The internet and consumer sharing of information and experiences open up new opportunities for self-help. The chapter concludes with an equivocal assessment of the consumer as victim. While not all consumers are victims in everyday life, victimhood haunts consumers in a society of extensive risks, whether perceived or real.

The idea that consumers are victims no longer enjoys quite the popularity it once did. The view that they can be easily manipulated and controlled by devious advertisers and marketers has now given place to the image of the discriminating, sophisticated and generally 'savvy' consumer. Victimhood is widely discussed in connection with particular disadvantaged social groups. The world of consumption, on the other hand, is not the first to come to mind when thinking of people suffering injustice and oppression. On the contrary, today's consumers are meant to be sovereign, capable of pursuing their interests and, as we saw in earlier chapters, seek excitement, identity and pleasure. Could the image of the consumer as victim therefore be a trifle excessive? Should it be restricted only to cases of major scandals where life and health were put at risk by dangerous products and dishonest practices?

We think not. In addition to being victims of blatant exploitation and fraud, consumers are exposed to many forms of victimhood, in some of which they may even collude themselves but the victimhood is nevertheless real. Does tobacco smoking constitute a moment of sovereign consumer choice or is it the result of a methodical campaign to get people addicted to nicotine? Was the 2013 discovery of horsemeat in a wide range of European processed meat products an instance of harmless misrepresentation by the sellers (nobody died as a result of it) or an example of scandalous fraud and misinformation? And is indebtedness and financial ruin the outcome of individual consumer miscalculation and foolishness or could it be laid down to the door of consumerism and its relentless encouragement to spend. In this chapter, we argue that consumers can easily become victims – be manipulated, used, exploited, defrauded, humiliated – and that today's globalized trade and internet shopping create new opportunities for victimhood. As we will show in Chapter 9, 'The Consumer as Activist', the experience or threat of victimhood can be a prime motivation for consumers getting organized and seeking to discover a collective voice with which to promote their interests.

Victimhood is as old as any market trading system where purchasers can be cheated or conned by sellers. Impersonal markets where buyers and sellers have no personal bond and no enduring relationship exacerbate the possibilities of deception and swindling. In the modern senses that we explore in this book, the image of victimhood took centre-stage in the post-war period when techniques of mass promotion and advertising came into their own. Vance Packard's book, *The Hidden Persuaders*, published in 1957, created a stir with its revelations of consumer manipulation by new techniques of depth psychology and mass advertising (Packard, [1957] 1981). Thenceforth, the consumer could be seen not only as a victim of age-old and unscrupulous commercial interests but also as fodder for the new sophisticated techniques of the emerging science of consumer psychology, which drew on the insights of Freud and their application in marketing (see 'Introduction: The Faces of the Consumer'). The hidden persuaders were eager to sell products to consumers by exploiting various unconscious vulnerabilities and needs, ranging from the need for social approval to the unconscious desire for immortality to the down-to-earth fear of suffering from bad breath or body-odour. Above all, merchandizers recognized the power of sex to sell products that reassured women that they were attractive and men that they were virile, in other words products that reaffirmed traditional gender stereotypes. Packard, however, went beyond this, arguing that merchandizers systematically *create* needs and vulnerabilities through their advertising, generating a whole host of 'problems', for which their offerings provided solutions. Unpicking people's worries about their identities, their bodies, their age, their value as human beings and so forth gave the marketer new insidious ways of manipulating consumers.

In *One-dimensional Man* (1964), a book that like Packard's achieved cult status, Herbert Marcuse launched a powerful attack on late capitalism as compounding the alienation of the worker by turning people into one-dimensional beings solely preoccupied with consumption. Capitalism and especially consumer culture, he argued, systematically generate and impose false needs that they then purport to satisfy through different material goods, automobiles, clothes, jewellery and so forth. These false needs serve the interests of capital but create dependence, aggression and unhappiness for the consumer, intensifying the discontents that feed them and creating a spiral of alienation, frustration and discontent. They also have the result of obliterating other real needs, whose fulfilment would threaten the interests of capital and its representatives. Late capitalism, argued Marcuse and followers, made the false needs more central than the real ones.

> We may distinguish both true and false needs. 'False' are those which are superimposed upon the individual by particular social interests in his repression: the needs which perpetuate toil, aggressiveness, misery, and injustice. Their satisfaction might be most gratifying to the individual, but this happiness is not a condition which has to be maintained and protected if it serves to arrest the development of the ability (his own and others) to recognize the disease of the whole and grasp the chances of curing the disease. The result then is euphoria in unhappiness. Most of the prevailing needs to relax, to have fun, to behave and consume in accordance with the advertisements, to love and hate what others love and hate, belong to this category of false needs. Such needs have a societal content and function which are determined by external powers over which the individual has no control; the development and satisfaction of these needs is heteronomous. No matter how much such needs may have become the individual's own, reproduced and fortified by the conditions of his existence; no matter how much he identifies himself with them and finds himself in their satisfaction, they continue to be what they were from the beginning – products of a society whose dominant interest demands repression. (Marcuse, 1964: 4–5)

Marcuse's 'one-dimensional man' is the individual locked in a vicious circle of false needs for different consumer products and experiences for which he or she sacrifices an ever increasing part of his or her life in alienated work. Such is the grip of false needs that people will forfeit the satisfaction of real needs (healthy food, decent clothes, a sound education, the love of others) in order to buy spurious goods that will provide short-lived euphoria and long-term disappointment.

Since the 1980s, interest in alienation has ebbed among scholars of consumption and the concepts of 'false needs' and 'false consciousness' have become almost anathema (see, for example, Soper, 2007; 2008). The post-Second World War critical tradition, associated with the Frankfurt School (Jay, [1973] 1996; Adorno, 1991), lost some of its glamour and momentum when, under the influence of postmodernism, many cultural commentators began to celebrate consumption as an active, affirmative and even joyful pursuit rather than a passive, driven, escapist activity. A new generation of Marxist cultural theorists began to argue that consumption holds not only creative but liberating potential (Hall and Jacques, 1989). In spite of attempts by Lasch (1991), Sklair (1995; 2002) and others to underline the continuing addictive qualities of contemporary consumption (see Chapters 5 and 6), it would be fair to say that cultural studies lost interest in the notion of the consumer as victim. Instead, it sought to cast the consumer as explorer, as semiotic puzzle-solver, as *bricoleur*, as identity-seeker, or as we shall see in Chapter 8, as rebel.

Oblivious to this view propounded by cultural theory, however, consumer advocates and a new wave of consumer organizations around the world have persisted in highlighting the continuing and even increasing vulnerabilities of consumers in an age of global consumer capitalism. In this chapter, we will explore some of the objective and subjective reasons that have fuelled this critique and why we see victimhood as an important face of the consumer. We will then discuss some of the mechanisms for consumer protection that have been undertaken by governments and, more recently, intergovernmental bodies against the claims that free markets offer the strongest source of protection by enabling consumers to abandon or 'punish' inefficient or unscrupulous organizations and products. In contrast to such claims, we will examine the argument that individual consumer action (i.e. 'voting with their dollar') is not enough to provide adequate consumer protection. This requires collective representation through consumer organizations and lobbies (see also Chapter 9, 'The Consumer as Activist'). Finally, we examine some of the corporate responses to calls for enhanced consumer protection and assess their effectiveness.

The experience of being a victim

Most consumers worry about being taken for a ride, about being sold overpriced, flawed or dangerous goods and services. The act of consuming taps a deep well of experience from childhood onwards. Few children have not experienced the excitement of the first meaningful purchase of a toy or sweet they longed for. As part of the preparation for this book's first edition, we interviewed consumer activists and employees of consumer organizations from several different countries. We asked some of them if they could remember their first significant purchase. After sometimes intense interviews discussing the complexities of consumer activism and the challenges ahead, their eyes would light up and smile as they told of a mother giving money to buy a sweet or some early excitement. One, brought up in an isolated, near self-sufficient community in a developing country, told of the awe of being allowed to buy a canned drink on a trip out to town, an unheard of luxury. To anticipate such pleasure or excitement on every occasion (explored in Chapter 6, 'The Consumer as Hedonist') is unrealistic. One is bound to be disappointed with purchases from time to time. The thrill of the early experience of consumer power, such as buying your own toy, is counterbalanced by the bitterness or disappointment from a purchase that fails to live up to expectations – the toy that quickly falls apart, the sweet that looked nice but tasted disgusting, the dress that didn't look good a few weeks later – or that went wrong.

Disappointment alone does not turn consumer into victim. Victimhood is the other side of the coin of the consumer as sovereign chooser (see Chapter 2, 'The Consumer as Chooser'). Instead of being agents who do things and make choices with full knowledge of their consequences, consumers as victims are coaxed into decisions that are against their interests; they suffer from actions of other people who seek to take advantage of them and over whom they have little control; or suffer from harmful long-term effects of their own actions. They generally incur financial loss or even financial ruin and are liable to experience intense feelings of anger, indignation, frustration and despair. They may spend much time seeking redress through the courts or through other organizations, but this can compound their frustration and anger as more energy, money and time are sacrificed in pursuit of some elusive vindication.

Victimhood can afflict consumers across the demographic spectrum. Children can be victims of unscrupulous marketing that highlights the fun aspects of breakfast cereals and confectionary at the expense of their health (Hawkes, 2007). But elderly people, too, can be victims in the hands of mercenary salespeople offering investments, holidays, home improvements and so on. In a culture that celebrates youthfulness and good looks, women have been vulnerable to the tyranny of the fashion, cosmetics and jewellery industries. Men, too, are vulnerable to campaigns aimed at enhancing their egos and masculinity, through symbols of power and status, including gym memberships and sports equipment. Ethnic groups are targeted for particular insecurities. Adolescents going through a period of fragility and prone to identity crises, are fraught with possibilities of victimhood, as they strive to gain acceptance from their peers under the tyrannical rule of 'cool'. Psychological vulnerabilities and ignorance, wilful or otherwise, are liable to turn any group of consumers into victims.

Consumers in different demographic and cultural positions may experience variable degrees of satisfaction and dissatisfaction, along a continuum that ranges from 'exceeds my expectations' to 'falls far short and causes me harm'. Whether people see themselves as victims and complain is not easily predictable by psychological models. They may be more or less passive, more or less vocal to the maker and seller. Singh produced a typology of dissatisfaction response: passives, irates, voicers and activists (Singh, 1990), suggesting the different routes that dissatisfaction can take. From a marketing perspective, well-publicized complaints are bad for brand image, sometimes prompting retailers to offer 'money back if dissatisfied' promises as an active part of their marketing strategy. Since brands account for a large part of a product's value, complaints tarnish the brand image, so the seller or maker is generally encouraged to clarify and tighten up procedures on the following: information to customers, guarantees, after-sales service and assistance, speed of response to complaints and so on (Loudon and Della Bitta, 1993: 575ff). But for the consumer, the welter of warranties can themselves become an additional burden. Recognizing that one has been duped is not something that most people willingly acknowledge unless either the disappointment and anger is acute or the advantage of going public is compensation or revenge. Overall, complaining about one's purchases stands against much of the rhetoric that sees consumers as sovereign agents capable of looking after their own interests, and making sound choices. Consistent with this, victimhood is more likely to be acknowledged when it affects children and other vulnerable sections of the population.

Why are consumers prone to victimhood?

At the heart of the reasons for victimhood lie the divergent interests of producers and consumers, interests that markets are supposed to reconcile. Observers of capitalism since Adam Smith have acknowledged that, under the sway of the profit motive, producers have an incentive to cut costs, cut corners, raise prices and increase their profitability. In addition, they have an incentive to sell goods and services of limited use-value to consumers, if they can entice them with a variety of more or less unrealistic promises. Throughout history and all the way to our times, there has been a long litany of scandals and abuses which highlight the vulnerability of consumers. Food adulteration, for example, is as old as the food trade itself and a regular cause of consumer victimhood. Some forms of adulteration may at first seem innocuous. 'Why sell food when you can sell water?' asked an inadvertently candid industry advertisement in the 1970s; a century earlier, a UK Parliamentary enquiry in 1874 had concluded that the addition of water may not have poisoned people but it certainly cheated them

(London Food Commission, 1987: 157). Other forms of adulteration pose serious dangers to public health.

In 1820, chemist and librarian at the Royal Society of Chemistry in London, Frederick Accum published his now classic *A Treatise on Adulterations of Food and Culinary Poisons*. He anticipated acclaim across the spectrum of British society for his exposé of extensive but routine adulteration of food and drink. Some forms were harmless – pea powder in coffee – while others were not – lead in Spanish olive oil, opium in beer (Accum, 1820). His tale was a sordid one, demonstrating the value of the new science of chemistry in exposing adulteration and showing how consumers were defrauded and poisoned. The book sold out but Accum was quickly subjected to a hate campaign, with powerful opponents eventually hounding him out of the country (Wilson, 2008). Despite his work, no laws or behaviours changed. An uneasy normality of routine adulteration resumed and it was not until three decades later that the issue returned to the forefront of British politics. A new band of researcher-campaigners in the 1850s repeated work pioneered by Accum (Hassall, 1855). Like him, they named the guilty parties and products but unlike him, they presented their findings under the auspices of the grandly titled Analytical Sanitary Commission, which was in fact themselves. Between 1851 and 1855, Arthur Hassall in the laboratory and Thomas Wakley a surgeon and Member of Parliament who also edited the medical journal *The Lancet* joined by the editor of *The Times* exposed adulteration in 2,500 different products (Paulus, 1974; Wilson, 2008). This scandalized public opinion and was an early example of a campaign both exposing and creating a sense of victimhood. It was also a 'textbook' illustration of a perfectly executed campaign, combining different appeals to victimhood. It produced irrefutable evidence of fraud, identified wrong-doers, generated political debates, used science to show there were threats to health and safety, alerted the public interest, fanned dissent, and made the case for reform. It culminated in the UK's first tough legal framework. Even this, however, did not materialize until the 1890s due to resistance from sections of the food industry (Lang, 2006). Thus, over the period 1820–90 the British public was exposed to a stream of evidence showing that consumers were victims, before they were offered legal protection by the state.

Awareness of consumer vulnerability and victimhood was also an issue across the Atlantic. In 1906, the radical journalist Upton Sinclair published *The Jungle*, a novel in which he depicted the dismal conditions of Chicago abattoirs and meat factories, where even when the occasional worker had fallen into the meat grinders, the machines did not stop and the products were still sold. This led to an immediate outcry in the US national press. President Theodore Roosevelt, sceptical at first, ordered an inquiry, which reported back in secret that the conditions in Chicago were, if anything, worse than Sinclair had chronicled. Within a year, the powerful US Pure Food and Drug Act 1906 was passed. Again, industry interests had initially rejected the allegations, and again, it took public outrage for the regulatory regime to address the source of scandal.

Exposure of the consumer to risks is not peculiar to food. Countless scandals and scares involving drugs, pesticides, tobacco, cars, children's toys, furniture and other products have sensitized us to consumer vulnerability. The thalidomide drug scandal in the 1950s broke after this drug, sold initially as a sedative, was found to curtail pregnant women's morning sickness. But it was subsequently discovered also to cause catastrophic limb malformation in utero. It later transpired that warnings about this drug's ill-effects had been ignored (Knightley et al., 1979). In the 1960s, US campaigner Ralph Nader made his reputation by revealing that the world's biggest car company was knowingly selling cars with a fatal structural flaw that led to loss of life and injuries (Nader, [1965] 1991). More recently, public health researchers have shown that tobacco companies knowingly sold products that were cancer-causing but suppressed this information and even enhanced the nicotine content of their products to make them more addictive (Bates and Rowell, 1998). In short, across the ages and across sectors, consumers have learned that operations in the marketplace engender serious risks.

In an increasingly inter-dependent world, possibilities of consumer victimhood are compounded by numerous additional factors. Well-functioning local markets, where producers meet their customers regularly, can reduce such difficulties. If you meet your butcher and know that he or she sources only from a few local farmers with whom they have a personal business relationship, then there is a close (and short) chain of responsibility. The farmer is unlikely to seek to deceive the butcher and the butcher is unlikely to seek to deceive the customer, if they are to maintain good business relations. Impersonal and highly complex supply chains, on the other hand, make this ideal hard to realize. When a supermarket sources its meat products from hundreds of suppliers and manages sales by various 'offers' or 'best buys', corporate responsibility becomes diffused. Suppliers and purchasers become more opportunistic, often seeking short-term benefit at the expense of a lasting business relationship. This becomes even more pronounced in the case of processed products such as ready-meals which may include ingredients from numerous suppliers across many countries. In 2005, when a batch of Worcester sauce was found to be contaminated by the banned dye Sudan 1, the UK's Food Standards Agency was forced to recall over 350 products, – including ready-meals, pizzas, sauces and sausages from all the main supermarket chains. Internationally, more than 550 products had to be recalled. The source of the contamination was eventually traced to some chilli powder imported from India that directly or indirectly found its way into all these products (Food Standards Agency, 2005a; Food Standards Agency, 2005b). Similarly, during the major European horsemeat scandal of 2013, horsemeat – which is cheaper than beef – was found to have been routinely used as a substitute in a wide range of processed foodstuffs, entirely unknown to the supermarkets and brands which were selling the products (Elliott, 2013). Unlike the chilli powder scandal, the horsemeat scandal exposed systematic consumer fraud, run by criminal gangs.

Highly elaborate supply chains and complex, multi-ingredient products are susceptible to poor information flow that impedes the sound working of markets. Product information today has become so complex that sometimes consumers would need to spend so much time studying labels or reading the small print that any transaction becomes nigh impossible. When hiring a car at an airport, for example, a customer would have to spend a long time reading the full list of terms and conditions (up to 20 pages long) to be able to sign them knowingly. In addition to impersonal markets, complex supply chains and complex products, today's relentless pace of innovation and highly sophisticated technologies make it virtually impossible for most consumers to draw direct comparisons between many products they use. While they can resort to testimonials from other customers and from 'experts', they are more likely to respond emotionally to brand image and advertisements. Is my computer or mobile phone as good as yours? What is the way of establishing that one package is a better deal than another? From this perspective, a considerable amount of new product development and marketing seems designed to create confusion in the mind of consumers, exploiting this confusion in what undoubtedly results in victimhood.

The tricky mix of factors involved in making a product choice is further complicated if a consumer has an environmental concern or wishes to minimize the environmental impact of his or her choices. At present, there are no environmental labels for food, as there are for 'white goods' (refrigerators, electrical goods, etc.) in the European Union. Even more, there are no agreed criteria for the different types of environmental impact – greenhouse gas emissions, recyclability, resource use, impact on biodiversity, etc. Could a label possibly convey all such information? It is unlikely. Under these circumstances, it is little wonder that many consumers give up taking the environment consistently into account when making purchasing decisions, even though they might want to in principle. The well-recognized split between intention and behaviour is reinforced.

Globalization creates still more opportunities for consumer victimhood, as it juxtaposes the individual consumer with ever more powerful corporations by greater market shares, and ever wider-reaching brands. At a time when most markets are dominated by a few corporate giants, dedicating vast budgets to marketing and advertising, the ability of the individual consumer to make sovereign choices is severely compromised. It is against this background then that calls for consumer protection by governments, international bodies and consumer advocates must be heard.

Consumer protection

Consumer protection in Europe can be traced back to mediaeval laws to stand-ardize weights and measures of goods, with different countries creating regulations and laws for products of particular sensitivity. Germany, for example, had its famous *Rheinheitsgebot* covering the purity of beers. In the UK, the world's first industrial nation, the need to protect the individual from the vagaries of the market led to the emergence of the co-operative movement in the middle of the 19th century and to the rise of trades unionism itself – the former to protect individuals as consumers, the latter as workers (see Chapter 9, 'The Consumer as Activist'). A number of prolonged anti-adulteration and health campaigns even-tually prompted the passing of the new Public Health Act 1848 and the Food Adulteration Act 1860, which provided early landmarks of consumer protection, outlined earlier. Prior to incorporation into the European Union's (EU) legisla-tive framework, consumers in the UK were protected when buying goods by the Sale of Goods Act 1979, which was elegant and simple. It stated that goods must be 'of satisfactory quality', that is, free from defects unless the purchasers have been informed about them; be 'fit for the purpose', for example, a washing machine is actually capable of cleaning clothes; and 'as described', that is, if the shirt was advertised or labelled as cotton, it should be just that. The law required goods to be free from even minor defects and of an appearance and finish 'reasonably' to be expected. For services, the law stated that they should be deliv-ered with reasonable care and skill, within a reasonable time and at a reasonable charge, if no price was fixed in advance (Office of Fair Trading, 1994: 4–10).

Other laws added and strengthened this basic provision. However, the key issue was in defining what is or is not reasonable, something over which argu-ments can rage. To enhance consumer protection, a new pan-EU legal framework was subsequently introduced – in the UK as the 1987 Consumer Protection Act – replacing all EU member states' national legislation. This new EU framework now provided a definition of product liability and consumer safety protection, attempting to balance consumer rights with producer liabilities. But producers could avoid liability if they could prove that they had shown *due diligence*, that is had not *knowingly* sold unfit products. If, for example, a defect emerged after the product had been sold and the seller had sold it in good faith, there would be no liability (Department of Trade and Industry, 2005). Thus, companies paid no damages or compensation to people who had purchased contaminated goods in the Worcester sauce and horsemeat scandals we mentioned earlier.

Now, the EU has a whole Directorate-General (that is, a ministry) dedicated to consumer affairs and health – DG SANCO. Announcing an ambitious pro-gramme of work up, DG SANCO claimed that its purpose was to 'protect citizens from risks and threats which are beyond the control of individuals and that can-not be effectively tackled by individual Member States [...] and to increase the ability of citizens to take better decisions about their health and consumer interests' (DG SANCO, 2005: 3). Most consumer protection law is now set at European rather than national level, because numerous products involve ingredients from many countries and are sold across numerous national borders. Likewise, consumer protection work, ranging from product labelling to contracts and compliance, structures and procedures that enable consumers to seek redress and minimise risks, are all carried out at supra-national level, a clear reflection of the increasingly global nature of today's capitalism.

In the USA, the El Dorado of consumerism and the land of the Fordist Deal, consumer protection emerged as an important theme of the political agenda long before globalization or the complexity of products and supply chains exacerbated consumer vulnerability. This came about as a result of a broad alliance of forces, most especially, the US government and consumer organizations themselves. Nadel, the author of an influential study of US consumer protection, argued that the success of legislative pressure depends on how well organized forces are across public interest groups, the Executive and Congress. US consumer protection has its roots in social processes that began after the Civil War and patterns were set then that persist to this day (Nadel, 1971: 5–6). Waves of legislation in the US followed periods of corporate excess when business interests came to dominate all others. As Robert Reich (former US Secretary of Labor) has argued, it came in three waves, 1887–1914, 1927–39 and 1962–78 (Reich, 1981), driven by a 'long-standing and uniquely American suspicion of large, powerful institutions, whether economic or political' and a fear that the little guy can be crushed (Tiemstra, 1992: 3). The first wave of regulation was promoted at the turn of the century by the Progressives, energized as we saw by Upton Sinclair's exposé, the middle phase was identified with Roosevelt's New Deal, and the third was associated with President John F. Kennedy's landmark statement to the US Congress in 1962. In this, Kennedy earmarked four fundamental consumer rights to be safeguarded by the state in order to protect consumers from the power of business:

> the right to accurate and complete information about products at the point of sale; the right to products that are reasonably safe in their ordinary and foreseeable uses; the right to choose among products of different specifications; and the right of consumers to be heard by government regulatory bodies. (Kennedy, 1962, emphasis added)

This third regulatory phase

> grew from a view that there was a need to redress the imbalance in the marketplace between buyer and seller. It [...] was symbolized by the behavior of the nation's largest corporation (General Motors) toward an individual (Ralph Nader) sharply critical of that firm. Conditions were right for the [consumer] movement. The increased complexity of products, the broadening of service channels and depersonalization of shopping, the growth of consumer services (of which consumers have more difficulty in judging quality), the broader availability of the 'material things of life' to those with newly expanded

discretionary buying power; and other factors – all combined to create strong 'consumer demand' for ideas and action that would help the public obtain a better deal in the marketplace. (Bloom and Greyser, 1981: 4)

Business, however, took a very different view of state regulation initiated in response to campaigns by consumer organizations in the 1960s and particularly by Ralph Nader and his new organization (Nader, [1965] 1991) (see Chapter 9, 'The Consumer as Activist'). Business argued that these provisions amounted to an infringement of its liberty to make and sell what it wanted. Fernstrom, a business apologist from the financial sector, scathingly called this transition of US regulatory policy an evolution from *caveat emptor* (buyer beware) to *caveat vendor* (seller beware), and suggested that the evolution went to a point where business leaders felt 'government had totally usurped the consumer's responsibility to think for or protect himself' (Fernstrom, 1984: 1–3). Others like Ross Cranston, author of the classic treatise on UK consumer law (later UK Solicitor General), were equally scathing about reliance on the market, claiming that 'it is difficult to take seriously the argument that the market will further consumer protection' (Cranston, 1984: 399). He argued that consumer protection should not be a rhetorical afterthought, and should be built into fully integrated regulatory frameworks.

What, then, has been the effect of regulation designed to protect the consumer? Nadel's assessment is that real protection occurred when there was a combination of forces, inside and outside the legislature, supported by well-briefed, 'onside' journalists, individualists in Congress, public goodwill and well-researched activists. All too often, however, consumers are too disparate, too individualized; consumer professionals are too small in number; and Congress is more of a follower than an initiator.

In the era of globalization, a fourth phase of consumer protection is emerging, designed to protect consumers from the liberalization of markets and global trade. In this fourth phase, national regulatory regimes are replaced by international agreements which put the onus on companies at different stages of the supply chain to ensure the safety of their products, as well as the accuracy and completeness of the information provided about them. The key concept is traceability. Being able to trace where ingredients and components originate has emerged as a key element of public protection (see studies in Regattieri et al., 2007; Coff et al., 2008). Providing full information about particular products and services becomes enshrined in international regulations and agreements. Although the new legal regime makes traceability the key tool for protecting consumers, the reality can be labyrinthine (Sharpe et al., 2008), and requires global networks of law enforcement, honest companies, good records and sophisticated information technology. In practice, traceability remains at best partial, while labelling and other sources of information have continued to be battlegrounds between companies, governments and consumer groups.

All in all then, how effectively can the law protect consumers? Of course, scams and scandals perpetrated at the expense of consumers have not been eradicated. Scares over health and food continue to grab public attention from time to time. Individual consumers continue to find themselves on the receiving end of unscrupulous operators. Criminals can target consumers through 'phishing' and identity theft. And large corporations continue to find ways of cushioning the impact of international agreements and evading some of the regulatory apparatus aimed at controlling them. All the same, compared to two centuries ago, the recognition of consumer victimhood and ensuing legislation at national and international levels has tempered some of the worst excesses of consumer exploitation.

Far less protection has been accorded to consumers in developing countries, where products deemed dangerous or environmentally unsound in the developed world can be dumped. In addition, products whose advertising and sales have been controlled and circumscribed in affluent countries – such as cigarettes, pesticides and drugs – may continue to be heavily promoted and distributed in developing countries. In such situations, vulnerable national governments are unable to protect their citizens by curtailing the actions of transnational corporations, some of which have turnover many times greater than the GNP of the countries where they trade. The protection of consumers in these countries is closely linked to the protection of their workers and the local residents, as the case of pesticides illustrates. A hazardous product jeopardizes individuals as consumers of unsafe products, as workers handling the pesticide, and as inhabitants of an environment where pesticides are dumped (Bull, 1982; Lang and Clutterbuck, 1991; Jacobs and Dinham, 2003; Taskforce on Systemic Pesticides, 2014). Thus, the ill-effects of pesticide application are disproportionately suffered by rural inhabitants of the South. In 1990, the World Health Organization (WHO) estimated that there were a minimum of 3 million acute cases of pesticide poisoning and 20,000 unintentional deaths a year, mostly in Third World countries (Jeyarraratnam, 1990; United Nations and UNEP, 1990). Fifteen years later, the UN reported some improvement but the situation continued to be bleak in developing countries with 'several thousand fatalities among agricultural workers'. Developing countries use only 25 per cent of the world's pesticides but account for a staggering 99 per cent of pesticide-related deaths (FAO, 2004).

Self help?

If national and international regulatory machinery provide at best partial protection to consumers, can consumers seek to protect themselves and further their interests through co-operation, like the early co-operative movement (see Chapter 9, 'The Consumer as Activist')? What presents insuperable problems to an individual – sifting through large amounts of information or product lists or acquiring the necessary scientific and technical knowledge – can be tackled more effectively if consumers act collectively. This is the rationale for persistent consumer activism: together we can make victimhood less likely and make well-being more likely; de facto, this can transform capitalism (Sklair, 1996). Thus, the Seikatsu Clubs, a successful system of consumer co-operatives in Japan formed in 1965, offers its over 300,000 mainly women members a product range of around 3,000 selected goods, on the basis that if they are the best products and meet consumers' needs, why offer a range of 30,000 as supermarket chains do? Shigeki Maruyama of the Seikatsu Club Union in Tokyo has stated: 'We refuse to handle products if they are detrimental to the health of our members or the health of the environment' (Seikatsu Club, 2005). The Mountain Equipment Co-op (MEC) in Canada is another interesting case. It is a member-owned, retail consumer co-operative, with more than 4 million members worldwide and a turnover of over $250 million in 2012. To purchase from its range of products – in outdoor clothes and pursuits – consumers have to sign up to become, in effect, co-owners by paying Canadian $5 for lifetime membership. This entitles them to vote for the board (MEC, 2014) but, more importantly, to purchase products that have been carefully scrutinized for their environmental qualities, ethical sourcing, sound design and production.

In the internet era, consumer co-operation has discovered a wide range of new forms. Individuals now routinely share their experiences of different products and services by leaving feedback on different sites. Some feedback is controlled by companies themselves – 'tell us what you think' – while other feedback is collected on sites specifically designed to collate such experiences, such as TripAdvisor. In addition, people routinely share experiences, good and bad, on Facebook and other social media, sometimes to the point of taking over a brand. At the time of writing this, a tweet from one of our students dissatisfied with the quality of a hotel's gym facility led to an instant refund and the offer of a free stay once the quality of the gym had been upgraded. In such ways, consumers can come to see themselves as communities of like-minded individuals, indeed, as what are known as 'communities of practice' (Wenger, 1998). By sharing information, they seek to pass their learning onto others with whom they share interests and values. They also seek collectively and publicly to sanction and reward particular providers.

Examples of consumer co-operation appear to be growing, even if they run opposite to the individualistic ethos of contemporary Western consumption. The images of the consumer presented in previous chapters of this book – whether as chooser or as identity-seeker, as communicator or as hedonist – accord the highest value to the rights and choices of the individual. So long as this ethic persists, consumers will continue to be vulnerable and the muscle that they can exercise in the marketplace will be limited. What form consumer self-help takes in the future is uncertain, although technology is likely to open up ever-increasing possibilities. The experience of shared victimhood and risk may see an enhanced sense of consumer solidarity and willingness to share product information. It may also see a growth of full-blooded co-operative models or forms of co-operation 'lite' such as car clubs and equipment pools. Or it may be co-opted by conventional business into yet another profit-generating avenue. Whatever happens, it is unlikely to obviate the need for legislative protection.

Can companies protect consumers?

Consumer advocates would regard the notion that companies might be trusted to protect consumers are almost laughable. Yet consumers themselves have more ambivalent attitudes when confronted by the might and sophistication of vast organizations and their brands. On the one hand, they place a great deal of trust in brands, giving corporations, if anything, the benefit of the doubt, unless major infringements are exposed (Greyser and Diamond, 1983). On the other hand, consumers are sceptical and cautious, willing to embrace various conspiracy theories, where there is a whiff of a corporation abusing its power or covering up its malpractices. Consumer advocates the world over often lament that consumers can be gullible and are fobbed off by excuses and rationalizations offered by the public relations and the image-making machine of corporations, yet consumers do on occasions collectively punish an organization and do so effectively. No case demonstrates this better than the almost overnight collapse of the Ratner brand, after its chief executive was publicized as having jokingly disparaged his cheap products in a large forum:

> We also do cut-glass sherry decanters complete with six glasses on a silver-plated tray that your butler can serve you drinks on, all for £4.95. People say, 'How can you sell this for such a low price?' I say, because it's total crap.[1]

Thus, while consumers may be victims (or naive, or gullible or undiscerning), they are unlikely to take kindly to someone who points this out to them.

And what about companies' own commitment to provide customer service and quality? Do they offer any protection to the consumer? At least since the publication of Peters and Waterman's management 'bible' *In Search of Excellence* (1982), few ideas have held as powerful a grip in management thinking as customer service and quality. Organizations devote billions every year to training their staff, to raising product safety and improving their environmental records, in order to keep the loyalty of their customers and to out-perform their competitors. A single, well-publicized case of a dissatisfied customer, a dangerous sub-standard product or one environmental disaster can be enough to undo the hard work of years of product development and image-making. Oil giant BP (re-branding itself at gigantic expense as 'Beyond Petroleum') found to its dismay that decades of nurturing its environmental credentials were undone in a few days by the Deepwater Horizon oil spill in the Gulf of Mexico in 2010. This disaster illustrates how quickly reputational damage can be done. It also illustrates that consumers and environmental protection cannot be left to the proclaimed good intentions of companies.

Most companies today are acutely aware of the capacity of their customers to feel risk and threat. Of course, companies are concerned to present a smiling face to their customer. Of course, they train their staff to give the impression that the customer is sovereign. Of course, they use the language of customer satisfaction. But for all the outpourings on quality and corporate culture, profit and raising market share remain the overpowering objectives of most companies. Why else are they in business? Necessary as customers are to ensure profits, the need to cut costs and corners, increase prices and reduce service poses a constant threat to consumers.

From risk to generalized hypochondria?

By confronting failures and championing the cause of the consumer, organized consumer groups and media programmes succeed in making visible the imperfections of markets and the resulting victimhood. Thanks to the tireless activity of campaigning consumer organizations, firms have come to accept minimum standards of service, information, quality and responsibility that they would not have conceded otherwise. Without pressures from consumer groups, these would have been seen as unnecessary extra costs undermining competitiveness. Initially regarded as irritating and anti-corporate, many companies now welcome consumer advocates. Some even welcome regulation on both environmental and consumer protection grounds, if only to safeguard their own reputation and to stop less scrupulous competitors from gaining competitive advantage.

Another consequence of the increasing exposure given to consumer scams and scandals has been to raise the profile of the risk that stalks consumers everywhere. Psychologists have long seen risk as inherent in all human decision-making (Lopes, 1987; Tversky, 1990; Breakwell, 2007). Games theorists, cognitive theorists, behaviourists all present a picture of the human brain constantly weighing up advantages and disadvantages among possible courses of action before settling into patterns of learned behaviour. There can be a disparity between the careful calculation of risks carried out by professionals like actuaries, epidemiologists and business analysts, on the one hand, and the risk calculations all humans make in everyday life, on the other hand. For example, well-publicized stories of a nightmare holiday, a mugging and a mishandled medical operation can feed generalized public anxieties, out of proportion to the actual probabilities of such events. Such anxieties are compounded by the sense that we now live in a world where major risks, ecological, health, scientific and financial, are what Giddens calls 'manufactured risks':

> *Manufactured risks are created by the very progression of human development, especially by the progression of science and technology. Manufactured risk refers to new risk environments for which history provides us with very little previous experience. We often don't really know what the risks are, let alone how to calculate them accurately in terms of probability tables. (Giddens, 1999: 4)*

Indeed, the sociologist Ulrich Beck made the case that modern life and modern consumer experience are characterized by constant and virtually unmanageable risks which are the product of modernization itself (Beck, 1992). Inoculating or insuring oneself and one's family against the risk of a nuclear reactor blowing up or an epidemic breaking out become impossible, due to the 'boomerang effect' – in a global world risks affect everyone, including those who create them and those who seek to avoid them. As a result of the daily reality of risk, constantly amplified and magnified by media coverage, modern culture is said to have become increasingly risk-averse. Consumers seek risk-free pleasure. If something goes wrong, someone or something must be to blame. The state is judged by how well it responds to disaster which may come in different forms, financial, ecological, familial and technological (Adam et al., 2000).

Policy-makers have responded to this risky side of modernity, turning to professionals, first, to identify and calculate risks (e.g. Bennett and Calman, 1999), then to identify the costs (in terms of money, mortality and morbidity), and then to manage the risks (Adams, 1995). The dominant public policy model of addressing risk now has three steps: risk assessment, risk management and risk communication, each underpinned by social assumptions (van Zwanenberg and Millstone, 2005). Elaborate systems of surveillance have been created by the state ostensibly to prevent victimhood and assuage public anxiety (Centers for Disease Control and Prevention, 2005), often at the cost of serious erosions of civil liberties and individual privacy. When scandals such as those outlined at the start of this chapter occur, these systems themselves come under scrutiny. Questions are asked about whether the calculations of risk were wrong, whether the risks were hushed up, whether responses were adequate, and what 'lessons' can be learned about their management. A veritable industry of risk analysis and management has thus grown. This industry has grown out of our obsession with risk and catastrophe. But it also feeds our insecurities and anxieties.

How then is it that consumers are so often seeking 'adventure' (see Chapter 4, 'The Consumer as Explorer'), if their sole objective is to minimize risk? What would life be like without risk? Would anyone venture beyond their front door or indeed out of their bed? In consumer studies, whole areas of leisure, outdoors and tourism activities are driven by consumers' desires for risky and even dangerous experiences: bungee jumping, white water rafting, mountain climbing, skiing. The drug-culture thrives on its 'devil-may-care' ethos. Many sports confront those who play them with the possibility of injury or even death. Gambling is a global industry which thrives on the thrills of risk. Consumers may be striving for risk and safety at the same time. All life, say the evolutionary psychologists, is shaped by humans' capacity to engage risk, to experiment and to seek the new. This casts risk-taking as a positive thing. When, however, someone gets hurt while chasing a risky prize, a blame game inevitably follows. Who is to blame? Were the regulations adequate? Were they followed? Was training adequate? Were consumers informed? Or were they reckless, causing their own undoing? (Fineman, 2015).

Risk is an inevitable part of consumer experience arising from many quarters. Perceptions of risk can be at odds with the actual hazards. A lot of the time, consumers avoid risks because of anxiety about potential consequences. These anxieties can sometimes assume the proportion of generalized hypochondria and even moral panic. Nevertheless, risk can be exciting and addictive, an experience which shows we are 'alive'. It can drive consumers to experiment with new and sometimes really dangerous products and experiences. We have argued in this chapter that while victimhood may not define today's consumers, it represents a very major threat that shapes their outlook. Victimhood is never far below the surface of consumer psychology. Like other faces of the consumer we are exploring in this book, the consumer as victim easily mutates into a different consumer face. The consumer as victim is almost the negative image of the consumer as sovereign chooser, a vulnerable and weak creature at the mercy of forces much greater than themselves, but also at the mercy of their own insecurities, vulnerabilities and fears. Yet, this creature may at times seek to turn the tables on the marketplace by becoming a rebel. The face of the consumer as rebel is the focus of the next chapter.

Note

1. www.telegraph.co.uk/news/uknews/1573380/Doing-a-Ratner-and-other-famous-gaffes.html (accessed 4 March 2015).

8

THE CONSUMER AS REBEL

People never rebel just because they have to carry a heavy load or because of exploitation. They don't know life without exploitation, they don't even know that such a life exists. How can they desire what they cannot imagine? The people will rebel only when, in a single movement, someone tries to throw a second burden, a second heavy bag onto their backs. The peasant will fall face down in the mud – and then spring up and grab an ax. He'll grab an ax, my gracious sir, not simply because he can't sustain this new burden – he could carry it – he will rise because he feels that, in throwing the second burden onto his back suddenly and stealthily, you have tried to cheat him, you have treated him like an unthinking animal, you have trampled what remains of his already strangled dignity, taken him for an idiot who doesn't see, feel, or understand. A man doesn't seize an ax in defence of his wallet, but in defence of his dignity. (Kapuscinski, 1983: 97)

CORE ARGUMENTS

People can use different objects and commodities to indicate rejection of the status quo. For a long time, the counterculture sought to demonstrate its opposition to the mainstream by adopting particular styles of consuming and totemic objects, such as music, cars and clothes. It is not surprising, therefore, that opposition to consumerism itself often assumes such forms. Opposition to consumerism can be conscious or unconscious, individual or collective, and it can be driven by rational, emotional or ethical motives. It ranges from unorthodox uses of everyday objects to rebellious acts like joy-riding, and includes ethical consumption, alternative consumption and even what is now known as anti-consumption which advocates consume less, consume differently and consume not at all. Consumerism, for its part, seeks to accommodate and incorporate different forms of resistance turning them into new opportunities to sell. Indeed, it can be argued that many consumer trends start as rebellions against the status quo. We disentangle different types of consumer rebellion, quasi-rebellions and pseudo-rebellions and assess whether they pose any real challenges to consumerism. What are such rebellions against?

Few aspects of the contemporary consumer have exercised as much fascination as that of the rebel, the consumer who uses the objects and images of consumerism to communicate opposition to the status quo and express a wide range of emotions such as anger, disenchantment, outrage, cynicism and disappointment. Equally consumers can and do express disenchantment and opposition by *refusing* to buy and use the goods and services of consumerist society, seeking alternative sources of meaning and pleasure. In resisting or rebelling against consumerism, consumers are not just standing up against consumerist goods and experiences but also against a set of social relations, which they view as exploitative and inhuman.

Both aspects of consumer resistance (oppositional uses of objects and refusal to consume) have posed threats to the architects and missionaries of the Fordist Deal, as outlined in this book. If consumers don't consume 'properly', jobs disappear, growth slows and the economy is threatened with collapse. When the Concorde resumed its flights to New York following the attacks of 9/11, Mayor Rudy Giuliani greeted the elite passengers – including politicians, businessmen and media representatives – inviting them to 'Spend! Spend! Spend!' The duty to consume in order to sustain the economy became a kind of patriotic duty in the face of the enemy (Soper, 2008). A few years later, when the burden of debt and negative equity curbed consumer spending, fears of a deflation that may lead to a downward spiral of shrinking consumption and economic collapse once again fuelled patriotic consumerism – it is the consumer's duty to consume.

In this chapter we explore the image of the consumer as rebel and its implications. It is an image with many layers. Many aspects of contemporary consumption have been seen as rebellions, from eating disorders to shoplifting and from urban graffiti to the movement for voluntary simplicity, the systematic shunning of the fruits of contemporary consumerism (see, for example, Kotler, 1986; Shaw and Newholm, 2002; Cherrier, 2009). In the last ten years, a substantial amount of interest has been generated by the notions of anti-consumption and the anti-consumer. But is it possible for anyone to be anti-consumption? Is life possible without consumption? Is anti-consumption just a fig-leaf for alternative consumption? If so, do alternative consumption practices represent a threat to consumerism?

Taken at face value, the image of the consumer as rebel flies in the face of the age-old wisdom, summed up in the Roman writer Juvenal's dismissive view of the Roman populace:

> They are only seriously bothered about two things – bread and circuses. (Juvenal, [AD 110–30] 1999): x, i, 80)

Consumption, he was arguing, buys peace; he was writing from the point of view of rulers, articulating the view that people will take the short-term pleasures of consumption and put them above 'higher' morals. People can be bought. Against this, there is a counterview – loudly articulated since the 1960s by one strand of Western anti-consumerism – that people can and should resist consumption. Consumption equals incorporation; it ties one to mainstream mass culture.

Thus, if possessing goods from this culture signifies conformity, it is more desirable to identify with other categories of goods which lack the undesirable connotations. A dichotomy of 'good' versus 'bad' goods underpins rebellious consumption – at times, this assumes the proportions of a Manichean split of virtuous and demonic products: bicycle is good, car is evil; vegetarian is good, meat is bad.

This juxtaposition – rejection versus acceptance, good versus bad – engenders rich discussions about the meaning of consumption, particularly the equation of rebellion with youth culture, youth being equated with a rejection of the lifestyles of their parents. In *The Conquest of Cool*, Thomas Frank argued that what starts as resistance can easily and quickly be incorporated into consumerism. In fact, it is the lifestyles of cool and rebellious youth that continuously fuel consumerism:

> *rebel youth culture remains the cultural mode of the corporate moment, used to promote not only specific products but the general idea of life in the cyber-revolution. Commercial fantasies of rebellion, liberation, and outright 'revolution' against the stultifying demands of mass society are commonplace almost to the point of invisibility in advertising, movies, and television programming. (Frank, 1997: 11)*

The view that rebellion can be incorporated into consumer capitalism has been profitably explored by armies of psychologists, not least those working in and for advertising, marketing and product development agencies. These professionals have accepted and even celebrated the notion that consumption can be rebellious, but have sought to tame its impulsiveness and unpredictability. Various goods claim: 'Come buy me; express opposition to [parents/mass society/ school/peer group] by owning me and being seen to use me'. Rebellious consumption is 'cool'. But this message has to steer a delicate dividing line between outright rebellion and partial or quasi-rebellion, conveying some threat but not too much. If what starts as rebellious and cool becomes mass, then its radical chic is lost. The function of marketing therefore is to retain the edge, to keep standardized products looking rebellious. According to this analysis, consumer rebellion is a kind of endless round of identity rebellion, with every cultural invention or rejection quickly picked up and turned mainstream.

In their book, *The Rebel Sell*, Joseph Heath and Andrew Potter reject the view of consumption as rebellion (Heath and Potter, 2005). Far from threatening, modern consumer rebels – from the 1960s hippie US counterculture to the 1990s Canadian Adbusters group, which wittily confronted the advertising industry with anti-ads or 'culture jamming' – have actually reinvigorated consumer capitalism. They are not peripheral but fundamental to consumerism. 'Culture jammers are not the first to try to break the system through consumer revolt. Countercultural rebels have been playing the same game for over forty years, and it obviously doesn't work. The counterculture was, from its very inception, intensely entrepreneurial' (Heath and Potter, 2005: 5). Rebellion, in Heath and Potter's account, is the lifeblood of consumerism. Far from being a threat, resistance is itself consumerist in that it expresses and breeds new ideas, products and ways of being. Far from the counterculture 'selling out', the youth rebelliousness of the 1960s generation actually enabled a new wave of consumption.

> With the hippies, nothing symbolized their rejection of the 'consumerism' of American society more than love beads, Birkenstocks and the VW Beetle. Yet during the '80s, the same generation that had 'tuned in, turned on and dropped out' presided over the most significant resurgence of conspicuous consumption in American history. The hippies became yuppies. [...] The crucial point is that (contrary to rumor) the hippies did not sell out. Hippie ideology and yuppie ideology are one and the same. There simply never was any tension between the countercultural ideas that informed the '60s rebellion and the ideological requirements of the capitalist system. While there is no doubt that a cultural conflict developed between the members of the counterculture and the defenders of the older American Protestant establishment, there never was any tension between the values of the counterculture and the functional requirements of the capitalist economic system. (Heath and Potter, 2005: 5)

Conscious or unconscious resistance?

Before the arrival of postmodernism, a whole generation of social critics in the 1960s and 1970s battled against consumerism, which they blamed for the disappearance of revolutionary ardour among the working classes of Western societies. Consumerism, as the bourgeois ideology of material possessions, was readily absorbed within the Marxist view of alienated consciousness, a consciousness alienated not only in the course of commodity production, but equally by the state, the machinery of mass media and other ideological apparatuses. For Marcuse, consumerism penetrates into the unconscious mental structures, becoming the basis for a 'biological' second nature:

> The so-called consumer society and the politics of corporate capitalism have created a second nature of man which ties him libidinally and aggressively to the commodity form. The need for possessing, consuming, handling, and constantly renewing the gadgets, devices, instruments, engines, offered to and imposed upon the people, for using these wares even at the danger of one's own destruction, has become a 'biological' need ... The second nature of man thus militates against any change that would disrupt and perhaps even abolish this dependence of man on a market ever more densely filled with merchandise – abolish his existence as a consumer consuming himself in buying and selling. The needs generated by this system are thus eminently stabilizing, conservative needs: the counter-revolution anchored in the instinctual structure. (Marcuse, 1969: 11)

That generation of social critics would have found images of the consumer increasingly prevalent since the 1980s highly problematic. For them, consumers were massively manipulated, passive hostages to the capitalist logic of production; mass consumption was frequently seen (as in the quote above) as a smoke-screen, a euphemism for mass production and mass alienation (Williams, 1976).

Since the 1980s, an entirely new set of images of the consumer started to appear; these images grew out of a rejection of earlier critiques of modern consumption and all its paraphernalia, its luxuries and absurdities, its emphasis on style, its seeming unconcern with the origins of the commodities on offer, its obsession with difference and its domination by mass advertising and marketing. In place of the managed, manipulated and duped images of consumers of old, the new images became brighter, more active, more creative. Heroic qualities started to creep into images of consumers as explorers, innovators and artists, images that came to dominate consumer culture theory (see, for example, Firat and Venkatesh, 1995; Firat and Dholakia, 1998; Arnould and Thompson, 2005). No image, however, captures these heroic qualities as vividly as that of the consumer rebel.

Symbols of rebellion

The view that social groups can find and express oppositional meanings in particular activities or objects is hardly new or original. In 2011, London's venerable Victoria and Albert Museum hosted an exhibition, 'Postmodernism – Style and Subversion 1970–1990', celebrating the widespread use of everyday objects as symbols of rebellion. Three years later, the same museum hosted the exhibition 'Disobedient Objects', claiming it to be:

> *the first to examine the powerful role of objects in movements for social change. It demonstrates how political activism drives a wealth of design ingenuity and collective creativity that defy standard definitions of art and design. Disobedient Objects focuses on the period from the late 1970s to now, a time that has brought new technologies and political challenges. On display are arts of rebellion from around the world that illuminate the role of making in grassroots movements for social change: finely woven banners; defaced currency; changing designs for barricades and blockades; political video games; an inflatable general assembly to facilitate consensus decision-making; experimental activist-bicycles; and textiles bearing witness to political murders.*[1]

Particular ways of looking, talking or walking, hairstyles, Camel cigarettes, Harley Davidson motorbikes, bleached jeans, Dr. Martens shoes, can all function as icons of disaffection and defiance. But are such tokens of modern anti-consumption, the adoption of branded commodities by the alienated or the rebellious to convey rejection of the system, really the acts of consumers-in-rebellion? Such groups do not rebel *against* commodities, but use commodities to express protest. According to this view, Dr. Martens, tough looks apart, are not even an instrument of rebellion (like the axe in the hands of Kapuscinski's rebel) but a symbol, which incidentally happens to be a branded commodity. In similar ways, punks used safety pins and razor blades as jewellery, signalling their protest through the use of cheap and unbranded items of everyday life. And Naomi Klein's *No Logo* (2000) and Adbusters' 'Culture-jamming', at first critiques, quickly became brands themselves; in 2004 Adbusters even produced its own brand of running shoes. The transition from opposition to becoming a brand was complete within two decades (Heath and Potter, 2005).

Symbols of disaffection, whether expensive branded items or cheap everyday ones, may be dismissed as tokens of youthful rebelliousness accompanied by submission to the rule of commodities. But on the other hand, is not this argument in danger of implying that the cynicism of the observer(s) is shared by the consumers? Not only disaffected young people, but many if not all consumers in industrialized societies of the North use commodities to rebel against the commoditization of everyday life. What unites the 1970s' use of safety pins as earrings with the 1980s' fashion of wearing torn jeans – the more frayed the better – as symbols of defiance is the discovery of *uses* for objects distinctly different from those assigned to them by manufacturers and merchandisers. This constitutes a rebellion against

> the authority of the producer [which] lies in the capacity to define the meaning of that which is consumed. Producers have more authority to the extent that the meaning or value of an object or service is defined by how the producer understands, interprets, [and] judges it. (Abercrombie, 1994: 51)

According to this view, unorthodox uses of standardized objects are not seen as merely semiotic games (see Chapter 4, 'The Consumer as Explorer'), but as genuine acts of rebellion against the authority of the producer.

This acceptance of the consumer's act of rebellion as real, heartfelt and potentially dangerous is the starting point in Michel de Certeau's *The Practice of Everyday Life* (1984), which seeks to loosen the connection between a commodity and its sign-value, defined by some omnipotent code. It is wrong, argues de Certeau, to equate consumption with the purchase of a particular item, its physical dissipation or the appropriation of its (pre-given) sign-value. Instead he argues that consumers can resist the dominant economic order even as they consume its outputs, its commodities and its images. This is done not by active resistance (such as consumer boycotts, discussed later) or by passively refusing to buy its products and images, but by using them in ways that are foreign or antagonistic to those intended by manufacturers, advertisers and so on. In this way, consumers may challenge the hegemonic order by rejecting the legitimacy of its claims, even if they do not reject its products.

Two interrelated metaphors are central to de Certeau's thinking: anti-colonization and guerrilla warfare. Native Americans resisted the religious, political and legal practices and representations imposed on them by Spanish colonialism, 'not by rejecting them or transforming them (though that occurred as well), but by many different ways of using them in the service of rules, customs or convictions foreign to the colonization which they could not escape' (de Certeau, 1984: 32). Like those native Americans, consumers operate in an occupied territory; like the native Americans, they appear to accept passively what they receive. Yet in practice, they transform it, distort it, undermine it, twist it and laugh at it. De Certeau uses the French anthropologist Claude Lévi-Strauss' idea of *bricolage*, a mixture of creative makeshift, improvization, cunning and guileful ruses, to describe how consumers experiment with latent symbolic properties of commodities and images, fashioning new and unexpected entities out of mass marketed components. This act is both creative and oppositional.

De Certeau criticizes those radical and conservative critics of consumption who regard the consumer as victim or at least passive recipient of standardized, glamorized products:

> *In reality, a rationalized, expansionist, centralist, spectacular and clamorous production is confronted by an entirely different kind of production, called 'consumption' and characterized by its ruses, its fragmentation (the result of the circumstances), its poaching, its clandestine nature, its tireless but quiet activity, in short its quasi-invisibility, since it shows itself not in its own products (where would it place them?) but in an art of using products imposed on it. (de Certeau, 1984: 32)*

In this conception, consumption emerges as guerrilla fighting in an occupied territory. The powerful define and construct 'places' like shopping streets and malls, houses, cars, schools and factories that they seek to control and rule, using strategies and plans. The weak, for their part, are forced to operate in these places, but are constantly seeking to convert them into their own 'spaces', using ruse, guile and deception and relying on suddenness and surprise. To the strategies of the powerful, the weak proffer tactics, operating in isolated actions, forever discovering cracks in the system and opportunities for gain. The joy of consumption, then, comes not from the temporary sating of an addiction or from the fulfilment of greed, but from outwitting a more powerful opponent who has stacked the cards:

> *Innumerable ways of playing and foiling the other's game, that is, the space instituted by others, characterize the subtle, stubborn, resistant activity of groups which, since they lack their own space, have to get along in a network of already established forces and representations. People have to make do with what they have. In these combatants' stratagems, there is a certain art of placing one's blows, a pleasure in getting around the rules of a constraining space. We see tactical and joyful dexterity of the mastery of a technique. Scapin and Figaro are only literary echoes of this art. (de Certeau, 1984: 31)*

Torn jeans

Fiske takes de Certeau's arguments a step further, arguing that 'consumption is a tactical raid on the system' (Fiske, 1989: 35). Consumption is neither passive nor purely individual, but is part of a 'popular culture [which] is made by the people, not by the culture industry. All the culture industries can do is produce a repertoire of texts or cultural resources for the various formations of the people to use or reject in the on-going process of producing their popular culture' (Fiske, 1989: 24). Meanings and pleasures, argues Fiske, are not conjured up by merchandisers of culture, trend-setters and other hirelings of capital; nor do meanings and pleasures reside in the texts themselves, whether they be TV programmes (Fiske, 1987), shopping malls, designer clothes or advertisements. Instead, the meaning and the pleasure emerge from the consumers' active engagement with such texts and frequent attempts to undermine them and subvert them. Fiske does not deny that today's cultural commodities

> bear the forces that we can call centralizing, disciplinary, hegemonic, massifying, commodifying. Opposing these forces, however, are the cultural needs of the people, this shifting matrix of social allegiances that transgress categories of the individual, or class or gender or race or any category that is stable within the social order. These popular forces transform the cultural commodity into a cultural resource, pluralize the meanings and pleasures it offers, evade or resist its disciplinary efforts, fracture its homogeneity and coherence, raid or poach upon its terrain. All popular culture is a process of struggle, of struggle over the meanings of social experience, of one's personhood and its relations to the social order and of the texts and commodities of that order. (Fiske, 1989: 28)

In contrast to de Certeau's consumer-guerrillas who, judging by the examples he provides in the latter parts of his book, seem engaged in rather timid and esoteric practices, Fiske's consumer-guerrillas sneer, jeer and shout. They despoil the landscapes of capital, with graffiti, rubbish and noise; they tear, they break, they steal (or 'shop-lift'). They challenge ceaselessly capital's attempts to define the meanings of things and discover pleasure in destroying the pleasures that capital ostentatiously offers. In this argument, Fiske taps an important tradition within Anglo-American criminology, which through a series of studies of working-class youth culture generated the idea that what mainline sociology defined as deviance amounted to symbolic rebellion (Matza, 1964; Taylor et al., 1973; Robins and Cohen, 1978). A dominant theme of this tradition was that what seemed like hoodlum or nihilism was in fact a statement, at times poorly, at times well articulated, against the values of respectable society, including those of the respectable working class.

Fiske transposes some of these ideas from the area of crime to the area of consumption. His discussion of the 'Jeaning of America' highlights the force of these arguments. Far from lamenting the hegemony of blue-jeans in American campuses as a sign of students willingly putting themselves in mass uniforms, while deluding themselves with images of youthful vigour and glamour (as Marcuse might have done), Fiske sees jeans as a cultural resource on which students set busily to work. Blue-jeans are a text on which students can write and read their own meanings. By disfiguring their jeans in particular ways, that is, by bleaching them, tie-dying them or, especially, tearing them, students can express oppositional meanings to those intended by manufacturers and advertisers. Thus, wearing torn jeans is 'an example of a user not simply consuming a commodity but reworking it, treating it not as a completed object to be accepted passively, but as a cultural resource to be used' (Fiske, 1989: 10). This is no idle fiddling, but 'a refusal of commodification and an assertion of one's right to generate one's own culture' (Fiske, 1989: 15).

Unlike de Certeau's cheerful *bricoleurs*, Fiske's rebels are angry, conscious and self-conscious; their tactics are not limited to semiotic games, jokes and fantasies, but extend into action. In Fiske's view, shoplifting is true guerrilla infiltration into enemy terrain. It affords the thrill and excitement of rebelling against a system in which everything has to be paid for, and, when successfully accomplished, it marks a temporary victory of cunning against the strategies of capital, its electronic eyes and surveillance apparatuses.

> *Shop-lifting is not a guerrilla raid just upon the store owners themselves, but upon the power block in general. The store owners are merely metonyms for their allies in power – parents, teachers, security guards, the legal system, and all agents of social discipline or repression. (Fiske, 1989: 39)*

Fiske's position highlights the on-going struggle over control of popular culture. Over the last 30 years (even as he was writing), jeans have been undergoing their designer make-over. They have moved from being personally adorned to being factory adorned, with tears, designs, logos, bleach and colour effects factored in at source. And the market fragmented, with cheap jeans being sold by discount retailers and own-label supermarkets, alongside others that were astonishingly expensive but superficially nearly identical being sold by upmarket fashion houses (Mintel, 2005). Behind the differences and nuances that could be instantly appraised by the cognoscenti, lies a rapidly changed world of production, now organized on global lines, with global chains of command (Icon Group International Inc., 2002).

So is Fiske's narrative of shoplifting and other raw acts of consumer rebellion to be rejected? We think not. At its most extreme, when there is media coverage of serious calamities such as earthquakes, power-cuts, riots or civil disturbances, it is noticeable how there is often property plunder. In societies marked by extreme poverty and disparities of wealth, social dislocation may be an opportunity. From this perspective, if individual shop-lifters may be seen as free-shooters or guerrilla snipers at consumer capitalism, urban rioters represent mass consumer rebellion, a by-passing of the cash nexus, an occasion to be opportunistic. TV screens conveying images of people plundering electrical stores and supermarkets may be an indication that consumption can, as Fiske proposed, be the focal point of social struggle and rebellion, as it was at the time of the food riots of two centuries ago (Rudé, 1959; Thompson, [1971] 1993).

Tactics of consumer rebellion

For a period in the 1990s, the quintessence of images of consumers as rebels was the joy-rider, who steals a smart car, drives it at tremendous speed, performs outrageous manoeuvres, causes as much havoc along the way as possible, and outsmarts attempts by police to stop him (the joy-rider is rarely 'her'). In some corners of society, such figures were celebrated, becoming quasi-folk heroes among disaffected youth. Joy-riders were as daring as they were unpredictable. They might enjoy the ultimate offering of consumer society, the fast car, without paying for it or being restrained by the responsibilities and burdens that such cars impose on their legitimate owners. Alternatively, they might choose slow, ugly and battered old cars to pit against the police, before wrecking them or torching them. In all cases, they appeared to take over a piece of the road, rebelling against and re-writing its rules and meanings (Parker, 1974; McCarney, 1981). To be sure, their victories may be short lived as are those of most rebels, but they are all the sweeter for it. They also create victims out of other consumers. It is telling that just as joy-rides declined in the 2000s as a result of greatly improved car security systems, the idea of joy-riding was embraced by mass culture spawning several films and popular computer games, demonstrating how consumerism can appropriate and profit from what were initially rebellious practices.

Another archetype of rebellion is the ram-raid, in which a powerful vehicle drives at speed into the window of a shop or any outlet with cash, usually late at night; the raiders empty as much of the contents of the shop into the van as they can and leave, while bystanders idly watch the spectacle or even cheer the ram-raiders. At one ram-raid in genteel Bath in the early 1990s, the bystanders physically stopped a policeman who tried in vain to arrest a group of ram-raiders (Ryle, 1993). This upsurge generated a moral panic for some in that city (local newspaper headline: 'A City Centre Held to Ransom'), whereas for others they became a weekly spectator sport (Pook, 1993). Ram-raiding is a worldwide phenomenon, with ram-raiders seeming to take literally the advertisers' message 'Come and get me', ignoring, as advertisers do, the other part of the bargain, the obligation to pay. Like joy-rides, ram-raids feed property-owning paranoias and are demonized by respectable society, which endlessly seeks to criminalize and control them. Like joy-rides, the number of ram-raids was greatly reduced through improved security measures, including physical obstacles, security guards and cameras. Yet, guerrilla tactics have always relied on tactical shifts, targeting the weakest points of the system; as soon as a particular tactic becomes ineffective a different one emerges.

A rather different type of rebellion against commodities has been identified by Susie Orbach (1978; 1986) and feminist analysts of obesity. For them, not only fat and over-eating, but also anorexia and related eating 'disorders' are forms of protest against consumer society; both over-eating and starving are rejections of the social roles that define women in industrialized societies. If fat is a rebellion against being an object of adornment and pleasure, anorexia is a symbolic rejection of the fruit of consumer society, a refusal of the poisoned chalice. Anorexia, like a hunger strike, is a political gesture, observes Orbach. Like shoplifting, joy-riding and ram-raiding, eating disorders can be interpreted as rebellions against the edicts of consumerism, rebellions that do not always seek to destroy the objects of consumption but to redefine them, reclaim them and re-appropriate them.

One range of tactics of consumer rebellion that has grown in the last 25 years is 'subvertising' or 'culture jamming', that explicitly targets advertising and the media. This was pioneered by the Canadian activist organization Adbusters, founded in 1989, whose agenda and rhetoric are well captured by Kalle Lasn (1999), one of its co-founders:

> *The old political battles that have consumed humankind during most of the twentieth century – black versus white, Left versus Right, male versus female – will fade into the background. The only battle worth fighting and winning, the only one that can set us free, is The People versus The Corporate Cool Machine. We will strike by unswooshing America™ by organizing resistance against the power trust that owns and manages the brand. Like Marlboro and Nike, America™ has splashed its logo everywhere. And now resistance to that brand is about to begin on an unprecedented scale. We will uncool its fashions and celebrities, its icons, signs and spectacles. We will jam its image factory until the day it comes to a sudden shattering halt. And then on the ruins of the old consumer culture, we will build a new one with a noncommercial heart and soul. (Lasn, 1999: xvi)*

Subvertising involves the deliberate and organized addition of disfigurement and re-appropriation of advertisements through graffiti, social hacking or culture jamming. Its purpose is to destroy the appeal of targeted products and images as consumerist icons (ECRA, 1994). The advertising industry is sensitive to accusations of infringing norms of decency, yet it also plays with the boundaries, knowing that to shock is to attract attention; and attention is a key measure of advertising's effectiveness. Subvertising therefore takes the subtlety and starkly confronts the disguised exploitation. The subvertising tactic is to be witty, pithy and daring and to expose hypocrisy and manipulation. Sexism and health have been two key areas of action. At times, it targets a particular product, as did the campaign to disfigure sexist posters advertising the Fiat Panda in the 1980s, or assumes a more generalized assault on advertising culture itself. As we were writing this chapter, what was claimed as 'the largest advertising takeover' took place, with 'guerrilla crews' swapping 365 poster advertisements with works of popular art, in ten UK cities.[2] In spite of the enduring success of subvertising and culture jamming in maintaining a critical commentary against consumerism, it is revealing that their tactics, like so much of consumer rebellion, is appropriated by the mainstream. It is not uncommon, these days, to see political commercials in the US, designed by consultants and advertisers, that seek to discredit or ridicule political opponents by subverting their commercials. Likewise, companies can now seek to turn subvertising to their advantage, as demonstrated by the logo used by supermarket giant Tesco that claims 'You shop, we drop', subverting the anti-consumerist message 'Shop till you drop'.

The ingenuity of critical and oppositional forces in subverting some of the icons of contemporary consumerism is often matched by the latter's enduring ability to incorporate such subversion and, at times, turn it into opportunities for profit. In a paradoxical way, the tactical raids on the system reinforce the rule of commodities and consumerism. They reinforce the power of consumerist signifiers and generate opportunities for companies and brands to innovate and renew themselves (see, for example, Holt, 2002; Cova and Cova, 2012; Rumbo, 2002). No sooner does a product become an icon of opposition than manufacturers seek to capitalize on it, by mass-producing it, often raising its price or discovering a niche for it. The experience of jeans discussed earlier is instructive. As soon as manufacturers discovered that jeans were no longer a uniform icon of youth, independence and freedom, they adapted their products accordingly. Macy's, the large US department store, eagerly started selling jeans that were already shrunk, bleached or torn. In this way, the big retailing outlet affects to become an accomplice to rebel-images of disfigured jeans, thereby compromising them and neutralizing them. To be sure, new marks and new distinctions are produced by consumers, for example, between 'really rugged' jeans and 'mock rugged' jeans. Yet, one suspects that rebellions that end up consumed with such minutiae, only reinforce a system that prospers on diversity and difference. These rebels, whether joyful or angry, may divert themselves and others with their creative *bricolage* and occasional raids on the system. They may be celebrated as triumphant tricksters who poke fun at the system, but ultimately they lack the moral indignation, the single-mindedness and the destructive fury of true rebels. As Holt has starkly put it, they only represent a vanguard revolutionary elite

> insofar as they assist entrepreneurial firms to tear down the old branding paradigm and create opportunities for companies that understand emerging new principles. Revolutionary consumers helped to create the market for Volkswagen and Nike and accelerated the demise of Sears and Oldsmobile. They never threatened the market

itself. What has been termed 'consumer resistance' is actually a form of market-sanctioned cultural experimentation through which the market rejuvenates itself. (Holt, 2002: 89)

A system that can institutionalize rebelliousness by channelling it into unorthodox uses of its staples, blue-jeans, motorbikes or cigarettes, it could be argued, commodifies rebelliousness itself. As steady stream of books from Vance Packard to Heath and Potter have noted, consumer capitalism has an extraordinary capacity to take what first directly threatens it and, after a deep intake of breath, convert it into a marketing opportunity (Packard, [1957] 1981; Heath and Potter, 2005). Instead of destruction and retribution, rebels vent their anger and frustration into commodities, buying them, stealing them, disfiguring them and investing them with meaning. In such ways, they become entrapped in the very mechanism from which they seek to escape.

Rebels with causes: consumer boycotts

Not all forms of consumer rebellion are quite as easily accommodated. If the tearing of jeans leaves the power block largely untroubled, the mere suggestion of consumer boycotts or sabotage of its products can, if not seriously damage a company's stock (except in dire circumstances), at least threaten its reputation and cause executives troubled nights. The term 'vigilante consumer' was coined to describe the activities of those organized or semi-organized consumers who take a serious interest in companies' ethical and environmental standards and lead public opinion against those companies that are found wanting (Dickenson, 1993). Even where consumers can hardly be described as vigilantes, however, there is evidence that an increasing number either use their spending as a form of voting to reward and punish different suppliers or are actively involved in consumer boycotts (Littler, 2005; Shaw et al., 2006; Willis and Schor, 2012). The UK magazine *Ethical Consumer* has tracked consumer boycotts in the UK since the 1990s (*Ethical Consumer*, 2005). These range from boycotts against banks for their involvement in Third World debt to supermarkets for building on green field sites, to cosmetic manufacturers for animal testing, to chemical companies for continuing production of CFC gases. Entire countries have been singled out for boycotts – Botswana for forcing bushmen out of national parks, Barbados for the export of monkeys for animal experimentation, Israel for 'decades of refusing to abide by UN resolutions', Norway for its commercial whaling, Taiwan for continuing to import rhino horn. The list on the website is long, but, given the existence of such boycotts in many free societies, it is reasonable to ask about their effectiveness and impact.[3]

Many of these boycotts attract limited media attention, although they may be significant enough to affect corporate policies (*Ethical Consumer*, 2005; Harrison et al., 2005). The threat of possible damage – to sales, reputation, staff morale, brand image – may be enough to generate change. Thus, Neutrogena, manufacturers of the Norwegian Formula hand cream, moved its production to France and declared that it was 'adamantly opposed to whaling' as a result of the anti-whaling campaign. All major supermarket chains in Britain either stopped buying Faroese fish or declared its origin on the label, in response to a campaign to protect the pilot whale. The cosmetics manufacturer, L'Oréal, succeeded in having a consumer boycott of its products lifted, by signing an agreement with PETA, a US animal rights organization, to stop animal testing on its products.

Against such success stories for consumer boycotts, it could be argued that there are too many boycott calls and that collectively they are often too parochial ('single issue') or too restricted to the fringes of consumption to have a serious effect. The majority of consumers, overloaded by moral causes and saturated by information, signs and messages, ends up resigned, confused, impotent or unprepared to bother. The latest boycott, if it does gain attention, quickly fuses with numerous other messages and images, and may vanish as meaningless noise rather than as a lasting call to action. Yet neither companies nor the masses of consumers can ignore the critical commentary on commodities sustained by continuing, mutating and merging consumer boycotts. Baudrillard's flying signifiers (1988) do not merely migrate from commodity to commodity as objects of desire, but also as objects of rejection and avoidance. So it does not matter so much what countries, companies or commodities are objects of current boycotts, as that a succession of boycotts constantly mobilizes consumers to remind manufacturers, merchandisers and retailers that they have moral and environmental responsibilities. The boycott tactic invites consumers to act in their individual capacity to a broader social end. Their effectiveness depends crucially on how well organized they are and how much media coverage they generate, issues that we shall examine in detail in Chapter 9, 'The Consumer as Activist'. Consumer activism seeks to organize consumer dissatisfaction, disappointment and indignation, converting them into political resources and pressure for change.

'Alternative' consumption: pop festivals

If consumer boycotts and vigilante consumers express a concern for the environment and ethics, they hardly undermine the deeper foundation of consumerism, that a good life is synonymous to rising living standards, better and bigger consumption. Alternative forms of consumption represent a different type of rebellion, one that repudiates the products and services of big capital, not because they happen to be ethically questionable and environmentally damaging, but because they are products and practices of a system that is ethically moribund and environmentally calamitous. Such rebellions are not expressed in unorthodox uses of products (although this may be part of it) nor in the rejection of targeted products as in boycotts. These rebellions reject Western-style consumption and seek to supplant it with a radically different type of consumption, which encompasses a number of principles:

- Consume less.
- Consume local products.
- Avoid products produced and merchandised by big capital.
- Avoid cash and use alternative modes of economic transactions.

The last two of these principles are graphically portrayed by Hetherington (1992) in his description of the Stonehenge pop festivals and New Age travellers, who have sought to recreate in the 1990s something of the ethos of the 1960s hippies. Hetherington provides vivid descriptions of consumer rebels who take over the places of the powerful and at least temporarily make them their own. What could be more symbolic than taking over Stonehenge, the archetypal heritage site turned consumerist theme park, and reducing it to a no-go area for respectable visitors, police and big capital. In this way, it becomes a shrine of alternative consumption, waste and excess. Noisy, extravagant, unrestrained – pop festivals represent one challenge to the strategies of modern consumerism. They too, however, can be compromised and hijacked by the cash nexus, as was illustrated when the recreation of the Woodstock free festival in 1994, 25 years after the original, turned into an all-ticket consumerist orgy. The Glastonbury festival in the UK set out from its inception in 1970 to raise money for good causes. It combined 'alternative' consumption with the mainstream. The initial charge for the first festival was £1; it was attended by 1,500 people. By 2005, the ticket cost £125 plus £4 booking fee and £4 for postage and packing; 112,000 people attended.[4]

The American Burning Man festival that takes place annually in Nevada prompted Robert Kozinets (2002) to ask whether it is possible for consumers to escape the market in alternative institutions that offer emancipatory opportunities and a different consumer logic from the one that dominates contemporary consumerism. Through an ethnographic study of the festival that takes place over a week and culminates in the burning of a wooden effigy, Kozinets observed numerous alternative exchange practices emphasizing gift exchanges and consumer practices as self-expressive art. He also noted the prevalence of a discourse supporting caring and communality while disparaging market logics and commercialization. Kozinets argues persuasively that the festival is neither a potentially revolutionary event, but nor is it a consumerist manifestation by another name. It is a temporary oasis for those who participate (many of whom are well-heeled city professionals) and an opportunity to explore different modes of selfhood and identity.

> *Burning Man is not about major social change, but minor changes in identity, taking place collectively and simultaneously. It is not a grand Utopia, but a more personally enriching youtopia – a good place for me to be myself, and you to be yourself, together. Rather than providing a resolution to the many extant social tensions in contemporary life – such as those surrounding the beneficial and oppressive elements of markets – it offers a conceptual space set apart within which to temporarily consider, to play with and within those contradictions. It falls short of some ideal and uncontaminated state, but it may be all the consumer emancipation most consumers want or need. (Kozinets, 2002: 36)*

In many respects, today's festivals represent revivals of the old spirit of carnival, when conventional norms and laws are suspended and replaced by free, familiar contact among people that defies social hierarchies and civilized conventions. As Bakhtin, famous student of the carnival, argued:

> *Carnival is not contemplative, it is, strictly speaking, not even played out; its participants live in it, they live according to its laws, as long as those laws are in force, i.e. they live a carnivalistic life. The carnivalistic life is drawn out of its usual rut, it is to a degree 'life turned inside out', 'life the wrong way round'. (Bakhtin, [1929] 1973: 100–101)*

Bakhtin saw the Renaissance as marking the 'zenith of carnivalistic life'; thereafter, the carnival declines, restricted mostly to literary expressions, notably Dostoevsky's polyphonic novel. Arguably, then, today's festivals as spaces and times of excess are not set against the demands of scarcity, oppressive social hierarchies and religious admonitions for restraint. Instead, they are set against the cornucopian ideal of today's consumerism where pleasure and excess can be enjoyed at any time and any place. In this regard, then, one is inclined to agree with Kozinets's assessment that 'much of what goes on at Burning Man is cathartic, a ritual of release or rebellion … that ultimately props up the market system by reinforcing it with labor and purchases' (Kozinets, 2002: 36).

LETS

Currency has long represented one of the rebels' traditional targets. It is not accidental that Cynics, antiquity's early anarcho-rebels, sought to deface and adulterate their cities' coinage, something that led to the expulsion of the famous Diogenes from his native Sinope. In our times, alternative currencies and media of exchange have been a platform for challenging the hegemony of consumerism. One such is the LETS, or Local Exchange Trading System. This is a form of cashless local system of exchange in which people trade with each other on a bartering basis. LETS provides a network of members, often computerized, who offer their services and goods in exchange for units of a notional currency. This notional currency is not convertible to cash, but can be used to buy goods and services from other LETS members. The services range widely from gardening and baby-sitting to legal advice and car maintenance, from music lessons to accountancy, and from leasing of equipment (computers, lawnmowers, washing machines) to architectural design. The first LETS experiments took place in a cash-starved area of British Columbia in 1982; since then the system has spread into the USA, New Zealand, Australia and elsewhere. In the UK, by 1996, there were over 40,000 people involved in schemes in 450 local currency systems (LETSlink UK, 2005). The membership of individual LETS may vary from about ten (the number required to set up a new system) to 500 and interest in the scheme has increased partly as a response to structural unemployment.

LETS is not merely a trading system at the margins of mainstream economy, devoid of ideology or a sense of mission. On the contrary, many of LETS' members regard it as a way of strengthening community links undermined by the cash nexus, and of regenerating local economies without relying on conventional capital. LETSlink declares:

> Capital flight deprives an area of a means to trade within itself. Many low-income areas, however, still possess skills, human energy and potential, and all kinds of material resources. All the components of real wealth are there, locked away, alongside a myriad of unmet needs. All that is missing, essentially, is a medium of exchange. We simply need a communications system, linking supply and demand. (LETSlink UK, 1994)

LETS enables those with limited cash resources to become involved actively in their local economies and communities. Everyone, including the poorest person, has something to offer; everyone, including the richest, has a need to be met. Many of those who joined LETS report that they joined for ideological reasons, but they discover that it makes good economic sense, especially in a period of recession when the number of transactions increases considerably, if they accept payment in the local LETS currency. Some local traders, like grocers, opticians or clothing stores, have opted to accept part of the payment in cash and part in local currency and have reported much increased trade.

One issue that divides LETS schemes is whether their members should all charge the same basic unit for their time or whether they should be allowed to charge depending on the demand for their products and services. Some local economies uphold two LETS schemes, one in each category. Predictably, this has a divisive effect, since higher-status occupations tend to favour the differential system, while lower-status occupations favour the uniform rate. At the moment, it is not clear which system will predominate or whether the two can co-exist side by side. In any case, LETS systems have provided a radical alternative to conventional consumption, in several different ways. First, they focus on unbranded, unadvertised and unmediated goods and services (advertising is limited to internal bulletins). They re-affirm the value of hand-made, home-made products and regenerate arts and crafts, ranging from organic farming to woodland management, cheese-making, spinning and weaving, which are swept aside by big capital. Second, they bring together the person as a producer and seller of goods and services with the person as buyer and consumer. In this way, they replace an impersonal cash-nexus with a visible, personal relationship between consumer and producer. Third, they enable individuals and groups whose lack of cash would exclude them both from the local economy and from involvement in the community. Fourth, they bring together people of different social classes in relations of mutuality that cross social boundaries and encourage accountability and responsibility. Fifth, they keep capital local. Finally, they find a legitimate way of generating economic activity that evades taxation and by-passes the legislative and other apparatuses of the state.

The ultimate consumer rebel: 'consume less'?

In all the ways described above, LETS schemes represent an organized alternative to mainstream consumption, challenging its ethos and breaking some of its taboos. It is a mild rebellion, a well-tempered rebellion. It even goes as far as to challenge the ultimate taboo against which few dare to express themselves – the equation of better life with more consumption. The ascetic line, once such a prominent element of the Protestant work ethic and later a central value of hippie lifestyles, seems to have disappeared from the public discourses of the mass media and mainstream political debate. TV, press, magazines, dependent as they are on advertising revenue, have warmly espoused the concerns of activist-consumers or even ethical consumers, but they shy away from any direct assault on the premise of consumerism. It is only in the last 30 years that some progressive environmental and ethical consumer groups have started to discuss seriously a frontal assault on the religion of 'Shop 'til you drop, spend 'til the end, buy 'til you die'. In the words of Ignacio Peon Escalante, a Mexican consumer/citizen activist:

> *Our vision is that we should live a more austere life, but also a better quality life; less quantity and more quality. Mexicans believe that if they want to be modern, they must imitate the Americans, aspire to their living standards. They confuse development with materialism, they think that being 'modern' means having instead of being. Consumerism is an absurd form of materialism; this is true of the Third World as well as of the First World. (Interview with the authors for first edition, 1994)*

'Consume less' is the focal point of these discussions – is it a recipe for political suicide, as the British Greens discovered when they seriously raised the issue as part of their electoral campaign in 1992, or is it a brave slogan today that will emerge as the commonsense of the future?

'Consume less' may become the final frontier of the consumer rebel, the consumer who does not merely seek living space within the present system or use the products of the system to express disaffection and protest, but decides that 'enough is enough'; anything less than a frontal assault on the core assumption of consumerism is inadequate. Such an assault would, of course, transcend the limits of rebellion and would amount to a major moral and political challenge to capitalist hegemony. As Sklair has eloquently argued, capitalism throughout the world has become so dependent on consumerism for its legitimation and reproduction that any threat to the equation of 'more' with 'better' would be deeply subversive:

> *The control of ideas in the interests of consumerism is almost total. The ideas that are antagonistic to the global capitalist project can be reduced to one central counter-hegemonic idea, the rejection of the culture-ideology of consumerism itself. Without consumerism, the rationale for continuous capitalist accumulation dissolves. It is the capacity to commodify all ideas and material products in which they adhere, television images, advertisements, newsprint, books, tapes, films and so on, not the ideas themselves, that capitalism strives to appropriate. (Sklair, 1991: 82)*

Calls to consume less are all too frequently ridiculed, especially if those who make them can be seen sporting anything more ostentatious than sackcloth and ashes (Lansley, 1994; Sklair, 2002). Yet the earth's finite resources and its finite tolerance for abuse and neglect are no longer what Lasch (1991) called the 'forbidden topic'. The notion of 'prosperity without growth' has now entered public debate, even if few politicians or policy-makers will be seen publicly contemplating it (Jackson, 2009). As long as individuals, organizations or even entire nations seek to maintain ever growing consumption standards, they have limited moral authority to pontificate to others on the need to respect the environment and to preserve the earth's natural resources (Korten, 2001; Stiglitz, 2002).

Yet, since the first edition of this book was published, practices and discourses opposing consumerism have gathered pace. While unable or unwilling to mount a frontal attack on the citadel of consumerism, they have set up camp outside it. Whether calling themselves voluntary simplifiers (Etzioni, 1998b; Cherrier, 2009; Shaw and Moraes, 2009), downshifters (Schor, 1998; Hamilton, 2003; Hamilton and Mail, 2003), culture-jammers (Rumbo, 2002; Littler, 2005; Cherrier, 2009), conscious consumers (Atkinson, 2012; Gotlieb and Wells, 2012; Shah et al., 2012; Willis and Schor, 2012), anti-consumerists (Soper, 2008; Black and Cherrier, 2010), or nothing at all, whether motivated by active aversion to the fruits of consumerism or by passive lack of interest and boredom (Wilk, 1997; Saren, 2012), these are people who consume (don't we all?) but refuse to be defined by their consumption (Nixon, 2013). Consumerism comes up with ever cleverer ways of enticing them into its citadel, but they stubbornly seem to persist in seeing themselves as anti-consumerist, even if they do not unite under a single banner, even if at times they succumb and enter the citadel. They, for their part, are quite successful at drawing some of those who had previously firmly inhabited the citadel out of it to explore what life outside can be like. The citadel itself maintains its size and clout, even if its omnipotence and legitimacy can no longer be taken for granted.

Beyond rebellion

Images of consumers as rebels that started to emerge in the 1980s grew out of a rejection of images of consumers as passive objects of manipulation, as victims. Yet these are precisely the images that have fuelled not only the anger, but also the tireless activity of self-confessed consumer advocates over the last two centuries (see Chapter 9, 'The Consumer as Activist'). In this chapter, two different forms of rebellion have emerged. On the one hand, we examined the rebellion of those consumers who challenge the authority of producers, not by completely rejecting their wares, but by rejecting, first, the meanings assigned to them, second, the methods of acquiring them, third, the methods of using them, fourth, the methods and costs, cultural and environmental, of their production. On the other hand, we looked at the rebellion of those who question consumerism, its products, its meanings, its suppliers and its glamorizers, who are beginning to map out a radical new vision:

> We are reaching the end of the line in terms of that kind of existence, materialism and consumerism. People have not enough time in their lives to live. They work for long hours for less pay. How do we move beyond consumerism and materialism? It is not enough to preach and critique. The only way away from materialism and consumerism is an alternative economic and social framework with which people can identify. People will have less time at work and more on alternative things. What do you do the rest of the time? You can spend it sitting in front of a TV and get packaged entertainment and remain a bloated consumer society, or there is a possibility that we can entice each other to become part of what I call the intimate society. This is a volunteer economy, in which there is no market coercive relationships which transform people into things, but on service and gift giving. The bottom line is that the more people identify themselves with a serving capacity or a stewardship capacity, the less they define themselves by the material things. I know that people who volunteer for work have less and less time for their possessions and are less possessed by their possessions. They are serving, they are giving, they are participating in a real way. Having said that I realize that you cannot have true participatory democracy in a market economy. Worker-run companies have

absolutely no way of invigorating principles of democracy based on volunteer work, so long as they have to survive in a market economy. (Jeremy Rifkin, in an interview with the authors, 1994)

The future of consumption, according to this vision, lies neither in rebellion, nor in activism limited to the area of consumption. The consumer must act beyond his or her interests as consumer, in short he or she must once again act as a citizen, taking responsibility for the future (See Chapter 10, 'The Consumer as Citizen').

In conclusion

Images of the consumer as rebel tend to be nervous and fragile, easily mutating into each other or into other images of the consumer such as activist and citizen. What most share is a disenchantment with contemporary consumerism and an ability to imagine and sometimes to enact an alternative. In the interest of clarity and at the risk of becoming somewhat formulaic, Table 8.1 identifies some of the core aspects of each strand of the consumer as rebel and indicates some of the ways into which it morphs into other images.

How convincing are images of consumers as rebels? As a corrective to images of consumers as infinitely malleable, seducible and manageable, the phenomena studied in this chapter are of considerable importance. De Certeau, Fiske, Abercrombie, Hermann and others have drawn attention to the unexpected, creative and unmanageable aspects of modern consumption. Their contributions parallel arguments concerning the resistance of workers to management's strategies of control. Just as organizations may contain unmanaged terrains in which individuals evade management controls through play, jokes, stories and fantasies (Gabriel, 1995), contemporary consumption entails wide, unmanaged dimensions, vividly portrayed by these writers. These unmanaged dimensions lie not so much in the rejection of consumer products, let alone in the rejection of consumption itself, but in unorthodox appropriation and uses of these products, especially in ways that express protest.

Finding heroic qualities in these activities seems more problematic. Teenagers enjoying fast rides in stolen cars may be romantically envisioned as rebels against a system that denies each man his own fast car. Anorexic women can be seen as hunger strikers, heroic in their defiance and self-sacrifice. Shop-lifters may be conjured as tricksters scoring victories at the expense of omnipresent electronic eyes. Young people piercing or tattooing their skins or (more temperately) disfiguring their blue-jeans may be seen as revolting against the values of respectable society. Yet, such constructions may reveal more about the enduring power of consumerism than challenge to it. Consumer rebellions like these often draw people back into the world of commodities where they can be compromised,

Table 8.1 The Consumer as rebel – different images

Image	Practices	Response to consumerism	Emotions and/or rationality	Morphs into/ close to …	Some key authors
Cool consumer and dandy	Choosing 'cool brands', unorthodox use of objects	Aesthetic rejection of mass consumerism	Boredom, disdain, superiority	Hedonist, identity-seeker	Fiske, 1987; 1989; Frank, 1997; Pountain and Robins, 2000; Holt, 2002
Youthful rebel 'without' a cause	Joy-rides, ram-raids, eating disorders	Symbolic rejection of consumerism and challenging of 'civilized' morality	Anger, anxiety, despair, nihilism, rage	Identity-seeker, victim	de Certeau, 1984; Fiske, 1987; 1989; Holt, 2002; Heath and Potter, 2005
Rioter	Looting, stealing, mass shoplifting	Property as theft, 'getting own back', redistribution and restoring natural justice	Exhilaration, self-righteousness, rage	Explorer, hedonist	Rudé, 1959; Moxon, 2011; Treadwell et al., 2013
Politically conscious consumers	Buying as voting, boycotts and buycotts, anti-particular brands (but not necessarily anti-brand), buying local	Ecological and civic responsibility	Seeking information and acting responsibly, discovering alternative types of pleasure	Chooser, citizen, activist	Holt, 2002; Shaw et al., 2006; Johnston, 2008; Soper, 2008; Barda and Sardianou, 2010; Atkinson, 2012; Carr et al., 2012; Gotlieb and Wells, 2012; Willis and Schor, 2012
Temporary rebel	Visiting festivals and engaging in 'alternative consumption' as carnivalesque interludes or breaks	Escapist, need for a break, alternative hedonism, seeking alternative consumerisms (gifts, aesthetic, non-market exchange)	Escape from boredom and disenchantment through discovery of alternative consumption oases	Chooser, explorer, victim	Hetherington, 1992; Kozinets, 2002; Soper, 2008
Ethical consumer	Local currencies, downshifting, voluntary simplicity, boycotts and buycotts, buying local	Environmentalism, anti-capitalist, moral rejection of consumerism	Acting responsibly, offering symbolic or material acts of resistance, fundamental lifestyle change	Activist, citizen, zealot	Etzioni, 1998b; Schor, 1998; Korthals, 2004; Harrison et al., 2005; Shaw and Newholm, 2002; Cherrier, 2009; Barnett et al., 2010; Schor, 2010; Willis and Schor, 2012;
Disenchanted and alienated consumers or anti-consumers	Stop buying ever wider ranges of products, anti-brand, make own, rediscover craft, prosumption	Self-sufficiency, asceticism, naturalism, nomadism	Withdrawal from consumerism, rediscovering balance and harmony, ranges from 'disgusted' to 'uninterested'	Citizen, activist	Wilk, 1997; Klein, 2000; Holt, 2012; Nixon, 2013

appropriated and commodified. Far from rejecting consumerism, one can become a rebel (and appropriate the heroic qualities of this image) simply by engaging in the appropriate type of consumption. Why pick up an axe (like Kapuscinski's rebel) when you can be a rebel merely by tearing up your blue-jeans or having a stud passed through your nose? Camus was one of the first to signal that rebellion can quickly degenerate into style, the rebel turning into a dandy or an aesthete:

> Romanticism demonstrates, in fact, that rebellion is part and parcel of dandyism: one of its objectives is outward appearances ... Dandyism inaugurates an aesthetic which is still valid in our world, an aesthetic of solitary creators, who are obstinate rivals of a God they condemn. (Camus, 1971: 49)

Camus castigated the sterility of this attitude, which accommodates, eviscerates and commodifies rebellion. By comparison to aesthetic rebels who denounce the god of consumerism without denying him, the rebels who preach alternative consumption, organize consumer boycotts, set up a local LETS or opt privately and quietly to consume less are far less romantic figures. Yet, it is these largely invisible rebels who may in the long run provide the greater, if not the only, challenge to consumerism. By saying 'No' or 'Less' or 'Do it differently', they may force a questioning of the core assumptions of consumerism and open up a range of choices that are currently if not silent, at least easily stifled by the din of commodities.

Notes

1. www.vam.ac.uk/content/exhibitions/disobedient-objects/disobedient-objects-about-the-exhibition/ (accessed 4 March 2015).
2. www.buzzfeed.com/brandalism/the-largest-advertising-takeover-in-world-history-px5q (accessed 4 March 2015).
3. www.ethicalconsumer.org/boycotts/boycottslist.aspx (accessed 9 March 2015).
4. www.efestivals.co.uk/festivals/glastonbury/2005/tickets.html (accessed 4 March 2015).

9

THE CONSUMER AS ACTIVIST

Consumption and leisure are not substitutes for power. (Lester Thurow, 1993: 121)

CORE ARGUMENTS

There is a long tradition of consumer activism in many different countries. The Irish gave the name to the boycott in the late 19th century, but the Americans had practiced it much earlier against the British when pressing for independence in the 18th century, as indeed did the Indians under Gandhi in the 20th. Throughout its history, consumer activism has assumed many different formats: campaigns, legal cases, education, individual and collective acts, whistle-blowing and other forms of direct action. We identify four waves of consumer activism, each with its own characteristics: the co-operative movement, which argued that consumers must take control of production; the value-for-money movement, which argued for scientific testing of products to provide comparative information on best value; Naderism, which proposed that consumer activists must fight against corporate greed; and a new wave of alternative or political activism, which is still developing but seeks to completely restructure and redefine consumption on ethical and socio-environmental grounds. While there are tensions between these waves of activism, elements of all four waves can be found to co-exist in many of today's initiatives.

In this chapter we reflect and build on the analysis of what in the first edition we called the active consumer: those people and movements setting out to promote the rights, consciousness and interests either of all or of particular groups of consumers. In the first edition of this book, we offered a historical and sociological analysis of consumer movements as 'active consumerism'. We depicted this as emerging in four waves. We posited that each wave proposed not only new forms of organizing, but different ways of looking at consumption. All of these waves have left traces that are still alive and effective in the world of consumer organizations today throughout the world. This chapter outlines those four waves of consumer activism and asks what, if anything, has changed since we first outlined our theory. We conclude that some interesting realignments are underway within and across the 'waves' of consumer activism, suggesting considerable dynamism and inventiveness.

Consumer activists have acquired a high profile in most affluent societies since the middle of the 20th century – appearing on the media, writing reports, appealing for support, giving governments, companies or products a hard time. The scope of their demands is extensive, ranging from calls for better goods and services, to bans or restrictions on existing ones, to new ways of producing, delivering and selling. Responding to consumer protests and demands has had to be factored into corporate strategy. Gone are the days when suppliers had to deal with advocates only in time of crisis – a faulty good or a mistake. Today, being aware of and anticipating consumer complaints almost before the activists have articulated them is routine corporate behaviour. Of course, public relations in the pejorative sense of 'spin' and playing with appearances is an important corporate defence, but even there the rhetoric can belie significant change. Companies do not merely seek to respond to or even anticipate criticism from active consumers; they also want to be *seen* to be doing so. This tussle between companies, the state as regulator and overseer of commerce and active consumerists is old. Happily, since we wrote the first edition, there have been several good, new studies that followed our call both to study and to engage with active consumerists (see, for example, Maclachlan, 2002; Caraher, 2003; Kozinets and Handelman, 2004; Harrison et al., 2005; Glickman, 2009; Hilton, 2009).

When consumer activists meet socially or in consumer congresses, there is no shortage of reflection or analysis. This is due in part to the high motivation of people attracted to work for such organizations. It is also due to the nature of the work; arguing a case for consumers requires constant attention to detail, the plans of the 'opposition', the forming of alliances and the shaping of strategies. It is also a reflection of the values to which activists subscribe. They are committed to making things better for others, for not just some but all consumers. Back in 1995, we judged that the consumer movement tended to do its most searing analysis in private, thereby leaving the theoretical terrain to academics. And we were underwhelmed by what we read. How different the situation is two decades later! There has been a rush of interest in studying and debating the shape and role of consumer activism and numerous academics have come out and engaged in some serious analysis of, with and for consumer groups.

This growth of interest is not unrelated to the growth of 'single issue' activism, replacing more conventional party politics. But it is also a reflection, perhaps, of a shift within the social sciences, which two decades or so ago were dominated by idealist debates associated with postmodernism (Trentmann, 2005). In the 1980s and early 1990s, academic approaches were dominated by cultural relativists looking at meanings, cultures and signs of markets rather than their material realities, overt power relations and 'brute facts'. This created an ideological and language divide with the more engaged activists who just sought to 'get on with it'. This is no longer so. New studies, happily, have broken down this schism. In the UK, for instance, around a half of the 25 projects funded by the £5 million 2002–7 'Cultures of Consumption' programme of the Economic and Social Research Council addressed consumerism in one way or other. In particular, as we prophesied, there has been increased interest in the harder end of consumer activism, on people who push against market realities and seek to redesign how markets operate (Hertz, 2001; Kozinets and Handelman, 2004). And here, as we will see later, what were fringe consumer actions have become more mainstream. Notions of fair trade, global justice or animal rights were deemed very marginal concerns indeed in the mid-1990s. They have now become accepted as part of the mainstream agenda.

Active consumers and campaigners

Boycotts have long had a seminal role in consumer activism because they symbolize a rejection of the damaging aspects of consumption and represent the consumer-activists' act of defiance. They have 'bite', not just heart. Named after Captain Boycott, an Irish land agent against whom landless Irish peasants organized in 1880, the tactic now known as boycotts dates from earlier. Solidarity action against particular products were known before, as Witkowski's study of the American non-importation movement in the late 18th-century shows (Witkowski, 1989). In the 20th century, Gandhi's *ahimsa* or non-violent direct action included the organization of consumer boycotts of British cloth and salt. Boycotts range from local to global in their scope and vary enormously in the degree to which they are organized. Craig Smith has argued that their effectiveness depends on their visibility and that business seeks to get round this, as when Argentinian corned beef was (reputedly) repackaged and labelled as Brazilian to sell it in the UK during the 1982 Falklands–Malvinas War (Smith, 1990). Smith also argued that consumer boycotts against food products tend to be more effective because food is a perishable good and consumed daily. Yet, the longest food boycott – against Nestlé for its sales of breastfeeding substitutes (Allain, 1991) – has been well organized, has won consciousness and, on occasions, has dented sales, but still has not achieved its goals. Studies on the effectiveness of consumer boycotts are inconclusive. Boycotts should neither be dismissed nor their effects glorified (Friedman, 1985; White and Kare, 1990; Friedman, 1999; Willis and Schor, 2012). Some boycotts, for example, led to the withdrawal of major banks from operating in apartheid South Africa while others have failed to shift the sale of powdered milk to developing countries in the long term. What all studies suggest is that successful boycotts have the capacity to affect a company's reputation, even if not its policies. In that sense, the Nestlé boycott has tarnished the brand if not its huge power.

Debating the direction of consumer activism is not new; nor is the attempt to organize disparate individual acts of consumption by appealing to higher moral or political ends. Consumerism has always been enlightened by active attempts to redirect consumer behaviour. A commitment to inject ethical and political values into a discourse dominated by the economics of free trade is not new. Most anti-colonial struggles appealed to external as well as internal populations not to consume products being made, owned or controlled by the oppressor. With the ending of colonialism in the mid-20th century, boycotts gradually shifted from political aims to more directly economic ones, becoming more of a refinement tool within marketplaces, to improve products, choice and information. The world's largest consumer organization, the US Consumers Union (CU), was itself born out of a long and bitter struggle in the 1930s within Consumer Research Inc., another consumer organization that the CU eventually superseded. The fight was partly an internal factional disagreement but partly ideological over whether consumer interests were aligned to the interests of the organized labour movement, and over whom consumers should ally with and how they should organize (Hermann, 1982). Are consumer organizations really no more than trades unions for consumers? Or are they 'soft' organizations smoothing inefficiencies within consumer capitalism? Arguably, whereas trades unions ultimately have the sanction of with-holding their labour to improve pay or conditions, consumer organizations ultimately can only try to organize their members to withhold or redirect their spending on a product or range until a perceived wrong is put right. Boycotts are thus the 'hard' weapon for consumer organizations. In the 1990s, for instance, the nascent anti-free trade sections of the consumer movement began once more to call for boycott action (Nader, 1991; Lang and Hines, 1993; Klein, 2000).

Is consumer activism inevitably oppositional? We think not. Through all the different manifestations of consumer activism explored here, there are some common characteristics:

- **A desire for change**: there is a moral edge to activism. Consumption is viewed as a vehicle for its own transformation; it can therefore be imbued with a mission to transform an important part of the social order.
- **Rights**: consumers are deemed to have rights that have to be fought for or else they will be lost or undermined.
- **Values**: consumption is not merely a set of economic transactions but has a profoundly ethical dimension too; consuming is a form of moral action.
- **Public good**: consumption affects other people, society and the environment that go well beyond the act or purchasing, using and discarding goods and services.
- **Collectivity**: individual actions can be hugely reinforced by acting in concert with others. Like workers in the workplace, individual consumers have little power; by acting together, they wield considerable power in achieving or precipitating change.
- **Organization**: consumer interventions are planned and organized to deliver a coherent set of objectives and to achieve maximum impact; consumer bodies are instrumental in this process.

First wave: co-operative consumers

The first widespread, organized consumer movement began as a reaction to excessive prices and poor quality goods, food in particular. The co-operative movement took off in its modern form in Rochdale in north-west England in 1844, at the height of the industrialization process and had both a producer and a consumer side. Exclusively producer co-operatives, in fact, date from even earlier and were corn mills established by skilled artisans. These were set up in opposition to local monopolies who in the words of one co-op historian 'had conspired to supply that most basic of commodities, bread, at very high prices' (Birchall, 1994: 4). As early as 1760s, there were co-operatively run mills as well as bakeries at Woolwich and Chatham in south-east London. The Woolwich co-op mill was burned down and local bakers were accused of arson.

Drawing on such experiences and the example of utopians such as Robert Owen, whose thoughts and practices had developed at New Lanark Mills in Scotland, the co-operative movement developed its creed. As Dr William King, one of the key early thinkers, said: 'These evils may be cured: and the remedy is in our own hands. The remedy is CO-OPERATION' (Birchall, 1994: 9). By 1832, there were 500 local co-operative societies, but the movement collapsed in 1834 in the face of outright state repression of working-class movements and internal weaknesses, which were exacerbated by lack of rights and legal status. In some cases, such as Brighton's 1830s co-op, the success was such that its members were lured into selling their shares for cash (Birchall, 1994: 31). This danger has peppered co-operative consumer history. If there are no profits to shareholders but the dividend comes to the consumer who owns the production, assets can quickly be built up. There is thus an inevitable temptation for asset-stripping, if the co-operative ethos is weakened, or there are 'insiders' who want to raise capital or act like conventional capitalist enterprises. This happened to the UK co-operative movement in 1997 when there was an attempt to break up and sell off the UK Co-operative Wholesale Society. The attempt was foiled and ended in court. And in 2013, the UK Co-operative Bank, having disastrously over-borrowed to take over what it thought was a too-good-to-miss opportunity for expansion by buying another enterprise (Myners, 2014), was forced to abandon century-old principles, and meekly submit to being largely taken over by bond holders. The bank is now 70 per cent owned by hedge funds, the antithesis of co-operative ideals.

Back in the 1830s, despite its faltering start, co-operation offered enough practical proof that consumers could exercise power over production to attract others to try. In the 1840s, another co-operative enterprise in Rochdale, England set up one shop – now a museum – to sell goods to those who joined up. Profits, instead of being allowed to be accumulated and ploughed back into manufacture, as in Owen's model, were divided among the co-operators, the consumers

(Redfern, 1913: 1–11). Co-operation rather than Adam Smith's self-interest should, so it was felt, be able to function as the basis for meeting consumer needs. It prospered.

The principle of this new movement, which was extraordinarily successful both in business and ideological terms, was 'self-help by the people'. No distinction was made between people as consumers and as producers. Conventional business, co-operators argued, divided producers from the output of their own hands. Co-operation was the great social alternative to the capitalists' economic armoury, which merely divided and ruled the mass of working people (Thompson, 1994). This principle was summed up by Percy Redfern in one of the classics of consumer activism:

> *In our common everyday needs the great industries of the world take their rise. We – the mass of common men and women in all countries – also compose the world's market. To sell to us is the ultimate aim of the world's business. Hence it is ourselves as consumers who stand in a central relation to all the economies of the world, like the king in his kingdom. As producers we go unto a particular factory, farm or mine, but as consumers we are set by nature thus to give leadership, aim and purpose to the whole economic world. That we are not kings, but serfs in the mass, is due to our failure to think and act together as consumers and so to realise our true position and power. (Redfern, 1920: 12)*

The appeal was to allow ordinary people to build from the bottom, to control the means of production, and not to accept their lot. Co-operation offered a richer, stronger, more fulfilled and supportive social existence, a chance for working people to build a better world. To allow this mass to participate, a new civic society had to be created, and vice versa. This was a radical vision, at odds with the Victorian ideals of individualism and enterprise, but in other ways exemplifying its values of thrift and decency. Co-operatives were a subversive combination of theory and practice, means and ends, which were and still are deeply threatening to prevailing market theory. The co-operator Holyoake parodied the movement's detractors as follows:

> *The working class are not considered to be very rich in the quality of self-trust, or mutual trust. The business habit is not thought to be their forte. The art of creating a large concern, and governing all its complications, is not usually supposed to belong to them. (Holyoake, 1872: 1)*

The movement grew rapidly and proved the Jeremiahs wrong. The Rochdale Pioneers, as they became known, had their own corn mill within six years. The practice of local co-ops spread like wildfire – and its legacy continues to this day (Thompson, 1994). Co-operation from below, rather than Owen's benign paternalist vision of production led from above, for mutual benefit, put the consumer in charge, probably for the only time ever. In the mid-19th century, the co-operative movement expanded into hundreds of local co-operative societies, each fiercely independent, but gradually merging over the 20th century. Despite hundreds of mergers, there are still numerous co-operative societies in the UK alone.

With time, and as 20th-century consumer abundance weakened the case for defensive co-operation, markets lost their threat and the mutuality principle weakened. For most British people by the mid-20th century, co-operation meant a process by which customers at only one chain, the Co-op, received a coupon with the bill at the check-out counter – the famous 'divi' or dividend. The scheme was closed in the 1960s, overtaken by the nakedly capitalist savings stamps schemes run by the rival private or stock-holder retailers, who in turn dropped it. These have now been overtaken by loyalty cards.

So has the co-operative path for consumer activism turned out to be a false one, subverted and incorporated? Actually, even though it may appear to have lost its cutting edge radicalism, the co-operative model has spread, and has shown that consumers can demand better service and investment for their good. This is radically different from the gloss of corporate social responsibility or 'community' initiatives sponsored by companies today. A century and a half after its foundation, the co-operative movement has spread throughout the world, finding gaps in provision, encouraging particularly disenfranchised or poor consumers to take back some control and to reject profiteering by commerce. As Kofi Annan, Secretary-General of the United Nations, wrote in 2003, the co-operative movement

> is one of the largest organized segments of civil society, and plays a crucial role across a wide spectrum of human aspiration and need. Co-operatives provide vital health, housing and banking services; they promote education and gender equality; they protect the environment and workers' rights. [...] they help people in more than 100 countries better their lives and those of their communities. (Annan, 2003)

There are 700 million people signed up to co-ops worldwide in those 100 countries. Banks, factories, insurance, farming and retailing companies all reside under the co-operative movement umbrella. In the UK, where the movement began, in the 1990s it began to sell off huge parts of its food industrial empire and in 2014 it sold its huge farm holdings to the Wellcome Trust. Vertical integration, owning everything from land to point of sale, for so long a strength of the movement, had by the end of the 20th century been defined by the movement's leaders to have become an economic liability. This was now the era of flexible specialization and post-Fordism, characterized by tough contracts and specifications policed by ruthless retail giants to cut prices (Burch and Lawrence, 2007). The co-op was one brand among many. This was a far cry from the 1840s co-operators' dream of an autonomous empire with everything kept within the co-op family. The active consumer could be born, eat, live and die, all serviced from within the movement. With time and scale of operations, the direct control of consumers slipped away and the co-operative societies were forced to retrench, amalgamate and restructure under pressure from new consumerist values. To some extent, the vision of the co-operative activists was incorporated by its retail rivals, providing a better service cheaper, with the perceived bonus of being seen to be 'modern'. Today the co-operative ethos in the UK has been buffeted by these consumerist values and undermined by its own managerial mistakes (Myners, 2014). In other countries, however, this ethos has found new supporters, like the Japanese Seikatsu Clubs, the Canadian Mountain Equipment Co-operative and credit unions in the USA and Southern Africa.

The 21st-century co-operative movement now has immense challenges: how simultaneously to address, confront, service and deliver on consumer appetites that are contradictory – on the one hand glamourized consumerist demands and on the other hand for no-nonsense tried and tested products. In the past, the co-operatives had an easier time; associated with decent but low-income working people, value-for-money was assumed to be a driver. The hard work, zeal and commitment of the 19th-century pioneers who built the local socie-ties, who saved and invested in new shops, factories and land to serve working people, who had the vision to aspire to create their own complete supply chains, all this brought good-quality goods and services to those who hitherto had lacked them. The co-ops made consumerism affordable. With the arrival of the mass consumer society in the late 20th century, however, that rationale for the movement weakened. Others could do it cheaper, faster, with modernity, without the ideological worthiness. The co-op's affairs were inevitably con-ducted by professional managers, whose vision became more pragmatic, though it never collapsed into quite the ethos of other retail organizations. Despite these limitations, the active co-operator/consumer retains some of its potency, even if today's global markets and the international division of labour make it hard to realize. Will co-operatives be able to rebuild and combine ethics with efficiency? Can they be once more associated with flair and panache rather than solid respectability, or recapture respectability as more potent than flair and excitement? It remains to be seen.

Second wave: value-for-money consumers

The second wave of the consumer movement is today by far the highest profile form of consumer activism, to such an extent that it is often wrongly regarded as being the entire consumer movement. We term this 'value-for-money' con-sumerism. This emerged in its modern form in the 1930s, but built upon tentative US consumer initiatives in the late 19th and early 20th centuries.

A Consumers League was formed in New York in 1891. In 1898, the National Consumers League was formed from local groups and by 1903 had 64 branches in 20 states. The movement took off after a celebrated exposé of wide-scale food adulteration and bad trade. Upton Sinclair, a radical journalist, was sent to write newspaper articles on the insanitary condition at the Chicago stockyards and the meat packing plants (see Chapter 7, 'The Consumer as Victim'). The result was *The Jungle*, a novel published in 1906 (Sinclair, [1906] 1985). A socialist, he hoped to proselytize with the political message that market forces served neither worker nor consumer; he hoped to bring down US capitalism – instead he changed US food law. 'I aimed at the public's heart and by accident hit it in the stomach', he wrote, anticipating many a single issue consumer campaign which launches a simple message, from which it generalizes (Sinclair, [1906] 1985). As a result of the reaction to Sinclair's book, legislation was rushed through Congress, the Pure Food and Drug Act of 1906 and the Meat Inspection Act of the same year, an extraordinary impact for a book (Forbes, 1987: 4). The Federal Trade Commission and a variety of anti-monopoly laws were also set up at the turn of the century.

These early US consumer groups placed heavy emphasis on the containment of the emerging powerful corporations. Their writings were full of concerns about the power of the new 'combines' over individuals, both as workers and as consumers. Unlike the first wave of consumerism, these groups were concerned about the threat posed to consumers by increasing concentration and monopoly capital. In the roaring 1920s with its unprecedented explosion of consumption, *Your Money's Worth* (Chase and Schlink, 1927) a best-selling book, tried to show how consumers were being exploited even as they were first tasting the fruits of mass production – the beginnings of what we term the Fordist Deal, pleasurable consumption as compensation for alienated work. A year later, one of the authors, Schlink, founded Consumers Research Inc. to carry out consumer product testing on a large scale. Its purpose was to provide research and information to consumers in the marketplace. This was the first time that consumer activism saw itself as enabling consumers to take best advantage of the market, rather than trying to undermine the market through co-operative action or political agitation and lobbying.

In 1936, following a bitter confrontation over Schlink's authoritarian management, a group from Consumers Research Inc. split to form the Consumers Union. This prospered and the Consumers Union is now a huge organization, with over 8 million subscribers, 1 million on-line activists to change legislation, 50 laboratories and offices, more than 600 workers and an annual turnover of over $200 million. It proudly states: 'Since 1936, our mission has been to test products, inform the public, and protect consumers' (Consumers Union, 2014). Its magazine *Consumer Reports* epitomizes the principle of second-wave consumerism enabling its members to get best value for money by offering authoritative information about marketplace products and services. The principle of value-for-money took root in the consumer movement and reached its heyday in President John F. Kennedy's 1962 'Consumer Message to Congress' (Forbes, 1987: 37).

Some value-for-money organizations besides those in the USA have grown into very substantial operations. The UK Consumers' Association now called *Which?* founded in the 1950s to emulate the US CU, has grown its subscriber list to over 1 million. The Dutch De Consumentenbond in 2014 had 500,000 members, the highest membership for any consumer movement in the West proportionate to national population. The Belgian *Test Achats*, which like *Which?* and De Consumentenbond was founded in the mid-1950s, has considerable extra weight due to its formal link with similar Spanish, Portuguese and Italian groups, and more recently with one in Brazil. Smaller organizations with the same ethos can be found in many other countries, such as Germany, Belgium, Denmark, Australia, New Zealand, and the ex-Soviet and Eastern bloc. In all of these countries, the arrival of the internet opened up new opportunities and resulted in increased membership and information sharing.

But the recipe is the same. These organizations test products for safety, ease of use, price, durability, task effectiveness; in short, overall value-for-money. Readers/members are informed about the 'best buy' and warned about 'cons' and bad buys. Large sums of money are spent conducting independent tests of products, usually in the consumer organization's own laboratories or test benches. And with the web, surveys and requests to hear stories and problems from members have grown, creating a new more interactive consumerism *inside* the consumer activist organizations themselves.

Unlike the co-operative movement, this second wave of consumer organizations has no pretensions of offering a radically different vision for society. Its adherents see their role as ameliorative, to make the marketplace more efficient and to champion the interests of the consumer within it. Their aim is to provide independent information and education for the consumer about the features that will enable them to act effectively as consumers (John, 1994). The value-for-money model places considerable stress on rights to information and labelling and the right of redress if something goes wrong. John Winward, former Director of Research at the UK Consumers' Association (now *Which?*), conceived of these non-profit organizations as 'information co-operatives' (Winward, 1994: 76–77).

Second-wave consumerism has faced a number of difficulties. Post-Fordist production methods and the proliferation of niche markets undermine the possibility of meaningful comparisons between broadly similar products. The pace and impact of technological change makes such comparisons still harder. As producers deliver ever more nuanced 'niche' products into the marketplace, product information becomes outdated almost before consumers get the data. If the sheer range and proliferation of products make testing harder and render benchmarking quickly obsolete, two compensations are that consumers have become more market savvy and that information can be disseminated more quickly. On the other hand, many consumers do not resort to these associations to obtain comparative information of products, relying instead on new arrivals such as BuzzFeed and, most importantly, price comparison websites and sites which give feedback from consumers themselves (see Chapter 11, 'The Consumer as Worker').

Four criticisms have been raised at second-wave consumerism. First, it downplayed or even failed to address longer-term environmental and social issues, taking a consumer perspective that strictly focused on the point of purchase, the act of choosing. Second, it has had an overwhelmingly middle-class orientation based on the assumption of ever-increasing standards of living. Third, as a child of affluent consumption, it tended not to focus on the plight of poorer consumers, or was perceived as not doing so. And fourth, it had an inappropriately conservative approach to consumption, in which consumption is a right, and is intrinsic to the American good life. It has

> rarely questioned the fundamental premise on which American industrialism is based: the desirability of technical efficiency and of technological and economic growth. Instead, consumerism has focused most of its attention on such problems as the lack of product safety or of adequate consumer information. (Bloom and Stern, 1978: 14)

Such criticisms found their mark within value-for-money consumer organizations, who have responded. They have conducted work on the pressures experienced by low income consumers, for instance, and monitoring how food prices rose more than wages in the Great Recession (*Which?*, 2013b; 2013a). And they have used the web to attract more occasional hits by non-paying members, putting more effort into disseminating study findings through the mass media, thus making them available to all. Adapting this way, value-for-money consumer activism has remained hugely successful. Its organizations have grown in influence. Second-wave consumerism has had a remarkable impact on business, holding companies and governments to account, and publishing a flood of authoritative reports which embarrass the powerful into change. Its independence, its unwillingness to accept advertising revenue and its sometimes almost religious obsession with accuracy has given an authority which companies and governments can only disregard at their cost.

Third wave: Naderism

The third wave of consumer activism, like the second, emerged in the USA. Its figurehead, Ralph Nader, became one of the most admired US citizens in national polls for years, until his presidential campaign in 2000 was blamed by many for allowing George W. Bush to win the presidency. His subsequent 2004 campaign barely registered and he received accordingly less opprobrium. Nader is not someone who worries about unpopularity. He initially shot into global, not just US, prominence with the publication of his book *Unsafe at Any Speed* in 1965, an exposé of the car industry (Nader, [1965] 1991). The book argued that one automobile model in particular, the Chevrolet Corvair, and automobiles in general were poorly designed and had built-in safety short-cuts. The industry had resisted giving priority to safety policy that, he alleged, resulted in an annual slaughter of Americans; he claimed it had been 51,000 in 1965. Highway accidents cost $8.3 billion in property damage, medical expenses, lost wages and insurance overhead expenses (Nader, [1965] 1991: vii). Relying on independent tests, Nader showed how the Corvair easily went out of control at 22 miles per hour, contrasting with its advertising claims of 'easy handling', being 'a family sedan' and a car that 'purrs for the girls' (Nader, [1965] 1991: 27). Yet the car's road-handling on corners meant that it demanded 'more driving skill in order to avoid collision than any other American automobile'. As though that was not bad enough, he catalogued how General Motors had failed to come clean on the Corvair's design faults and how when aware of these, it calculated that it would be cheaper not to correct them. Overnight, Nader became a consumer activist hero. What marked his approach as special was that he not only generalized from the particular, documenting how the Corvair may have been an extreme case of consumer safety being a low priority, but that he spelt out at great length how the case was only the tip of an iceberg. His perspective – much expanded and expounded – positioned the consumer activist against the corporate giants. In so doing, he brilliantly voiced the interests of mainstream as well as radical consumers emerging in the affluent US society of the 1960s.

Nader, a Harvard-educated lawyer, quickly expanded his activities, setting up the Center for Study of Responsive Law and the Project for Corporate Responsibility in 1969. By the end of the 1970s he had spawned a series of organizations, staffed by young professionals, nick-named 'Nader's Raiders', many of them lawyers like himself, young, keen and prepared to be David to corporate Goliaths. By the 1990s, there were 29 organizations with combined revenues of $75–$80 million, founded by Nader or under the Nader umbrella (Brimelow and Spencer, 1990). The common themes of these organizations were a distrust of corporations, a defence of the individual against the giants, a demand that the state protect its citizens and above all, an appeal for Americans to be citizens, not just consumers. Naderism assumed that the consumer is relatively powerless in a world dominated by corporate giants, whether these are automobile or insurance companies, the health sector or the government–industry complex. The nature of commerce is stacked against the customer, unless regulations or standards of conduct are fought for. This is a hard fight, so consumer activists have to be tough, well briefed, well organized and able to make optimum use of the mass media.

Nader brought a new punch to consumer politics and tapped a deep well of public unease about the power of large corporations vis-à-vis the individual customer. He saw the role of consumer organizations as going beyond getting the consumer the best deal in the marketplace. He made the case for confronting the market itself. Writing about the US food industry in 1970, for instance, Nader made a number of charges about what it will do if left to its own devices:

> Making food appear what it is not is an integral part of the $125 billion food industry. The deception ranges from the surface packaging to the integrity of the food products' quality to the very shaping of food tastes. [...] In fact, very often the degradation of these standards proceeds from the cosmetic treatment of food or is its direct cost by-product. [...] For too long there has been an overwhelmingly dominant channel of distorted information from the food industry to the consumer. [...] Company economy very often was the consumer's cost and hazard. As a result, competition became a way of beating one's competitor by racing for the lowest permissible common denominator. (Nader, 1970: v)

The role of the state, in the absence of consumer pressure, is to collude with this downward spiral, which disadvantages good businesses. The consumer activist's role was and is to confront, to expose, to stand up for public rights, to be a citizen. A persistent theme is to bring the corporate state under the control of democratic forces, and away from the grip of big business (Krebs, 1992: 440–443).

Like the second wave of the consumer movement, Naderism is adamant on the role of information and that information should be free and fair. If the first wave saw capitalism as something to be stepped away from (co-ops are non-profit organizations that share out rather than accumulate or privatize profits), the second wave sees its own role as that of providing information for the consumer to be able to operate more effectively in the marketplace. And the third wave, Naderism, sees capitalism as something to be accepted, but which has to be worked hard on to prevent its excesses becoming its norms.

Naderism places great emphasis on information from consumer bodies as debunking the misinformation systematically disseminated by companies unless held to account. For Nader, the situation is simple and clear. 'It is time for consumers to have information that will provide them with an effective understanding of the secrecy-clouded situation' (Nader, 1970: vii). Freedom of information – rather than product information or mere labelling on a packet – has been a persistent theme for Nader. He helped inspire the UK Campaign for Freedom of Information in its uphill task to reform the British state's reflex for secrecy. (Britain only achieved an overarching Freedom of Information Act in 2000, although there had been some incremental improvement prior to that.) For Nader, secrecy symbolises a collusion between state and commercial interests, and it is the duty of the consumer activist to break that collusion, or else she or he becomes an accomplice to it.

Only vigilant consumers can break the pact, said Nader:

> Major corporations like their consumers to remain without a capacity for group purchasing action, group legal action, group participating action before regulatory agencies. [...] The possibility that consumers banding together can muster their organised intelligence to play a major role in shaping economic policy and the future of our political economy is an unsettling one for the mega corporations that play much of the world's economy. So too would be an organised consumer initiative to assess the hazards of technology or forestall the marketing of products which use consumers as test subjects or guinea pigs. (Quoted in Beishon, 1994: 9)

Nader's views have fed on the deep apprehension of American consumers, and the public in general, towards anything big and unfettered, corporate power in particular. Unlike second-wave organizations, Nader and his colleagues believe that only active involvement by citizens at the local level can counteract these forces. Whereas second-wave groups are reformist and 'top-down' in their strategies, preferring lobbies to rallies, Naderism has been equally content to lobby and rally, priding itself upon building up grassroots citizen action. In the marketplace, the message is to be frugal, to get wise in 'the vital art of self defense' to 'protect yourself in the marketplace', whether buying a car, health insurance, food or a house (Nader and Smith, 1992). These are terms that echo the early American non-importation movement resisting the British in the late 18th century (Witkowski, 1989).

Unlike second-wave consumerism, Naderism, though admired, has not easily been grafted onto the consumer cultures of other countries. Neither the political culture nor the legal system nor the scale of consumption in other countries has until recently favoured the growth of Nader-like organizations. But with global de-regulation in the 1990s and the emergence of regional trade blocs such as the EU and NAFTA, and in bi-lateral regional trade agreements negotiated in the 2010s such as the Trans-Atlantic Trade and Investment Partnership (TTIP) or Trans-Pacific Partnership (TPP), Naderism's persistent charge at the collusion of big business and the state found new allies. These have included environmental groups, animal welfare groups, trades unions, as well as other consumer groups. Although at times controversial, Naderism has been a powerful force among activists. The appeal to stand up and be counted is thrilling and inspiring. It has provided a new model for a media-hungry world, the activist who dares to take on the powerful, thus turning the consumer activist into a civilising force.

The globalization of consumer activism

Consumers' International, formerly the International Organization of Consumers Unions (IOCU), is a global network founded in 1960, which had over 240 affiliated organizations from 120 countries in 2014 (Consumers International, 2014).

These vary in size and wealth, with the larger and wealthier tending to be in affluent Western countries, but activists are now strong in developing countries too and the Western groups have funded consumer activism in new markets of the South and, for instance, in the former Eastern bloc after the USSR collapsed in the late 1980s. As consumption has grown in Asia, for example, consumer activism of different varieties has emerged. A new generation of consumer activists such as Anwar Fazal, Martin Khor, Vandana Shiva and others have not only applied the lessons of Naderism in their own countries but championed all four waves of consumer activism outlined in this chapter. They have taken on corporations outside their national boundaries, too, building an international consumer activism. Their vision has tended to be more societally focused than just the pursuit of individual choice, and has championed developing country concerns. They were particularly active in the anti-globalization movement from the 1990s. Developing countries, they argue, are particularly vulnerable to the globalization of capital and new 'free' trade rules, which they saw as threatening the well-being of their consumers, as well as workers. For this generation, the consumer activist aspires to citizenship rather than value-for-money consumerism. In the words of Khor:

> *Traditional value-for-money consumerism (what brand of washing machine to buy) is not important for the Third World. What is important is pollution, world resources, what products should be promoted and what products should be banned. Should we have washing machines at all? (Interview with the authors, January 1994)*

The presence of this more questioning approach to consumerism has been problematic. Consumers International states that it:

> *promotes the establishment of legislation, institutions and information that improve quality of life and empower people to make changes in their own lives. It seeks to ensure that basic human rights are recognised, and promotes understanding of people's rights and responsibilities as consumers. (Consumers International, 2004)*

Rights and responsibilities are equally important. The rights are: for basic needs to be satisfied, for safety, to be informed, to choose, to be heard, to redress, for consumer education and for a healthy environment. Consumer responsibilities should also 'use their power in the market to drive out abuses, to encourage ethical practices and to support sustainable consumption and production'. Organizations which are members of Consumers International now subscribe to the belief that developing and protecting consumers' rights and their awareness of their responsibilities are integral to the eradication of poverty, good governance, social justice and respect for human rights, fair and effective market economies and the protection of the environment (Consumers International, 2004). This is a shift from the values of second-wave consumerism in its purest form.

Fourth wave: alternative, ethical and political activists

A new wave of consumer organizations emerged slowly in the 1970s and accelerated in the 1980s, which in 1995 we termed 'alternative consumerism'. At that time, we sensed that while this fourth wave had many elements – green, ethical, Third World solidarity, labour rights, health, animal welfare and fair trade orientations – it as yet lacked any coherence. We wondered if these strands would remain separate and fragmented. Nonetheless, we felt there was sufficient commonality for these apparently disparate groups to be viewed as one wave. We called it 'alternative consumerism' to capture its general opposition to mainstream consumerism (the way we have used the term throughout this book until this point). Since then, a degree of coherence has started to emerge. A new progressive consumer activism is building an ethical, social and ecological dimension into marketplace thinking (Harrison et al., 2005; Stolle and Micheletti, 2013). It is now being called by some 'political activism' or 'political consumerism' (Kozinets, 2002; Kozinets and Handelman, 2004; Bevir and Trentmann, 2007; Gotlieb and Wells, 2012; Holt, 2012; Willis and Schor, 2012). Fourth-wave claims and arguments are increasingly confident and are finding audiences among consumers, governments and companies.

An increasing number of consumers from all social classes are influenced by one or more of the strands which collectively we identified as making up fourth-wave activism. They are prepared to undertake actions to further them, including adjusting their buying and consuming patterns through to boycotts, adbusting and culture jamming (see, for example, Littler, 2005; Atkinson, 2012; Gotlieb and Wells, 2012; Holt, 2012; Shah et al., 2012; Willis and Schor, 2012). Undoubtedly some of the strands become co-opted into the mainstream and remain reformist (see Chapter 11, 'The Consumer as Worker'), but others are more radical, charting a different concept of what consumption is. They feed on having a target against which to focus their moral outrage and build a movement. Targets can range from particular companies, like Nestlé and Nike, to particular processes like factory farming or sexist advertisements, to particular products like fur and junk food, to particular labour practices like sweatshops or child labour, and to particular environmental threats like nuclear power or pesticides. Most of these began to emerge in the 1970s and 1980s and can be seen as having gained their inspiration from the green and counter-cultural movements, but they draw their inspiration more widely, injecting an ethical and moral dimension alongside the material (or anti-material) dimension of consumer activism.

Like previous waves of consumer activism, fourth-wave activism has generated its own concept of how to empower consumers against an adversary. The co-operative wave sought to empower people through collective action against what it saw as profiteering and unscrupulous business. The value-for-money wave sought to empower consumers to operate smarter in the marketplace and more rationally against the wiles of commerce. Naderism, the third wave, appealed to consumers to make their voices heard against the might of the corporation and the overweening power of the state. In contrast, the fourth wave seeks to empower people by challenging unfettered consumerism itself, its brands, its symbols, its practices and its products. While there is no common overarching enemy, all strands of the fourth wave seek to distance people from the narrow dictates of consumerism. They seek to reclaim and refashion what the good life is all about, and to enable people to discover new avenues for meaningful action and existence if not wholly outside the world of commodities, then at least downgrading its importance.

The more reformist strands within the fourth wave have charted different paths for a green or ethical consumerism broadly seeking to reform the existing marketplace and structures of capitalist society. They envisage a world of benign consumerism, which reconciles the demands of the environment and various social and animal rights with the pursuit of happiness through *informed* consumer choices. They champion, for example, swapping from a petrol car to an electric fully recyclable car; or shifting from a car to a bicycle, while retaining the right to choose from among hundreds of different types and models. An interesting illustration of reformist activism has been the attack on what are seen as unethical brands and their replacement by 'benign' brands that can be trusted to act more ethically and responsibly.

The story of Fairtrade products illustrates this trend (Lamb, 2008; Barratt Brown, 1993). Fairtrade is a concept that came into existence to ensure that primary producers in developing countries received a larger part of the money that consumers spent on their goods. Frequently this was less than 1 per cent (Fairtrade International, 2013). Over the last 40 years, Fairtrade has become a formidable brand in its own right, with a wide recognition factor for its logo and a large presence worldwide. One particularly successful product in Europe has been a coffee branded as Cafédirect in the UK and as Max Havelaar in the Netherlands. The Dutch name is a reference to a famous Dutch novel, published in 1860, which denounced the use of slaves in the coffee trade, and made an early appeal to consumers to choose differently (Multatuli, [1860] 1987). Currently, over half the bananas in Switzerland are Fairtrade; so too is over 40 per cent of sugar in the UK and 20 per cent of roses sold in Germany. Over 30,000 Fairtrade products are currently sold in more than 125 countries. Worldwide in 2012, shoppers spent over €4.8 billion on Fairtrade certified products with Germany accounting for 10 per cent of this. Giant companies like Starbucks and Costa Coffee now promote fair trade and source a large part of their raw materials from certified suppliers. The Pret A Manger chain switched all its filter coffee (15 per cent of sales) to fair trade sources in 2002. Such change by commerce has been seen by the Fairtrade movement as a measure of its success, confirming the view that it represents an essentially reformist strand of alternative consumerism. The motives for the consumers' switch to Fairtrade are important. When people consume food or drink, they are mostly uncomfortable with connotations of harm. In brand terms, this had a triple message: this is a good product in its own right *and* it has extra connotations and positional goods *and* by consuming it, one can do good. Three 'wins' in one sip.

Another strand of the fourth wave has been green consumerism. Like the Fairtrade movement, the green consumer movement began in Europe and spread to North America. Seemingly overnight, aerosols with CFCs and apples with pesticide residues became no-go areas in the supermarket, and activists appealed to buy differently for the environment (Elkington and Hailes, 1988). The green consumer movement forced companies to listen to them and spawned new ranges of products such as phosphate-free detergents and cars with recyclable components, which gave consumers the option of choosing 'green'. Many of these products that started at the margins of consumption rapidly became mainstream, particularly when regulation mandated their use, as happened with the shift to low energy light bulbs, and the phasing out of old-style incandescent bulbs first in Latin America in 2005, then in Europe from 2009, and in the USA from 2014.

A strong reformist thread of green consumer activism set out to transform capitalism into making only 'good' goods (Elkington and Burke, 1987; Elkington, 1997). The appeal to the consumer is 'consume carefully' rather than 'don't consume' or 'consume less'. A mechanism it championed was that companies should undertake environmental audits, either alongside other traditional financial reporting or as an internal driver for more comprehensive efficiency and gaining competitive advantage (Kaplan and Norton, 1993). External sector-wide audits have also grown, comparing companies and their products for their environmental soundness and the green credentials. Activists have audited governments, too, conducting 'end of term' performance reports, and governments have even adopted this in uncomfortable self-monitoring processes ascribed to arms-length bodies or reviews (e.g. Environmental Audit Committee, 2011).

By the 21st century, environmentalism had consolidated its position as a dominant discourse in consumption but had fragmented into numerous different mainstream products and initiatives and other less mainstream campaigns. A whole new category of green businesses and green product ranges had emerged, ranging from cosmetics to electrical goods and even cars, leading to a green producer–consumer nexus, where environmentalists began to act as prompts to innovation and referees of corporate behaviour. Green consumer activism had generated a near-universal ideology that genuflects before the word 'the planet', even if its practical applications are patchy.

Tensions between reformists and radicals among consumer activists persist. In one camp were the proponents of a more caring, considerate capitalism: use purchasing power to reduce energy use or other desired environmental qualities (Gilg et al., 2005). The Factor Four approach, for instance, argues that technologically it is possible to reduce products' energy use by a factor of four and to become much more efficient than at present, thus staving off ill-effects of emissions, and climate change (von Weizsäcker et al., 1996). A new more energy-efficient washing machine is more desirable than an older one. In the other camp were those who argued that the thrust of green consumers should be to consume less altogether (Irvine, 1989; Durning, 1992a; Schor, 1998; Schor, 2010). In some respects, the first camp was charged by the latter with coming to the rescue of consumer capitalism and giving it new opportunities for niche products, at the very moment when traditional markets were being saturated. Looking back over four decades of modern green consumerism, like earlier generations of reformers, green activists have been victims of their own success, a process recognized by activists themselves, many of whom have harboured no illusions about the limitations of green activism if restricted to consumption. For all its variations, green consumerism had become mainstream by the end of the 20th century.

Ethical consumerism is poised to do likewise. Ethical consumerism stresses the moral dimension of consumer choice, grading all products and services against a mix of criteria such as the following used by the Ethical Consumer Research Association (*Ethical Consumer*, 2012):

- **Environmental:** environmental reporting, nuclear power, climate change, pollution and toxics, habitats and resources.
- **Animals:** testing, factory farming, animal rights.
- **People:** human rights, workers' rights, supply chain management, irresponsible marketing, arms and military supply.
- **Politics:** genetic engineering, boycotts, political activity, anti-social finance.
- **Positives:** company ethos, product sustainability.

These criteria have altered and deepened since first formulated in the 1990s (Adams et al., 1991; *Ethical Consumer*, 1994; Harrison and Turner, 2014). When the Ethical Consumer Research Association was founded in Manchester, close to Rochdale of co-operative pioneer fame, in 1989, it was advised not to use the word 'consumer' in its title 'because the word is too narrow a definition of what people do' (Rob Harrison, interview with the authors, February 1994). The word 'consumer' places an emphasis on only one aspect of people's behaviour, one that tends to deny the political and moral goals the organization had come into existence to promote. By the mid-1990s, Harrison could argue that the organization's goal is really to change culture and to promote a consumer awareness of the global implications of Western consumption. Issues such as fair trade, aid and exploitation of Third World workers, far from being marginal to the ethics and politics of Western consumption, lie at its very heart (Wells and Jetter, 1991; FTEPR, 2014; Sylla, 2014). Unlike green consumerism which was quickly incorporated into the mainstream, parts of the ethical consumer movement have maintained their radical edge and their oppositional stance to business, persistently encouraging boycotts. They view themselves as holding a mirror to those aspects of business that business itself would rather not acknowledge. Unlike more extreme forms of fourth-wave activism, like those surveyed by Kozinets and Handelman (2004), the ethical consumer movement does not view the ordinary consumer in the street as its enemy, but as someone who needs to be educated, sensitized, helped, appealed to and supported to get better organized.

Animal activism has become yet another important – and arguably the 'noisiest' – strand in the fourth wave of consumer activism, not least because it addresses consumerism at the level of species and because some of its proponents have resorted to violent action against their adversaries. The history of these consumer activists begins in the early 19th century. The UK Royal Society for the Prevention of Cruelty to Animals, for instance, was founded in 1824 mostly to protest about the treatment of working animals – pit ponies down mines and farm draught horses. What brought animal activism under the umbrella of consumer activism in the late 20th century, however, was the moral outrage caused by exposés of animals suffering in the production and testing of transitory consumer goods such as cosmetics, furs and fashion. Only a tiny minority of activists have followed the route of the Animal Liberation Front which bombed scientific laboratories in protest about the use of live animals for product safety tests. Most animal activists agree a civilized society cannot use animals purely as resources the way it uses oil to fuel cars. Animals must be treated with respect and compassion as sentient beings. For them, factory farming, along with testing, have been core targets (Korthals, 2004; d'Silva and Webster, 2010; Lymbery and Oakeshott, 2014). Vegetarianism and veganism have been promoted as ethical consumer responses to the issue of animal welfare and as key platforms for alternative consumption (Singer and Mason, 2006). Peter Singer, the Australian utilitarian philosopher who opened up the new ethical interest in food with his book *Animal Liberation* (Singer, 1975), went on record to welcome the development of laboratory 'meat' in 2013 as heralding the possibility of a cruelty-free meat era (Singer, 2013).

The future: convergence or continued divergence?

Since we outlined our account of the four waves of consumer activism, a number of important changes have occurred all pointing to some convergence and cross-fertilization across the waves. First, the fourth wave's ethical and environmental values began to be absorbed by the dominant and powerful second-wave or value-for-money consumer groups. Corporate social responsibility (CSR) advocates became influential in auditing company behaviour. The crises and bankruptcies of giant firms such as Enron in the USA and Parmalat in Italy encouraged some financiers to see the economic value of viewing companies through an ethical and longer-term filter (Harrison, 2003). CSR has been, in part, a response to consumer activists whose legitimacy grew with the crises (Crane and Matten, 2007).

Second, co-operatives, the original first wave of consumer activism, took note of, helped and began to embrace the vitality and appeal of the fourth wave by making new commitments to position co-operatives as more trustworthy sources of the necessities of life. The small Co-operative Bank pioneered this return to ethics-led banking and proved ethics could be good for business, until it over-stretched itself, nearly collapsed and reverted to being an ordinary bank in 2013, as we described above. The Co-op's food retailing division also tentatively began to revitalize its ethical and green credentials, launching a 'responsible retailing' campaign in the mid-1990s (Co-operative Group, 2004), and seeing this re-branding grow its business in the 2000s.

Third, in December 1999, several disparate strands of consumer activism, real-ising they had common interests, came together in Seattle, USA, in opposition to the proposed revision of the World Trade Organization's world trade rules (Solnit et al., 2009). Activists began to realize that what had been 'single issues' in the past were all being threatened by a restructuring of world trade rules to facilitate more cross-border trade. The general threat of weaker regulations and standards brought advocates together, whether interested in animal welfare or public health, the environment or labour rights, fair trade or food poverty (Monbiot, 2003). Wider political events – in this case restructuring of trade rules to suit commerce – drew activists together, searching for their common interest. Thus, globalization reinvigorated consumer activism across the waves (Klein, 2000), in a manner anticipated by political theorists wondering if single issue politics might replace formal political parties as the agenda setters of the future (Richardson, 1995). Indeed, this has happened; membership of formal political parties has declined, even though activism has not, and civil society member-ships have grown astronomically worldwide.

Fourth, as we argued in our notion of the 'twilight of consumerism', a certain ennui set in within consumer society, compounded by the indebtedness and insecurity brought about by the Great Recession of 2007–13. John Maynard Keynes – even shortly after the 1929 Wall Street Crash – in a celebrated essay, pondered on what a world characterized not by shortage but by plenty would be like for consumers. The challenge posed by a world where machines replaced labour, he thought, would be how to fulfil ourselves when we have so much 'free' time (Keynes, 1933). He asked whether societal well-being might better be pur-sued if we became clear about the point at which 'sufficiency' is achieved. How much do we need? When is enough enough? Keynes reminded his audience that these are moral questions. This debate has surfaced again with a new generation of behavioural economists questioning any colleagues who pursue economic growth at any costs. Consumerist societies, these latter-day Keynesians argue, are

Table 9.1 Some dimensions of consumer activism

Issue	1 Co-operative	2 Value for money	3 Naderism	4 Fourth wave
Origins	1840 (UK)	1900s (USA)	1960s (USA)	1970s (internationally)
Organizational form	Co-operative	Associations, club membership with bureaucratic core	Charismatic	Network and collaboration
Goals	Reform and create parallel markets	Make market more efficient, champion the consumer	Support the 'little guy', expose bad practice	Constrain or reduce markets
Values	Solidarity among consumers and producers, co-ownership	Rationality, education, information	Accountability, responsibility	Social justice, rights, environmental care
Attitude towards markets	Collective action	Informed comparisons to help consumer choose	Litigation, exposés, surprise	Alternative or tamed markets
Enemy or target	Greedy unscrupulous employers and sales	Inefficiency, shoddy goods	Over-powerful and immoral corporates	Corporations and sometimes thoughtless consumers
Nature of activism	Build your own system	Comparative testing to improve rational choice	Research to 'dig the dirt'	Moral outrage and single target campaigns
Radical or reformist?	Was radical, now reformist	Reformist	Radical	Radical and reformist
Highpoint campaign	Internationalization of the co-operative ideal and practice	Consumer protection acts, freedom of information	Exposing corporate malpractice	Implementing bans and prompting legislation
Sign of cross-fertilization with other waves	Some with fourth wave	With ethical and environmental issues	With fourth wave	Morphing into citizen-consumer

not necessarily endlessly happier as societies get wealthier (Daly et al., 1990; Jackson, 2009; Daly and Farley, 2011; Skidelsky and Skidelsky, 2012). These arguments resonate deeply with fourth-wave activists who have persisted in asking questions: how much can one consume? What is good consumption? How many goods or services or downloads transform life? That said, there are no signs of an end to consumption globally – far from it, political leaders seem desperate to encourage it as the way out of recession – but activists worldwide have captured attention with their critique of escalating consumerism, and their questions assumed greater significance following the banking crisis and Great Recession.

This review has outlined four waves of the consumer as activist. Each has its own characteristic but consumer-activists unite in rejecting the anarchism of the market. They stress that right and wrong are concepts that cannot be written out of consumption. The vast majority of consumers recognize this, even if they continue to be seduced by the marketplace and its cornucopia of offerings. The activists, each in their different ways, engender scepticism among all consumers. Their success lies in making consumers smarter. Table 9.1 summarizes some key characteristics of each of the four waves of consumer activism considered in this chapter.

Many activists acknowledge that consumer capitalism can redefine itself in ways that accommodate some of their demands. This may take the form of creating niche markets (for ethical or green products) or by accepting a degree of regulation as a necessity for its continuing legitimation. Some consumer-activists recognize this as an inevitable limitation of much reformist activity. This in no way negates the value of their efforts or undermines their objectives, but it does mean that there is a ceaseless process of incorporation and accommodation, as ideas are 'cherry-picked' leading to modifications made to products and processes, ranging from slight to significant. Cynics might argue that this relegates consumer activism to being unpaid revisionists of advanced capitalism. In some respects, this is inevitable, but in important ways, the contribution of activists lies in acting as the moral conscience of the existing system, aiming for a set of principles that is above price or minor product amelioration and diversification. Other activists go further and view palliative reform as inadequate in stopping the ruinous path of consumer capitalism. For them, the concept of the consumer must now be itself overcome, having become fatally flawed and compromised. Only by redefining how they think and act can individuals today individually and collectively recover some of the control that they have lost to the organizations and objects that now dominate their lives and through which they express themselves.

In this important sense, the new wave of consumer activism incorporating animal welfare, fair trade, ethical consumption and more, maps one clear if complex path for consumers, a route for translating consumerism into citizenship. The contrast between consumers and citizens is a long standing distinction to which we now turn.

10

THE CONSUMER AS CITIZEN

We are witnessing the swift debasement of the concept of 'citizen' – the person who actively participates in shaping society's destiny – to that of 'consumer', whose franchise has become his or her purchasing decisions. (Stuart Ewen, 1992: 23)

CORE ARGUMENTS

The increasing power of consumerism has eroded an older tradition that approached people as citizens with rights and responsibilities. This looked at political action as the key to ensuring a better and fairer quality of life. In the 20th century, this democratic tradition delivered a welfare system in many countries where the state acted as the guarantor that core human needs, such as education and health, be met independently of the ability to pay. All citizens were in principle equal. Consumerism, on the other hand, proposes a model of freedom and happiness through individual choice exercised in a marketplace, unconcerned about social inequalities or the well-being of others. This ideology has been articulated and championed by the New Right since the 1980s, resulting in consumerism encroaching the terrain of citizenship. Privatization, outsourcing and New Public Management have opened up public services to market forces in the hope that they would deliver improvements in quality and costs, but the results have been patchy. Some companies for their part have sought to address their customers as citizens through the lens of corporate social responsibility. This has led to the hybrid concept of the consumer-citizen, which has been received with some scepticism by academics. While the citizen may appear to be in retreat, under pressure from consumerism, there are also signs that environmental, community and political concerns are restoring the idea of collective spaces and rights, and the shared responsibility to defend them.

The idea of the citizen to some Anglo-Saxon ears has a rather quaint, old-fashioned ring to it; citizenship was what liberal political theorists referred to, civics was what children were taught in class. For other cultures, following the legacy of the French Revolution, the concept of citizen is foundational to their national and political identity. The contrast between consumer and citizen has been the subject of considerable debate. Does the triumph of consumerism and the omnipotence of markets seriously erode the notion of citizenship or even consign it to history textbooks? Can consumerism replace citizenship as the guarantor of social rights? Does the notion of citizenship add any value in societies where markets dominate social relations? Can the consumer replace the citizen as the agent of social change and become the basis of a platform of opposition?

Many consumer activists, as we saw in Chapter 9, have also sought to proclaim the ideal of citizenship in contradistinction to the notion of the individualistic consumer, which they saw as too individualistic, restrictive, in short irrecoverably hijacked by the political Right (Nader, [1965] 1991; Monbiot, 2000; Goldsmith and Mander, 2001; Khor, 2001; Korten, 2001; Martin, 2002; Shiva, 2002; Sassatelli, 2006; Johnston, 2008; Atkinson, 2012; Gotlieb and Wells, 2012; Shah et al., 2012; Willis and Schor, 2012). In this way, they have resurrected an older idea propounded by the founder of the UK's *Which?* (formerly the Consumers' Association) and National Consumer Council, Michael Young, who had envisaged organized consumers as a new third force for the citizenry, alongside organized labour and organized capital and management. Even earlier in 1920, the co-operative theorist, Percy Redfern, had called on consumers to unite to

> *build a new social order – an order which may restore the primitive social unity, but now upon a world scale instead of within the narrow circle of the township and village. ... In the past the consumer has paid. In the future he and she together must live and act as citizens in the commonwealth of man. (Redfern, 1920: 42 and 57)*

Yet almost as soon as the idea of citizenship re-emerged as the focus for progressive opposition in the late 1980s, attracting to it demands for freedom of information, written constitutional rights, electoral reform and so on, the idea was seized by the New Right (Pirie, 1991; Cockett, 1994) as a lifeline to keep the neo-liberal project on course, even as it was beginning to be questioned. More recently, the idea of choice that has prospered on the back of a consumerist ethos has been re-introduced into discussions of citizenship to the point where consumerism may have colonized citizenship.

In this chapter, we examine the chronic tension that has existed between the idea of the consumer and that of the citizen, and assess whether the two represent conflicting tendencies. We also examine whether one of them can usurp the other or whether there remains a place for both of them in contemporary culture. Finally, we provide a provisional assessment on whether the concept of the citizen can form the basis of a co-ordinated opposition to consumer capitalism. We will see that the idea of citizenship is itself often commodified and corrupted by consumer capitalism and the political and ideological powers that underpin it. Yet we shall also note that whenever a vocabulary of opposition and defiance is required, as the Occupy Movement which began in 2011 and related protests amply demonstrate, it is as likely as not to proceed from the ideal of the citizen.

Citizens and consumers

People have no serious difficulty thinking of themselves as consumers. Thinking of ourselves as citizens is more problematic, even for those of us who spent our childhood saluting the flag daily. 'In this society, citizenship is an archaic term. It is not part of the language of everyday life. Its value for understanding this life is not evident either' (Wexler, 1990: 166). Demands for citizenship and the right to vote might be high on the popular agenda in a country engaged in mass struggle for enfranchisement, such as South Africa during the five apartheid decades, but in the so-called mature democracies like the USA and countries of the EU, the right to vote and broader notions of citizenship have become more problematic. Voting rates have declined, though citizenship reasserts itself whenever voters question a political agenda, such as the European Constitution.

The idea of citizen implies mutuality and control as well as a balance of rights and duties that is neither evident nor necessarily especially attractive; how attractive that mix is depends on the balance of advantages versus demands. Citizens are active members of communities, at once listened to, but also prepared to defer to the will of the majority. Citizens have to argue their views and engage with the views of others. In as much as they can make choices, citizens have a sense of superior responsibility. Making choices as a citizen leads to a very different evaluation of alternatives than if one chooses as a consumer. As a citizen, one must confront the implications of one's choices, their meaning and their moral value. The notion of citizenship has at its core a 'bond', as T. H. Marshall noted, 'a direct sense of community membership based on loyalty to a civilization which is a common possession' (Wexler, 1990: 169).

Consumers, on the other hand, need not be members of a community, nor do they have to act on its behalf. They operate in impersonal markets, where they can make choices unburdened by guilt or social obligations. Both Marx and Simmel remarked on how the cash nexus dissolves social bonds, the former to criticize it as the root of alienation under capitalism, the latter to praise it as the liberation from the fetters of the gift economy (Marx, [1844] 1972; Marx, [1867] 1967; Simmel, 1978). Unlike citizens, consumers can indulge their appetites and passions without worrying that they will be accused of intemperance and excess. Moral restraints need not hold them back; so long as they can pay, they can do as they please. Morality, in fact, is systematically kept out of the world of the consumer or, better, it is readily cast as sanctimonious moralizing intent on spoiling the other's carefree happiness.

The citizen and the consumer ideas have very different pedigrees. The citizen, the foundation of Athenian democracy and reinvented and expanded by the American and French revolutions, implies an equality among citizens, even if it denies it to others – slaves, immigrants or refugees. It is essentially a political concept, defining individuals as standing within a state and a community, according them rights and responsibilities (Rawls, 1971: 699). The citizen is an impersonation of what Philip Rieff called 'political man', the ethical ideal based on the notion that the good life, justice and happiness can be attained through political action, rather than through religious faith; the latter had been the recipe for salvation of political man's predecessor, the 'religious man' (Rieff, 1959; 1966). Common to both religious and political ideals was the presupposition that each individual is an organic part of a whole, unable to achieve full individuality and happiness except as a member of that whole. Where the ideal of the citizen dramatically deviated from that of the religious believer was in the inalienable rights of citizens to hold their own opinions and views. One can be a citizen while disagreeing and criticizing the government; this was a new form of freedom.

The consumer, on the other hand, originates in a very different ideal, referred to by Rieff as 'economic man', who seeks the good life in markets. Few variants of this ideal are as clear-cut as the Protestant work ethic, or, in the 20th century, the backbone of modern consumerism, the Fordist Deal (see Chapter 1, 'The Emergence of Contemporary Consumerism'). Here individuals act as atoms, unencumbered by social responsibilities and duties, free from the obligation to account for their preferences and choices. They are never required to endure sacrifices for a superior goal, nor do their actions represent anybody other than themselves. They need not defer to any collective majority. So long as they act within the law, they have no need to worry whether their choices are right or wrong, good or bad, so long as they give them pleasure. In brief then, citizens feel responsible to others and demand that the state takes responsibility for the common good, consumers only feel responsible to themselves, request no support from others or from the state and accept the bad as well as the good consequences of their actions.

The notion of the citizen can become easily idealized, the focus of nostalgia for a time when individuals were meant to be active members of political communities and when economies where conceived as having national boundaries, when a vote created a political assembly which could control a national economy. However, if such a notion of citizenship implies control, commitment and bonding, it also carries since its earliest origins disturbing resonances of exclusion and discrimination. Women (for the largest part of human history and in most countries), children, non-citizens, stateless persons, immigrants, refugees, prisoners (in some countries), exiles, people without official papers and fixed addresses, mentally sick people and vagrants, these are people who are excluded from the rights of citizenship and may therefore be harassed, exploited and discriminated against in most societies, especially those which place a high premium on citizenship. The outsider can be used as a mechanism of social division. Consumers, on the other hand, generally face no such discrimination, so long as they can afford to pay, irrespective of age, creed or anything else. Through money they may acquire a wide variety of things, including in many cases 'citizenship', the right to participate in a way of life, a dream. Consumerism gives the vote to groups traditionally disenfranchised by citizenship discourses. This has been the argument regularly deployed by the promoters of free markets.

How then is it possible that two ideas so different as citizen and consumer can become part of the same discourse? Two main political avenues have led to this convergence. The left, having lost faith in the consumer as the hero of right-wing economics, has sought to enlarge the consumer into a responsible consumer, a socially aware consumer, a consumer who thinks ahead and tempers his or her desires by social awareness, a consumer whose actions must be morally defensible and who must occasionally be prepared to sacrifice personal pleasure to communal well-being. In other words, the left has stretched the idea of consumer in the direction of citizen. The US organization Public Citizen and all the other organizations started by Nader (see Chapter 9, 'The Consumer as Activist') have been prolific in campaigning and promoting the idea of the citizen and of consumers as citizens. So concerned was Nader and his team about the decline of meaningful US citizenship by the early 1990s that they produced a civics package for use in schools (Isaac and Nader, 1992). This profiled a number of key citizens' movements representing the rights of women, minorities, consumers, unions and the environment. More importantly, the civics package took students through the options a citizen has for participating in civil society: whistle-blowing, pamphleteering, getting organized, arranging meetings, conducting research, legal action, direct action, becoming a shareholder activist and so on. The book, to some extent, was a 'how to' and 'what' summary of much of third- and fourth-wave consumer activism and was a classic statement, as Nader wrote in the 'Foreword', of 'practicing civics, becoming a skilled citizen, using one's skills to overcome apathy, ignorance, greed or abuses of power in society at all levels ...' (Nader, [1965] 1991: iv). Similar moves followed the election of New Labour (a centrist rather than left government) in 1997 in the UK. The message was that the only route to rebuilding citizenship from a consumer starting point was involvement with others. Since then, many have lamented the further decline of citizenship, especially among young people. Putnam (2000) in his best-selling *Bowling Alone* has argued that the threads that hold US communities together have frayed. A study by Carr and colleagues (2012), based on extensive survey data, showed that generation X – born in the 1960s and 1970s – exhibits the highest rates of over-consumption and competitive consumption of any in the USA. By contrast, they found that the earlier civic generation (born in the 1930s and early 1940s) and baby-boom generation (born between 1945 and 1964) demonstrate a far stronger citizenship orientation and politically conscious consumption. Their findings do not support the view that younger people use consumer activity as a surrogate for political action.

The right (which has repeatedly reinvented itself) has sought to incorporate the citizen into its image of the consumer by using the concept of 'votes' and ballots. According to this argument, consumers vote in the marketplace in exactly the same way as citizens voted in the Athenian agora of old. The marketplace becomes a surrogate for political discourse or, in their view, incorporates political discourse, rendering it redundant, not least because the shopping vote is quick, precise and decisive. The citizen is being redefined as a purchaser whose 'ballots ... help create and maintain the trading areas, shopping centres, products, stores, and the like' (Dickinson and Hollander, 1991: 12). Buying becomes tantamount to voting, market surveys the nearest we have to a collective will (Ewen, 1992: 23). In this way, the more wealth or purchasing power the consumer has, the more 'votes' she or he gets, thus transmogrifying the old political principle of one-person-one-vote. The concept of dollar-votes, initially conceived by right-wingers, is now increasingly discussed across the political spectrum (Arnould, 2007; Jubas, 2007; Johnston, 2008; Soper, 2008; Gotlieb and Wells, 2012).

With such divergence of interpretation, it is not surprising that, when the idea of the citizen emerges in discussions of consumption, it assumes different mean-ings. Nowhere is this more clear than in discussions of TV (McRobbie, 1994; 1999). Market enthusiasts want unregulated TV, where individuals choose to watch what they want. In an age of multi-channel, satellite and internet TV, if they do not like a programme, they vote by switching to a different channel or by switching off and turning to their game consoles, their computer or other personal entertain-ment systems. Public service advocates, on the other hand, believe that if individuals act merely as consumers, they end up with a profusion of virtually indistinct chan-nels appealing to the lowest common denominator. Their choice is narrowed to minutiae (Brown, 1991). If, however, they act as citizens, they seek to control and regulate what is shown on their screens, voting for a particular range of options and stopping others. Ultimately, the citizens do not take markets as given but will seek to regulate them, control them and tame them. They seek to do so either through direct action and active participation, or indirectly, through the state or other mechanisms, which set generalized frameworks that 'filter' choice and set common standards. A range of viewing options, from child pornography to tobacco advertising to decapitations of captives and public executions, would no doubt find some viewers wishing to take them – however, these have been regulated out of the television screens. And this is where the state comes into discussions of citizens and contemporary consumption.

The dilution of the citizen? Or resurrection?

The nature of the state is and always has been furiously contested. On the traditional left, critics have long seen the state as the club of the ruling class, a mechanism for facilitating the interests of capital and oiling the wheels of commerce (Miliband, 1969; Poulantzas, 1975). Social democrats and liberals have taken a more accommodating position, arguing that the state can be used to ameliorate the conditions of the poor, notably through welfare, educational and health provisions (e.g. Beveridge, 1942). Conservatives of the older paternalist school did not deviate much from the idea of the state as safety-net, though they would draw a line between those deserving assistance and those not.

> *[Conservatism] regards it as the duty of the modern State to ensure to the subject pure air and water, to see that his food is unadulterated, and to assist him to maintain himself and his family in sickness and old age. It lays it down as a cardinal principle that every citizen shall have a right, so far as is humanly possible, to a good education, open spaces, and healthy conditions of life. The modern State is the assurance company which assures these benefits to its citizens. (Bryant, 1929: 17)*

Under the New Right of the 1980s, the state disowned such paternalist responsibilities. Throughout the 1980s and 1990s (the Thatcher–Reagan years and their legacy), it set out, first, to dismantle the welfare philosophy through privatization and contracting services to independent firms, and then explicitly they sought to redefine it (Cockett, 1994), turning citizens into consumers (HM Government, 1991). According to this view, it is up to the citizens as consumers to decide whether they want a service from the state and what quality they are prepared to pay for. In simple terms, why bother voting for politicians to provide public parks and clean air, if parks can be privately supplied by Disneyland and others? Public space, from parks to pavements, is seen as an opportunity to sell, not to commune; it becomes a marketplace, not a social place (Worpole, 2000). This marketization has been most rigorously applied in the education, healthcare and pension sectors, with even the social democratic welfarist countries under pressure to reform their public sectors. The principles of consumer choice and individual responsibility are subverting the idea of universal rights to health, education and pensions.

Critics of marketization draw upon three stands of analysis, broadly, sociological, economic and political. One strand argues that government has been taken over by totally unaccountable forces that corrupt the possibility of anyone having control, whether termed consumer or citizen (Greider, 1992; Monbiot, 2000; Korten, 2001; Held, 2006). For both citizens and consumers, rights have become dependent upon wealth. For Bauman, the poor have been made to look like failed citizens who mishandled their exercise of choice and are now forced to accept the state's choices on their behalf (Bauman, 1998). As Golding has said, 'to be poor is to endure conditional citizenship' (Lister, 2004: vii). The poor, of course, are marginalized by consumerism but further fractionalized by gender and position in the workforce (Toynbee, 2003; Lister, 2004).

The second strand of criticism asserts that the very idea that consumers or market forces can govern affairs of state is absurd and that a public sector, distinct from the private sector, has to be retained.

> *The analogy between government and firms doesn't hold water. Since the public sector is not driven by the same profit motive – citizens' priorities are different from stockholders' – it has no inherent reason to price its services more expensively. (Lynch and Makusen, 1993: 128)*

According to this view, fundamental resources such as water, air, open space and wildernesses should not be treated as commodities but as common goods to be husbanded and cared for by agencies that are not penetrated by market forces (Kaul et al., 1999; Barlow and Clarke, 2002; Morgan, 2003).

The third strand set out to reclaim the notion of citizenship from the clutches of the New Right (Crick, 2001; Crick, 2004). This strand argues that the modern Anglo-American 'hands off' state with its individualistic and pro-business orientation marks the nadir of true citizenship (Pollock and Leys, 2004). David Rieff views the US citizen as no more than a supermarket cultural browser: 'For better or worse (probably both), ours is a culture of consumerism and spectacle, of things and *not* ideas' (Rieff, 1993: 63).

The consumer-citizen hybrid

Some progressive companies have sought to address their customers as though they were citizens, keenly interested to act responsibly in line with environmental, ethical, human rights and other social values. This has led some authors to propose the concept of the consumer-citizen, a new hybrid (Campbell, 2004; Jubas, 2007; Johnston, 2008; Shah et al., 2012). This hybrid is based on the assumption that markets can be tamed by ideological and cultural forces that seek to reaffirm collective values like sustainability and human rights. There need not be a contradiction between consumerism and citizenship, they proclaim; one can be a responsible citizen while enjoying all the choice and privileges of consumerism. Johnston carried out a detailed study of the giant US Whole Foods Market (WFM) whose stores offer vast arrays of organic, diverse, exotic produce and processed products. She examined the extent to which the ideals of consumer and citizen can be drawn together under the aegis of a socially responsible corporation. She found that the citizen-consumer hybrid is riven with contradictions:

> *Rather than meeting the requirements of consumerism and citizenship equally, the case of WFM suggests that the citizen-consumer hybrid provides superficial attention to citizenship goals in order to serve three consumerist interests better: consumer choice, status distinction, and ecological cornucopianism. I argue that a true 'citizen-consumer' hybrid is not only difficult to achieve, but may be internally inconsistent in a growth-oriented corporate setting. (Johnston, 2008: 229)*

Others have further questioned the happy marriage of consumer and citizen. Jubas, a feminist scholar, is sceptical of the view that consumerism, a deeply unequal ideology, can ever be compatible with the democratic ideal of equality among citizens of whatever income level and irrespective of gender, race or creed (Jubas, 2007). Consumption, she argues, cannot function as an effective corrective, let alone a strategy of resistance, to inequality and privilege. Campbell (2004) goes further and suggests that the consumer-citizen hybrid is an oxymoron.

Where does the consumer movement stand in all this? In the 1980s, the consumer movement was divided by the New Right's attempt to redefine the citizen as consumer. The second-wave value-for-money organizations (See Chapter 9, 'The Consumer as Activist') generally supported with only minor reservations initiatives such as the UK Citizen's Charter (which attempted to obliterate any distinction between citizen and consumer) and privatization (HM Government, 1991). They believed that such moves offered a better deal by raising the quality of service and widening the range of options. They were swayed by the rhetoric that nationalized industries and public services were arthritic and unresponsive. In doing so, second-wave consumer organizations acknowledged the argument of the New Right that the state is unable to conduct economic activity effectively, whether this amounts to running a transport network, a health service or an automobile manufacturer.

The third and fourth waves of consumer organizations, on the other hand, were sceptical about the consumer-citizen hybrid and dismissive of privatization and marketization of the state sector (Harrison et al., 2005). Privatization is seen as accelerating the dilution of citizenship, accentuating social inequality and making public services contingent on the ability to pay (Pollock and Leys, 2004). If the ideological principle of progressive taxation is on the defensive, the idea that all citizens are entitled to certain services on an equal basis is also under attack from dominant political culture. Some third- and fourth-wave thinkers were disparaging of the New Right's efforts to resurrect an ideal of citizen, even as it fostered inequalities and divisions within their societies. If this is citizenship, they said, it is of a lightweight form. These efforts were even more risible when seen against the tone of political and cultural discourse set by the mass media. The days of the Athenian agora, of reasoned debate and personal involvement have long been overtaken by the politics of the sound-bite, the image, the simulation and the passive evaluation of policies and politicians after the manner of soap-powders. Even governments genuinely committed to the ideal of citizenship would find it hard to take independent political or economic action in an age of free trade, capital globalization and transnational institutions (Nader, [1965] 1991; Lang and Hines, 1993: 49; Held and Koenig-Archibugi, 2005).

The rest of this chapter explores further the arguments above as they play out in three different arenas: privatization and sub-contracting of public services, consumer advice and information, and the environmental impact of consumption.

Privatization and sub-contracting

The privatization of the state sector is one of the central arenas in which these arguments have been fought over. State industries were targeted by the New Right as inefficient, failing to give value for money to the customer and ripe for market discipline. Earlier, certain consumer bodies had already argued the case for increased competition in public services (National Consumer Council, 1978; National Consumer Council, 1979), a plea that was eventually to lead to their own demise! The Thatcher government went well beyond all earlier recommendations and, in a wave of spectacular privatizations, sold off water, telephone, electricity, gas, the state airline and even public transport all to the private sector. Other areas of the state sector, like sections of the prisons and security services, were partially contracted out. Many others were off-loaded to charities or third sector organizations. The overall principle was to relieve the state of the responsibility for the quality of services run under its auspices, to offer better value for money to the tax payer and to introduce market discipline in the delivery of such services, thus enhancing quality and innovation. Thatcher's pioneering example was emulated worldwide, in countries as diverse as Italy, India and Russia. In some countries, however, there was strong reaction against privatization; in Latin American countries, like Venezuela and Brazil, there have been fierce debates over retention of public assets such as oil (Gott, 2000).

The main opposition to privatization and outsourcing of public services, outside party politics, came from trades unions and, occasionally, environmental groups which took a broader citizen's approach, expressing a series of concerns regarding standards, public health and safety implications, increased costs for low-income groups and lack of democratic accountability. The consumer might in the short term benefit from competition, smarter packaging, greater choice, they acknowledged, but citizens stood to lose massively from these moves. Not only were a number of national assets taken away from them, but, subject to the market mechanism, unprofitable operations were run down. More importantly, these moves symbolized the ideological triumph of the neo-liberal and neo-conservative creed that only free enterprise could run business efficiently and that all state-run enterprise was doomed to dip endlessly into the tax-payers' pocket. A service or a commodity that did not attract purchasers in the market, according to the Thatcherite logic, could be dispensed with. A wedge had been driven between citizen and consumer. Under the rhetoric of a share-owning democracy, the concept of the citizen was itself being privatized.

Another prong of the strategy to reduce citizens to consumers consisted of outsourcing, such as via the introduction of compulsory competitive tendering for local authority services. In the UK, services such as street cleaning, school meals and direct labour organizations in building maintenance were all contracted out in the early 1980s (Whitfield, 1983). Subsequently in the 1990s, middle-class professional services such as architects, legal services and residential care homes were all contracted out too. What had previously been a nexus of national and local services regarded as integral parts of the British state's support structure for the citizen, became markets. An entire new ethos of managerialism, called New Public Management (Ferlie et al., 1996), was introduced wholesale into the management of public services, borrowing from the private sector. Terms like 'benchmarking', 'performance indicators', 'incentivization', 'best practice' and 'targets' superseded the older tradition of public administration and its notions of public goods and public service. The outsourcing and mana-gerialist ethos spread to many other countries worldwide (e.g. Walker and Wang, 2005), ostensibly bringing consumer pressure to modernise public services.

The introduction of a new language of 'empowerment', 'internal markets' and 'mixed economy of care', 'public–private partnerships' and 'private finance initiatives' into public service organizations is significant. A service becomes a commodity, even as a hollow vocabulary of empowerment, choice and quality was rehearsed to justify it (Mather, 1991; Pirie, 1991; Walker and Wang, 2005). What the rhetoric of the consumer achieved beyond doubt was to put business in the driving seat, offering it profit-making opportunities, while constantly undermining the idea of citizens with rights and obligations. The buzz-word of empowerment, hijacked from minority right movements, was to provide both the *coup de grâce* to the old notion of citizen and its banalization in the Citizen's Charter, a UK government initiative launched in 1991 promising certain 'rights' for customers of state ser-vices (HM Government, 1991). This was a misnomer and might have been more accurately described as a customers' charter for public services about to be privat-ized. Academic critics viewed it as 'an exercise in improving supplier responsiveness to customers but unaccompanied by any real shift in power to consumers' (Hambleton and Hoggett, 1993: 106). Utilities were made to promise targets such as the length of delay before answering a phone, the percentage of trains arriving within a few minutes of the promised arrival time, the number of crime enquiries completed and so on. Over decades, this discourse took root and became accepted as the normal framework for public policy-making.

Consumer advice, information and education

Another issue that highlights the distance between older traditions of citizenship and its reinvention by the neo-liberals has been over what it means to be an effec-tive consumer in the marketplace and what information consumers require to operate effectively. Older traditions of citizenship, since the 19th century, emphasized the value of education to provide the tools by which effective resource manage-ment could be undertaken. Thus, reading and writing as well as more specialist offerings like domestic science or home economics were meant to enable people to make sensible decisions as consumers, to manage their money and other resources effectively and to get the best out of the marketplace. Consumer activists, for their part, made their impact by stressing the role of information, including product and price information, packaging and labelling. As seen in the previous chapter (Chapter 9, 'The Consumer as Activist'), one of their earliest arguments was that markets cannot operate as effective mechanisms against unscrupulous or ineffi-cient suppliers *unless* consumers have the requisite information and right of redress. All strands of consumer activism have been in agreement that it is essential for consumers to know their rights in front of the law (Cranston, 1984).

In the 1970s, the UK government still saw as its role both to provide opportunities for consumer redress, but also to ensure that information was available to ensure the smooth operation of the markets. It set up a national system of law centres offering legal advice to consumers, irrespective of their ability to pay. Prompted by the Consumers' Association (now *Which?*), it also set up a system of Consumer Advice Centres, drawing on experience elsewhere in Europe. The aims of these centres were to offer pre-shopping advice to help people decide which product to purchase, as well as to assist them with complaints when purchases had gone wrong. In practice, people did not use the pre-shopping advice that much, but they did make extensive use of the complaint support schemes (National Consumer Council, 1977). Some of the centres handled as many as 40,000 enquiries a year, no mean index of interest at a local level. By 1977, there were 120 centres, processing over half a million com-plaints a year (Fulop, 1977: 22–23). Better evidence of the consumers' thirst for support and information cannot be supplied than the success of this scheme. This was possibly the high point of the state, acting on behalf of the citizen, providing information and legal services to the consumer.

One of the very first things that the Thatcher government did was to cut central government funds to the Consumer Advice Centres and then to close them down altogether. Information about redress was transferred to Citizens Advice Bureaux, staffed mostly by voluntary labour, while product information and advice was left to the consumers themselves to search and find wherever they could. The state was no longer accepting responsibility for people's choices as consumers. If they made wrong or unwise decisions, they should face the consequences. They should also have the burden of risk whenever things go wrong. It took several disastrous episodes, like rail accidents, mad cow disease and other epidemics, to remind the public of the limits of information and the amount of control they had. Once the state's duties to its citizens had been replaced by sovereign con-sumers making independent choices in pursuit of their own well-being, the government could wash its hands of responsibility. As with the example of pri-vatization, in the case of information, advice and education, we observe a diminution of the state's roles and an eclipsing of the citizen by the consumer.

Since then, the arrival of the internet has completely revolutionized the channels through which consumers obtain information and has forced consumers into the driving seat of seeking information to protect themselves. The idea that the state might actually be needed to provide such information seems almost quaint. Consumers appear to have taken up this challenge with relish, going as far as freely and generously sharing this information with fellow-consumers. In the next chapter, 'The Consumer as Worker', we will explore how this may be re-injecting a degree of citizenship into contemporary consumption. We should also note that the older media, TV, radio and newspapers, have seized the consumers' need for information as an opportunity to turn information into a game of mass entertainment – auctions, reality shows, quizzes, magazine programmes and other opportunities for pundits. As entertainment becomes a substitute for education, the citizen is once again eclipsed by the consumer.

Citizens, consumers and the environment

The environment is another key location from which to explore the differing outlooks between consumer and citizen. It also is a litmus test for distinguishing between the citizen as a mechanism for self-discipline and control and the citizen as a vehicle for seeking to re-establish a deeper spirit of community and general welfare. The consumer's role in either damaging or protecting the environment is an issue that has generated considerable rancour within the organized consumer movement, sections of which initially did not see the environment as a consumer issue at all. Some of them went as far as seeing environmental regulations as anti-consumer, a back door into protectionism and, therefore, higher prices in the shops. 'The environment is not a consumer issue' is a position that now only rarely, if at all, appears in consumer circles. The older waves of the consumer movement were slow to integrate environmental criteria into their value-for-money appraisals of consumer goods. But today it is *de rigeur* for responsible consumerism to include environmental elements. These range from pale green to dark green, the former focusing on environmental labelling, energy audits and niche products with marginal green gain, the latter advocating stringent recycling and product footprints (see below) to a more generalized promotion to consume local products and even to consume less.

Environmentalists, for their part, have since the 1970s urged retailers to cut down on packaging and shoppers to recycle or reuse wherever possible. As a result, appeals to consumers to clean up their own back-yard and use their purchasing power to force industry to tidy up its act have become part of the cultural landscape. Jay Hair, then President of the National Wildlife Federation, urged Americans to take ten practical steps if they wish to act as citizens rather than consumers (Hair, 1989). These included actions such as cutting down on trash, using cloth diapers (nappies), not leaving water running needlessly, reusing grocery bags, planting a tree and using public transport or car pools. A quarter of a century later, this list does not seem outdated! Such encouragements to act responsibly, to consume wisely, to cut waste, and to think of the eco-sphere as one consumes seek to reintroduce a citizen's ethic of social responsibility, which goes beyond the consumer's narrow self-interest, countering the ethos of a throw-away society (The Ecologist, 2001). This vision of planet-earth citizenship was accused of lacking any wider notion of social solidarity, civic debate, co-ordinated action or sacrifice. It individualized the idea of citizenship, as if acting responsibly was a matter of individual choice alone. In this way, citizenship became a life-style, however praiseworthy and necessary, which could easily degenerate into tokenism and was hardly likely to alter the politics of consumption.

A more collective appeal to consumers as citizens resorts to collective action to restrain free markets and introduce 'green' measures through legislation or taxa-tion, whether at international, national or local levels. European environmental and fourth-wave consumer groups have turned to the EU as the forum on which campaigns for the protection of the environment and individual consumers could be debated and acted. It was at this level that measures such as the setting of standards for controlling pesticide residues, genetic engineering and water pollution, as well as access to environmental information, recycling electrical goods and cars and eco-labelling (such as labelling washing machines or refrig-erators for their energy efficiency) were debated. Some of these debates were decided in the environmentalists' favour and some went against, but the balance shifted distinctly in the environmental direction. European institutions emerged as an important new terrain for citizenship and as political bodies delivering environmental protection. From the New Right perspective, European institu-tions have taken over the role of the nanny from national governments.

Citizenship, at a local level, can go beyond individual lifestyle choices (whether to recycle an aluminium beer can) into acting in concert with other citizens in local communities. The landmark UN Conference on Environment and Development in 1992 enshrined this basis for community citizenship and con-sumption in the Local Agenda 21 strategy (UN, 1992). This proposed that localities should define their own community objectives, in consultation with local popula-tions, and should then receive central government support to attain these objectives. This strategy built upon the experience of pioneering green citizen local economies, even when this meant a reduction of choice for individual con-sumers or costlier products. One is denied the option of choosing to pollute, just as one may, on public health grounds, be denied the right to spit on pavements.

A different attempt to reclaim terrain from the consumer and hand it over to the citizen is through the indicators of 'environmental space' or 'ecological footprints' (van Brakel and Zagema, 1994; Wackernagel et al., 1996). This notion proposes that every consumer action leaves a 'footprint' on the eco-system and that every consumer takes up a certain amount of physical space which includes land and resource use. By using a battery, by driving a car, by purchasing a computer, or by eating meat every day, contemporary Western consumers are leaving disproportionately large and deep imprints on the environment, in comparison to earlier generations and to the rest of the world's consumers (Global Footprint Network, 2010). In order to achieve any degree of sustainable development, let alone allow some of the world's poorer people to enjoy a larger part of the earth's resources, rich Northern consumers will have to reduce substantially their ecological footprints (Royal Society, 2012). From this analysis, rampant consumerism and citizenship are incompatible (Durning, 1992b; Skidelsky and Skidelsky, 2012). Consumer capitalism, say these thinkers, cannot continue at the current pace without meeting its nemesis – resources will run out, the eco-sphere will be irreparably damaged, and the choices of future generations severely curtailed to the point, say the more apocalyptic proponents of this view, where life itself is threatened (see also Chapter 1, 'The Emergence of Contemporary Consumerism').

In summary, the first two examples above – privatization and consumer advice – represent areas where consumerism has encroached on citizenship. The third example suggests a rearguard action by citizens in defence of the environment against the ravages of consumerism.

Consumerism as democracy

The efforts of environmentalists and the more radical elements of the consumer movement have played a part in reasserting the importance of citizenship in recent years. However, is it possible for the citizen to have any serious influence in the modern world when politics itself threatens to collapse into an offshoot of consumption? 'The culture and entertainment industries have helped make politics a spectator sport. The pursuit of happiness now means amusement and diversion ...' (Barnet and Cavanagh, 1994: 41). When politicians compete for votes via sound-bites and television commercials, and when political debate is conducted at the level of slogans, advertising and gladiatorial encounters, does not the idea of citizenship itself collapse too? When so many political decisions are taken outside the public's view or in another country (the problem of multi-level governance), could it be that the idea of citizenship has become a smoke-screen behind which green fundamentalists are pushing their own political agendas, as the ideologues of the free market sometimes claim? And could the idea of the EU as a forum for the new citizenry not be laughed out of court by those who have sought to portray all European institutions as arthritic bureaucracies? Can it not be argued that behind the ideal of the global or European citizen, unelected civil servants and unaccountable politicians keep themselves in jobs by dreaming up unwarranted regulations and standards that tie up the hands of business and restrict the choice of consumers?

The question of whether the battle over the citizen is worth fighting against the narrow self-interest of the consumer is not one that environmental groups and other progressive forces have resolved yet. Some are arguing that instead of setting up the citizen to fight the beast of consumerism, as a latter-day St George against the dragon, a preferable strategy might be to tame the beast and redirect its powers. In this chapter, we have examined the battle that is being fought over the concept of the citizen. We have considered the efforts to present the consumer as citizen as a force that may potentially oppose contemporary Western consumerism, as well as those forces that seek to reduce the citizen to but another face of the consumer, like those investigated in other chapters of this book.

At the moment, the prospects for the citizen do not look good. For the last 40 years, voters in Western countries have listened to appeals to act in more socially responsible ways. However, by and large, in the privacy of the ballot booth they have often voted for governments that promise them tax cuts, who redefine public space as private goods and who favour increased opportunities for individuals to spend their pay packets as they wish. The balance seems to favour the consumer over the citizen who appears a timid figure at the borders of contemporary consumption. Embarrassed by the right's attempts to embrace them or set them up as a bulwark against unwanted aliens, citizens feel uneasy amidst the din of modern advertising and the clamour of the mass media. Yet citizens are figures who, from time to time, raise their voices, to the surprise of many. It is too early to assess their ultimate impact, but by the beginning of the 21st century, all over the world citizen-like movements (like Citizen UK) and protests (like Occupy) demanded new rights, as well as the assertion of old ones (Klein, 2000; Sassatelli, 2006; Johnston, 2008; Gotlieb and Wells, 2012; Shah et al., 2012; Willis and Schor, 2012).

It can be argued today that the channel through which many citizens make their voices heard comes in the form of single issue politics, marginal activities or local communities. Equally, the sacrifices of local campaigners against hypermarketization, environmental protesters or human rights activists can be decoded as media stunts and attempts at sensation, devoid of commitment and moral force. No sooner do individuals discover in citizenship one of the last remaining defences against the rule of markets, than they also discover what a precarious defence it can turn out to be. All the same, it is telling that whenever a vocabulary of organized and conscious opposition to consumer capitalism and its powerful accoutrements is required, citizenship, especially global citizenship, citizenship without frontiers, citizenship defending the interests of future generations, even if it is an assertion and celebration of the community, invariably appears on the agenda. It remains to be seen whether, under the force of things to come, the idea of citizen, redefined and reformulated, can form the basis of an alliance that mounts a serious challenge to consumer capitalism.

11

THE CONSUMER AS WORKER

This divorce of production from consumption, which became a defining feature of all industrial or Second Wave societies, even affected our psyches and our assumptions about personality. Behavior came to be seen as a set of transactions. Instead of a society based on friendship, kinship, or tribal or feudal allegiance, there arose in the wake of the Second Wave a civilization based on contractual ties, actual or implied. The cleavage between these two roles – producer and consumer – created at the same time a dual personality. The very same person who (as a producer) was taught by family, school, and boss to defer gratification, to be disciplined, controlled, restrained, obedient, to be a team player, was simultaneously taught (as a consumer) to seek instant gratification, to be hedonistic rather than calculating, to abandon discipline, to pursue individualistic pleasure – in short to be a totally different kind of person ... to perform a patriotic service by keeping the wheels of the economy turning. (Toffler, 1980: 58)

CORE ARGUMENTS

Work and consumption have long been seen as separate spheres of life. Work is where value is generated, while consumption is where value is dissipated. The Fordist Deal demonstrated that there is a strong link between how people earn and how they spend their money. In recent years, there has been an increasing realization that consumption itself entails a substantial amount of work done by consumers. This work, for which we propose the term consumption-work, can involve hard physical and intellectual labour, entailing a wide variety of skills. In the internet era, a large part of what is known as digital labour fuses the experiences of working and consuming. The face of the *consumer as worker* presented in this chapter draws on recent concepts of the 'prosumer' and the 'working customer', seeking to capture the core elements of this fusion. Manifested in phenomena such as crowdsourcing, co-creation and co-production, the category of the consumer-worker is going beyond the 20th-century idea of the consumer who serves him or herself in a supermarket or a fast food restaurant. In the 21st century, the dematerialization of consumption and production are running apace, blurring the boundaries between the two. Every place has the potential to become a social factory, epitomized by the internet café where people can both consume and work. And every form of consumption-work has the potential of unleashing new human potential or turning into a new form of alienation and exploitation.

Work and consumption: two spheres or one?

An essential premise of this book since it was first conceived has been that the world of consumption and the world of work have *not* been separate spheres of life, even if the experience of consumption and the experience of work appear at times to be polar opposites. Through our concept of the Fordist Deal (see Chapter 1), we tried to capture the close interrelationship between the two spheres at one particular historical moment. This was the moment that witnessed the birth of mass consumption allied to the birth of mass production, epitomized in Henry Ford's recognition that if he paid his workers sufficiently they could afford to buy his products. This Fordist Deal, which relied on alienated and mostly deskilled labour in exchange for ever-higher standards of living became the underpinning of 20th-century consumerism.

A large amount of scholarship since the first edition of this book has started to recognize that consumption itself involves an element of work. Some authors have gone as far as to say that this is so obvious that it was a blind spot of earlier consumer studies (Ritzer, 2014). Suddenly, consumers are seen as actively engaged in the co-creation of brands (see, for example, Prahalad and Ramaswamy, 2004a; Prahalad and Ramaswamy, 2004b; Arvidsson, 2005; Arvidsson, 2006; Cova and Dalli, 2009; Hatch and Schultz, 2010), product ideas and even the actual generation of marketable goods such as advice and information for other consumers. The view that consumers do work for themselves, for other consumers and for businesses has come into sharp relief as a result of the spread of new information technologies, including social media, the blogosphere and Web 2.0, the areas of internet activity where content is generated by users (e.g. Kleemann et al., 2008; Cova and White, 2010). This rapid development in the last 15 years has been so significant that, we felt, it warranted this present chapter which proposes an additional face of the consumer – the Consumer as Worker – alongside the nine we depicted earlier. In this chapter we examine the different types of work that consumers do, the debates about its meaning and its economic contribution, and consider whether work done by consumers represents new forms of alienation and exploitation or of creativity and empowerment. We conclude by drawing some lines of continuity and discontinuity between the consumer as worker and the other nine faces of the consumer in this book.

Hard working consumers

Consumers work. This seems quite self-evident. Going to a marketplace and making a purchase involves the expenditure of human physical and mental energy.

The same goes for cooking a meal at home and eating it with one's family. For Karl Marx, this type of labour belonged to his category of reproduction rather than production. It ensured that the workforce was maintained in order to work in the productive sphere; to carry out its productive role in the economy, a workforce had to be fed, clothed and sheltered (Marx, [1867] 1967). Fundamental to Marx was the view that exploitation is entirely restricted to the productive sphere, not the reproductive one, which therefore received little attention from either him or his followers until feminists made it central to their agenda and critique (Hartmann, 1979). Throughout the 20th century, and with the rise of consumerism, an ever increasing part of the work involved in the production and especially the circulation of goods came to be assigned to consumers. Why pay workers to do work that consumers could do more or less happily? Whereas a traditional grocer would serve customers from behind the store counter one at a time, the supermarket self-service model enables consumers to go behind the counter and serve themselves.

Indeed, today's supermarket turns the customer into the cashier and security guard too, with self-checkout technology. In a similar way, fast food turns customers into waiters and even table-clearers. IKEA and other stores turn consumers into carpenters by inviting them to assemble their own furniture. Between choosing an IKEA product and seeing it as material object assembled in one's room, a huge amount of labour and time have to be expended by the customer travelling to the store, identifying the components against a catalogue, self-checking it out, loading it on their vehicle, returning home, carrying and assembling it. Still more work has to be done getting rid of the packaging, and yet more if some components are missing or the product is in some way defective. The incentives for consumers are high quality, better designed products at ostensibly lower prices. Arguably, some consumers feel some sense of pride and achievement when they have assembled a product that, if assembled industrially by employees would be a source of tedium and alienation. These incentives have proved highly successful with millions of consumers. In spite of the stress they may feel by the time they conclude their purchases, people across social classes, national cultures and age groups appear eager to work hard for their home furnishings.

It should be stressed that not only the middle class works hard at consumption. Nor is this a purely contemporary phenomenon. Upper-class consumers may work hard with an architect to design their new house, with their tailor to design their new suit, or with an artist to design their new installation or portrait. People on low or no incomes arguably have to work even harder for their consumption in order to make their limited resources stretch further (Viswanathan et al., 2012). In order to obtain credit – which to the more affluent is easy – the poor have to work hard to prove their credit-worthiness. As we shall see presently, work done by consumers can be experienced in vastly different ways, depending on a range of circumstances – from deeply alienating to hugely rewarding.

Given how much work is done by consumers, why is it that academic interest in consumer-work is so recent? This is partly due to the devaluation of the domestic sphere and unpaid labour by theorists of production, and the systematic disinterest by theorists of consumption into anything that smacked of work. It is also a result of disciplinary boundaries across the social sciences. The arrival of the internet and the huge new areas of consumer-work that it opened up made academics sit up, take notice and begin to generate theories and concepts that would begin to acknowledge this work and draw closer together the spheres of work and consumption. A simple and elegant way of doing so has been to propose the concept of the 'working customer'. According to Rieder and Voss (2010), working customers are active not passive. They do not wait to be serviced like royalty but, rather, assume the position of co-workers who take over specific elements of the productive process, usually unpaid. The work done by working customers is frequently closely managed – they are guided across the aisles of the supermarket by the store's lay-out and electronically monitored to ensure they pay for all their goods – and designed into the process. Working consumers gradually acquire various skills, argue Rieder and Voss, which are valuable resources for the corporate structures that control the process; companies will invest a lot of time and resources in 'educating' the consumer in how to do the work while servicing themselves – hence the helpful employee hovering near the self-checkouts to teach consumers what to do or the patient call-centre worker in India explaining to the UK bank customer over the phone how to use the bank's latest electronic fraud-fighting gismo.

Examples of the working customer phenomenon are legion. They mushroomed with the arrival of the internet. The ATM, allied to various online operations, for example, has almost completely replaced the bank teller. Much of the travel agency industry has been wiped out by online travel booking and holiday planning. Large numbers of bookshops have closed as customers busily browse and buy online, often e-books that require no physical labour to produce them, warehouse to store them or drivers to deliver them. Some of this extends the self-service economy, noted by earlier social scientists (Gershuny, 1978). Where, however, the working customer improves on the self-serving consumer is in initiating innovations, offering support to other customers, and participating in product development and configuration through the phenomenon of crowdsourcing. Crowdsourcing goes beyond filling one's own supermarket trolley. The customers tell the retailer what items to put on the shelves, which new products to obtain, how to market them, how to improve their design and quality and so forth (Kleemann et al., 2008; Howe, 2009; Bayus, 2013). Crowdsourcing involves the building of communities of non-expert but dedicated and smart users, who generate, collect and sift ideas, and examine their potential for exploitation. In some regards, they take the older 'suggestions box' principle one stage further by involving the person who makes the suggestions in the subsequent steps. Crowdsourcing is now widely applied by an ever increasing number of companies (including companies like Unilever, Fiat, Tesco and Honda) to refine and develop products. Hackathons, a special type of crowd-sourcing, involves intensive sessions, sometimes lasting several days, by groups of computer specialists drawn together and aimed at generating particular soft-ware innovations. The value of user generated ideas and innovations has rapidly become an item of faith in the corporate sector. One study that compared product innovation by in-house experts with suggestions from a network of customers found that ideas provided by the latter group scored significantly higher in terms of novelty and customer benefit, even if they were somewhat lower in terms of feasibility than the ideas generated by the specialists (Poetz and Schreier, 2012).

Customers do not only take active part in generation of product ideas. They also become involved in their translation into actual products and the marketing of these products. Brand co-creation is now widely viewed as a characteristic of progressive brands, those that do not seek to bludgeon consumers with pre-packaged values but allow them and even invite them to participate actively in generating symbols, logos and images that define a brand (e.g. Holt, 2002; Brown et al., 2003; Arvidsson, 2005; Pongsakornrungsilp and Schroeder, 2011). This has the advantage of allowing brands to evolve and adapt to changing fash-ions and circumstances; thus the brand is now viewed as fitting into an 'ecology' in business, capable of regenerating themselves with the help of their users or becoming moribund and extinct.

Somewhat more controversially, customers are also knowingly or unknowingly used to monitor and evaluate the performance of employees. This is accom-plished through various types of feedback – from on and off-line comment boxes to stickers on the back of trucks. The mere presence of customers acts as a more or less discreet disciplining force to the paid employees who find themselves stuck behind a 'glass cage', a form of management control that is gradually replacing what Max Weber described as the 'iron cage' of bureaucracy (Gabriel, 2005). It is no longer impersonal and fixed rules which discipline the worker and monitor performance but the exposure to the external, critical gaze of the con-sumer. In this way, employees and customers become interlocked as ingredients of the brand. Their looks, their clothes, the tone of their voice, their public involvement, all become elements of the brand. Zwick and colleagues (2008: 163) argue that co-creation is itself a form of controlling consumers, 'a [new] political form of power aimed at generating particular forms of consumer life at once free and controllable, creative and docile'. In a subsequent paper, Zwick and Knott (2009) go further still, and claim with some justification that, even when pas-sively visiting websites, consumers are unknowingly working for the corporation by furnishing data about themselves, their lifestyles, their predilections, which enable the company to profit by selling such data to others. In this way, Google's profits come from the 'hits' produced by its users merely as they touch their key-pads. Once Google realizes that consumer X is in the market for a new greenhouse, consumer X is liable to be subjected to alluring special offers from various suppliers. A positive interpretation of this is that consumers only receive advertisements for goods and service in which they have an interest. The opposite is the increasingly common view that Google has now emerged as the perfect form of Big Brother. His younger siblings love him, even as they submit to him.

Consuming work

If the co-creating consumer and the working customer open up consumption to the world of work, the world of work has been opening up to the world of consumption. As employers seek to incorporate their employees into the corporate brand, they engage increasingly in the practice of 'internal branding' (Punjaisri et al., 2009) or the promotion of a company's brand among its own members (Müller, 2013). Human resource (HR) departments gradually come to resemble marketing departments, as companies try to sell themselves to current and prospective employees as exciting places to work, offering them electrifying opportunities to 'grow' themselves and enhance their CVs/resumés (Korczynski, 2007; Chertkovskaya, 2013). A marketing and branding orientation first noted by Fromm ([1947] 1965) suffuses the entire organization, including its products, employees and customers. Image and appearances assume tremendous importance as aspects of the brand. The clothes worn by workers, their hairstyles, jewellery and other aspects of their persona, become crucial features in supporting the brand. This applies to every 'front-line' occupation where employees come in contact with the customer – receptionists, bar work, retailing, cosmetics, advertising, architecture, media, public relations. But it also increasingly comes to apply to services like health and education where an employee's entire personality as a representative of the organization can be gradually appropriated as a feature of the brand. As Karen Dale suggests in her paper titled 'The employee as "dish of the day"' (2012), employees becomes both consumers and consumed, actively engaged in the commodification of themselves. Gender is a core feature of this process of commodification, as is the sexualization of the relation between employee and customer, which manifests itself as a 'sexual simmer' (Tancred-Sheriff, 1989; Hall, 1993).

The marketing orientation turns employees into brands in their own rights. It also opens the door to the emergence of the nanny corporation, which says that, in order to support the brand, you must be fit and healthy, go to the gym, eat healthy meals and basically take better care of yourself. Nanny corporations are liable to subsidize services to enhance employee health and fitness, although undoubtedly this can also be a way of controlling their lives outside the workplace.

Being lean and fit is seen as a necessary requirement for the job; failing to live up to such standards may jeopardize suitability for the company as a risk of contaminating the brand. Viewed from afar, this can be interpreted as a new form of paternalism or as an insidious form of control (Fleming and Spicer, 2004; Fleming, 2009).

The resurrection of the prosumer

The increasing overlap and possible amalgamation of the spheres of production and consumption have seen the unexpected return of a term first introduced by futurologist Alvin Toffler in 1980 (Toffler, 1980), which fuses the words producer and consumer into the neologism 'prosumer'. In his book *The Third Wave*, Toffler had argued that the ideas of producer and consumer were themselves the product of the industrial revolution. Prior to industrialization, people made most of their own clothes, grew most of their own food, made their own entertainment and so forth. The Industrial Revolution marked a point when the purpose of production shifted from domestic use to exchange. Domestic production was left out of the formal economy as it continues to this day to be left out of official statistics and economic indicators. In a post-industrial age, argued Toffler, the separation between producer and consumer would fade away. Physical labour would gradually decline, not least due to automation, work and consumption would fuse, and producers and consumers would merge into prosumers, people who produce an increasing range of their own use-values in goods and services.

> *Producer and consumer, divorced by the industrial revolution, are reunited in the cycle of wealth creation, with the customer contributing not just the money but market and design information vital for the production process. Buyer and supplier share data, information, and knowledge. Someday, customers may also push buttons that activate remote production processes. Consumer and producer fuse into a 'prosumer'. (Toffler, 1980: 239)*

Toffler's concept was picked up a few years later by marketing guru Philip Kotler (1986), who identified two prosumer profiles: the hobbyists who fill their leisure time with hobbies and do-it-yourself (DIY) activities and arch-prosumers who opt for a lifestyle of voluntary simplicity that is close to nature, producing as many things they can themselves – growing their own vegetables, knitting their own clothes, and avoiding mass consumption where possible. Both these groups, he said, posed special challenges to marketers.

It took 20 years for this idea to come into mainstream social science as a crucial feature of early 21st-century society. The reason for this uptake is undoubtedly the arrival of the internet and information society, and the new opportunities these opened up for consumers to engage in production. Ritzer has been one of the strongest advocates of the view that a revolutionary change is underway with the arrival of the new prosumer:

> First, prosumers are performing tasks (e.g. checking themselves in and out of hotels and at airport kiosks) that they rarely, if ever, did before. Second, many people are no longer employed, or they are doing different kinds of work, because of the various things pro-sumers are now doing themselves without pay. Third, many companies are earning unprecedented profits because they are able to employ far fewer people than they would have if prosumers did not perform various tasks without pay. Fourth, people now get lots of things free of charge, especially on the internet, in part because of the free labor of prosumers. [...] Fifth, many of these developments have been made possible by new technologies – the computer, internet, self-scanners, 3-D printers – and they are leading to further technological advances that will, among other things, further expand prosumption. (Ritzer, 2014: 13)

Agreeing with Toffler, Ritzer has gone as far as to argue that the rise of the prosumer is sooner or later going to sound the death knell of the consumer as previously known. He posits that there is a continuum of prosumption; at one end, there is 'prosumption-as-production', in the middle a 'balanced prosumption', and at the other end 'prosumption-as-consumption'. Somewhat controversially, he offers IKEA as an example of prosumption-as-production, where prosumers have to do a lot of work, and Massive Open Online Courses (MOOCs) as an example of prosumption-as-consumption, where much of the burden of education is put into students to control. It could be argued that setting up a bookcase – IKEA's best-selling Billy case – requires much less work than following an entire course online or marking other students' coursework. The rather trivial example of withdrawing money from an ATM is offered to illustrate 'balanced prosumption', as it involves both the work of withdrawing and that of using the needed cash. Despite perhaps inappropriate examples, Ritzer's key point – that prosumption is highly profitable from the capitalist's point of view since it replaces paid with unpaid labour and therefore is likely to increase in future – is entirely plausible.

In his study of crowdsourcing, Howe agrees with Ritzer that the image of the consumer as well as that of the producer are soon to be overtaken by that of the prosumer. Unlike Ritzer, however, he believes that this will see a weakening of the role of companies and a strengthening of the part played by amateurs.

> Once upon a time there were producers and consumers. Their roles were static and well defined. But thanks to the Internet and the falling cost of the silicon chip, the line between producer and consumer has begun to blur. Amateurs provide the crowdsourcing engine with fuel, and the open source software movement provided it with a blueprint. But it's the widespread availability of the means of production that empowers the crowd to take part in a process long dominated by companies. As a result, the 'consumer,' as traditionally conceived, is becoming an antiquated concept. (Howe, 2009: 71)

Table 11.1 Conceptualizations of the consumer as worker

Conceptualization	The idea	Example	Key writers	Comment
Self-serving customer	The shopper is drawn into work previously done by paid employees	The supermarket replaces the grocer, fast food replaces the restaurant	Gershuny, 1978; Ritzer, 1993	A feature of McDonaldization, this contributes to deskilling and standardization
Working customer	Quasi-employee who produces value for the company without pay	Amazon customers advise other customers by writing product reviews and uploading lists of favourite books	Rieder and Voss, 2010	The customer becomes unpaid employee and co-worker
Crowdsourcing	Unpaid innovators, product developers and customer supporters offer solutions to both managers and other customers	The *Fiat Mio* car, the world's 'first outsourced car'	Kleeman et al., 2008; Howe, 2009; Bayus, 2013; Poetz and Schreier, 2012	Overlaps with working customer but tends to be on a mass scale and the worker may be any user (not necessarily a customer)
Prosumer	The fusion of worker and consumer	Wikipedia, MOOCs	Toffler, 1980; Kotler, 1986; Arvidsson and Colleoni, 2012; Ritzer et al., 2012; Fuchs, 2014; Ritzer, 2014	People contribute content, monitor and use it, they simultaneously produce and consume value
Co-creator/co-producer	Consumers are co-creators of value and brands, and possibly exploited in this process	Napster or Netflix	Prahalad and Ramaswamy, 2004a; Prahalad and Ramaswamy, 2004b; Zwick et al., 2008; Hatch and Schultz, 2010; Pongsakornrungsilp and Schroeder 2011	The consumer co-creates a new brand or modifies an existing one with the producers
Produser	Users become producers of 'participatory' news and co-creators of stories	Citizen journalism websites such as Indymedia and Slashdot	Deuze et al., 2007	Creates news and news hierarchies on the basis of the users interests rather than the significance accorded by editors or journalists

Different terms we have introduced so far, like the self-serving customer, the working customer, crowdsourcing, prosumer, co-creator/co-producer and the produser, all suggest an increasing overlap of the spheres of work and consumption. Table 11.1 summarizes some of the features of each of these conceptualizations. Although distinct, these conceptualizations overlap extensively as a result of the agreement that they all come out into sharper relief as a result of technological forces to which we will turn below. Subsequent sections in this chapter will investigate whether the work done by consumers amounts to exploitation of their free labour or to a new form of self-actualization, and will draw bridges between the consumer as worker and the images of the consumer we painted earlier in this book.

New technology

All of the conceptualizations of the consumer-worker in Table 11.1 recognize the extraordinary changes brought about in recent decades by the arrival of the internet, social media, the blogosphere and Web 2.0 (any website reliant on user-generated content). These have truly revolutionized some aspects of consumption since this book was first conceived. We now inhabit a digital world in which the technologies we use transform our ways of thinking, the ways we see ourselves and even our moral priorities. Our everyday lives have been 'virtualised', drawing upon a world of games and simulations which, as Baudrillard prophesied, can seem more real than reality. Our online personas, avatars and touched-up photo-shopped images become embedded in our identities every bit as firmly as our actual clothes or jewellery or haircuts (Belk, 1988; 2013).

A dominant feature of this digital world is the dematerialization of commodities but also the dematerialization of the processes of consumption and production themselves. Where an earlier generation of consumers relished real objects such as books with beautiful covers, cars with gleaming surfaces or antique furniture with ageing patina, today's consumers are as likely to turn to *experiences* on- and off-line, such as attending festivals, physically visiting theme parks and tourist destinations or online browsing, pornography and gaming (Pine and Gilmore, 1999). Purchasing and owning an object is quite different from having an experience. Instead of having physical CDs, one gets a year's subscription to Spotify. In such a world, spectacle assumes paramount significance, way beyond the dystopia outlined by Guy Debord in the *Society of the Spectacle*, his Situationist manifesto (Debord, 1977; Merrifield, 2005). Images circulating in social media become facts. The power of the image is such that it arguably even takes precedence over the experience. Images that show you attending a party, a festival or a wedding, or meeting a TV celebrity or a former

US President become more real than the fading memories of the event itself (Boorstin, 1962; Sontag, 1977; Gabriel, 2008).

Maybe even to a greater extent than is the case for consumption, production itself becomes dematerialized. The production of ideas, symbols, images and other texts replaces the production of a wide range of physical objects and services. What was once viewed as intellectual labour is now being subsumed into digital labour. Every minute that we spend in front of a computer can be seen as digital labour, both in the simple sense that our digits (fingers) are being used to type on the keyboard and in the sense that information is digitally produced and processed. As Ritzer, Dean and Jurgenson noted (2012), most of this digital labour takes place outside designated locations such as offices or factories, and instead spreads into public spaces like parks, commercial spaces like cafés or private spaces like homes. Visit a Starbucks today and you are likely to get an image of a diverse and polychrome gang of workers assiduously interacting with their laptops. They hardly seem to take notice of each other, wrapped up in bubbles far more hermetically than any group of factory or office workers. In this way, the Starbucks outlet becomes both a minor chapel of consumption and a micro-factory of digital production.

Digital labour extends the logic of the worker society into every nook and cranny of our lives, so that we work 24 hours a day. As Cederström and Fleming say, 'we now live in a "worker society" ... a hermetically sealed society in which *we are always at work*' (Cederström and Fleming, 2012: 17). A workaholic culture becomes endemic and almost impossible to avoid. Workaholism, previously viewed as an extreme self-induced addiction, argue Cederström and Fleming, becomes an escapist social addiction, one that directly parallels and complements shopaholism. No better evidence for the addictive quality of digital labour can be provided than the first question people ask when away from work or home: 'Is it on the internet?' or 'Is there wi-fi access?' The mere thought of being out of contact induces a kind of panic. Human existence becomes inconceivable outside digital existence. Being disconnected from digital or internet contact becomes tantamount to non-existence. Equally, internet-based work turns every space and opportunity into a social factory where people work hard without ever having a boss to look over their shoulder.

A large amount of unpaid digital labour takes place on social media or on what is now called Web 2.0. These allow users to interact and collaborate with each other, creating networks or even virtual communities which share user-generated content. This has opened up countless opportunities that blur the distinctions between work and consumption, such as updating one's profile, ticking 'like' and 'dislike' boxes, commenting on friends' photos and postings, publicizing one's triumphs and failures, and sharing the most mundane incidents in daily life. For celebrities who use Twitter, this becomes an art form, in which spilling egg on one's tie can be tweeted to millions of followers, whose day is thus enhanced for a millisecond! For the majority of users, this type of activity makes any distinction between work and consumption entirely meaningless. What is not meaningless, however, is the great deal of value that companies derive from the unpaid work that consumers do in sharing experiences, providing reports and sorting out problems for others. The phenomenal expansion of online book-seller Amazon is surely in part due to the product reviews that consumers contribute to its platform and which are an invaluable resource for other consumers. Consumers thus both work for Amazon and provide valuable information about themselves, a resource which can be sold on.

Consumption-work

What is work and how does it differ from labour? Marx argued that labour is what makes humans distinctively human. Through labour, humans mould nature to their own needs. Through labour, they develop their intellectual and spiritual capabilities. Hence labour is not merely the expenditure of energy, but also the use of imagination, creativity and intelligence. Capitalist production, argued Marx, alienates people from their labour, something that results from alienation from the product of their work, and results in further alienation of people from each other and from their creative potential (Marx, [1844] 1972). Under capitalism, labour becomes equated with oppression, dehumanization and exploitation rather than creativity and fulfilment.

Unlike labour, a term proselytized by political economy, work is predominantly a concept used by sociologists and psychologists encompassing a wide range of cultural assumptions. What is the meaning of work? What is the value of work? What is the purpose of work? Traditionally work was divided up into intellectual and manual work, the former enjoying higher status than the latter. In the 20th century, the idea of work was further enlarged to include the attainment of psychological aims. Thus coming to terms with death and loss was attributed by Freud to mourning work, just as the process of constructing an identity is attributed more recently to identity-work (e.g. Sveningsson and Alvesson, 2003; Beech et al., 2012). Breaking the dualism of intellectual and manual work, Hochschild proposed the concept of emotional work, later turned into emotional labour (Hochschild, 1979; 1983). This concept has been widely incorporated into different disciplines to indicate the fact that much of the work we do has an emotional dimension, an interplay of our own emotions and those of others. In line with this, some theorists have developed the concept of aesthetic labour to describe the work that goes into clothes, cleaning and grooming oneself is a vital part of the service by the worker to the brand (e.g. Hancock and Tyler, 2000; Korczynski and Ott, 2004; Warhurst and Nickson, 2009).

In a similar way, we can now describe the work done as part of consumption as 'consumption-work'. This includes traditional, new and emerging aspects of labour that people do as consumers. All the aspects of work we noted above with regard to a self-assembly purchase from IKEA would constitute consumption-work. So too would every form of shopping, browsing, travelling, carrying, comparing, complaining, consulting, sharing, selling and so forth. The food sector has been a major advocate of enlarging consumption-work in the form of recipe development and home cooking at the expense of ready-made meals. Consumers are enticed into developing a meal whose ingredients are chosen, weighed and measured and assembled prior to taking them or having them delivered at home in order to use them in their cooking. This service is offered by both retailers and celebrity chefs in artisanal and online versions. The entire DIY and hobby sectors involve large amounts of consumption-work. Much of the digital labour noted above – updating social network profiles, offering advice to other consumers, providing product reviews, involvement in crowdsourcing, 'likes' and 'dislikes' – are all forms of consumption-work.

One of the interesting questions posed by this trend is whether consumption-work entails various new types of skill or whether it boils down to new forms of deskilling. In our view, the digital world calls for a wide range of new skills, even as old skills are made obsolete by social and technological factors. These new skills are both necessary and valuable. Knowing how to navigate numerous websites in order to purchase a successful package of goods or a holiday, knowing how to programme a mobile phone, a camera or a computer, knowing how to choose a cosmetic surgeon, knowing how to filter out false claims and time-wasters, all these and many others processes require skills that are by no means self-evident or easy to accrue. For many middle-aged or older people, they represent daunting challenges, prompting them to outsource their consumption-work to others – for love or money. Thus, a grandmother calls in a grandson to help sort out her recently acquired computer and to navigate and master the updated software. A son working in New York can order and have delivered to his infirm father in England a decent meal every day. A car buyer can outsource the finding and location of a particular vehicle online to a specialist. Outsourcing becomes a generalized principle of our age, something that extends into all aspects of what Hochschild calls the 'outsourced self' (Hochschild, 2012).

The more one reflects about consumption-work, the more one recognizes how extensive this has become in our daily lives. We also realize how the acquisition and development of skills in consumption-work are what generally distinguish between savvy and sophisticated consumers and clumsy ineffective ones. This also gives opportunities for consumers to become more skilled, and over time to become more sophisticated. As we suggested in earlier chapters (e.g. Chapter 4, 'The Consumer as Explorer'), some people become consumer virtuosos, offering their skills to others either for money or as gifts. Bargain-hunting is clearly one area of consumer virtuosity, but is by no means the only one. So too is the ability to ferret out rare objects, to spot items of unrealized value or to discover complementary goods that increase each other's value. The antiques trade thrives on this kind of skilled consumption-work, in providing opportunities for spotting and identifying valuable items (often amidst useless junk) and recognizing their value – the rarer the better. In this regard, antique-spotting is not unlike bird-spotting. Skills required to carry this out effectively can be expanded in breadth, depth and range with time and effort. Even amateurs can create value through this type of consumption-work, as illustrated by the annual Big Garden Birdwatch, co-ordinated by the Royal Society for Protection of Birds, which invites every person in the UK with a garden to report the birds they see over a period of one week (RSPB, 2014). On the basis of this, an annual survey of the changing population count is published, providing a useful snapshot. This is a good example of crowdsourcing (over half a million British people participated in 2014) and an illustration of mass rather than individualized consumption-work. It also highlights how voluntary consumer-work turns amateurs into contributors to scientific research dedicated to the public good (Vandzinskaite et al., 2010).

While some consumption-work is unpaid, some can be monetized. This is particularly the case with digital labour such as what is published on the blogosphere. Many bloggers are amateurs in the proper sense of the word – they blog for the love of it. Others blog hoping to generate advertising revenue. The reality, however, can be very different as Chia has strongly argued:

> *Suspended between a vibrant vision of blogging as a surefire ticket to fame and fortune and a sobering structural reality of obscurity and tedium, bloggers are recalibrating their collective delusions of grandeur by constructing alternative economies of exchange. Instead of valuating their self-professed labor monetarily or quantitatively, bloggers are reverting to more attainable small-scale social exchanges that are qualitative in form. More than hits, links, and votes, bloggers appear to value a virtual pat on the back, a reassuring remark, a sincere conversation. (Chia, 2012: 421)*

This raises the question of whether consumption-work is an empowering and creative outlet or yet another illustration of alienated and exploited labour, this time done by consumers. Quite a few authors have rushed to castigate crowdsourcing and other forms of digital labour as a rip-off, getting consumers to work for nothing, and even selling them goods for money which other consumers have provided free (for different arguments, see Zwick et al., 2008; Arvidsson, 2010; Rieder and Voss, 2010; Arvidsson and Colleoni, 2012; Fuchs, 2014; Ritzer, 2014). Indeed, some companies such as TripAdvisor and Airbnb would be inconceivable without massive input provided by consumer-workers free of charge; and the value of the service provided by Amazon and Google would surely decline considerably without consumer inputs. All the same, millions of people find great satisfaction and achieve a degree of self-actualization through this type of consumer-work. Consider, for example, the solidarity, advice and support now generated by women over the experience and travails of motherhood through sharing experiences and tips in what in the USA are called 'mommy blogs' (Doucet and Mauthner, 2012). If alienation entails isolation, estrangement and meaningless activity, this surely provides an antidote. In this respect, we do not share the bleak view of consumer-work offered by some of its critics (Comor, 2010). We do, however, recognize the delicacy and personalization of what shifts the experience from one category to the other.

An interesting feature of digital labour is how consumers can construct their identities around it (Ibarra and Petriglieri, 2010). Gaming and other forms of digital work create hierarchies of success and measure the performance of different users against their peers; gaming sites have rankings just as websites such as Amazon provide rankings of leading reviewers and commentators. Other sites compare numbers of 'hits' and 'likes', creating hierarchies of success, which tend to be mainly ephemeral but remain quite important for the identities of their users. When Yahoo closed many of its online game sites (mainly under attack by hackers as well as users who heaped abuse on others), users complained that suddenly they had lost their 'rankings' – from 'somebodies' they had become 'nobodies'. Competition for status is an important motive for this kind of consumption-work. However, another even more important motive may be the desire to help other people. This takes the form of sharing knowledge and information on how to solve common problems ranging from acute medical conditions to minor software glitches, from annoying gardening difficulties to identity-threatening fashion crises, from how to cope with a drug-addicted child to how to deal with a branch of state bureaucracy or a corporation. This desire to help others and offering advice, support and time stands at odds with the individualism and self-centredness of much contemporary consumerism, and provides a rationale for some communitarian thinking (Etzioni, 1993; Etzioni, 1998a; Putnam, 2000). In communities and networks of online users, whether evolving out of shared interests or shared objectives, quasi-gift transactions become an important currency of exchange. Taking the time to respond to a person one has never met, purely because one feels an empathy with their predicament, is an aspect of this new form of solidarity that has thrived in the internet age.

Links to other faces of the consumer

In adding this new face of the consumer to the nine we outlined in 1995, we are acknowledging the far-reaching transformation that the arrival of the internet has brought about, drawing consumption closer to work. Like the faces of the consumer we originally identified then, the consumer as worker is but an artefact, a way of looking at people's experience and what Habermas called lifespace (Habermas, 2003). It accords with an ever-rising awareness that consumption involves work and sometimes hard and risky work. Like the other faces of the consumer, the consumer as worker easily mutates. As a creative conceptualization of the consumer, the consumer as worker readily turns to consumer as rebel, dreaming up different ways to subvert dominant culture (Cova and Cova, 2012). It highlights consumer agency and the productive aspects of consumption (Arnould and Thompson, 2005). Thus consumers create value for themselves, for others and the public good, as well as for corporations, whether knowingly or unknowingly. They can work in more or less skilful ways and hone their skills with practice, and with input from others.

The consumer as worker, at times striving for self-actualization and creativity, and willing to share the fruits of his or her labour with others, would appear to sit at the opposite end of the spectrum from the consumer as victim – passively manipulated by business and PR. Yet as Fuchs, Comor and others have opined, this may represent a new form of exploitation and even alienation (Comor, 2010; Fuchs, 2010; 2014). As Cederström and Fleming (2012) forcefully argued, digital labour may now be inducing a non-stop, 365-day a year addiction to being and working online, converting every space into a workplace. What greater victimhood could there be than this?

The consumer as worker also has clear links with the consumer as explorer, communicator, identity-seeker and so forth. An interesting connection ties him or her with the last, the consumer as citizen. As we have shown in the present chapter, there is a tension at the heart of the consumer as worker, as to whether the kind of work generated by the internet individualizes and isolates people in their personalized bubbles, or whether, on the contrary, it brings them into ever closer contact, and enables them to have discussions with fellow consumer-workers, drawing them towards a new ideal of online citizenry. Readers will readily identify further connections between the consumer as worker and other images.

In our view, the rise of the consumer-worker – the face we have sketched above – is further evidence for the unravelling of the simplicity of the Fordist Deal. A century on from Henry Ford, the image of the consumer as worker almost turns the Fordist Deal on its head. The Fordist 'thou shalt work hard for enjoyment' assumes a new meaning.

A concluding question

The addition of the consumer as worker to our portrait gallery of the consumer raises an interesting question. Is it that people have now started doing things as consumers that they did not do before, and that the consumer as worker is a genuinely new type of consumer? Or is it simply that academics (including the present authors) have not previously noticed what had been happening? No wonder Marxists and radical analysts have become interested in this issue, because if it is the former, then a new stage in the evolution of capitalism is underway, requiring new categories and threatening any long held existing tenets, such as where value originates and who is being exploited or alienated. The heat of the debate between Fuchs and Arvidsson over the issue of whether consumers generate 'surplus value' and, if so, how, demonstrates how much is at stake. The evidence presented in this chapter suggests that work always had a part in consumption, and that Toffler in 1980 was reminding us of the obvious and merely prophesying that this type of consumption-work would become more commonplace. If this is true, then what is emerging is a growth of pace and scale of the process rather than something that is altogether new.

Our view is that something qualitatively new *is* indeed unfolding. We do not, however, think that this will result in the consumer's complete obliteration as Ritzer and Howe suggest, consumers becoming prosumers. If anything, we would argue that this represents yet another version of the tendency we identified in our initial argument – the tendency of different stakeholders to claim a single face of the consumer as sovereign and to diminish or ignore all others. Our argument suggests that the prosumer as a strand of the working consumer is too volatile a concept, too ready to mutate into one of the existing images of the consumer, with accompanying dynamics, to take the combined burden of production and consumption. We envisage workers and consumers surviving as towering concepts for some considerable time more.

12

THE UNMANAGEABLE CONSUMER

The world is too much with us; late and soon, Getting and spending, we lay waste our prowess: Little we see in nature that is ours; We have given our hearts away, a sordid boon! (William Wordsworth, 'The World')

CORE ARGUMENTS

The idea of the consumer is claimed by many interest groups and intellectual traditions, yet no one owns it. Why is the consumer such a contested and troublesome concept? The different faces of the consumer outlined in this book each has a discrete presence and validity, yet they all demonstrate a readiness to mutate into each other or melt away. The concept of the consumer has therefore become an 'essentially contested concept', one that is unstable and hard to pin down. This is the basis for arguing that today's consumer is intrinsically unmanageable, a status compounded by the demise of the Fordist Deal. Under the Fordist Deal, the desires and actions of consumers were more manageable. Today, changes in production, rapid technological innovation, population and environmental pressures, political uncertainties and globalization, have all conspired to unravel the stability that once was the hallmark of the Fordist Deal. Consumerism, we argue, faces a number of challenges, including environmental, demographic, religious and ethical. In spite of its ability to colonize ever wider parts of the world and social life, consumerism has been chronically unable to honour its promise of making people happy. Its future remains uncertain.

Few concepts have been claimed by so many interest groups, ideologies and academic traditions as that of the consumer. It is rare for an idea to have such diverse meanings as 'to consume'. As we have seen, economists, sociologists, social psychologists, cultural critics, postmodernists, Marxists, Conservatives, advertisers, journalists, pop-semioticians, marketers and marketeers, historians of ideas, environmentalists and activists all come up with their own visions and images. The consumer has become a cultural fetish, an obsession.

This book has, from the beginning, brought together traditions that do not normally address each other enough. Each chapter has critically assessed a core idea of who consumers are, how they behave, what drives them, what concerns them and how they see the world. Each one can be thought of as a landscape of consumption, highlighting different features and disguising others. We have disagreed with some, supported others and offered our own. We are not suggesting that contemporary consumption is the totality of these, nor do we recommend that readers should pick and choose which image they most or least identify with and discard the others. What we are suggesting is that each image represents a position within a contested terrain. It is what the French refer to as a *prise de position*, in other words an initial gambit on which one is prepared to place a stake.

Why has the consumer become such a hotly contested terrain, the point at which so many contradictions of contemporary society converge? Why do so many claim it as their own and, if it is not, struggle to appropriate it? Why do so many political parties now claim to speak on consumers' behalf? Why do so many different academic traditions seek to define the consumer, criticize the consumer or praise the consumer? At the outset of the book, we stated that numerous historical factors have contributed to raising the consumer to the top of recent academic and political debates. These include the decline of the Protestant work ethic in the West, the ideological role of Western consumerism throughout the Cold War, and the adoption of the consumer by the political right epitomizing freedom to choose in an unfettered marketplace. The consumer came to symbolize modernity, equality and happiness. Emerging technologies have opened up millions of new choices that reinforce people's experience of consuming, whether at home, at work or in public spaces.

Through the pages of this book we have established that much depends on how the consumer is viewed, whether for example, he or she is seen as sovereign (requiring no self-appointed spokespeople to defend his or her interests) or victim (easily manipulated and outwitted by the apparatuses of capital), explorer (thirsting after new experiences and meanings) or activist (campaigning on behalf of collective rights), communicator (using objects as bridges to relate to fellow humans) or rebel (using objects to express rejection and rage), identity-seeker (trying to find a real self in the objects he or she consumes) or hedonist (concerned above all with personal pleasure). These are all attempts to frame the consumer and, more often than not, to sell particular self-views to consumers themselves, either by flattery, by cajoling, by moralizing, by seduction or by straight manipulation.

Each of the faces we have sketched is discrete, having a separate and defined character. Some are active, others are passive, some are adventurous, others are conservative, some are rational, others are impetuous, some are conformist, others are rebellious. They all, however, show a propensity to fragment or to mutate into a different face. We have noted, for example, how readily the image of the consumer as chooser turns into victim, or the consumer as rebel turns into identity-seeker. Different social and economic circumstances are liable to draw out one or other face. In periods of austerity and debt, for example, the political appeal of the rational, thrifty consumer outshines that of the consumer as compulsive, hedonistic and spendthrift. We also noted the enduring tension between consumer and citizen defined by a split between collective and individual interests. The consumer is free to choose without constraint or oversight, whereas the citizen has civic obligations. In this edition of the book, we have introduced a new face of the consumer-as-worker that is coming into sharper definition all the time, which results from an increasing integration of the spheres of production and consumption. More and more, consumers are working unpaid as part of production and distribution, for example when they assemble goods from IKEA, or book travel online, or provide information and advice to each other about the quality of their holiday. Both these two images of the consumer – as citizen and worker – undermine the notion of consumption as a free-standing and autonomous sphere of experience.

While the battle over who owns and can define the consumer rages above the consumer's head, people get on with their everyday lives, trying to make the best of their situation, whatever their lot, and also to make sense of their lives. It would be plausible and attractive to envisage consumers in this way, that is, as oblivious to the consternation they are causing to business, politicians, the chattering classes and theoreticians. At a stroke, this analysis would halt any systematic attempt to understand people's behaviour as reflexive, self-conscious consumers, leaving the terrain to those who have an interest in defining them in particular ways. Market researchers and opinion pollsters, for instance, would claim the consumer as theirs, but so too would consumer activists and political parties. We are profoundly opposed to ending our pursuit of consumers in this book in this fashion, by abandoning them to whoever speaks on their behalf with the loudest voice.

For better or for worse, many of us think of ourselves, at least part of the time, as consumers. Whether reading the consumer pages of newspapers, listening to exhortations from politicians or consumer organizations, visiting theme parks and supermarkets, or trying to stretch the household budget at the end of a week, we unavoidably have to confront ourselves as consumers, and make decisions as consumers. Why else do individuals become so preoccupied with what they buy, give and eat? Why do they seek advice, turning to the consumer pages of the media, or family or the internet for advice? For the most part, one cannot opt out of being a consumer, living in a non-consumer fashion, in a non-consumer landscape. Even those who find themselves excluded from the bonanzas of consumerism – including an estimated 1.3 billion of our fellow humans who live on less than $1.25 per day – cannot escape defining themselves in terms of lack and dreaming of a better life. Consumerism, in the diverse forms examined in this book, has become a reference point for all of humanity. This does not mean that it is uncontested; it is possible to resist and even reject consumerism while continuing to be a consumer. It is even possible to consume without being defined by the things that you consume, while seeking to generate meaning and happiness for yourself and those around you in other ways outside the sphere of consumption altogether.

The demise of the Fordist Deal

We began this book by suggesting that modern consumers have to be understood in their relationship to production, as the outcome of what we called the Fordist Deal. By this we meant the unwritten understanding that ever-increasing living standards and steady employment would be the reward for accepting alienating work without excessive dissent. From birth, the modern consumer has been connected to the methods and politics of mass production, just as earlier generations of consumers, too, had been dependent on the vagaries of production, harvests and warfare for their subsistence. Like earlier consumers who had relied on the beneficence of the Church or their masters, consumers under the Fordist Deal relied on secure, regular and rewarded (if not rewarding) work.

The Fordist Deal is currently unravelling under pressure from multiple causes that affect production as deeply as consumption. New technologies and the instantaneous transmission of information have resulted in a dramatic dematerialization of production and a restructuring of the international division of labour – who makes what, where and how. The ideas of a 'steady job' or a 'job for life' in much of the industrialized West, to say nothing of the formerly centrally planned economies of the Communist bloc, have virtually lost their meaning. Instead, many jobs have become casualized and careers have become fragmented, characterized by rapid job moves, being constantly on the lookout for better opportunities and work prospects, and frenetic periods of work on specific projects followed by almost certain periods of self-employment or underemployment. This has been associated with the rise of a social class which Standing (2011) calls the 'precariat'. Casualization does not necessarily mean unemployment; on the contrary, it implies impermanence in work as the new benchmark. Indeed, vast new opportunities of employment have been created in the service sectors, involving either the manipulation of symbols on screens and the clicking of computer mice, or alternatively frontline work with customers in hospitality, entertainment, retail, sport and tourist sectors. The Fordist Deal has also collapsed with the rise of the working customer or the 'prosumer' (Rieder and Voss, 2010; Ritzer, 2014). Why pay your workers to do the work if your customers will do it without pay *and* thank you for it!

Another reason for the unravelling of the Fordist Deal lies in deep-rooted changes in consumption patterns. On the one hand, consumerism is colonizing ever larger spheres of social and personal life. New areas of consumption, such as education (e.g. higher education in the UK), health (e.g. fertility treatments and voluntary euthanasia), voluntary organizations (now marketed as though they are detergent brands) and public services (e.g. transport) are being taken over by a consumer ethos of choice and markets. Affluent people these days even find it perfectly acceptable to 'outsource' their children's parties to party organizers and the care of their elderly to strangers (Hochschild, 2012). On the other hand, the collapse of the property bubble in the Great Recession saw a resurrection of the value of thrift and a reluctance to spend, as people were reminded how much consumerism had been fuelled by a vast expansion of credit (e.g. Ivanova, 2011; Hyman, 2012).

If consumerism is being tested or challenged in the older developed economies, it has found new areas of growth in rapidly developing countries. New parts of the world are seized by the excitement of consumerism. Western brands have found explosive new markets, first among rich elites and then among the wider emerging middle classes. In sectors such as call centres and software development, it could be argued that a new variant of the Fordist Deal is emerging between employers and employees, allowing for islands of Western hedonist lifestyles and aspirations to exist side by side with highly regimented and monitored work – all this in the midst of 'old-style' and widespread deprivation and poverty.

If the comfortable co-habitation of mass consumption and mass production that characterized the Fordist Deal is coming to an end, production and consumption continue to be tied together. Understanding consumption requires that we understand production, and understanding production requires that we understand consumption. This is not a new insight. A century and a half ago, Marx was keenly aware that production and consumption cannot be separated: 'Without production, no consumption; but also, without consumption, no production' (Marx, [1859] 1993). What *is* new is the increasing integration of consumption and work that we noted in the previous edition of this book and that has now proceeded apace (see Chapter 11, 'The Consumer as Worker'). Some consumption, such as working out in a gym or reading this book is almost *just work*. By the same token, a great deal of consumption, especially including what are referred to as 'corporate hospitality' and 'corporate travel', takes place while we are notionally *at work*.

How does this integration come about? At the level of societies, internet-based technologies have been a major factor, requiring consumers to learn new skills and work longer in the process. At the individual level, a new politics of meaning and identity has blended the experiences of work and consumption. Meaning and identity are not fashioned solely in the realm of consumption as some theorists of postmodernity argued, or solely in the workplace as others have argued. They emerge from what Bourdieu (1979) called the *habitus* and associated lifestyles – loosely connected sets of tastes, behaviours, ideas and values that integrate work with consumption (Gershuny, 1988; Chaney, 1996; Du Gay, 1996). These lifestyles may entail coherence in work, leisure and home, or may entail dissonances and discontinuities. The holiday, that lifestyle emblem, may complement work, home and income or, equally, may be extravagantly out of tune with them. Under the regime of the Fordist Deal, identity and meaning were tied to one's work and one's living standards as enabled by their working situation, themselves the product of class position (Sennett, 1998). Today, by contrast, identity and meaning are more fluid, tentative and inconsistent.

Unmanageability and the consumer

In the first edition of this book, we argued that the Fordist Deal was weakening and suggested that Western consumerism may have entered a twilight phase. During the high noon of consumerism in the latter half of the 20th century, we argued, the face of the consumer was clear, as was the significance of his or her every movement. The pursuit of happiness through consumption seemed a plausible, if morally questionable, social and personal project. Today, this argument seems dated. The economic conditions have become more fraught. There has been a major recession which exposed how consumerism had relied on a debt-ridden bubble. As a result, enduring insecurities were created in the West and emerging prosperity in the East was threatened. Social inequalities have widened further within and between societies. The American Dream has lost its allure because it seems unrealizable for so many people, trapped in insecure jobs, with stagnant wages and feeling a squeeze on their living standards. Spending fatigue threatens to overcome even some of the better-off, who opt for simpler lives, underpinned by spiritual and community values. The Fordist Deal has become a museum piece.

The demise of the Fordist Deal has had one very clear-cut consequence. It has made the consumer more unmanageable, lending continuity to the core argument of our book since its first edition. Casualization of work is accompanied by casualization of consumption. People lead more precarious and uneven existences, one day enjoying unexpected boons and the next feeling overwhelmed by insecurity and debt. Precariousness, unevenness and fragmentation will continue to characterize Western life prospects. Marginality has paradoxically become central. The notion of an average consumer has become a fiction. Affluent members of professional and managerial cadres can find themselves overnight laid off and in abject financial and emotional difficulties. Many of them opt for drastic changes in their lives; senior bank managers become home decorators;

marketing executives that used to handle accounts worth millions are now delivering wine from white vans (Gabriel et al., 2010; Gabriel et al., 2013). By the same token, today's unemployed person can become tomorrow's start-up 'app' millionaire or TV celebrity, adopting the lifestyle of the super-rich. For a sizeable proportion of society, however, the likeliest prospect is to end up a member of the 'precariat'.

In this uncertain world, the consumer must now be deemed *unmanageable*, claimed by many, but controlled by nobody, least of all by consumers themselves. The very term 'the consumer' in these circumstances becomes what the philosopher W. B. Gallie called an 'essentially contested concept' (Gallie, 1964). Such a concept, he proposed, entails a variety of meanings; different arguments draw out particular meanings while excluding the others. There is no way to adjudicate between different meanings, yet not all meanings have an equal claim to be valid. Our presentation of the consumer fits Gallie's definition of an essentially contested concept perfectly, as we have sought to show in the different chapters of this book. The notion of unmanageability becomes even more appropriate in an era where the capacity to plan must give way to opportunism, living for the present. Deeming the consumers to be unmanageable does not mean that vast resources are not expended in seeking to control them, cajole them, predict and mould their behaviour and consciousness. Vast amounts of information are collected at the point of sale, the point of thinking about a purchase, in order to make consumers appear predictable and amenable to typologies of marketing efforts. And yet, the best attempts at managing consumers easily come undone, as when a fad or a fashion seizes their imagination and, just as quickly, goes. Even as they are constantly typecast and pigeon-holed, consumers are becoming more unmanageable, eccentric and paradoxical.

The argument then is that, like today's producers, today's consumers (after all, even in a globalized division of labour they are often the same people) must rely on opportunism, and seeking to be in the right place at the right times. As Bauman has argued, when the rules of the game keep changing,

> the sensible strategy is [...] to keep each game short – so that a sensibly played game of life calls for the splitting of one big all-embracing game with huge stakes into a series of brief and narrow games with small ones. [...] To keep the game short means to beware long-term commitments. To refuse to be 'fixed' one way or the other. Not to get tied to the place. Not to wed one's life to one vocation only. Not to swear consistency and loyalty to anything and anybody. Not to control the future, but to refuse to mortgage it: to take care that the consequences of the game do not outlive the past to bear on the present. (Bauman, 1996: 24)

To retailers and producers of goods and services, this unmanageability may not be a terminal difficulty and, for some, it may represent an opportunity. So long as a certain proportion of the population at any one time is in a position to spend, there will be markets, and entrepreneurs will discover opportunities to capitalize on people's desire to celebrate, enjoy themselves and improve their lifespace. After all, the opportunism of consumers is matched by the opportunism of business. Co-creation of value and co-production of brands represents the fruit of the cross-fertilization of these two opportunisms. Market researchers and the agents of production endlessly pursue the Holy Grail of control, seeking to anticipate consumer trends on behalf of capital, which stands to gain massively from accurate predictions, coupled with investment, in attempts to shape or tempt consumption to its benefit. The task of those who seek to anticipate trends is inevitably partisan, their goal is to mould the future to their ends.

Planning a future for the consumer is one thing; delivering it is another. Even at the mundane level of anticipating what objects will be popular in the future, prognostication is fraught with danger. In the short term, companies are remarkably adept at anticipating the weekly or daily demands of consumers. Modern information technology and data storage perform miracles in short-term forecasting. Supermarkets are particularly skilled in combining such forecasting with stock control and just-in-time production systems. Like the weather, however, longer-term forecasting is more problematic. Indeed, the history of consumption is full of failed prophesies. Products that pundits were once sure would become objects of mass consumption and desire in the future now stand as quaint reminders of the pitfalls of futurology. In the 1960s, for instance, the merchants of tomorrow's world were offering us throw-away paper clothes, holidays on the moon, living in geodesic domes, eating food in tablet form, undertaking less work. In practice today, precious few houses are in dome form; there has been a meteoric rise in nutritional supplements but only in addition to more 'ordinary' food; no one has been to the moon almost since the first landings; mountains of paper are thrown away – despite the promise that the age of the electronic office would be paperless – but not having been worn on human bodies; and people who are in work often work harder and longer, just as consumers work harder and longer for free.

There is a disparity, however, between the fantasies of industrialists and retailers and those of consumers themselves. The former ever dream of managing consumers, while the latter's dreams make them ever unmanageable. The former seek to put their vision into practice; the latter subvert, refuse, accept, interpret, surrender or embrace, in the manner this book has explored. Consumers have proven that in spite of the best efforts to constrain, control and manipulate them, they can act in ways that are unpredictable, inconsistent and contrary.

Challenges to consumerism

Unpredictability, inconsistency and contrariness all characterize today's consumption. At the same time, governments and commercial interests persist in pursuing 'business as usual' where well-being is equated to economic growth and higher spending power. Faith in the market as the mechanism that will deliver this higher standard of living is undiminished among the world's power elite, even if it is being more openly contested by some critics and some oppositional movements. An increasing number of voices is heard arguing that environmental, demographic and social factors will combine in the longer term to undermine this conception of well-being as increased wealth. Religious fundamentalism of different faiths and the resurgence of political parties of the extreme right also threaten the dominant model of consumerism and its ability to deliver the good life.

The environmental challenge to consumerism is now clear to almost all thinking people. The evidence is very strong for coming shortages of key resources that have underpinned the consumerist expansion. These include oil, water, land, soil, clean air and minerals. Without these, even a largely dematerialized economy cannot function. There may be techno-fixes to some of these environmental and material threats; renewable sources of energy and fracking may become substitutes for Middle East oil. The success of such technical fixes as complete solutions should not be relied upon. Even tougher environmental challenges are at hand. The most significant of these is undoubtedly climate change, which heralds dramatic discontinuities and ruptures in current forms of consumption. Pollution, waste and desertification are also looming.

The demographic challenge is likely to prove as severe and politically unsettling. The world population passed 6 billion at the beginning of the 21st century, was 7 billion in 2013 and is predicted by the UN Population Fund to rise to 9–10 billion by 2050. Feeding, housing and providing water for such numbers is a formidable challenge. This is exacerbated by the environmental problems noted above and by the demographic disequilibria created by ageing populations of most industrialized countries, alongside the youthfulness of other countries. This combination of environmental and demographic factors has led some analysts to speculate that social unrest, disease and warfare will reach unprecedented scale in the longer term, leading to vast new migrations across continents, and spawning the militarization of borders. Others, on the other hand, argue that the problem is not absolute numbers of people and production but relative inequalities and distribution of public goods within and across those populations. Whichever is the case, the challenge to consumerism remains.

All of these challenges might have mobilized political and social forces to bolster consumerism, if only it had managed to deliver its promise to make people happy. This is far from the case. There is overwhelming evidence that decades of consumerism have not delivered unequivocal happiness. If anything, they have created discontents of their own. Mental illness, family dislocation and enduring social inequalities are in themselves measures of the failure of consumerism to fulfil its promise, as is the growth of therapies, 'mindfulness' and self-help. It is not surprising that many people question or abandon consumerism altogether, opting for lower-levels of consumption and simpler lifestyles. Happiness, they seem to claim, is not a destination to travel towards, but a way of travelling; build happiness into your life now.

Speaking at the peak of the Fordist Deal in the USA, Robert F. Kennedy, then running for President and shortly before his assassination, captured the limitations of equating consumption, as measured by economic indicators, with social well-being.

> *For too long we seem to have surrendered personal excellence and community value in the mere accumulation of material things. Our gross national product now is over 800 billion dollars a year, but that gross national product, if we judge the United States of America by that, that gross national product counts air pollution, and cigarette advertising, and ambulances to clear our highways of carnage. It counts special locks for our doors and the jails for people who break them. It counts the destruction of the redwoods and the loss of our natural wonder in chaotic squall. It counts Napalm, and it counts nuclear warheads, and armored cars for the police to fight the riots in our city. It counts Whitman's rifles and Speck's Knives and the television programs which glorify violence in order to sell toys to our children. Yet, the gross national product does not allow for the health of our children, the quality of their education, or the joy of their play. It does not include the beauty of our poetry or the strength of our marriages; the intelligence of our public debate or the integrity of our public officials. It measures neither our wit nor our courage; neither our wisdom nor our learning; neither our compassion nor our devotion to our country; it measures everything, in short, except that which makes life worthwhile ... (University of Kansas, Lawrence, Kansas, 18 March 1968)*

Half a century ago, a leading politician such as Kennedy could see clearly the limits of consumerism for the richest consumer society in the world. Today, as the Fordist Deal is moribund, even as more nations are sucked into its consumerist legacy, leaving us with a far more fragile promise of happiness and a far greater burden for future generations, there are more people, across nations, who have started to share his concerns and foreboding. It remains to be seen whether these concerns will find organized expression in new popular movements or in a political will to bring about genuine social change.

REFERENCES

Abercrombie, N. (1994) 'Authority and consumer society', in R. Keat, N. Whiteley and N. Abercrombie (eds), *The Authority of the Consumer*. London: Routledge, pp. 43–57.

Accum, F. (1820) *A Treatise on Adulterations of Food and Culinary Poisons*. London: Longman.

Adam, B., Beck, U. and Loon, Jv. (2000) *The Risk Society and Beyond: Critical Issues for Social Theory*. London: Sage.

Adams, J. (1995) *Risk*. London: UCL Press.

Adams, R., Carruthers, J. and Fisher, C. (1991) *Shopping for A Better World: A Quick and Easy Guide to Socially Responsible Supermarket Shopping*. London: Kogan Page.

Adorno, T. (1991) *The Culture Industry*. London: Routledge.

Allain, A. (1991) 'Breastfeeding is politics: a personal view of the international baby milk campaign', *The Ecologist*, 21: 206–213.

Alvesson, M. (2013) *The Triumph of Emptiness: Consumption, Higher Education, and Work Organization*. Oxford: Oxford University Press.

Anderson, B. (1983) *Imagined Communities*. London: Verso.

Anderson, S. and Cavanagh, J. (2000) *Top 200: The Rise of Corporate Global Power*. Washington, DC: Institute of Policy Studies.

Annan, K. (2003) 'Message for International Cooperation Day', 25 June, UN Press Release SG/SM/8762 OBV/359. New York: United Nations.

Appadurai, A. (1990) 'Disjuncture and difference in the global cultural economy', *Theory, Culture and Society*, 7: 295–310.

Arnould, E. J. (2007) 'Should consumer citizens escape the market?', *Annals of the American Academy of Political and Social Science*, 611: 96–111.

Arnould, Eric J. and Thompson, Craig J. (2005) 'Consumer culture theory (CCT): twenty years of research', *Journal of Consumer Research*, 31: 868–882.

Aron, R. (1967) *18 Lectures on Industrial Society*. London: Weidenfeld & Nicolson.

Arvidsson, A. (2005) 'Brands a critical perspective', *Journal of Consumer Culture*, 5: 235–258.

Arvidsson, A. (2006) *Brands: Meaning and Value in Media Culture*. London: Routledge.

Arvidsson, A. (2010) 'The ethical economy: new forms of value in the information society?', *Organization*, 17: 637–644.

Arvidsson, A and Colleoni, E. (2012) 'Value in informational capitalism and on the internet', *Information Society*, 28: 135–150.

Atkinson, L. (2012) 'Buying in to social change: how private consumption choices engender concern for the collective', *The ANNALS of the American Academy of Political and Social Science*, 644: 191–206.

Bakhtin, M. ([1929] 1973) *Problems of Dostoevsky's Poetics*. New York: Ardis.

Barda, C. and Sardianou, E. (2010) 'Analysing consumers' "activism" in response to rising prices', *International Journal of Consumer Studies*, 34: 133–139.

Barlow, M. and Clarke, T. (2002) *Blue Gold: The Battle Against Corporate Theft of the World's Water*. London: Earthscan.

Barnet, R. J. and Cavanagh, J. (1994) *Global Dreams: Imperial Corporations and the New World Order*. New York: Simon & Schuster.

Barnett, C., Cloke, P., Clarke, N. and Malpass, A. (2010) *Globalizing Responsibility: The Political Rationalities of Ethical Consumption*. Chichester: Wiley-Blackwell.

Barratt Brown, M. (1993) *Fair Trade: Reform and Realities in the International Trading System*. London: Zed Press.

Barthes, R. ([1966] 1977) 'The rhetoric of the image', in S. Heath (ed.), *Image – Music – Text*. Glasgow: Collins, pp. 32–51.

Barthes, R. (1973) *Mythologies*. London: Paladin Books.

Bates, C. and Rowell, A. (1998) *Tobacco Explained: The Truth About the Tobacco Industry ... in its Own Words*. London: Action on Smoking.

Bateson, G. (1972) *Steps to an Ecology of Mind*. London: Intertext Books.

Baudrillard, J. ([1968] 1988) 'The system of objects', in M. Poster (ed.), *Jean Baudrillard: Selected Writings*. Cambridge: Polity Press, pp. 10–28.

Baudrillard, J. ([1970] 1988) 'Consumer society', in M. Poster (ed.), *Jean Baudrillard: Selected Writings*. Cambridge: Polity Press, pp. 29–56.

Baudrillard, J. (1983) *Simulations*. New York: Semiotext(e).

Baudrillard, J. (1988) 'Simulacra and simulations', in M. Poster (ed.), *Jean Baudrillard: Selected Writings*. Cambridge: Polity Press, pp. 166–184.

Baudrillard, J. and Gane, M. (1993) *Baudrillard Live: Selected Interviews*. London and New York: Routledge.

Bauman, Z. (1988) *Freedom*. Milton Keynes: Open University Press.

Bauman, Z. (1992) *Intimations of Postmodernity*. London: Routledge.

Bauman, Z. (1996) 'From pilgrim to tourist: or a short history of identity', in S. Hall and P. Du Gay (eds), *Questions of Cultural Identity*. London: Sage, pp. 18–36.

Bauman, Z. (1998) *Work, Consumerism and the New Poor*. Buckingham: Open University Press.

Bauman, Z. (2001) 'Consuming life', *Journal of Consumer Culture*, 1: 9–30.

Baumeister, R. F. (1986) *Identity: Cultural Change and the Struggle for Self*. Oxford: Oxford University Press.

Bayus, B. L. (2013) 'Crowdsourcing new product ideas over time: an analysis of the Dell IdeaStorm community', *Management Science*, 59: 226–244.

Beck, U. (1992) *Risk Society: Towards a New Modernity*. London: Sage.

Beech, N., Gilmore, C., Cochrane, E. and Greig, G. J. (2012) 'Identity work as a response to tensions: a re-narration in opera rehearsals', *Scandinavian Journal of Management*, 28: 39–47.

Beishon, J. (1994) 'Consumers and power', in R. John (ed.), *The Consumer Revolution: Redressing the Balance*. London: Hodder and Stoughton, pp. 1–11.

Belk, R. W. (1982) 'Gift giving behavior', *Research in Marketing*, 2: 95–126.

Belk, R. W. (1988) 'Possessions and the extended self', *Journal of Consumer Research*, 15.

Belk, R. W. (2013) 'Extended self in a digital world', *Journal of Consumer Research*, 40: 477–500.

Bell, D. (1976) *The Cultural Contradictions of Capitalism*. New York: Basic Books.

Benjamin, W. and Tiedemann, R. (1999) *The Arcades Project*. Cambridge, MA: Belknap Press.

Bennett, P. and Calman, K. (1999) *Risk Communication and Public Health*. Oxford: Oxford University Press.

Berger, P. and Luckmann, T. (1967) *The Social Construction of Reality*. Garden City, NY: Anchor.

Bertens, J. W. (1995) *The Idea of the Postmodern: A History*. London: Routledge.

Beveridge, S. W. (1942) 'Social insurance and allied services', Cmd 6404. London: HMSO.

Bevir, M. and Trentmann, F. (2007) *Governance, Consumers and Citizens: Agency and Resistance in Contemporary Politics*. Basingstoke, Hampshire: Palgrave.

Birchall, J. (1994) *Co-op: The People's Business*. Manchester: Manchester University Press.

Black, I. R. and Cherrier, H. (2010) 'Anti-consumption as part of living a sustainable lifestyle: daily practices, contextual motivations and subjective values', *Journal of Consumer Behaviour*, 9: 437–453.

Bloom, P. N. and Greyser, S. A. (1981) 'Exploring the future of consumerism', research program, July 1981. Cambridge, MA: Marketing Science Institute (USA).

Bloom, P. N. and Stern, L. W. (1978) 'Consumerism in the year 2000: the emergence of anti-industrialism', in N. Kangun and L. Richardson (eds), *Consumerism: New Challenges for Marketing*. Chicago: American Marketing Association, pp. 183–200.

Boje, D. M. (2001) *Narrative Methods for Organizational and Communication Research*. London: Sage.

Boorstin, D. J. (1962) *The Image or What Happened to the American Dream*. New York: Atheneum.

Bourdieu, P. (1979) *Outline of a Theory of Practice*. Cambridge: Cambridge University Press.

Bourdieu, P. (1984) *Distinction: A Social Critique of the Judgement of Taste*. London: Routledge.

Breakwell, G. M. (2007) *The Psychology of Risk*. Cambridge: Cambridge University Press.

Brewer, J. and Trentmann, F. (2006) *Consuming Cultures, Global Perspectives: Historical Trajectories, Transnational Exchanges*. Oxford: Berg.

Brimelow, P. and Spencer, L. (1990) 'Ralph Nader Inc.', *Forbes*, 146: 117–129.

Brown, D. H. (1991) 'Citizens or consumer: US reactions to the European Community's directive on television', *Critical Studies in Mass Communication*, 8: 1–12.

Brown, R. L. (1958) 'Wrapper influence on the perception of freshness in bread', *Journal of Applied Psychology*, 42: 257–260.

Brown, S., Kozinets, R. V. and Sherry, J. F. (2003) 'Teaching old brands new tricks: retro branding and the revival of brand meaning', *Journal of Marketing*, 67: 19–33.

Bryant, A. (1929) *The Spirit of Conservatism*. London: Methuen & Co.

Bull, D. (1982) *A Growing Problem: Pesticides and the Third World Poor*. Oxford: Oxfam.

Bunting, M. (2004) *Willing Slaves: How the Overwork Culture Is Ruling Our Lives*. London: HarperCollins.

Burch, D. and Lawrence, G. (2007) *Supermarkets and Agri-food Supply Chains*. Cheltenham: Edward Elgar.

Burnett, J. (1969) *A History of the Cost of Living*. Harmondsworth: Penguin.

Campbell, C. (1989) *The Romantic Ethic and the Spirit of Modern Consumerism*. Oxford: Macmillan.

Campbell, C. (2004) 'The citizen-consumer: is this term an oxymoron?', Consumers as Citizens seminar, 22 April, HM Treasury, London.

Camus, A. (1971) *The Rebel*. Harmondsworth: Penguin.

Caraher, M. (2003) 'Food protest and the new activism', in S. John and S. Thomson (eds), *New Activism and the Corporate Response*. Basingstoke: Palgrave, pp. 185–205.

Carmel, E. and Papadolpoulos, T. (2009) 'Governing social security: from protection to markets', in J. Millar (ed.), *Understanding Social Security: Issues for Policy and Practice*. Bristol: Policy Press, pp. 93–110.

Carr, D. J., Gotlieb, M. R., Lee, N.-J. and Shah, D. V. (2012) 'Examining overconsumption, competitive consumption, and conscious consumption from 1994 to 2004: disentangling cohort and period effects', *The ANNALS of the American Academy of Political and Social Science*, 644: 220–233.

Castells, M. (1996) *The Information Age: Economy, Society and Culture. Vol. 1: The Rise of the Network Society*. Oxford: Blackwell.

Cederström, C. and Fleming, P. (2012) *Dead Man Working*. Winchester: Zero Books.

Centers for Disease Control and Prevention (2005) *Behavioral Risk Factor Surveillance System: Kansas vs Missouri Physical Activity*. Atlanta: Centers for Disease Control and Prevention.

Chaney, D. (1996) *Lifestyles*. London: Routledge.

Chase, S. and Schlink, F. J. (1927) *Your Money's Worth: A Study in the Waste of the Consumer's Dollar*. New York: Macmillan.

Cherrier, H. (2009) 'Anti-consumption discourses and consumer-resistant identities', *Journal of Business Research*, 62: 181–190.

Chertkovskaya, E. (2013) 'Consuming work and managing employability: students' work orientations and the process of contemporary job search', unpublished PhD thesis, Loughborough University.

Chia, A. (2012) 'Welcome to Me-Mart: the politics of user-generated content in personal blogs', *American Behavioral Scientist*, 56: 421–438.

Clammer, J. (1992) 'Aesthetics of the self: shopping and social being in contemporary Japan', in R. Shields (ed.), *Lifestyle Shopping: The Subject of Consumption*. London: Routledge, pp. 195–215.

Clammer, J. (2011) *Contemporary Urban Japan: A Sociology of Consumption*. Oxford: Wiley-Blackell.

Clarke, J., Newman, J., Smith, N., Vidler, E. and Westmarland, L. (2007) *Creating Citizen-consumers: Changing Publics and Changing Public Services*. London: Sage.

Cluley, R. and Dunn, S. (2012) 'From commodity fetishism to commodity narcissism', *Marketing Theory*, 12: 251–265.

Cockett, R. (1994) *Thinking the Unthinkable: Think-Tanks and the Economic Counter-Revolution, 1931–1983*. London: HarperCollins.

Coff, C., Barling, D., Korthals, M. and Nielsen, T. (eds) (2008) *Ethical Traceability and Communicating Food*. The International Library of Environmental, Agricultural and Food Ethics. New York: Springer.

Cohen, M. J. (2013) 'Collective dissonance and the transition to post-consumerism', *Futures*, 52: 42–51.

Comor, E. (2010) 'Digital prosumption and alienation', *Ephemera*, 10: 439–454.

Consumers International (2004) *About CI: Rights and Responsibilities*. London: Consumers International.

Consumers International (2014) 'About us'. Retrieved from: www.consumersinternational.org/who-we-are/about-us (accessed 19 August 2014). London: Consumers International.

Consumers Union (2014) 'Mission'. Retrieved from: www.consumersunion.org/about/mission (accessed 19 August 2014). Yonkers, NY: Consumers Union.

Co-operative Group (2004) *Shopping with Attitude*. Manchester: Co-operative Group.

Cova, B. and Cova, V. (2012) 'On the road to prosumption: marketing discourse and the development of consumer competencies', *Consumption Markets & Culture*, 15: 149–168.

Cova, B. and Dalli, D. (2009) 'Working consumers: the next step in marketing theory?', *Marketing Theory*, 9: 315–339.

Cova, B., Kozinets, R. V. and Shankar, A. (2007) *Consumer Tribes*. London: Routledge.

Cova, B., Maclaran, P. and Bradshaw, A. (2013) 'Rethinking consumer culture theory from the postmodern to the communist horizon', *Marketing Theory*, 13: 213–225.

Cova, B. and White, T. (2010) 'Counter-brand and alter-brand communities: the impact of Web 2.0 on tribal marketing approaches', *Journal of Marketing Management*, 26: 256–270.

Cox, A. D., Cox, D. and Anderson, R. D. (2005) 'Reassessing the pleasures of store shopping', *Journal of Business Research*, 58: 250–259.

Crane, A. and Matten, D. (2007) *Corporate Social Responsibility*. Thousand Oaks, CA and London: Sage.

Cranston, R. (1984) *Consumers and the Law*. London: Weidenfeld and Nicolson.

Crick, B. R. (2001) *Citizens: Towards a Citizenship Culture*. Oxford: Blackwell.

Crick, B. R. (2004) *Essays on Citizenship*. London: Continuum.

Csikszentmihalyi, M. and Rochberg-Halton, E. (1981) *The Meaning of Things: Domestic Symbols and the Self*. Cambridge: Cambridge University Press.

Culler, J. ([1981] 2001) *The Pursuit of Signs: Semiotics, Literature, Deconstruction*. London: Routledge.

Dale, K. (2012) 'The employee as "dish of the day": the ethics of the consuming/consumed self in human resource management', *Journal of Business Ethics*, 111: 13–24.

Daly, H. E. (1996) *Beyond Growth: The Economics of Sustainable Development*. Boston: Beacon Press.

Daly, H. E., Cobb, J. B. and Cobb, C. W. (1990) *For the Common Good: Redirecting the Economy Toward Community, the Environment, and a Sustainable Future*. London: Green Print.

Daly, H. E. and Farley, J. C. (2011) *Ecological Economics: Principles and Applications*. Washington, DC and London: Island Press.

Davidson, M. P. (1992) *The Consumerist Manifesto: Advertising in Postmodern Times*. London: Routledge.

Davis, L. J. (2008) *Obsession: A History*. Chicago: University of Chicago Press.

Deaton, A. and Muellbauer, J. (1980) *Economics and Consumer Behavior*. Cambridge and New York: Cambridge University Press.

Debord, G. (1977) *Society of the Spectacle*. Detroit: Black and Red.

de Certeau, M. (1984) *The Practice of Everyday Life*. Berkeley, CA: University of California Press.

Defra (2014) *Agriculture in the UK 2013* (29 May update). London: Department for Enviornment, Food and Rural Affairs.

Department of Trade and Industry (2005) *Guide to the 1987 Consumer Protection Act*. London: DTI Consumer Affairs Directorate.

Deuze, M., Bruns, A. and Neuberger, C. (2007) 'Preparing for an age of participatory news', *Journalism Practice*, 1: 322–338.

DG SANCO (2005) 'Health and Consumer and Protection programme 2007–2013'. Retrieved from: http://europa.eu.int/comm/consumers/overview/programme_2007-2013_en.htm (accessed 3 July 2005). Luxembourg: Commission of the European Communities.

Dhar, R. and Wertenbroch, K. (2000) 'Consumer choice between hedonic and utilitarian goods', *Journal of Marketing Research*, 37: 60–71.

Diamond, J. (2005) *Collapse: How Societies Choose to Fail or Survive*. London: Penguin Books.

Dichter, E. (1964) *Handbook of Consumer Motivations*. New York: McGraw-Hill.

Dickenson, N. (1993) 'Catering for the ethical shopper: a look into a growing consumer trend', *Financial Times*, 15 April.

Dickinson, R. and Hollander, S. C. (1991) 'Consumer votes', *Journal of Business Research*, 22: 335–342.

Dittmar, H. (1991) 'Meanings of material possessions as reflections of identity: gender and social-material position in society', *Journal of Social Behavior and Personality*, 6: 165–186.

Doucet, A. and Mauthner, N. (2012) 'Tea and Tupperware: mommy blogging as care-work and consumption', in C. Rogers and S. Weller (eds), *Critical Approaches to Care: Understanding Caring Relations, Identities and Cultures*. Abingdon: Routledge, pp. 92–104.

Douglas, M. (1975) 'Deciphering a meal', in M. Douglas (ed.), *Implicit Meanings: Essays in Anthropology*. London: Routledge, pp. 179–192.

Douglas, M. and Isherwood, B. (1978) *The World of Goods: Towards an Anthropology of Consumption*. London: Allen Lane.

d'Silva, J. and Webster, J. (2010) *The Meat Crisis: Developing More Sustainable Production and Consumption*. London: Earthscan.

Du Gay, P. (1996) *Consumption and Identity at Work*. London: Sage.

Durning, A. T. (1992a) *How Much Is Enough?* Washington, DC and London: Worldwatch Institute/Earthscan.

Durning, A. T. (1992b) *How Much Is Enough? The Consumer Society and the Future of the Earth*. New York: Norton.

ECRA (1994) 'Culture-jamming', *The Ethical Consumer*, 20–21.

Edge, A. (1999) *Faith of Our Fathers: Football as a Religion*. Edinburgh: Mainstream.

Ekins, P. (1999) *Economic Growth and Environmental Sustainability: The Prospects for Green Growth*. London: Routledge.

Elkington, J. (1997) *Cannibals with Forks: The Triple Bottom Line of 21st Century Business*. Oxford: Capstone.

Elkington, J. and Burke, T. (1987) *The Green Capitalists: Industry's Search for Environmental Excellence*. London: V. Gollancz.

Elkington, J. and Hailes, J. (1988) *The Green Consumer Guide: From Shampoo to Champagne: High-street Shopping for a Better Environment*. London: V. Gollancz.

Ellen Macarthur Foundation and McKinsey (2013) *Towards the Circular Economy*. Cowes, Isle of Wight: Ellen Macarthur Foundation.

Elliott, C. (2013) *Elliott Review into the Integrity and Assurance of Food Supply Networks: Interim Report*. Retrieved from: www.gov.uk/government/publications/elliott-review-into-the-integrity-and-assurance-of-food-supply-networks-interim-report (accessed 4 March 2015). London: HM Government.

Elliott, R. (1997) 'Existential consumption and irrational desire', *European Journal of Marketing*, 31: 285–296.

Environmental Audit Committee (2011) *Embedding Sustainable Development across Government. First Report of Session 2010–2011*. HC 504. London: House of Commons Environmental Audit Comittee.

Erikson, E. H. (1959) *Identity and the Life Cycle*. New York: Norton.

Erikson, E. H. (1968) *Identity: Youth and Crisis*. London: Faber and Faber.

Ethical Consumer (1994) 'The Ethical Consumer: special anti-consumer issue', *The Ethical Consumer*: whole issue.

Ethical Consumer (2005) 'About boycotts'. Retrieved from: www.ethicalconsumer.org/boycotts/aboutboycotts.htm (accessed 27 June 2005). Manchester: ECRA.

Ethical Consumer (2012) 'Food'. Retrieved from: www.ethicalconsumer.org/buyers-guides/food.aspx (accessed 4 March 2015). Manchester: ECRA.

Etzioni, A. (1988) *The Moral Dimension: Toward a New Economics*. New York: The Free Press.

Etzioni, A. (1993) *Spirit of Community*. New York: Simon & Schuster.

Etzioni, A. (1998a) *The Essential Communitarian Reader*. Lanham, MD: Rowman and Littlefield.

Etzioni, A. (1998b) 'Voluntary simplicity: characterization, select psychological implications, and societal consequences', *Journal of Economic Psychology*, 19: 619–649.

Etzioni, A. (2009) 'Spent: America after consumerism', *New Republic*, 240: 20–23.

European Commission (2014) *Towards a Circular Economy: A Zero Waste Programme for Europe*. Brussels: Commission of the European Communities.

Ewen, S. (1990) 'Marketing dreams: the political elements of style', in A. Tomlinson (ed.), *Consumption, Identity and Style: Marketing, Meanings and the Packaging of Pleasure*. London: Routledge, pp. 41–56.

Ewen, S. (1992) 'From consumer to citizen', *Intermedia*, 20: 22–23.

Eyre, A. (1997) *Football and Religious Experience: Sociological Reflections*. Oxford: Religious Experience Research Centre.

Fairtrade International (2013) *Unlocking the Power: 2012–13 Annual Report*. Bonn: Fairtrade International.

FAO (2004) 'Farmworkers need to be better protected against pesticides'. Retrieved from: www.fao.org/newsroom/en/news/2004/50709/print_friendly_version.html (accessed 3 July 2005). Rome: Food and Agriculture Organization of the United Nations.

Featherstone, M. (1991) *Consumer Culture and Postmodernism*. London: Sage.

Ferlie, E., Ashburner, L., Fitzgerald, L. and Pettigrew, A. (1996) *The New Public Management*. Oxford: Oxford University Press.

Fernstrom, M. M. (1984) *Consumerism: Implications and Opportunities for Financial Services*. New York: American Express Company.

Fineman, S. (2015) *The Blame Business*. London: Reaktion Books.

Firat, A. F. (1992) 'Fragmentations in the postmodern', *Advances in Consumer Research*, 19: 203–206.

Firat, A. F. and Dholakia, N. (1998) *Consuming People: From Political Economy to Theaters of Consumption*. London: Routledge.

Firat, A. F. and Venkatesh, A. (1995) 'Liberatory postmodernism and the reenchantment of consumption', *Journal of Consumer Research*, 22: 239–267.

Fiske, J. (1987) *Television Culture*. London: Methuen.

Fiske, J. (1989) *Understanding Popular Culture*. London: Unwin Hyman.

Flatters, P. and Willmott, M. (2009) 'Understanding the post-recession consumer', *Harvard Business Review*, 87: 106–112.

Fleming, P. (2009) *Authenticity and the Cultural Politics of Work: New Forms of Informal Control*. Oxford: Oxford University Press.

Fleming, P. and Spicer, A. (2004) '"You can checkout anytime, but you can never leave": spatial boundaries in a high commitment organization', *Human Relations*, 57: 75–94.

Food Standards Agency (2005a) 'Action taken to remove illegal dye found in wide range of foods on sale in UK'. Retrieved from: www.food.gov.uk/news/newsarchive/2005/feb/worcester (accessed 4 March 2015). London: Food Standards Agency.

Food Standards Agency (2005b) 'Sudan I consolidated product list'. Retrieved from: www.food.gov.uk/multimedia/pdfs/sudanlistno.pdf (accessed 13 January 2011). London: Food Standards Agency.

Forbes, J. D. (1987) *The Consumer Interest*. Beckenham: Croom Helm.

Fotaki, M. (2006) 'Choice is yours: a psychodynamic exploration of health policymaking and its consequences for the English National Health Service', *Human Relations*, 59: 1711–1744.

Fotaki, M. (2011) 'Towards developing new partnerships in public services: users as consumers, citizens and/or co-producers in Health and Social Care in England and Sweden', *Public administration*, 89: 933–955.

Fotaki, M., Roland, M., McDonald, R., Scheaff, R., Boyd, A. and Smith, L. (2008) 'What benefits will choice bring to patients? Literature review and assessment of implications', *Journal of Health Services Research & Policy*, 13: 178–184.

Frank, T. (1997) *The Conquest of Cool*. London: University of Chicago Press.

Frenkel, S. J., Korczynski, M., Shire, K.A. and Tam, M. (1999) *On the Front Line: Organization of Work in the Information Economy*. Ithaca, NY: Cornell University Press.

Freud, S. ([1914] 1984) 'On narcissism: an introduction', *On Metapsychology: The Theory of Psychoanalysis*. Harmondsworth: Pelican Freud Library, pp. 59–97.

Freud, S. (1920) *Beyond the Pleasure Principle*. London: Hogarth Press.

Freud, S. ([1921] 1985) 'Group psychology and the analysis of the ego', *Civilization, Society and Religion*. Harmondsworth: Pelican Freud Library, pp. 91–178.

Freud, S. ([1923] 1984) 'The ego and the id', *On Metapsychology: The Theory of Psychoanalysis*. Harmondsworth: Pelican Freud Library, pp. 341–406.

Freud, S. ([1930] 1985) 'Civilization and its discontents', *Civilization, Society and Religion*. Harmondsworth: Pelican Freud Library, pp. 91–178.

Friedman, M. (1962) *Capitalism and Freedom*. Chicago: University of Chicago Press.

Friedman, M. (1985) 'Consumer boycotts in the United States, 1970–1980: contemporary events in historial perspective', *Journal of Consumer Affairs*, 19: 96–117.

Friedman, M. (1999) *Consumer Boycotts: Effecting Change through the Marketplace and the Media*. London: Routledge.

Friedman, M. and Friedman, R. D. (1980) *Free to Choose: A Personal Statement*. New York: Harcourt Brace Jovanovich.

Fritsch, A. J. (1974) *The Contrasumers: A Citizen's Guide to Resource Conservation*. New York: Praeger.

Fromm, E. ([1947] 1965) *Man for Himself: An Inquiry into the Psychology of Ethics*. New York: Fawcett Premier.

FTEPR (2014) *Fairtrade, Employment and Poverty Reduction in Ethiopia and Uganda: Final Report to DfID*. London: School of Oriental and African Studies, University of London.

Fuchs, C. (2010) 'Labor in informational capitalism and on the internet', *Information Society*, 26: 179–196.

Fuchs, C. (2014) 'Digital prosumption labour on social media in the context of the capitalist regime of time', *Time & Society*, 23: 97–123.

Fukuyama, F. (1992) *The End of History and the Last Man*. New York: Free Press.

Fulop, C. (1977) *The Consumer Movement and the Consumer*. London: Advertising Association.

Furnham, A. and Okamura, R. (1999) 'Your money or your life: behavioral and emotional predictors of money pathology', *Human Relations*, 52: 1157–1177.

Gabriel, Y. (1993) 'Organizational nostalgia: reflections on the golden age', in S. Fineman (ed.), *Emotion in Organizations*. London: Sage, pp. 118–141.

Gabriel, Y. (1995) 'The unmanaged organization', *Organization Studies*, 16: 481–506.

Gabriel, Y. (1999) *Organizations in Depth: The Psychoanalysis of Organizations*. London: Sage.

Gabriel, Y. (2000) *Storytelling in Organizations: Facts, Fictions, Fantasies*. Oxford: Oxford University Press.

Gabriel, Y. (2005) 'Glass cages and glass palaces: images of organizations in image-conscious times', *Organization*, 12: 9–27.

Gabriel, Y. (2008) 'Spectacles of resistance and resistance of spectacles', *Management Communication Quarterly*, 21: 310–327.

Gabriel, Y., Gray, D. E. and Goregaokar, H. (2010) 'Temporary derailment or the end of the line? Managers coping with unemployment at 50', *Organization Studies*, 31: 1687–1712.

Gabriel, Y., Gray, D. E. and Goregaokar, H. (2013) 'Job loss and its aftermath among managers and professionals: wounded, fragmented and flexible', *Work, Employment & Society*, 27: 56–72.

Galbraith, J. K. (1967) *The New Industrial State*. New York: Signet.

Galbraith, J. K. (1974) *Economics and the Public Purpose*. London: Deutsch.

Gallie, W. B. (1964) 'Essentially contested concepts', in W. B. Gallie (ed.), *Philosophy and the Historical Understanding*. London: Chatto & Windus, pp. 157–191.

Gershuny, J. (1978) *After Industrial Society? The Emerging Self-service Economy*. Atlantic Highlands, NJ: Humanities Press.

Gershuny, J. (1988) 'Lifestyle, innovation and the future of work', *International Journal of Development Banking*, 6: 65–72.

Gershuny, J. (1992) 'Are we running out of time?' *Futures*: 3–22.

Giddens, A. (1991) *Modernity and Self-identity: Self and Society in the Late Modern Age*. Stanford, CA: Stanford University Press.

Giddens, A. (1999) 'Risk and responsibility', *The Modern Law Review*, 62: 1–10.

Gilbert, J. (2008) 'Against the commodification of everything: anti-consumerist cultural studies in the age of ecological crisis', *Cultural Studies*, 22: 551–566.

Gilg, A., Barr, S. and Ford, N. (2005) 'Green consumption or sustainable lifestyles? Identifying the sustainable consumer', *Futures*, 37: 481–504.

Gilmore, F. (1999) *Brand Warriors: Corporate Leaders Share Their Winning Strategies*. London: HarperCollinsBusiness.

Gilmore, F. (2003) *Warriors on the High Wire: The Balancing Act of Brand Leadership in the Twenty-first Century*. London: Profile.

Ginzburg, C. (1980) 'Morelli, Freud and Sherlock Holmes: clues and scientific method', *History Workshop*, 9: 5–36.

Glickman, L. B. (2009) *Buying Power: A History of Consumer Activism in America*. Chicago: University of Chicago Press.

Global Footprint Network (2010) *Living Planet Report 2010: Biodiversity, Biocapacity and Development*. Gland, London and Oakland: WWF, Institute of Zoology, Global Footprint Network.

Goldsmith, E., Allen, R., Allaby, M., Davoll, J. and Lawrence, S. (1972) 'A blueprint for survival', *The Ecologist*, 2: 1–43.

Goldsmith, E. and Mander, J. (2001) *The Case Against the Global Economy and for a Turn Towards Localization*. London: Earthscan.

Goldstein, D. G., Johnson, E. J., Herrmann, A. and Heitmann, M. (2008) 'Nudge your customers toward better choices', *Harvard Business Review*, 86: 99–105.

Gotlieb, M. R. and Wells, C. (2012) 'From concerned shopper to dutiful citizen: implications of individual and collective orientations toward political consumerism', *The ANNALS of the American Academy of Political and Social Science*, 644: 207–219.

Gott, R. (1993) *Land Without Evil*. London: Verso.

Gott, R. (2000) *In the Shadow of the Liberator: Hugo Chavez and the Transformation of Venezuela*. London: Verso.

Goulart, R. (1970) *The Assault on Childhood*. London: Gollancz.

Gray, J. (1993) *Beyond the New Right: Markets, Government and the Common Environment*. London and New York: Routledge.

Gray, J. (1994) *The Undoing of Conservatism*. London: Social Market Foundation.

Gray, J. (2002) *Straw Dogs: Thoughts on Humans and Other Animals*. London: Granta.

Gray, J. (2003) *Al Qaeda and What it Means to Be Modern*. London: Faber.

Greider, W. (1992) *Who Will Tell the People: The Betrayal of American Democracy*. New York: Simon & Schuster.

Greyser, S. A. and Diamond, S. L. (1983) 'US consumers' views of the marketplace', *Journal of Consumer Policy*, 6: 3–18.

Habermas, J. (2003) *Lifeworld and System: A Critique of Functionalist Reason*. Boston: Beacon Press.

Hair, J. D. (1989) 'Changing from "consumers" to citizens', *EPA Journal*, 15: 37–39.

Hall, E. J. (1993) 'Smiling, deferring and flirting: doing gender by giving good service', *Work and Occupations*, 20: 452–471.

Hall, S. (1996) 'Who needs "identity"?', in S. Hall and P. Du Gay (eds), *Questions of Cultural Identity*. London: Sage, pp. 1–17.

Hall, S. and Du Gay, P. (eds) (1996) *Questions of Cultural Identity*. London: Sage.

Hall, S. and Jacques, M. (1989) *New Times*. London: Lawrence and Wishart.

Hambleton, R. and Hoggett, P. (1993) 'Rethinking consumerism in public services', *Consumer Policy Review*, 3: 103–111.

Hamilton, C. (2003) *Downshifting in Britain: A Sea-change in the Pursuit of Happiness*. Canberra ACT: The Australia Institute/Australian National University.

Hamilton, C. and Mail, E. (2003) *Downshifting in Australia: A Sea-change in Pursuit of Happiness*. Canberra ACT: The Australia Institute/Australian National University.

Hampden-Turner, C. and Trompenaars, A. (1993) *The Seven Cultures of Capitalism: Value Systems for Creating Wealth in the United States, Japan, Germany, France, Britain, Sweden, and the Netherlands*. New York: Currency/Doubleday.

Hancock, P. and Tyler, M. (2000) '"The look of love": gender and the organization of aesthetics', in J. Hassard, R. Holliday and H. Willmott (eds), *Body and Organization*. London: Sage, pp. 108–129.

Harrison, R. (2003) 'Corporate social responsibility and the consumer movement', *Consumer Policy Review*, 13 (4): 127–31.

Harrison, P. and Turner, J. (2014) '25 years of ethical shopping', *Ethical Consumer*: 38–41.

Harrison, R., Newholm, T. and Shaw, D. (2005) *The Ethical Consumer*. London: Sage.

Hartmann, H. I. (1979) 'The unhappy marriage of Marxism and feminism: towards a more progressive union', *Capital and Class*, 3: 1–33.

Harvey, D. (1990) *The Condition of Postmodernity: An Enquiry into the Origins of Cultural Change*. Oxford: Blackwell.

Hassall, A. H. (1855) *Food and its Adulterations: Comprising the Reports of the Analytical Sanitary Commission of 'The Lancet' for the Years 1851 to 1854*. London: Longman.

Hatch, M. J. and Schultz, M. (2010) 'Toward a theory of brand co-creation with implications for brand governance', *Journal of Brand Management*, 17: 590–604.

Hawkes, C. (2007) *Marketing Food to Children: Changes in the Global Regulatory Environment 2004–2006*. Geneva: World Health Organization.

Heath, J. and Potter, A. (2005) *The Rebel Sell: How The Counter Culture Became Consumer Culture*. Chichester: Wiley.

Held, D. (1999) *Global Transformations: Politics, Economics and Culture*. Cambridge: Polity Press.

Held, D. (2006) *Models of Democracy*. Cambridge: Polity.

Held, D. and Koenig-Archibugi, M. (2005) *Global Governance and Public Accountability*. Oxford: Blackwell.

Hennessy, P. (1992) *Never Again: Britain 1945–51*. London: Jonathan Cape.

Hermann, R. O. (1982) 'The consumer movement in historical perspective', in D. A. Aaker and G. S. Day (eds), *Consumerism: Search for the Consumer Interest* (4th edn). New York: Free Press, pp. 23–32.

Hertz, N. (2001) *The Silent Takeover: Global Capitalism and the Death of Democracy*. London: Heinemann.

Hetherington, K. (1992) 'Stonehenge and its festival: spaces of consumption', in R. Shields (ed.), *Lifestyle Shopping: The Subject of Consumption*. London: Routledge, pp. 83–98.

Hilton, M. (2009) *Prosperity for All: Consumer Activism in an Era of Globalization*. Ithaca, NY: Cornell University Press.

Hirsch, F. (1976) *Social Limits to Growth*. Cambridge, MA: Harvard University Press.

Hirsch, J. (1991) 'Fordism and post-Fordism: the present crisis and its consequences', in W. Bonefeld and J. Holloway (eds), *Post-Fordism and Social Form: A Marxist Debate on the Post-Fordist State*. Houndmills, Basingstoke, Hampshire: Macmillan Academic and Professional, pp. 8–34.

Hirschman, E. C. and Holbrook, M. B. (1982) 'Hedonic consumption: emerging concepts, methods and propositions', *The Journal of Marketing*, 46: 92–101.

HM Government (1991) *The Citizen's Charter*. White Paper. Cmnd 1599. London: HMSO.

Hobsbawm, E. J. (1994) *Age of Extremes: The Short Twentieth Century, 1914–1991*. London: Michael Joseph.

Hobsbawn, E. and Ranger, T. (1983) *The Invention of Tradition*. Cambridge: Cambridge University Press.

Hochschild, A. R. (1979) 'Emotion work, feeling rules, and social structure', *American Journal of Sociology*, 85: 551–575.

Hochschild, A. R. (1983) *The Managed Heart: Commercialization of Human Feeling*. Berkeley: University of California Press.

Hochschild, A. R. (2012) *The Outsourced Self: Intimate Life in Market Times*. New York: Metropolitan Books.

Holt, D. B. (2002) 'Why do brands cause trouble? A dialectical theory of consumer culture and branding', *Journal of Consumer Research*, 29: 70–90.

Holt, D. B. (2012) 'Constructing sustainable consumption: from ethical values to the cultural transformation of unsustainable markets', *The ANNALS of the American Academy of Political and Social Science*, 644: 236–255.

Holyoake, G. (1872) *The History of Co-operation in Rochdale*. London: Trubner and Co.

Homer (1974) *Iliad*. Harmondsworth: Penguin.

Horkheimer, M. and Adorno, T. ([1947] 1997) *The Dialectic of Enlightenment*. New York: Herder and Herder.

Howe, J. (2009) *Crowdsourcing: Why the Power of the Crowd Is Driving the Future of Business*. New York: Three Rivers Press.

Hull, C. L. (1974) *A Behavior System: An Introduction to Behavior Theory Concerning the Individual Organism*. Westport, CT: Greenwood Press.

Hutton, W. (1995) *The State We're In*. London: Jonathan Cape.

Hyman, L. (2012) 'The politics of consumer debt: U.S. state policy and the rise of investment in consumer credit, 1920–2008', *The ANNALS of the American Academy of Political and Social Science*, 644: 40–49.

Ibarra, H. and Petriglieri, J. L. (2010) 'Identity work and play', *Journal of Organizational Change Management*, 23: 10–25.

Icon Group International Inc. (2002) *The 2003–2008 World Outlook for Men's Outerwear Jeans*. San Diego, CA: Icon Group.

Irvine, S. (1989) 'Beyond green consumerism', Discussion Paper No. 1, September. London: Friends of the Earth.

Isaac, K. and Nader, R. (1992) *Ralph Nader Presents Civics for Democracy: A Journey for Teachers and Students*. Washington, DC: Essential Books.

Ivanova, M. N. (2011) 'Consumerism and the crisis: wither "the American Dream"?', *Critical Sociology*, 37: 329–350.

Jackson, T. (2009) *Prosperity without Growth: Economics for a Finite Planet*. London: Earthscan.

Jacobs, M. and Dinham, B. (2003) *Silent Invaders: Pesticides, Livelihoods, and Women's Health*. London: Zed Books.

James, O. (2007) *Affluenza: How to Be Successful and Stay Sane*. London: Vermilion.

James, W. (1891) *Principles of Psychology*. London: Macmillan.

James, W. ([1892] 1961) *Psychology: The Briefer Course*. New York: Harper and Row.

Jameson, F. (1983) 'Postmodernism and consumer society', in H, Foster (ed.), *The Anti-aesthetic: Essays on Postmodern Culture*. Port Townsend, WA: Bay Press.

Jay, M. ([1973] 1996) *The Dialectical Imagination: A History of the Frankfurt School and the Institute of Social Research 1923–1950*. Berkeley, CA: University of California Press.

Jenkins, R. (1992) *Pierre Bourdieu*. London and New York: Routledge.

Jessop, B. (2001) *Regulation Theory and the Crisis of Capitalism*. Cheltenham and Northampton, MA: Edward Elgar.

Jeyarraratnam, J. (1990) 'Acute pesticide poisoning: a major problem', *World Health Statistics Quarterly*, 43: 139–144.

John, R. (1994) *The Consumer Revolution: Redressing the Balance*. London: Hodder and Stoughton.

Johnston J. (2008) 'The citizen-consumer hybrid: ideological tensions and the case of Whole Foods Market', *Theory and Society*, 37: 229–270.

Jubas, K. (2007) 'Conceptual confusion in democratic societies: understandings and limitations of consumer-citizenship', *Journal of Consumer Culture*, 7: 231–254.

Juvenal ([AD110–30] 1999) *Satires*. Oxford: Oxford University Press.

Kahneman, D. (2011) *Thinking, Fast and Slow*. New York: Farrar, Straus and Giroux.

Kahneman, D. and Tversky, A. (1979) 'Prospect theory: an analysis of decision under risk', *Econometrica: Journal of the Econometric Society*, 47: 263–291.

Kahneman, D. and Tversky, A. (2000) *Choices, Values, and Frames*. New York: Cambridge University Press.

Kant, I. (1952) *Critique of Judgement*, trans. James Creed Meredith. Oxford: Clarendon Press.

Kaplan, R. S. and Norton, D. P. (1993) 'Putting the balanced scorecard to work', *Harvard Business Review*, 71: 134–142.

Kapuscinski, R. (1983) *The Emperor*. New York: Harcourt.

Kasser, T. (2002) *The High Price of Materialism*. Cambridge, MA: MIT Press.

Kaul, I., Grunberg, I. and Stern, M. A. (1999) 'Defining global public goods', in I. Kaul, I. Grunberg and M. A. Stern (eds), *Global Public Goods: International Cooperation in the 21st Century*. Oxford: Oxford University Press/United Nations Development Programme, pp. 2–19.

Kellner, D. (1989) *Jean Baudrillard: From Marxism to Postmodernism and Beyond*. Cambridge: Polity Press.

Kennedy, J. F. (1962) Special Message on Protecting the Consumer Interest: Statement read to Congress by President John F. Kennedy, Thursday, 15 March. Washington DC.

Keynes, J. M. (1933) 'National self-sufficiency', *The Yale Review*, 22: 755–769.

Khor, M. (2001) *Rethinking Globalization: Critical Issues and Policy Choices*. London: Zed Books.

Kleemann, F., Voss, G. G. and Rieder, K. (2008) 'Un(der) paid innovators: the commercial utilization of consumer work through crowdsourcing', *Science, Technology & Innovation Studies*, 4: 5–26.

Klein, N. (2000) *No Logo: Taking Aim at the Brand Bullies*. London: Flamingo.

Knightley, P., Evans, H., Potter, E. and Wallace, M. (1979) *Suffer The Children: The Story of Thalidomide*. London: Andre Deutsch.

Korczynski, M. (2001a) 'Communities of coping: collective emotional labour in service work', *Work, Employment and Society*. Nottingham University.

Korczynski, M. (2001b) 'The contradictions of service work: call centre as customer-oriented bureaucracy', in A. Sturdy, I. Grugulis and H. Willmott (eds), *Customer Service: Empowerment and Entrapment*. Basingstoke: Palgrave, pp. 79–101.

Korczynski, M. (2007) 'HRM and the menu society', in S. Bolton and M. Houlihan (eds), *Searching for the Human in Human Resource Management*. Basingstoke: Palgrave Macmillan, pp. 103–114.

Korczynski, M. and Ott, U. (2004) 'When production and consumption meet: cultural contradictions and the enchanting myth of customer sovereignty', *Journal of Management Studies*, 41: 575–599.

Korczynski, M. and Ott, U. (2006) 'The menu in society: mediating structures of power and enchanting myths of individual sovereignty', *Sociology: The Journal of the British Sociological Association*, 40: 911–928.

Korten, D. C. (2001) *When Corporations Rule the World*. Bloomfield, CT: Kumarian Press Inc.

Korthals, M. (2004) *Before Dinner: Philosophy and Ethics of Food*. Dordrecht NL: Springer.

Kotler, P. (1986) 'The prosumer movement: a new challenge for marketers', *Advances in Consumer Research*, 13: 510–513.

Kozinets, R. V. (1999) 'E-tribalized marketing? The strategic implications of virtual communities of consumption', *European Management Journal*, 17: 252–264.

Kozinets, R. V. (2002) 'Can consumers escape the market? Emancipatory illuminations from burning man', *Journal of Consumer Research*, 29: 20–38.

Kozinets, R. V. and Handelman, J. M. (2004) 'Adversaries of consumption: consumer movements, activism, and ideology', *Journal of Consumer Research*, 31: 691–704.

Krebs, A. V. (1992) *The Corporate Reapers: The Book of Agribusiness*. Washington, DC: Essential Books.

Kyrtatas, D. J. (2004) 'Paradise in heaven and on earth: Western ideas of perfect (non)-organization', in Y. Gabriel (ed.), *Myths, Stories and Organizations: Premodern Narratives for Our Times*. Oxford: Oxford University Press, pp. 66–80.

Lamb, H. (2008) *Fighting the Banana Wars and Other Fairtrade Battles*. London: Rider/Ebury.

Lang, T. (2006) 'Food, the law and public health: three models of the relationship', *Public Health*, 30–41.

Lang, T. and Clutterbuck, C. (1991) *P is for Pesticides*. London: Ebury.

Lang, T. and Hines, C. (1993) *The New Protectionism: Protecting the Future Against Free Trade*. London: Earthscan.

Lansley, S. (1994) *After the Goldrush: The Trouble with Affluence*. London: Century Business Books.

Lasch, C. (1980) *The Culture of Narcissism*. London: Abacus.

Lasch, C. (1984) *The Minimal Self: Psychic Survival in Troubled Times*. London: Pan Books.

Lasch, C. (1991) *The True and Only Heaven: Progress and Its Critics*. New York: Norton.

Lasn, K. (1999) *Culture Jam: The Uncooling of America*. New York: Eagle Brook.

Layard, R. (2005) *Happiness: Lessons from a New Science*. London: Allen Lane.

Lebergott, S. (1993) *Pursuing Happiness: American Consumers in the Twentieth Century*. Princeton: Princeton University Press.

Le Bon, G. ([1985] 1960) *The Crowd: A Study of the Popular Mind*. New York: The Viking Press.

Lee, M. (1993) *Consumer Culture Reborn: The Cultural Politics of Consumption*. London: Routledge.

Lee, M. (2000) *The Consumer Society Reader*. Oxford: Blackwell.

LETSlink UK (1994) *LETS Information Pack*. Warminster, Wiltshire: LETSlink UK.

LETSlink UK (2005) *So What Are LETS?* Warminster, Wiltshire: LETSlink UK.

Lévi-Strauss, C. (1978) *Myth and Meaning: The 1977 Massey Lectures*. London: Routledge.

Levy, S. (1982) 'Symbols, selves and others', *Advances in Consumer Research*, 9: 542–543.

Levy-Bruhl, L. (1966) *The 'Soul' of the Primitive*. New York: Praeger.

Lewis, M. (2014) *Flash Boys: A Wall Street Revolt*. New York: W. W. Norton.

Lister, R. (2004) *Poverty*. Cambridge and Malden, MA: Polity.

Littler, J. (2005) 'Beyond the boycott: anti-consumerism, cultural change and the limits of reflexivity', *Cultural Studies*, 19: 227–252.

London Food Commission (1987) *Food Adulteration and How to Beat It*. London: Unwin Hyman.

Lopes, L. L. (1987) 'Between hope and fear: the psychology of risk', *Advances in Experimental Social Psychology*, 20: 255–295.

Loudon, D. L. and Della Bitta, A. J. (1993) *Consumer Behavior: Concepts and Applications*. New York: McGraw-Hill.

Lury, C. (1996) *Consumer Culture*. Cambridge: Polity.

Lury, C. (2004) *Brands: The Logos of Global Economy*. London: Routledge.

Lymbery, P. and Oakeshott, I. (2014) *Farmageddon: The True Cost of Cheap Meat*. London: Bloomsbury.

Lynch, R. and Makusen, A. (1993) 'Can markets govern?', *The American Prospect*, 16: 125–124.

Mack, J. and Lansley, S. (1985) *Poor Britain*. London and Boston: G. Allen & Unwin.

Maclachlan, P. L. (2002) *Consumer Politics in Postwar Japan: The Institutional Boundaries of Citizen Activism*. New York and Chichester: Columbia University Press.

Maffesoli, M. (1995) *The Time of Tribes: The Decline of Individualism in Mass Society*. London: Sage.

Mander, J. (1991) *In the Absence of the Sacred: The Failure of Technology and the Survival of the Indian Nations*. San Francisco: Sierra Club Books.

Marcuse, H. (1964) *One-dimensional Man: Studies in the Ideology of Advanced Industrial Society*. Boston: Beacon Press.

Marcuse, H. (1969) *An Essay on Liberation*. London: Allen Lane.

Martin, J. (2002) *Nader: Crusader, Spoiler, Icon*. New York: Basic Books.

Marx, K. ([1844] 1972) 'Economic and philosophic manuscripts of 1844', in R. C. Tucker (ed.), *Marx-Engels Reader*. New York: Norton, pp. 53–103.

Marx, K. ([1859] 1993) *Grundrisse: Outline of the Critique of Political Economy*. Harmondsworth: Penguin.

Marx, K. ([1867] 1967) *Capital (Vol. 1)*. New York: International Publishers.

Maslow, A. ([1954] 1970) *Motivation and Personality*. New York: Harper and Row.

Mather, G. (1991) 'The race to improve public services', in M. Pirie (ed.), *Empowerment: The Theme for the 1990s*. London: Adam Smith Institute.

Matza, D. (1964) *Delinquency and Drift*. New York: Wiley.

Mauss, M. ([1925] 1974) *The Gift: Forms and Functions of Exchange in Archaic Societies*. London: Routledge.

McCarney, W. G. (1981) 'Joy-riding: a quest for identity', *Youth in Society*, 16–17.

McCracken, G. (1988) *Culture and Consumpton: New Approaches to the Symbolic Character of Consumer Goods and Activities*. Bloomington, IN: Indiana University Press.

McKendrick, N., Brewer, J. and Plumb, J. H. (1982) *The Birth of a Consumer Society: The Commercialization of Eighteenth-century England*. Bloomington, IN: Indiana University Press.

McRobbie, A. (1994) *Postmodernism and Popular Culture*. London: Routledge.

McRobbie, A. (1999) *In the Culture Society: Art, Fashion, and Popular Music*. London and New York: Routledge.

Meadows, D. H., Meadows, D. L., Randers, J. and Behrens, W. W. (1972) *The Limits to Growth: A Report for the Club of Rome's Project on the Predicament of Mankind*. New York: Universe Books.

MEC (2014) About MEC. Retrieved from: www.mec.ca/AST/ContentPrimary/AboutMEC/AboutOurCoOp.jsp (accessed 4 March 2015). Vancouver: Mountain Equipment Co-op.

Mendelson, R. A. (Committee on Communications (1992) 'The commercialization of children's television', *Pediatrics*, 89 (2): 343–344.

Merrifield, A. (2005) *Guy Debord*. London: Reaktion Books.

Mick, D. G. and DeMoss, M. (1990) 'Self gifts: phenomenological insights from four contexts', *Journal of Consumer Research*, 13: 322–332.

Miliband, R. (1969) *The State in Capitalist Society*. New York: Basic Books.

Millennium Ecosystem Assessment (Program) (2005) *Ecosystems and Human Well-being: Synthesis*. Washington, DC: Island Press.

Miller, D. (1987) *Material Culture and Mass Consumpton*. Oxford: Blackwell.

Mintel (2005) *Jeans – UK*. London: Mintel International Group Ltd.

Mishan, E. J. (1967) *The Costs of Economic Growth*. London: Staples P.

Monbiot, G. (2000) *Captive State: The Corporate Takeover of Britain*. Basingstoke: Macmillan.

Monbiot, G. (2003) *The Age of Consent: A Manifesto for a New World Order*. London: Flamingo.

Morgan, B. (2003) *Social Citizenship in the Shadow of Competition: The Bureaucratic Politics of Regulatory Justification*. Aldershot: Ashgate.

Moxon, D. (2011) 'Consumer culture and the 2011 "riots"', *Sociological Research Online*, 16: 19.

Mukerji, C. (1983) *From Graven Images: Patterns of Modern Materialism*. New York: Columbia University Press.

Müller, M. (2013) 'Brandspeak: understanding internal branding as a new form of control', unpublished PhD thesis, Innsbruck: Innsbruck University.

Multatuli ([1860] 1987) *Max Havelaar or the Coffee Auctions of the Dutch Trading Company*. Harmondsworth: Penguin.

Myners, P. (2014) *The Co-operative Group: Report of the Independent Governance Review*. Manchester: The Co-operative Group.

Nadel, M. V. (1971) *The Politics of Consumer Protection*. Indianapolis: Bobbs-Merrill.

Nader, R. ([1965] 1991) *Unsafe at Any Speed: The Designed-in Dangers of the American Automobile*. New York: Knightsbridge Publishing.

Nader, R. (1968) 'The great American gyp', *New York Review of Books*, 11: 28.

Nader, R. (1970) 'Foreword', in J. S. Turner (ed.), *The Chemical Feast: The Ralph Nader Study Group Report on Food Protection and the Food and Drug Administration*. New York: Grossman.

Nader, R. (1991) Keynote Speech to the world Consumer Congress. Hong Kong: International Organization of Consumers Unions.

Nader, R. and Smith, W. J. (1992) *The Frugal Shopper*. Washington, DC: Center for Study of Responsive Law.

National Consumer Council (1977) *The Fourth Right of Citizenship: A Review of Local Advice Services*. London: National Consumer Council.

National Consumer Council (1978) *Real Money, Real Choice*. London: National Consumer Council.

National Consumer Council (1979) *The Consumer and the State: Getting Value for Public Money*. London: National Consumer Council.

Nixon, E. (2013) 'Indifference in a culture of consumption', PhD thesis, School of Management, University of Bath.

Nixon, S. (1992) 'Have you got the look? Masculinities and shopping spectacle', in R. Shields (ed.), *Lifestyle Shopping: The Subject of Consumption*. London: Routledge, pp. 149–169.

Norberg-Hodge, H. (1991) *Ancient Futures: Learning from Ladakh*. San Francisco: Sierra Club Books.

Nove, A. (1983) *The Economics of Feasible Socialism*. London and Boston: G. Allen & Unwin.

Office of Fair Trading (1994) *A Buyer's Guide*. London: HMSO.

Omi, M. and Winant, H. (1987) *Racial Formation in the United States*. London: Routledge.

Orbach, S. (1978) *Fat Is a Feminist Issue*. London: Hamlyn.

Orbach, S. (1986) *Hunger Strike: The Anorectic's Struggle as a Metaphor for Our Age*. London: Faber and Faber.

O'Riordan, T. and Lenton, T. (2013) *Addressing Tipping Points for a Precarious Future*. Oxford: Oxford University Press/British Academy.

Orwell, G. (1962) *The Road to Wigan Pier*. Harmondsworth: Penguin.

Packard, V. ([1957] 1981) *The Hidden Persuaders*. Harmondsworth: Penguin.

Pandya, A. and Venkatesh, A. (1992) 'Symbolic communication among consumers in self-consumption and gift-giving: a semiotic approach', *Advances in Consumer Research*, 19: 147–154.

Panigyrakis, G. and Zarkada, A. (2014) 'A philosophical investigation of the transition from integrated marketing communications to metamodern meaning co-creation', *Journal of Global Scholars of Marketing Science*, 24: 262–278.

Parker, H. J. (1974) 'The joys of joy-riding', *New Society*, January.

Paulus, I. (1974) *The Search for Pure Food*. Oxford: Martin Robertson.

Pearce, F. (1991) *Green Warriors: The People and the Politics Behind the Environmental Revolution*. London: Bodley Head.

Perry, M. (1994) 'The brand: vehicle for value in a changing marketplace'. London: Advertising Association, President's Lecture, 7 July.

Peters, T. and Waterman, R. H. (1982) *In Search of Excellence: Lessons from America's Best-run Companies*. New York: Harpers & Row.

Piercy, N. F., Cravens, D. W. and Lane, N. (2010) 'Marketing out of the recession: recovery is coming, but things will never be the same again', *The Marketing Review*, 10: 3–23.

Pine, B. J. and Gilmore, J. H. (1999) *The Experience Economy: Work as Theatre and Every Business as Stage*. Boston MA: Harvard Business School Press.

Pirie, M. (1991) *Empowerment: The Theme for the 1990s*. London: Adam Smith Institute.

Poetz, M. K. and Schreier, M. (2012) 'The value of crowdsourcing: can users really compete with professionals in generating new product ideas?', *Journal of Product Innovation Management*, 29: 245–256.

Pollock, A. and Leys, C. (2004) *NHS plc: The Privatisation of Our Health Care*. London: Verso.

Pongsakornrungsilp, S. and Schroeder, J. E. (2011) 'Understanding value co-creation in a co-consuming brand community', *Marketing Theory*, 11: 303–324.

Pook, S. (1993) 'Ram-raids spark talks on security', *Bath Evening Chronicle*, 2 August.

Postman, N. (1986) *Amusing Ourselves to Death*. London: Heinemann.

Poulantzas, N. A. (1975) *Political Power and Social Classes*. London and Atlantic Highlands, NJ: NLB/Humanities Press.

Pountain, D. and Robins, D. (2000) *Cool Rules: Anatomy of an Attitude*. London: Reaktion Books.

Prahalad, C. K. (2004) *Fortune at the Bottom of the Pyramid: Eardicating Poverty through Rrofits*. Philadelphia, PA: Wharton School Publishing.

Prahalad, C. K. and Ramaswamy, V. (2004a) 'Co-creating unique value with customers', *Strategy & Leadership*, 32: 4–9.

Prahalad, C. K. and Ramaswamy, V. (2004b) 'Co-creation experiences: the next practice in value creation', *Journal of Interactive Marketing*, 18: 5–14.

Punjaisri, K., Evanschitzky, H. and Wilson, A. (2009) 'Internal branding: an enabler of employees' brand-supporting behaviours', *Journal of Service Management*, 20: 209–226.

Putnam, R. D. (2000) *Bowling Alone: The Collapse and Revival of American Community*. New York: Simon & Schuster.

Rawls, J. (1971) *A Theory of Justice*. Cambridge, MA: Harvard University Press.

Redfern, P. (1913) *The Story of the C. W. S.: The Jubillee History of the Co-operative Wholesale Society, Limited. 1863–1913*. Manchester: The Co-operative Wholesale Society Limited.

Redfern, P. (1920) *The Consumers' Place in Society*. Manchester: Co-operative Union Limited.

Reekie, G. (1992) 'Changes in the Adamless Eden: the spatial and sexual transformation of a Brisbane department store 1930–90', in R. Shields (ed.), *Lifestyle Shopping: The Subject of Consumption*. London: Routledge, pp. 170–194.

Regattieri, A., Gamberi, M. and Manzini, R. (2007) 'Traceability of food products: general framework and experimental evidence', *Journal of Food Engineering*, 81: 347–356.

Reich, R. (1981) 'Business is asking for it again', *New York Times*, 22 November.

Richardson, J. (1995) 'The market for political activism: interest groups as a challenge to political parties', *West European Politics*, 18: 116–139.

Rieder, K. and Voss, G. G. (2010) 'The working customer: an emerging new type of consumer', *Psychology of Everyday Activity*, 3: 2–10.

Rieff, D. (1993) 'Multiculturalism's silent partner: it's the newly globalized consumer economy, stupid', *Harper's Magazine*, August.

Rieff, P. (1959) *Freud: The Mind of a Moralist*. New York: Doubleday.

Rieff, P. (1966) *The Triumph of the Therapeutic*. New York: Harper and Row.

Ritzer, G. (1993) *The McDonaldization of Society: An Investigation into the Changing Character of Contemporary Social Life*. London: Pine Forge Press.

Ritzer, G. (1999) *Enchanting a Disenchanted World: Revolutionizing the Means of Consumption*. Thousand Oaks, CA: Pine Forge Press.

Ritzer, G. (2014) 'Prosumption: evolution, revolution, or eternal return of the same?', *Journal of Consumer Culture*, 14: 3–24.

Ritzer, G., Dean, P. and Jurgenson, N. (2012) 'The coming of age of the prosumer', *American Behavioral Scientist*, 56: 379–398.

Robins, D. and Cohen, P. (1978) *Knuckle Sandwich: Growing up in the Working-class City*. Harmondsworth: Penguin.

Rockström, J., Steffen, W., Noone, K., et al. (2009a) 'Planetary boundaries: exploring the safe operating space for humanity', *Ecology and Society*, 14 (2): 32. Retrieved from: www.ecologyandsociety.org/vol14/iss2/art32/ (accessed 4 March 2015).

Rockström, J., Steffen, W., Noone, K., et al. (2009b) 'A safe operating space for humanity', *Nature*, 461: 472–475.

Rose, G. (1978) *The Melancholy Science: An Introduction to the Thought of Theodor W. Adorno*. London: Macmillan.

Roszak, T. (1970) *The Making of a Counter Culture: Reflections on the Technocratic Society and Its Youthful Opposition*. London: Faber and Faber.

Royal Society (2012) *People and the Planet*. London: Royal Society.

RSPB (2014) 'Big garden birdwatch'. Retrieved from: www.rspb.org.uk/birdwatch/ (accessed 4 March 2015). Sandy: Royal Society for the Protection of Birds.

Rudé, G. F. E. (1959) *The Crowd in the French Revolution*. Oxford: Clarendon Press.

Rumbo, J. D. (2002) 'Consumer resistance in a world of advertising clutter: the case of Adbusters', *Psychology & Marketing*, 19: 127–148.

Rutherford, J. (1990) 'A place called home: identity and the cultural politics of difference', in J. Rutherford (ed.), *Identity: Community, Culture, Difference*. London: Lawrence and Wishart, pp. 1–20.

Ryle, S. (1993) 'Crowds cheer as gang hits Jolly's', *Bath Evening Chronicle*, 23 October.

Sahlins, M. D. (1972) *Stone Age Economics*. Chicago: Aldine-Atherton.

Salecl, R. (2010) *The Tyranny of Choice*. London: Profile.

Samuelson, P. A. (1970) *Economics*. New York: McGraw-Hill.

Saren, M. (2012) 'Boredom and consumer culture: is marketing the antidote or the poison?', *Boredom: Life and Work After the Experience Economy*, 12–14 April, Copenhagen, Denmark.

Sassatelli, R. (2006) Virtue, responsibility and consumer choice: fraing critical consumerism', in J. Brewer and F. Trentmann (eds), *Consuming Cultures, Global Perspectives: Historical Trajectories, Transnational Exchanges*. Oxford: Berg, pp. 219–250.

Schor, J. B. (1998) *The Overspent American: Upscaling, Downshifting and the New Consumer*. New York: HarperCollins.

Schor, J. B. (2010) *Plenitude: The New Economics of True Wealth*. New York: Penguin.

Schwartz, B. (2004) *The Paradox of Choice: Why More Is Less*. New York: HarperCollins.

Schwartz, H. S. (1990) *Narcissistic Process and Corporate Decay*. New York: New York University Press.

Scitovsky, T. (1976) *The Joyless Economy: An Inquiry into Human Satisfaction and Consumer Dissatisfaction*. New York: Oxford University Press.

Seabrook, J. (1978) *What Went Wrong? Why Hasn't Having More Made People Happier?*. New York: Pantheon Books.

Seabrook, J. (1985) *Landscapes of Poverty*. Oxford: Blackwell.

Seabrook, J. (2004) *Consuming Cultures: Globalization and Local Lives*. Oxford: New Internationalist.

Seikatsu Club (2005) 'Consumers' Cooperative Union of Japan'. Retrieved from: www.iisd.org/50comm/commdb/desc/d08.htm (accessed 3 July 2005). Tokyo: Seikatsu Club Consumers' Cooperative Union.

Sen, A. (1988) *On Ethics and Economics*. Oxford: Blackwell.

Sennett, R. (1998) *The Corrosion of Character: The Personal Consequences of Work in the New Capitalism*. New York: Norton.

Seth, A. and Randall, G. (2001) *The Grocers: The Rise and Rise of the Supermarket Chains*. London: Kogan Page.

Shah, D. V., Friedland, L. A., Wells, C., Kim, Y. M, and Rojas, H. (2012) 'Communication, consumers, and citizens: revisiting the politics of consumption', *The ANNALS of the American Academy of Political and Social Science*, 644: 6–19.

Shankar, A., Whittaker, J. and Fitchett, J. A. (2006) 'Heaven knows I'm miserable now', *Marketing Theory*, 6: 485–505.

Sharpe, R. P., Barling, D. and Lang, T. (2008) 'Ethical traceability in the UK wheat-flour-bread chain', in C. Coff, D. Barling, M. Korthals and T. Nielsen (eds), *Ethical Traceability and Communicating Food*. New York: Springer, pp. 125–165.

Shaw, D. and Moraes, C. (2009) 'Voluntary simplicity: an exploration of market interactions', *International Journal of Consumer Studies*, 33: 215–223.

Shaw, D. and Newholm, T. (2002) 'Voluntary simplicity and the ethics of consumption', *Psychology & Marketing*, 19: 167–185.

Shaw, D., Newholm, T. and Dickinson, R. (2006) 'Consumption as voting: an exploration of consumer empowerment', *European Journal of Marketing*, 40: 1049–1067.

Shiva, V. (2002) *Water Wars: Privatization, Pollution and Profit*. London: Pluto Press.

Sievers, B. (1986) 'Beyond the surrogate of motivation', *Organization Studies*, 7 (4): 335–351.

Simmel, G. ([1903] 1971) 'The metropolis in mental life', in D. Levine and G. Simmel (eds), *On Individuality and Social Form*. Chicago: Chicago University Press, pp. 324–339.

Simmel, G. ([1904] 1971) 'Fashion', in D. Levin and G. Simmel (eds), *On Individuality and Social Form*. Chicago: Chicago University Press, pp. 294–323.

Simmel, G. (1978) *The Philosophy of Money*. London: Routledge and Kegan Paul.

Simon, H. A. (1947) *Administrative Behavior*. New York: Macmillan.

Sinclair, U. ([1906] 1985) *The Jungle*. Harmondsworth: Penguin.

Singer, P. (1975) *Animal Liberation: A New Ethics for our Treatment of Animals*. New York: Random House.

Singer, P. (2013) 'The world's first cruelty-free hamburger'. Retrieved from: www.theguardian.com/commentisfree/2013/aug/05/worlds-first-cruelty-free-hamburger (accessed 4 March 2015). *The Guardian*. London.

Singer, P. and Mason, J. (2006) *Eating*. London: Arrow.

Singh, J. (1990) 'A typology of consumer dissatisfaction response styles', *Journal of Retailing*, 66: 57–99.

Skidelsky, R. and Skidelsky, E. (2012) *How Much Is Enough? The Love of Money and the Case for the Good Life*. London: Allen Lane.

Skinner, B. F. (1972) *Beyond Freedom and Dignity*. New York: Vintage Book.

Sklair, L. (1991) *Sociology of the Global System*. London: Harvester Wheatsheaf.

Sklair, L. (1995) *Sociology of the Global System* (2nd edn). London: Prentice Hall/ Harvester Wheatsheaf.

Sklair, L. (1996) 'Social movements and global capitalism', *Sociology*, 29: 495–512.

Sklair, L. (2002) *Globalization: Capitalism and Its Alternatives*. Oxford: Oxford University Press.

Sklair, L. (2010) 'Iconic architecture and the culture-ideology of consumerism', *Theory, Culture & Society*, 27: 135–159.

Slater, D. (1997) *Consumer Culture and Modernity*. Cambridge: Polity.

Slater, D. and Tonkiss, F. (2001) *Market Society: Markets and Modern Social Theory*. Cambridge: Polity.

Smith, A. ([1776] 1970) *The Wealth of the Nations*. Harmondsworth: Penguin.

Smith, N. C. (1990) *Morality and the Market: Consumer Pressure for Corporate Accountability*. London: Routledge.

Solnit, D., Solnit, R. and Mittal, A. (2009) *The Battle of the Story of the Battle of Seattle*. Edinburgh and Oakland, CA: AK Press.

Sontag, S. (1977) *On Photography*. New York: Farrar Straus and Giroux.

Soper, K. (2007) 'Re-thinking the "good life": the citizenship dimension of consumer disaffection with consumerism', *Journal of Consumer Culture*, 7: 205–229.

Soper, K. (2008) 'Alternative hedonism, cultural theory and the role of aesthetic revisioning', *Cultural Studies*, 22: 567–587.

Soper, K. (2012) 'Beyond the scarcities of affluence: an alternative hedonist approach', *Architectural Design*, 100–101.

Standing, G. (2011) *The Precariat: The New Dangerous Class*. London: Bloomsbury Academic.

Stiglitz, J. E. (2002) *Globalization and Its Discontents*. New York: W. W. Norton.

Stolle, D. and Micheletti, M. (2013) *Political Consumerism: Global Responsibility in Action*. Cambridge: Cambridge University Press.

Sveningsson, S. and Alvesson, M. (2003) 'Managing managerial identities: organizational fragmentation, discourse and identity struggle', *Human Relations*, 56: 1163–1193.

Sylla, N. S. (2014) *The Fair Trade Scandal: Marketing Poverty to Benefit the Rich*. Athens, OH: Ohio University Press.

Tajfel, H. (1974) 'Social identity and intergroup behaviour', *Social Science Information*, 13: 65–93.

Tajfel, H. (1979) 'Individuals and groups in social psychology', *British Journal of Social and Clinical Psychology*, 18: 183–190.

Tancred-Sheriff, P. (1989) 'Gender, sexuality and the labour process', in J. Hearn (ed.), *The Sexuality of Organization*. London: Sage, pp. 44–55.

Taskforce on Systemic Pesticides (2014) 'Report of the taskforce'. Retrieved from: www.tfsp.info/worldwide-integrated-assessment/ (accessed 5 July 2014). Gland, Switzerland: International Union for Conservation of Nature.

Tatzel, M. (2002) '"Money worlds" and well-being: an integration of money dispositions, materialism and price-related behavior', *Journal of Economic Psychology*, 23: 103–126.

Tawney, R. H. ([1922] 1969) *Religion and the Rise of Capitalism*. Harmondsworth: Penguin.

Taylor, I., Walton, P. and Young, J. (1973) *The New Criminology*. London: Routledge.

Thaler, R. (1980) 'Toward a positive theory of consumer choice', *Journal of Economic Behavior & Organization*, 1: 39–60.

Thaler, R. and Sunstein, C. (2008) *Nudge: Improving Decisions About Health, Wealth, and Happiness*. New Haven, CT: Yale University Press.

The Ecologist (2001) *Go M-A-D: Go Make a Difference – 365 Daily Ways to Save the Planet*. London: Think Publishing Limited.

Thompson, D. J. (1994) *Weavers of Dreams: The Origins of the Modern Co-operative Movement*. Davis, CA: Center for Cooperatives University of California.

Thompson, E. P. ([1971] 1993) 'The moral economy of the English crowd in the eighteenth century', in E. P. Thompson (ed.), *Customs in Common*. Harmondsworth: Penguin, pp. 185–258.

Thurow, L. C. (1993) *Head to Head: The Coming Economic Battle among Japan, Europe, and America*, New York: Warner Books.

Tiemstra, J. P. (1992) 'Theories of regulation and the history of consumerism', *International Journal of Social Economics*, 19: 3–27.

Toffler, A. (1970) *Future Shock*. New York: Random House.

Toffler, A. (1980) *The Third Wave*. New York: Morrow.

Tomlinson, A. (1990) 'Introduction: consumer culture and the aura of commodity', in A. Tomlinson (ed.), *Consumpton, Identity and Style: Marketing, Meanings and the Packaging of Pleasure*. London: Routledge, pp. 1–38.

Townsend, P. (1993) *The International Analysis of Poverty*. Hemel Hempstead: Harvester Wheatsheaf.

Townsend, P. and Gordon, D. (2002) *World Poverty: New Policies to Defeat an Old Enemy*. Bristol: Policy Press.

Toynbee, P. (2003) *Hard Work: Life in Low-pay Britain*. London: Bloomsbury.

Treadwell, J., Briggs, D., Winlow, S. and Hall, S. (2013) 'Shopocalypse now consumer culture and the English riots of 2011', *British Journal of Criminology*, 53: 1–17.

Trentmann, F. (2005) *The Making of the Consumer: Knowledge, Power and Identity in the Modern World*. New York: Berg.

Tversky, A. (1990) 'The psychology of risk', *ICFA Continuing Education Series*, 73–78.

Tye, L. (1998) *The Father of Spin: Edward L. Bernays and The Birth of Public Relations*. New York: Crown Publishers, Inc.

UN (1992) *Report of the United Nations Conference on Environment and Development* (Rio de Janeiro, 3–14 June 1992). New York: United Nations Conference on Environment and Development.

UNCTAD (2013) *Wake Up Before It Is Too Late: Trade and Environment Review 2013*. Geneva: UN Conference on Trade and Development, 341.

UNEP (2011) *Towards a Green Economy: Pathways to Sustainable Development and Poverty Eradication*. Retrieved from: www.unep.org/green economy (accessed 4 March 2015).

United Nations and UNEP (1990) *The Public Health Impact of Pesticides Used in Agriculture*. Geneva: World Health Organization.

van Brakel, M. and Zagema, B. (1994) *Sustainable Netherlands*. Amsterdam: Friends of the Earth.

Vandzinskaite, D., Kobierska, H., Schmeller, D. S. and Grodzińska-Jurczak, M. (2010) 'Cultural diversity issues in biodiversity monitoring: cases of Lithuania, Poland and Denmark', *Diversity*, 2: 1130–1145.

van Zwanenberg, P. and Millstone, E. (2005) *BSE: Risk, Science, and Governance*. Oxford and New York: Oxford University Press.

Veblen, T. ([1899] 1925) *The Theory of the Leisure Class*. London: George Allen and Unwin.

Viswanathan, M., Sridharan, S., Ritchie, R., Venugopal, S. and Jung, K. (2012) 'Marketing interactions in subsistence marketplaces: a bottom-up approach to designing public policy', *Journal of Public Policy & Marketing*, 31: 159–177.

von Weizsäcker, E. U., Lovins, A. B. and Lovins, L. H. (1996) *Factor Four: Doubling Wealth – Halving Resource Use: The New Report to the Club of Rome*. London: Earthscan.

Wackernagel, M., Rees, W. E. and Testemale, P. (1996) *Our Ecological Footprint: Reducing Human Impact on the Earth*. Gabriola Island, BC: New Society Publishers.

Walker, A. and Wang, Z. (2005) *East Asian Welfare Regimes in Transition: From Confucianism to Globalisation*. Bristol: Policy Press.

Warhurst, C. and Nickson, D. (2009) '"Who's got the look?" Emotional, aesthetic and sexualized labour in interactive services', *Gender Work and Organization*, 16: 385–404.

Weber, M. (1930) *The Protestant Ethic and the Spirit of Capitalism*. London: Unwin University Books.

Wells, P. and Jetter, M. (1991) *The Global Consumer: Best Buys to Help the Third World*. London: Victor Gollancz.

Wenger, E. (1998) *Communities of Practice: Learning, Meaning and Identity*. Cambridge: Cambridge University Press.

Wernick, A. (1991) *Promotional Culture: Advertising, Ideology and Symbolic Expression*. London: Sage.

Wexler, P. (1990) 'Citizenship in the semiotic society', in B. A. Turner (ed.) *Theories of Modernity and Postmodernity*. London: Sage, pp. 164–175.

Which? (2013a) *Cutting Back and Trading Down: The Impact of Rising Food Prices*. London: Which?

Which? (2013b) *Weathering the Economic Storm: Gloom Lightens, But People Still Struggling to Put Money Aside for a Rainy Day*. London: Which?

White, R. E. and Kare, D. D. (1990) 'The impact of consumer boycotts on the stock prices of target firms', *The Journal of Applied Business Research*, 6.

Whitfield, D. (1983) *Making It Public: Evidence and Action Against Privatisation*. London: Pluto Press.

Wilk, R. R. (1997) 'A critique of desire: distaste and dislike in consumer behavior', *Consumption Markets & Culture*, 1: 175–196.

Wilkinson, R. G. and Pickett, K. (2009) *The Spirit Level: Why More Equal Societies Almost Always Do Better*. London: Allen Lane.

Williams, R. (1976) *Keywords: A Vocabulary of Culture and Society*. London: Fontana.

Williams, R. H. (1982) *Dream Worlds: Mass Consumption in Late Nineteenth-century France*. Berkeley: University of California Press.

Williamson, J. (1986) *Consuming Passions: The Dynamics of Popular Culture*. London: Marion Boyars.

Willis, M. M. and Schor, J. B. (2012) 'Does changing a light bulb lead to changing the world? Political action and the conscious consumer', *The ANNALS of the American Academy of Political and Social Science*, 644: 160–190.

Willis, P. (1990) *Common Culture: Symbolic Work at Play in the Everyday Cultures of the Young*. Milton Keynes: Open University Press.

Wilson, B. (2008) *Swindled: From Poison Sweets to Counterfeit Coffee – The Dark History of the Food Cheats*. London: John Murray.

Winnicott, D. W. (1962) *The Maturational Processes and Facilitating Environment*. London: Hogarth Press.

Winnicott, D. W. (1964) *The Child, the Family and the Outside World*. Harmondsworth: Penguin.

Winward, J. (1994) 'The organized consumer and consumer information co-operatives', in R. Keath, N. Whiteley and N. Abercrombie (eds), *The Authority of the Consumer*. London: Routledge, pp. 75–90.

Witkowski, T. H. (1989) 'Colonial consumers in revolt: buyer values and behavior during the nonimportantion movement, 1764–1776', *Journal of Consumer Research*, 16: 216–226.

World Bank (2012) *Inclusive Green Growth: The Pathway to Sustainable Development*. Washington, DC: World Bank.

Worpole, K. (2000) *Here Comes the Sun: Architecture and Public Space in Twentieth-century European Culture*. London: Reaktion.

Zavestoski, S. (2002) 'The social-psychological bases of anticonsumption attitudes', *Psychology & Marketing*, 19: 149–165.

Zwick, D., Bonsu, S. K. and Darmody, A. (2008) 'Putting consumers to work: "co-creation" and new marketing governmentality', *Journal of Consumer Culture*, 8: 163–196.

Zwick, D. and Knott, J. D. (2009) 'Manufacturing customers: the database as new means of production', *Journal of Consumer Culture*, 9: 221–247.

INDEX

This index has been compiled by the authors to indicate where significant references are made to the terms below. It does not indicate the only instances where the terms occur in the text.

Page numbers below followed by the letter f refer to entries that continue through to the next page; Page numbers below followed by ff refer to entries continuing over several following pages